Hard Disk
Management
with DOS 5

3rd Edition

Dan Gookin

WINDCREST®/McGRAW-HILL

THIRD EDITION
SECOND PRINTING

© 1992 by **Dan Gookin**.
Published by Windcrest Books, an imprint of TAB Books.
TAB Books is a division of McGraw-Hill, Inc.
The name ''Windcrest'' is a registered trademark of TAB Books.

Library of Congress Cataloging-in-Publication Data

Gookin, Dan.
    Hard disk management with DOS 5 / by Dan Gookin. — 3rd ed.
       p.   cm.
    Rev. ed. of: Hard disk management with DOS. 2nd ed.
    Includes index.
    ISBN 0-8306-3521-1 (h)   ISBN 0-8306-3520-3 (p)
    1. Hard disk management.   2. MS-DOS (Computer file).   3. PC-DOS
(Computer file)   I. Gookin, Dan. Hard disk management with DOS.
II. Title.
QA76.9.H35G67   1992
005.74—dc20   91-34949
                                                             CIP

TAB Books offers software for sale. For information and a catalog, please contact
TAB Software Department, Blue Ridge Summit, PA 17294-0850.

Acquisitions Editor: Ron Powers
Book Editor: John C. Baker
Director of Production: Katherine G. Brown
Book Design: Jaclyn J. Boone
Cover: Sandra Blair Design and Brent Blair Photography, Harrisburg, PA   WP1

Contents

_____ PART ONE _____

HARD DISK ORGANIZATION

APPENDICES

Acknowledgments

The first edition of this book wouldn't have been possible without the contribution of Andy Townsend, my original co-author. I also would like to acknowledge Debbie Hess of Central Point Software; Jan Jacob of Fifth Generation Systems, Inc.; and Katherine Hinsch of Microsoft for their kind assistance. Thanks also to Bill Gladstone and Matt Wagner of Waterside Productions and to Ron Powers at TAB/McGraw-Hill. Special thanks go to Sandra and Jordan for the love and diversionary tactics.

Introduction

There is a revolution taking place in the personal computer industry. While this revolution is driven by technology, it's affecting the type and range of applications for which personal computers are used. At the heart of this revolution is the declining cost of computer power.

Dramatic cost reductions have taken place in the computer industry. Today you get much more computer power for your dollar than ever before. For example, back in 1980, the cost of disk storage was more than $100 per megabyte. Now, you can buy a megabyte of disk storage for as little as $6. Because of this cost reduction, having a hard drive with a computer system has evolved from a luxury to a necessity to a standard.

The hard drive is no longer the single most expensive item in your computer. It's not even considered outlandish to have a 100 Mb hard drive in a home system. This amount of storage might seem silly, considering that the first PC hard drive stored only 10 Mb—and that was rarely filled. Today, however, it's hard to find any computer software that doesn't require at least several megabytes of hard drive storage. So, the question really isn't whether or not you have a hard drive but how much storage that hard drive can provide. (Using DOS, a word processor, a spreadsheet, and nothing else requires a minimum of at least 40 Mb of disk storage.)

Alas, there is a downside to the revolution. While you always will be able to get more computer bang for your buck, the demands of computer software will never keep up with the hardware. Modern PC applications are power hungry, with a huge appetite for disk space.

The increasing need for hard disk computer systems to run larger applications and manage more data, coupled with the decreasing cost of hard disk technology, has led to a growing number of hard disk personal computer systems in operation. To keep the revolution in check and to keep your computer system under control, you need a system—a plan of attack—under which you'll control and master your PC. That's what this book helps you accomplish.

What this book is about

This book is about taming your hard disk. The subject of hard disks is a bewildering one. Even experienced computer users can become lost in the maze of megabytes and special commands associated with hard disks. The issue isn't having a hard drive, but rather managing the information on it.

Hard disk management really is the art of organizing and using a computer with a hard drive. It's the coordination of several elements: you and your needs, your software, DOS, and the hard disk itself.

The special problems associated with hard disks can be broken down into four major areas of concern:

- Organization
- Administration
- Security
- Performance

The first, and most obvious, concern is the need for organizing the massive storage potential of a hard disk. Unless the drive is being used to maintain a single, enormous database, it's likely that there will be thousands of different program and data files stored on it. Keeping track of programs and data can be a daunting proposition, especially to someone who is unfamiliar with computers in the first place.

The first part of this book describes several methods for organizing your hard disk into manageable units called subdirectories. You also will learn how to use DOS to keep everything organized and running at peak efficiency. Unlike other books, this one actually tells you what to do and how to do it; there's no guessing or assumptions. Why? Because good hard disk management starts with organization; there's no other way to do it.

The second concern is administration of your hard drive—the management in hard disk management. The second part of this book teaches you about DOS batch files, menu systems, and shells, which can be used to assist you in running your hard drive system. You'll discover how to create professional-looking menus for accessing your programs and data. These techniques will take the hassle out of your hard disk and leave the power readily available at your fingertips.

The third concern is security, which includes both data and program security. Primarily, you want to make sure your data is secure from accidental loss or hard disk failure. The third part of this book describes methods for duplicating the data stored on your hard disk to prevent the permanent loss of valuable data. Special DOS data preservation techniques and virus prevention and cures also are covered.

The other side of the security issue is privacy. If one computer system is shared between several users or if your computer is accessible to unauthorized use, you'll want some extra protection. Password security and data encryption are two features that can be added to your system to protect confidential data. This book describes a variety of techniques and programs that can be employed to ensure your data against security violations.

The fourth and final concern of hard disk users is performance. Hard drives are always getting faster. They're definitely faster than using the old, floppy-only systems of yore. Because you'll never go back in time and use a floppy-only system, you'll take the increased speed benefits of a hard drive for granted. However, for reasons discussed in the fourth part of this book, a hard disk's performance deteriorates as more files are added to it. This deterioration can significantly slow down your computer system. Part IV describes a number of techniques and tricks for enhancing the performance of your hard disk—stuff all DOS users should concern themselves with.

Who this book is for

If you're new to computers or if this is your first PC system, you will find a wealth of information describing the technology and terminology involved. You also will find step-by-step instructions for setting up your hard disk and storing programs on it. You probably will find these instructions easier to follow than those provided with your DOS manual.

Novice and advanced users will appreciate the information on subdirectories and the various commands associated with multiple directories. The information covered in the first five chapters of this book is devoted to discussions of hard disk technology, preparing hard disks for use, and commands associated with subdirectories and paths. As you become comfortable working with files and programs stored in different subdirectories, you'll want to move onto the more advanced subjects covered in the later chapters.

Advanced users will find the information on menu systems and batch file programming particularly useful. Using the information and programs provided with this book and the supplemental programs diskette, they will be able to design and create professional looking menu systems for use by themselves and less experienced users. The topics of data security and improved performance, which are covered in parts III and IV of this book, also will be of interest to advanced users.

Power users will find the utilities provided on the companion diskette to be worth the price of the book and diskette. These utilities offer sophisticated file management; a fast, professional menu generator; file encryption and attribute manipulation; and other exciting goodies. Power users also will find some of the tricks for providing file security and logging computer usage of interest. Some of these tricks are not documented in the DOS reference manual.

The companion diskette

Everything you need to practice good hard disk management is provided with DOS (except for the instructions, which you'll find directly in this book). Beyond DOS, there are third-party programs and utilities you can buy—specific applications to augment DOS or boost hard disk performance.

This book discusses many third-party programs you can buy and discusses their merits. Additionally, this book comes with a supplemental disk containing many public domain and shareware programs, as well as software written specifically for this book.

You can order the diskette offered with this book directly from TAB Books. All the programs are discussed in the text; they'll each help you master your hard drive.

If you're interested, you also can order the diskette offered with the previous editions of this book. Contact the PC-SIG Library at (800) 245-6717 or (800) 222-2996 in California. Ask for diskette #786.

What's new in the third edition

Wow! Three editions. Who would have ever thought that the simple hard disk management book Andy Townsend and I originally wrote back in 1987 still would be around today? Back then, hard drives were rare; hard disk management was a vague subject and few authors bothered with it. Today—three versions of DOS later—hard disk management still is a required subject for any PC hard disk owner, which by now means almost everyone.

Previously, this book was updated to include DOS versions 3.3 and later 4.0. Now, everything is centered on the new, best version of DOS: version 5.0. Incredible things have happened since that version was announced. DOS now can support very large hard drives and huge amounts of memory. DOS commands have been upgraded and new, life-saving commands have been added. This upgrade demanded that a new edition of this book be created to meet the needs of DOS 5 hard drive users.

As far as basic hard disk management goes, nothing much has changed. Hard disk management still is organization, administration, security, and optimization. For the next generation of DOS—as well as the new, hyperfast and supercool PCs—this book had to be updated. This third edition deals with all the changes that have taken place in the past few years, letting you know how to manage your hard disk in an ever-advancing computer world.

Conventions used in this book

This book isn't technical, yet it's about a technical subject. I don't like to write in computer jargon probably as much as you don't like to read it. So, to help ease you into technical concepts, any new terms will appear in italics. The term will be defined in the paragraph in which it is introduced. This method should avoid any confusion.

Throughout this book, you'll be introduced to various DOS commands, some of which probably will be new to you. To be consistent, I'm going to follow the same command syntax format as is used in the DOS user's manual: commands are shown in uppercase, with options and such following it in lowercase:

DEL *filename* [/P]

Items shown in brackets are optional; anything else shown is required. Either-or options are shown using a vertical bar, or pipe, character. These options will all be explained in the text along with the function of each command.

Note that, although all DOS commands are displayed in uppercase in this book, DOS doesn't require the commands to be entered that way. DOS is case insensitive and doesn't care whether the command is typed in all caps or not (although DOS is persnickety about spelling, options, and command order).

I also am going to assume that you know to press the Enter key after each command. Still, you should always double check what you've just typed, using the Backspace key to back up and erase if need be. Press Enter when you're sure the command is properly typed.

When it comes to DOS, this book is referring to Microsoft MS-DOS version 5.0 and later. If you have an earlier version of DOS, upgrade it. Seriously, just about everything here will apply to all versions of DOS, 3.3 or later. However, I heartily recommend an upgrade to DOS 5.0.

Incidentally, the term DOS (Disk Operating System) applies to all varieties of MS-DOS version 5.0; whether you're using PC-DOS, Tandy DOS, Compaq DOS, or Outer Wambooli DOS, it's all DOS in this book.

The term PC here applies to any computer running DOS. However, there are three distinct flavors of PC: the low-end, 8088/8086 systems, also called PC/XTs; the mid-range 80286 or AT systems; and the high-end 386 systems. In this book, the term *386* applies to any DOS computer with an 80386, 386SX, i486, or similar chip.

Every attempt has been made to ensure that the information contained within this book is as easy to follow as possible. While the subject matter occasionally can be difficult or technical, the style of the book is always unintimidating and friendly. I hope you find this book interesting and useful in helping you tame that wild and savage territory—your PC's hard disk.

Part I
Hard disk organization

In the beginning, using a floppy disk-only computer was easy—as far as organization was concerned. It worked like an old Wurlitzer jukebox. You had a pile of program diskettes and a pile of data diskettes. To use a program, you stuck its diskette into the disk drive, closed the drive's door, typed the program's name at the DOS prompt, pressed ENTER, and—voilá—you're there. For organization, you alphabetized the stack of diskettes. However, the hard drive you have on your PC now is just one big disk. It holds all your programs and data—possibly thousands or more files.

How a hard drive works and keeping it organized and running is the subject of this part of the book. Chapter 1 deals with the basics of disk storage and defines terms used throughout this book. Chapter 2 discusses preparing hard drives for use by DOS and your computer. Chapter 3 is on filenames and directories, which are fancy terms that describe how your computer stores and organizes information on disk. Chapter 4 introduces you to a few useful DOS commands. Chapter 5 introduces you to the concept of subdirectories. Chapter 6 is a tutorial on a useful DOS tool, the MS-DOS Editor. Chapter 7 is about system configuration with the all-powerful CONFIG.SYS file. Chapter 8 introduces you to the concept of batch files and batch file programming. Chapter 9 is on the AUTOEXEC .BAT file, a special program you create that sets up your computer the way you like it.

1

The basics of disk storage

Hard disks, with their massive storage capabilities and black box appearance, might seem a bit mysterious, especially for novice computer users, who often find the thought of all that storage space intimidating. If you feel this way about your hard disk, don't worry. This book will dispel the mysteries of megabytes, paths, and partitions and put you firmly in command of your hard disk.

This chapter exposes you to some practical theory relating to hard disk technology. Although there is no how-to information involved, the concepts and jargon talked about here will serve as the foundation for the remainder of the book. If terms like *sector*, *recording density*, and *access time* are unfamiliar to you, you should definitely read this chapter before proceeding. If you already have some understanding of magnetic storage, feel free to skim over this material.

Hard disk know-how

A computer is just a tool, albeit a very powerful one, that you ultimately control. As tools go, your computer really is quite simple to learn and use—especially when compared to tools such as hammers and band saws, which have a tremendous yearning to damage you and your thumbs. Computers, however, represent a different type of tool, what's often referred to as a *mind tool*. It's an apt description, because they can drive you crazy.

Although computers consist of various hardware components, such as keyboards, screens, microprocessors (the computer's brain), and storage devices, what causes them to run the way you want them to is the *software*. You can't see software; you can't touch it. Although you can see and hold the floppy diskette that contains the software, the diskette itself isn't the software—just as a compact disc, or CD, isn't the music. The musical simile is a good one: your computer is an orchestra and software is the music. Music—the software—is what makes the orchestra—the hardware—productive.

Software is the ultimate mind tool; you control it by understanding how it works. As you have probably learned by now, an excellent computer program with poor documentation (a rotten manual) is a pretty useless tool. The software itself is just as good, whether it's described well in the manual or not. However, the program's value as a tool is limited by your understanding of it. If you can't read about it in the manual, how can you do it with the software?

This same concept applies to your hard disk. Whether you've just purchased a new system with a hard drive or are an old-timer who's recently upgraded, you must gain some basic understanding of how it operates before you can use it successfully. This fact is true of any powerful tool. How useful would your car be if you didn't know how to start it, drive it, and maintain it?

Consider the two types of knowledge you need to use your car effectively. First, you need how-to knowledge—commonly called *know how*. You need to know how to turn it on, operate the various switches and pedals, steer, brake, and so on. You also need some why knowledge as well. At a minimum, you need to know why the car goes when you press on the accelerator pedal. What would happen if your car ran out of gas on the freeway and you hadn't a clue as to why it stopped running? (Most people who run out of gas never assume that at first because they reason they should know better.)

Your basic understanding of how your automobile works helps you to maintain it in proper working order and diagnose what's wrong when it doesn't work as expected. This type of knowledge is frequently referred to as *practical theory*. While you don't have to know all the technical details about how your automobile works, a little practical theory can go a long way.

Bits and bytes

The first step in understanding how computer storage works is to master the concept of bits and bytes. A *bit* is a binary digit, which has a value of either zero or one. *Binary* refers to the base two counting system. Humans, which should include about everyone reading this book, use the decimal, or base ten, counting system. In binary, values are zero and one. In decimal, they range from zero to nine.

Bits are the basic units of information storage in a computer. Each bit stores a value of either zero or one, represented as on or off switches inside the computer.

The octal and hexadecimal counting bases, shown in Table 1-1 along with binary and decimal, are other computer counting bases, though they're used mostly by programmers. Base ten, decimal, is used by most humans for counting, balancing checkbooks, and obeying traffic laws. Binary is used by computers. Why? Because computers only really have two things to count: an on current (usually 5 or 12 volts) and an off current (no volts). That system is the basis of how computers store all information.

Table 1-1 Computer counting bases.

Name	Base	Values
Binary	2	0 1
Octal	8	0 1 2 3 4 5 6 7
Decimal	10	0 1 2 3 4 5 6 7 8 9
Hexadecimal	16	0 1 2 3 4 5 6 7 8 9 A B C D E F

However, a single zero or one (an on or off current) doesn't store much information. For this reason, bits are grouped together in clusters called *bytes* (Fig. 1-1). In microcomputers, which include all PCs, bytes are composed of eight bits. It takes at least one byte to represent any useful data, such as a character or a number. This method works because eight bits in a byte can be arranged in 256 patterns of on/off. The computer interprets each of those patterns as a different value, ranging from 0 through 255. So, it's possible to have a single byte—eight bits—represent up to 255 of something, which could be values, codes, characters, or symbols.

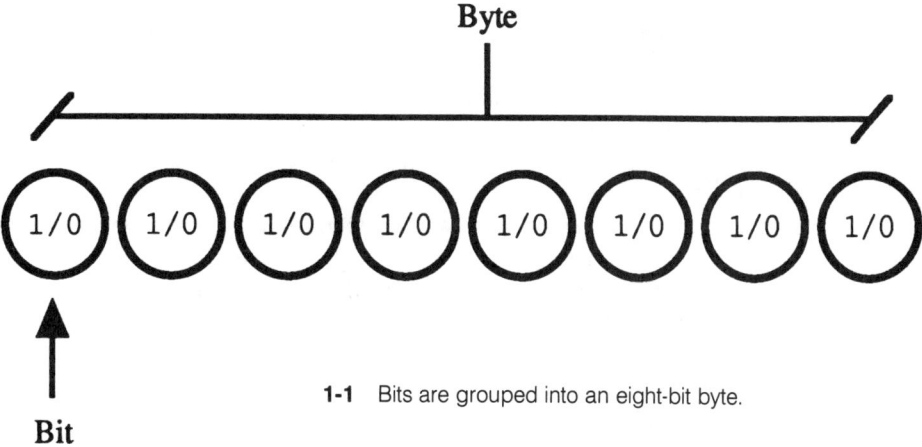

Byte

Bit

1-1   Bits are grouped into an eight-bit byte.

Data representation

When working with data, your computer is able to distinguish between alphanumeric and numeric data. *Alphanumeric data* includes text and digits (0 through 9)—note that the digits have no arithmetic value. A street address, such as 123 Any St., is an example of alphanumeric data. 123 isn't a value. The value 123 also can be stored in a computer, but it's numeric data, not alphanumeric.

To represent alphanumeric data, your computer uses a coding scheme known as ASCII (American Standard Code for Information Interchange). It's a system of code numbers from 0 through 127, each of which corresponds to a character—a letter, number, or punctuation symbol. There also are codes that represent certain *control characters*, such as the Enter key, the Esc key, Backspace, Tab, and so on.

Every character on the keyboard, including both upper- and lowercase letters, has its own ASCII code value. For example, the capital letter *A* has the ASCII value 65; the digit *9* has the value 57. Whenever you type a capital letter *A*, the ASCII byte value 65 is transmitted up the keyboard cable to your computer for input. In binary, the 65 looks like 01000001. The value for *9*, 57, looks like this in binary: 00111001.

Numeric data is encoded differently. With numeric data, the bit values actually represent the arithmetic value of the data—not the corresponding ASCII code. Storing values is accomplished using the binary place values of the individual bits within a byte. Figure 1-2 shows the binary place values for the first eight-bit positions.

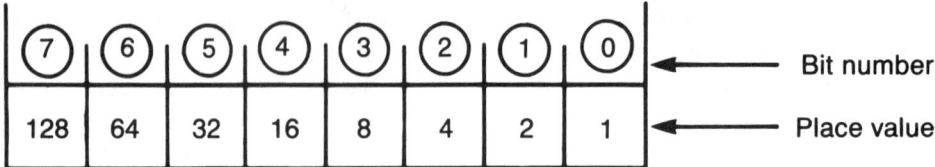

Bit number							
7	6	5	4	3	2	1	0
128	64	32	16	8	4	2	1

1-2   The binary place values for the first eight-bit positions of a binary number.

Using this binary arithmetic approach, the number nine (the value) has the binary code value 00001001. There's a 1 in the eight's place and another 1 in the one's place; all the other bit positions contain zeros. Because eight and one add up to nine, this specific sequence of bits represents the number nine. Notice that the binary coded number nine differs from the ASCII digit nine (00111001).

Don't worry if binary arithmetic isn't one of your stronger subjects; you won't need to convert decimal numbers to their binary equivalents. The computer does it for you automatically, all the time.

Your computer is able to differentiate between numeric and alphanumeric data as it's told by the software you're using. You don't have to worry about data representation. Instead, you just type at the keyboard or load information from a disk and leave it to the software and the computer to wrestle with the bits and bytes while you concentrate on the job at hand.

A comparison of binary and decimal

Because the binary number system is the basis for data representation, people who work with computers often measure things in binary. For trivial purposes, Table 1-2 contains a few common values converted into binary.

Table 1-2   Common values converted into binary.

Common value	Decimal	Binary
Fingers on one hand	5	00000101
Planets in the solar system	9	00001001
Sweet and sour pork	16	00010000
Hours in a day	24	00011000
Baskin-Robbins flavors	31	00011111
States in the U.S.	50	00110010
The national speed limit	55	00111011
Squares on a chess board	64	01000000
How fast we really drive	75	01001011
Degrees in a right angle	90	01011010
A "C" note	100	01100100
A gross	144	10010000
Water boils	212	11010100

Doesn't binary conversion make the metric system seem easy? Don't let it bother you. Usually, it's only the computer types who stick to binary numbers only. You can consider binary numbers as byte values that can represent characters, letters, and numbers.

Kilobytes, megabytes, and gigabytes

Just as bits are grouped into bytes, bytes are grouped into larger quantities. These quantities are used primarily when dealing with computer storage. They're represented by the following abbreviations: K, Mb, and Gb.

The K stands for a *kilobyte*, which means one thousand bytes. Well, actually, one K isn't strictly 1,000; it's really 2^{10}, which equals 1,024. Because that's so close to 1,000, most people are willing to neglect the difference and consider a K to be 1,000. *Close enough for government work* is one way of looking at it.

Mb, for a *megabyte*, means a K of Ks, or 1,048,576. You can compute this amount for yourself by multiplying 1,024 times 1,024. One megabyte is roughly a million bytes of storage. This amount might seem like a lot of storage until you start thinking in terms of gigabytes.

The Gb is for a *gigabyte*—a K of Mbs, which is a whopping 1,073,741,844 bytes. Again using round numbers, this is roughly equivalent to a billion bytes. These large numbers are used because bytes of data really are quite small compared to the large volumes of data that a computer can access, store or process.

Computer storage

How does your computer keep track of all the bytes of programs and data you use? To do so, it must rely on various storage devices. Computers use two different types of storage: electronic and magnetic.

Electronic storage

Electronic storage, usually in the form of RAM (random access memory), is used by the computer while it's in operation. The computer needs some place to store the program instructions that tell it what to do. It also must keep track of what it has done. In addition, it might need to remember the results of computations temporarily so that it can use those results in future computations.

Consider a word processing program. Before you can execute the word processing program, its software must be transferred from a disk (long-term storage) into the computer's memory. Only in memory (RAM) can the computer's microprocessor read and execute the software instructions. Additionally, the software needs its own storage space (more RAM) in which to put your prophetic words or prose. Eventually, this information will be printed or saved long-term to disk. For the computer to work on and manipulate it, however, the information must be in RAM.

The actual storage of information (bits and bytes) is done through the use of microscopic gates, or switches, which can be opened or closed according to the instructions of the word processing (or any computer) program. These switch settings remain in effect through the force of electricity. If the power to the computer were interrupted, as in the case of a power outage, the switch settings would return to their original state—the information stored in RAM then is lost. In terms of the word processing example, the program and the document under construction would both be lost. It's for this reason that most types of electronic storage, including RAM, are considered to be volatile. If you have ever lost important data because you inadvertently turned off your computer before saving (or the power company did it for you), then you know the true definition of volatility.

Another problem with electronic storage is its limited capacity. You are limited in the amount of RAM available to you by two factors: design and DOS. *Design* refers to the physical design of your computer. It can hold only so many RAM chips and those chips can hold only so many bits. RAM chips are categorized according to the number of gates they contain, which directly translates into bits. Common RAM chips contain 64 K, 256 K, or 1 Mb of storage space (the tiny gates). Note that, when referring to RAM chips, K and Mb stand for kilobits and megabits—not bytes. You need eight RAM chips—a bank—to make the full 64 K, 256 K, or 1 Mb of data. (Actually, for technical reasons not worthy of discussion here, you need nine RAM chips in one bank.)

The old IBM PC had space for only 256 K of RAM. By using expansion cards, you could upgrade RAM to 640 K. That was it. The PC/AT and all PCs with an 80286 microprocessor can have 1 Mb of RAM storage, with a potential for up to 8 Mb. 386 systems come with 1 Mb installed and typically can be upgraded to 16 Mb. That's a lot of storage and great potential, but the second limiting factor plays a role here—that's DOS.

Presently, DOS limits you to 640 K of RAM. This limitation stems from DOS's original design around the first IBM PC, as well as the need for DOS to be compatible with all PCs. For example, although a 386 system can have up to 16 Mb of RAM installed, DOS can only use 640 K to run programs—the same amount as the original PC. Starting with version 5.0, DOS uses some interesting tricks to access more memory, but it still places a ceiling on the total amount of RAM your software can use in a PC.

Magnetic storage

Because it's volatile, electronic storage is often referred to as temporary storage in a computer. For long term storage, you need something that still will be there long after the power is off. That second type of storage, more permanent than electronic storage, is *magnetic storage*.

Magnetic storage usually involves placing a magnetic imprint of the stored data on some medium, such as disk or tape—like a cassette recording or taping *I, Claudius* on your VCR. Magnetic storage enjoys several advantages over electronic storage. For one thing, magnetic storage media requires no power at all because it doesn't rely on electronic switch settings to represent data. If you turn off the power, the data still stays on the magnetic media. Another advantage is that magnetic media is very space efficient. On a high-capacity disk drive, a single 5¹/₄-inch diskette can hold 1.2 Mb of storage. A high-capacity 3¹/₂-inch diskette can hold 1.44 Mb of storage. Considering how compactly floppy disks can be stored, it is possible to store over a gigabyte of data on a single shelf of a bookcase.

The basic principles of magnetic storage are the same whether the medium used is tape, floppy diskette, or hard disk. A surface, usually mylar for tape and floppy diskette and aluminum for hard disks, is coated with a thin film containing molecules of ferric oxide (FeO_2) or a similar metallic oxide. The molecules exhibit a property known as *polarity*, which means that they have tiny magnetic poles—just as a magnet does.

Initially, these polarized molecules are randomly dispersed across the surface of the medium, so that their individual magnetic fields cancel each other. (Figure 1-3 illustrates this random situation.) However, by manipulating areas of the disk surface with a strong magnetic force, it's possible to align the poles of these molecules so that they create a magnetic field—they're all lined up, as opposed to being random. Because the poles can be either negatively or positively aligned, they can be used to represent on/off instances or, what you've come to know and love in computer storage, they can represent bits (Fig. 1-4).

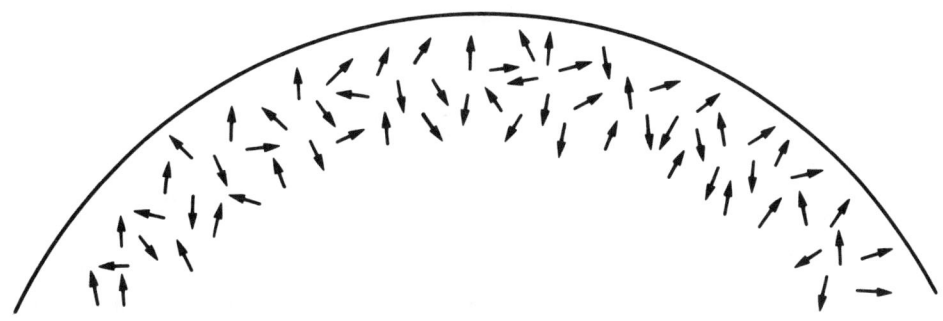

1-3   Randomly dispersed molecules of ferric oxide on the surface of a disk.

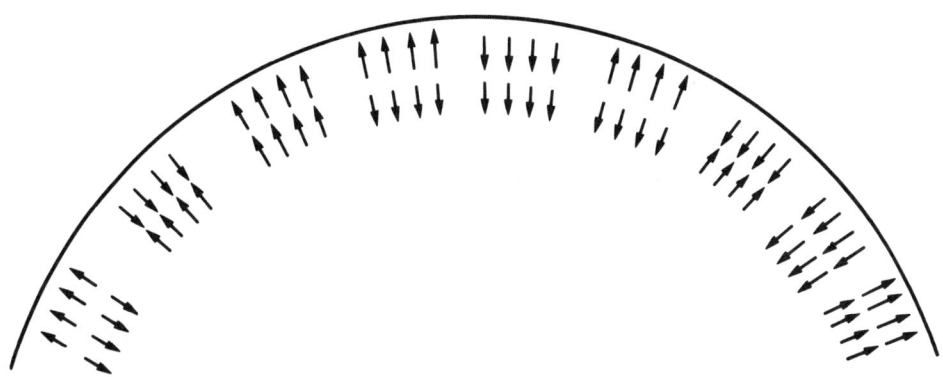

1-4   Molecules of ferric oxide that have been aligned by the read/write head.

The magnetic particles on a disk are aligned by a device called the *read/write head*. Like the recording head on a VCR or tape recorder, the read/write head passes closely above the surface of the disk, exerting a magnetic force. The magnetic particles that pass under the head are aligned according to the force exerted.

Once data has been stored on a disk, it can be read later. The data is read by passing the read/write head over the disk's surface, where it can detect the magnetic alignment of the magnetic particles. The data will remain on the surface of the storage medium until it's either intentionally changed or the medium becomes damaged.

How can you damage the media or destroy your data? Magnetic storage media can become damaged in a variety of ways. Fingerprints, soft drinks, dirt, dust, and exposure to magnets or electromagnetic fields all cause data to disappear. How the data is lost depends upon the cause. The thin film containing the ferric oxide molecules can be scratched or corroded away. In these cases, the oxide molecules literally are lost.

It also is possible for the molecules to become scrambled through exposure to errant electromagnetic fields. Even the most innocent-looking appliances, such as telephones and answering machines (which tend to congregate with computers on desktops), can be the source of electromagnetic radiation. (Every phone has a magnet in the mouthpiece.) The mere ringing of a telephone can be enough to scramble data on a nearby floppy disk.

Because data stored on magnetic media can be lost, it's important to create multiple copies, or *backups*, of your data. You will learn more about creating backups in chapter 16, "Backing up data and programs."

Hard disks versus floppy diskettes

In the microcomputer world, the two most common magnetic storage media are *floppy diskettes* and *hard disks*. This situation wasn't always the case. The earliest microcomputers used cassette tapes to record programs and data. Even the first IBM PC had a special Cassette BASIC program to use with cassette tapes. Unless you were involved in the pioneering days of the microcomputer revolution, however, you probably are more familiar with floppy diskettes and hard drives.

Before 1988 or so, only business systems were equipped with hard drives. Most home systems used floppies only, with a few hard drive systems available. Since about 1990, nearly all computers are sold with hard drives as well as floppy drives. Thankfully, the days of the floppy-only computer are over (save for some laptop systems).

The switch from floppy drive-only systems to those with both hard and floppy drives was gradual. Primarily, it occurred due to competition and lower prices. However, the advantages of hard disks over their floppy cousins have always been apparent:

- Increased storage capacity
- Faster access time
- Greater convenience

You might not directly notice any of these. If not, feel lucky about it; using a floppy-only system was a pain. Truly, the hard drive is a blessing to any computer system.

Early hard disk history

Interestingly enough, hard disk technology actually preceded floppy diskette technology. Hard disks evolved from magnetic drum storage. A drum symbol is used to represent auxiliary storage in systems design flow charts and near the hard drive LED on the face plate of some present-day computers.

Magnetic drums were hard metallic cylinders with an oxide coating. The drum rotated under a read/write head that read and recorded data on its surface. There were many disadvantages to drum storage, not the least of which was the physical size of the drums.

One of the earliest forms of hard disk was developed by IBM in the early 1970s. These disks were capable of storing 30 Mb of data per side. This characteristic quickly gained them the code name *Winchester disks*, after the famed 30/30 rifle. (Contrary to popular myth, *Winchester* doesn't refer to a disk manufacturer or any specific type of hard drive.)

The first Winchester disks were a whopping 14 inches in diameter and survive today only in the form of coffee tables. Contemporary hard disks (no longer called Winchester drives—save for a few old timers) are typically $5^1/4$ or $3^1/2$ inches in diameter, sometimes smaller. The basic design concepts of Winchester disks, however, still are used in most hard disk drive units.

Fixed hard disks

Winchester disks are *fixed disks*. Some computer manuals (notably IBM's) refer to them that way. FDISK, a hard disk initialization program that comes with DOS, stands for Fixed DISK. (You'll read about FDISK in the next chapter.)

Fixed disk means that the disk drive motor, the read/write head, and the disk itself are all enclosed within a sealed unit. For reasons that will become apparent in a moment, hard disk units need to operate in a sealed environment, which is one of the reasons why hard disk drives are more expensive than floppy drives.

Rigid disk surface   The reason hard disks can store so much more data than floppy diskettes involves the rigidity of disk itself. Floppy diskettes are exactly that—floppy. When they revolve in their jacket, they actually wobble. This wobbling effect means that, at any given point in time, the surface of the diskette might be fairly far away from the read/write head. This wobbling in turn requires that the magnetic fields recorded on the diskettes be relatively strong to be sensed by the read/write head. Due to the strength of the magnetic fields on the diskette's surface, each localized, magnetically recorded bit must be separated from its neighbors. Otherwise, the magnetic fields would interfere with each other, resulting in unreliable data. Figure 1-5 illustrates this situation, although in an exaggerated manner.

Hard disks, on the other hand, are rigid. They don't wobble—even at high revolutions. For this reason, the read/write head in a hard disk drive can be placed very close to the surface of the disk, typically on the order of one millionth of an inch. As a consequence, the magnetic fields recorded on the disk can be much weaker and can be placed

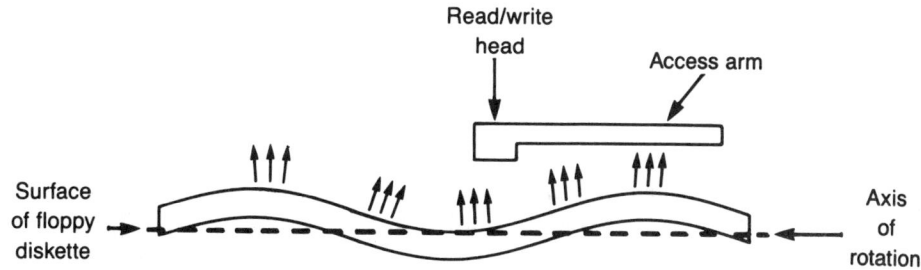

1-5   The floppy surface of a diskette requires stronger magnetic fields to represent data.

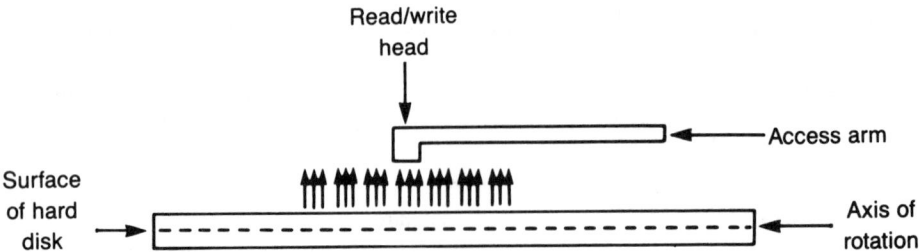

1-6 The rigid surface of a hard disk allows the heads to float very close to the disk surface, permitting the use of weak magnetic fields to represent data.

much closer together. Compare Figs. 1-5 and 1-6; the overall result is far greater storage capacity on hard disks than floppy diskettes.

Increased storage capacity doesn't come without a price. Because the head clearance is so microscopically small, the hard drive must operate in a specially sealed environment (as was mentioned earlier). Figure 1-7 shows the relative size of some common airborne particles in comparison to the clearance of a typical hard drive's read/write head. Note that even a fingerprint exceeds this clearance.

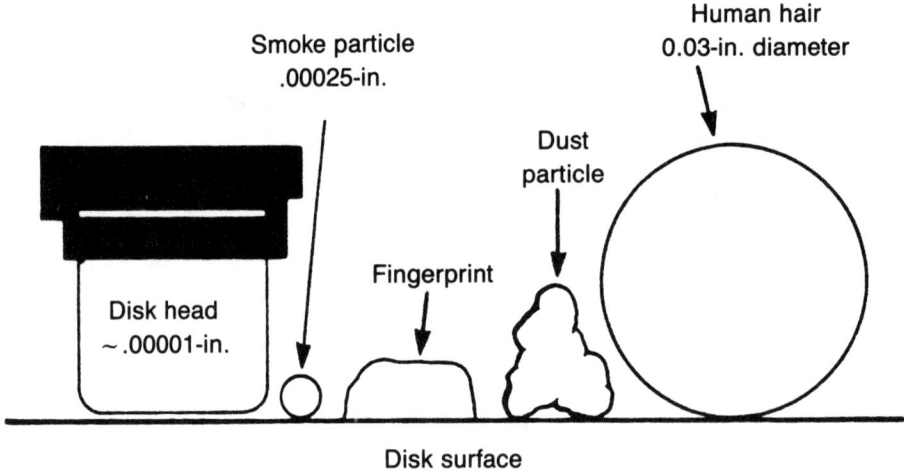

1-7 Head tolerances on the order of one micron compared to a variety of airborne particles.

Rapidly spinning Due in part to their rigidity, hard disks can revolve very rapidly in their drives, often as fast as 3600 RPM. The read/write heads used in these drives are aerodynamically designed so that they float, or fly, on the cushion of air created by the rapidly revolving disk. This design is why the heads will often be referred to as a *flying head* (which brings up interesting, science fiction-like concepts).

At such high speeds and with such low tolerances, any particulate matter that got in the way would cause the head to literally crash into the surface of the disk. The resulting collision would scratch the surface of the disk, rendering it unusable. Because the disk is an integral part of the hard drive unit, the entire drive would have to be replaced. Such head crashes are by no means unheard of and are one of the primary reasons for performing hard disk backups.

Fixed disks versus removable disks

The fixed disk is currently the most commonly used type of hard disk. Almost all internally mounted hard disk drives are of this type. As mentioned previously, fixed disk drives include the read/write head, the drive mechanism and the disk itself in a single, integrated vacuum-sealed unit. Fixed disk technology is well-established. Costs for hard drives have fallen dramatically so that such drives are affordable for even modest computing budgets.

There are limitations to fixed disk technology, however. Because the hard disk is physically fixed inside the drive unit, it cannot be removed if it becomes damaged or completely filled with data. A damaged disk means a damaged drive, which must be returned to the factory for repair. While you might not believe it right now, someday all your megabytes of storage are going to be used up. Then what?

To overcome these limitations, several different alternative technologies have been developed. All involve some method of separating the hard disk itself from the drive and read/write mechanism. These hard drive units are referred to as *removable disks* or *Bernoulli disks*, depending upon the technology employed. These removable disk devices will be discussed along with tape backup units in chapter 21.

The techniques for hard disk management are the same whether you are working with a fixed disk or a removable disk. For this reason, the term *hard disk* will be used throughout this book to refer to either a fixed or a removable disk.

Disk formats

As I mentioned earlier, the recording surface of the disk consists of a thin layer of randomly dispersed molecules of ferric oxide. Data is magnetically imprinted on the disk by aligning the poles of these molecules. Once a byte of data has been stored on the disk, the disk drive must have some method of retrieving that byte. If the surface of the disk were truly uniform, it would be impossible for your computer to locate data once it had been recorded. To overcome this problem, your computer uses an addressing scheme when storing and retrieving data from disk. This addressing scheme utilizes a series of magnetic markers on the surface of the disk. These markings constitute the disk's format.

Tracks and sectors

Disk formats differ from one brand of computer to another and even from one version of DOS to another. Despite the seemingly bewildering array of disk formats, certain key elements remain the same from one format to another. All disk formats use tracks and sectors to accomplish their particular formatting schemes.

Tracks consist of concentric rings, which start from the outer edge of the disk and continue inward. Each track is assigned a number, or address, starting with zero for the outermost track. The tracks are further divided into segments called *sectors*. The sectors within each track also are assigned a number. In Fig. 1-8, you see a simplified representation of a formatted disk. The number of actual tracks and sectors varies depending upon the disk format.

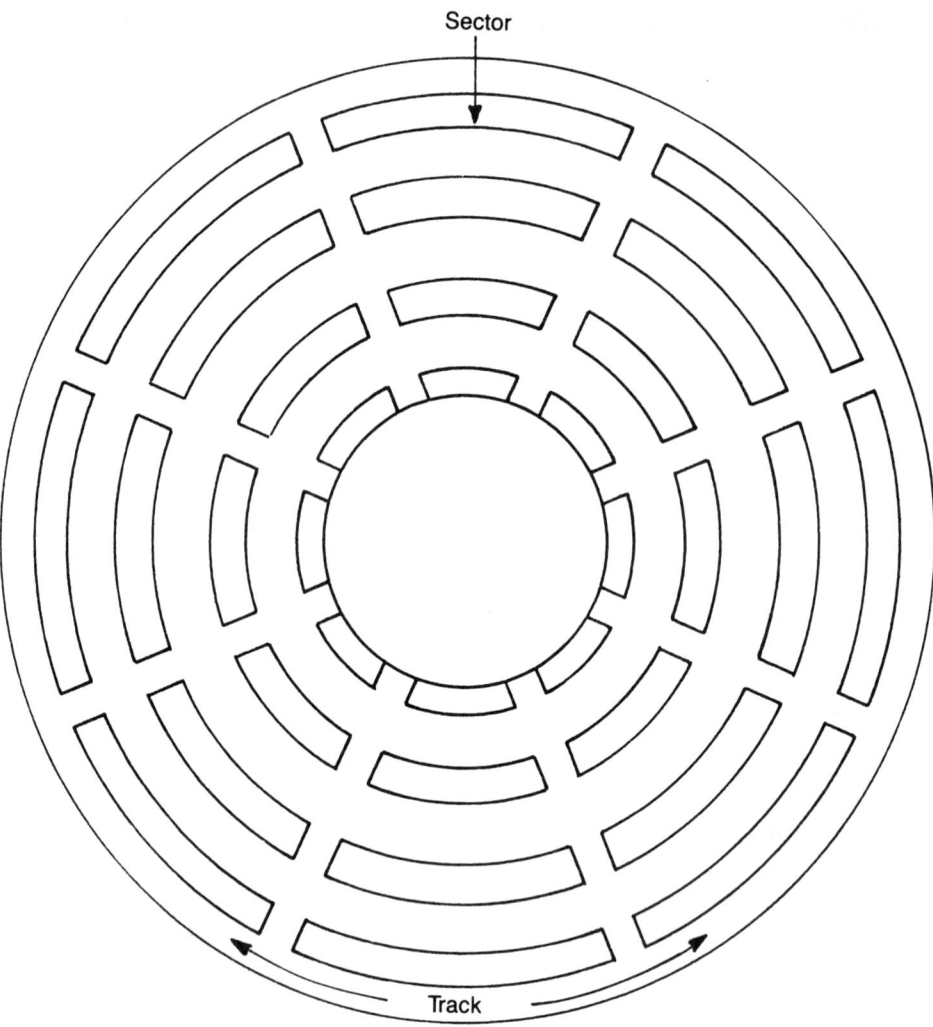

1-8 A simplified scheme representing the tracks and sectors of a disk.

Disks normally don't come with the tracks and sectors imprinted on their surface. Instead, they are sold blank, or *unformatted*. The disks are not formatted so you can use them in whichever computer you have. It's up to you to format the blank disks using a special formatting program. (Note that many hard disks are preformatted. For more on this topic, see chapter 2, "Preparing hard disks.")

The standard PC floppy diskette is formatted at 40 tracks to a side. High-capacity diskettes are formatted with 80 tracks per side. Hard disks usually have hundreds of tracks, even up to 1000 tracks in some cases.

Tracks per inch and disk density

Surprisingly, the tracks do not cover the entire surface of the disk. The distance between the outermost and innermost tracks is just about 2 centimeters (roughly three-quarters of an inch). The number of tracks per inch (abbreviated tpi) depends on the disk density.

The standard 360 K 5¼-inch diskette is referred to as a *double-density diskette*; 1.2 Mb diskettes are *high-density diskettes*. Double-density diskettes, which record 48 tpi, are physically different from high-density diskettes, which record 96 tpi. Although 360 K double-density diskettes can be used in 1.2 Mb drives, they can be formatted only at 48 tpi. To format at the higher 96 tpi, you must purchase the special high-density diskettes.

Why is this so? Because the surface of each diskette, the actual magnetic particles, is physically different between a double-density and a high-density diskette. Think of it like grains of sand. A high-density diskette has finer grains than a double-density diskette. If formatting were like dragging a rake through the sand, then you can create more ridges (tracks) in finer sand than in coarser sand.

The number of sectors per track also differs depending upon the format. The original DOS version 1.1 used a format with eight sectors per track. Subsequent versions of DOS (2.0 and above) have a nine sector format. There are 15 sectors per track on high-density diskettes. Hard disk drives normally are formatted with 17 sectors per track. Each sector contains the same number of bytes (512 bytes), regardless of its location on the disk.

Because the width of the sectors remains constant across all tracks, you might think that there should be more sectors in the outer tracks than in the inner ones. However, this would interfere with the addressing scheme, which depends upon a constant number of sectors from track to track. Instead, there are unused gaps between the sectors in the outer tracks. Much of the surface of the disk goes unused.

The problem of unused space is exemplified in DOS 1.1, which can format only one side of a floppy diskette. Why? When DOS 1.1 was introduced, most floppy drives contained only one read/write head and could record data only on one side of the diskette. Following the old adage that two heads are better than one, later drives contained heads for both sides of the diskette. Thus, DOS versions 2.0 and higher are capable of formatting both sides of the diskette.

Unfortunately, this situation has given rise to some misleading terminology. Diskettes manufactured for use in drives with only one head are called *single-sided*, while diskettes intended for use in dual-headed drives are referred to as *double-sided* or *dual-sided* and are marketed as such. Table 1-3 should shed some light on the density/side madness.

Table 1-3   Diskette capacities, tracks, sectors, and sizes.

Capacity	Tracks	Sectors	Sides	Description
360 K	40	9	2 Double-sided	Double density
1.2 Mb	80	15	2	High density
720 K	80	9	2 Double-sided	Double density
1.4 Mb	80	18	2	High density

Platters, surfaces, and cylinders

Hard drive units usually contain a number of disks, or *platters*. The sides of these platters are referred to as *surfaces*. Most hard drives contain two platters. It's possible, though, to purchase disk drives containing many platters. The number of platters contained in a drive unit in part determines the amount of storage it provides. Although a hard disk drive might contain several platters, it's common to refer to these enclosed platters as a single hard disk. You can say, "My hard disk holds 30 megabytes of data," when, in fact, the drive actually might contain two physical disks.

When discussing hard disks, track locations are described in terms of *cylinders*, because the same-numbered track on multiple surfaces essentially constitutes a cylinder in space. Instead of describing the location of data by surface, track, and sector, you use the surface, cylinder, and sector. Using the information provided for a given disk drive, you can determine the amount of formatted storage it can hold.

Consider, for example, a disk drive containing two platters, with a recording density of 690 tpi (resulting in 612 usable tracks per surface). If the disk is formatted with 17 sectors per track with 512 bytes per sector, the format creates 5,326,848 bytes of storage per surface, or 21,307,392 bytes in all—a 20 Mb hard drive. (Remember, the drive contains four recording surfaces.)

Disk access

In addition to their increased storage capacity, hard disk drives have the advantage of providing much faster access to the data they contain. *Access time* is a measure of the time required to locate and retrieve a sector of data. Although data might not come in nice, neat 512 byte blocks, the disk drive always reads and writes a sector at a time. (Technically, however, this statement is incorrect. See the section entitled "Directories and file access tables" in chapter 3 for a more accurate description.)

Access times for hard disks typically are around 40 milliseconds or faster (one millisecond is $1/1000$ of a second). The original PC/XT hard drive had an access time of 85 to 100 ms. That speed might seem slow by today's standards, but consider that floppy disk drive access times fall in the range of 175 to 300 milliseconds. Presently, some high speed hard drives have access times under 18 milliseconds. The access time keeps getting faster and faster. (Non-hard-disk-technology RAM drives have access times well under one millisecond.)

The reason for the striking differences in access times between hard and floppy drives is due to the mechanical differences between the two types of drives. To appreciate these differences, you need to have a basic understanding of how disk drives operate. Certain components are common to every drive, whether the drive is designed to hold floppies or hard disks.

Disks, floppy or hard, are held by a spindle much like a phonograph record. This spindle is rotated by the drive motor. There is a separate read/write head for each recording surface of the disk. Because the read/write head must be able to access data on any of the tracks, it's movable. The read/write head is placed on an access arm similar to the arm of a phonograph turntable. The access arm can be directed to move in or out according to the location of the track containing the sector to be accessed (Fig. 1-9).

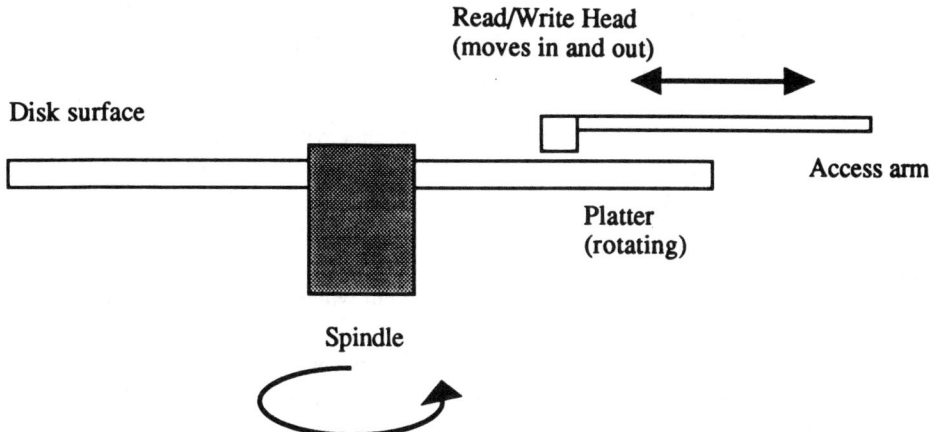

1-9 The access arm moves the read/write head across the rotating disk surface, allowing it to access any area of the disk.

The difference in rotation speed between hard and floppy drives is one reason hard drives have faster access times. Hard drives revolve at 3600 RPM, as opposed to 360 RPM for floppy drives. Even though hard drives have twice the number of sectors per track, it takes only one tenth as long to position the read/write head over a given sector in a hard drive. This time lag is known as *latency*.

Another element of access time is the amount of time it takes the access arm to move over the appropriate track. This time is referred to as *seek time*. In floppy drives, the read/write head usually is mounted on a pair of rails; track seeking is accomplished by moving the head in and out through the action of a stepper motor. With most hard disk drives, each read/write head is mounted on its own access arm; the access arms swing in or out as a single unit. Due to the mechanics involved, seek times tend to be faster for hard drives than for floppy drives.

Random versus sequential file storage

Hard disk devices are designed to hold large volumes of data and programs. Although the disk is divided into tracks (or cylinders) and sectors, it isn't very helpful to know that the data you are looking for is stored on surface two, cylinder seven, and sectors five, six, seven, and eight. Instead, you want to assign some easy-to-remember name to the data. For this reason, data and programs are given filenames, either by the program or the user creating them. In chapter 3, "Filenames and directories," the rules for filenames will be described in detail. For now, all you need to know is that both programs and data are considered as files by the operating system and are saved accordingly.

There are two methods for storing and retrieving files from disk: sequential storage and random storage.

With *sequential storage*, the entire contents of the file is written to the disk onto adjacent sectors within a given track. If one track is insufficient for all the data in the file, the head moves onto the next track and continues writing data.

Sequential storage requires that there be enough empty consecutive tracks and sectors to hold the entire file. Because this isn't always the case, sequential file storage isn't normally used. Instead, files are stored randomly.

Random storage, as its name implies, means that files are stored randomly on the disk according to the availability of sectors. For reasons that will be explained in chapter 3, sectors are grouped together into clusters. DOS keeps track of the used and unused clusters in an area of the disk known as the *File Allocation Table*, or *FAT*. When it saves a new file to disk, DOS searches the FAT for unused clusters and stuffs the file into them—sometimes in many pieces. A file in several clusters all over the disk sounds bad, but DOS keeps track of them and can properly reassemble them when you access the file a second time.

The random method of storage makes more efficient use of disk space than sequential access. However, it eventually leads to a situation known as *fragmentation*. Fragmentation occurs when so many files are split between so many clusters that overall disk performance slows as a result. The subject of fragmentation and how to deal with it is discussed in part IV of this book.

Summary

This chapter has provided you with an overview of disk storage. Most experienced computer users are familiar with the concepts and terms included in this chapter. However, there are many more technical details pertaining to disk formats and file storage that you must be aware of when working with hard disks. These will be introduced in the next chapter, which is on preparing hard disks for use.

2
Preparing hard disks

Preparing hard disks for use involves three separate procedures: *partitioning*, *formatting*, and *sysgening*. Usually, one or more of these steps are performed by the hard disk manufacturer or your computer dealer prior to sale. If you've been using your hard disk for some time and these three terms still are unfamiliar to you, the chances are that your hard disk was prepared for you. In this case, you might wonder why you should bother reading this chapter.

Unfortunately, nothing in the world of microcomputers is static (unless you rub your feet on the carpet and touch your computer's metal case). Both computer technology and your individual needs will change, often more rapidly than you expect. Because of changing software needs, through the addition of a network, or merely as a result of your increased sophistication, you might find that the original setup of your hard disk is no longer appropriate.

In this chapter, you'll learn how to partition, format, and install the operating system (DOS) on your hard disk for initial use. You also will learn how to repartition and reformat your hard disk, as well as install, or upgrade, different versions of DOS on your hard disk to accommodate your changing software and computing needs. Each of these operations is explained in detail. What's not covered here is the physical aspect of upgrading your hardware; that's covered in part IV.

Logical versus physical formatting

Recall from the first chapter that disks must be formatted prior to use. Formatting is the process of preparing the diskette for use by a particular computer or operating system. All disks must be formatted, regardless of their size or type; even hard disks must be formatted.

DOS disk formats actually consist of more than just the tracks and sectors laid down on the surface of the disk. In addition to these physical data addresses, a DOS disk format includes what's considered *logical information*. This information includes technical details regarding the disk format, as well as two work areas: the directory and the FAT (File Allocation Table).

With hard disks, the processes of physical and logical formatting often are performed separately. These two formats are sometimes referred to as the disk's *low-level format* and *high-level format*. Before discussing these two components of a hard disk's format, it might be helpful to follow the process of formatting a floppy diskette, in which the processes of physical formatting and logical formatting are done at the same time.

The format operation

The DOS command to format a diskette is FORMAT. (It actually is a file on disk, FORMAT.COM; therefore, it's considered an external DOS command.) FORMAT is typed at the DOS prompt and followed by the letter of the drive containing a diskette to be formatted. As is always the case, the drive letter is followed by a colon.

For example, to format a diskette in drive B, the following version of the FORMAT command is used:

    FORMAT B:

You probably have done this dozens of times to format floppy diskettes. You also might recall that it's possible to format a diskette so that it can be used as a system (DOS, or bootable) diskette by including the /S option:

    FORMAT B: /S

This and other formatting options will be explained in greater detail later in this chapter.

The physical format

When you enter the FORMAT command, DOS prompts you to insert a diskette in drive B (or whichever drive you've specified) and press the Enter key when you're ready. Once given the go-ahead, DOS proceeds to format the diskette.

For floppy diskettes, the formatting process consists of several steps. First, DOS tests the diskette to determine if it's already formatted. If not, DOS lays down the magnetic tracks and sectors on the diskette's surface, starting with the outermost track. As each track is formatted, the individual sectors within the track are established. The number of tracks per surface and the number of sectors per track are dictated by the version of DOS you are using. Also, DOS knows certain characteristics of the disk drive containing the diskette you're formatting. It will always attempt to format the highest capacity diskette for that drive, unless you direct it to do otherwise using FORMAT's optional switches. The tracks and sectors created by this initial step constitute the diskette's physical format.

In the case of floppy diskettes, DOS initializes each sector as it's created by filling in the individual bytes with dummy data. The actual value used by DOS is the decimal number 246 (F6 in hexadecimal; 11110110 in binary). Once each sector is initialized, the physical format is done and the new floppy diskette is ready for its logical format.

If the diskette already has been formatted, DOS skips the physical format step. Instead of creating new tracks and sectors, and filling each byte with the value 246, DOS merely scans the disk to verify that the diskette still can hold data. If any sectors cannot pass muster, DOS might physically format them or just mark them as bad and continue scanning. Once the scan is complete, the diskette then is logically formatted.

Why not do a physical reformat of a floppy diskette? Because it really is not necessary if the diskette already was formatted. By merely verifying each sector, DOS is assuring itself that the disk can hold data. If you really want to physically reformat the diskette, you can use the FORMAT command's optional /U switch. Conversely, if you want to skip the verifying step (and save lots of time), you can use the /Q switch and Quickformat the diskette.

The advantage to the non-destructive verify step, as well as Quickformatting diskettes, is that it allows DOS's handy UNFORMAT command to quickly recover an accidentally-formatted diskette. This subject is covered in part III of this book, chapter 15.

The logical format

After the physical formatting is complete, DOS proceeds with the logical diskette format. The logical format basically creates three things on the diskette: the boot record, FAT table (there are two of them), and the directory. This level of formatting basically establishes the work areas that DOS will use on the diskette.

The boot record is stored on the first track of the diskette, in the first sector. It's basically a tiny program your PC's hardware loads in from disk when the computer starts. The program is less than 512 bytes long (the size of a sector) and it assists in booting, or loading the operating system on computer startup. (This function of the boot record will be discussed further later in this chapter.)

Along with the boot program is various information about the diskette, information which the computer can easily access because the boot record is always located in a diskette's first sector. Some of that information includes the version of DOS used to format the disk, details of the disk's physical format (tracks and sectors), and where other important information is located on the disk. Figure 2-1 shows the boot record from a 1.4 Mb DOS 5.0 data diskette.

The special information contained in the boot record assists DOS in determining the diskette's physical format and in locating and reading files stored on the diskette. You can think of the boot record as the diskette's dog tags. For example, Table 2-1 describes some of the details about the boot record illustrated in Fig. 2-1. The values listed are in base 16, hexadecimal.

Table 2-1   Boot record details.

Offset	Value	Meaning
003	"MSDOS5.1"	It's a DOS 5-formatted diskette
00B	200	Bytes per sector (200 hexadecimal is 512 decimal)
011	E0	Maximum files in the root directory (E0 hexadecimal is 224 decimal)
015	F0	Type of media (F0 is a 1.4 Mb, $3^1/_2$-inch diskette)
018	12	Sectors per track (12 hexadecimal is 18 decimal)
01A	2	Number of read/write heads (it's a double-sided disk drive)
01E	n/a	Boot loader program
02B	"BOOT DISK"	The disk's volume label
036	"FAT12"	The type of FAT table used

Offset (in hexadecimal)

```
     00 01 02 03 04 05 06 07-08 09 0A 0B 0C 0D 0E 0F
000  EB 34 90 49 42 4D 20 20-33 2E 33 00 02 02 01 00    .4.IBM  3.3.....
010  02 70 00 D0 02 FD 02 00-09 00 02 00 00 00 00 00    .p..............
020  00 00 00 00 00 00 00 00-00 00 00 00 00 00 00 12    ................
030  00 00 00 00 01 00 FA 33-C0 8E D0 BC 00 7C 16 07    .......3.....|..
040  BB 78 00 36 C5 37 1E 56-16 53 BF 2B 7C B9 0B 00    .x.6.7.V.S.+|...
050  FC AC 26 80 3D 00 74 03-26 8A 05 AA 8A C4 E2 F1    ..&.=.t.&.......
060  06 1F 89 47 02 C7 07 2B-7C FB CD 13 72 67 A0 10    ...G...+|...rg..
070  7C 98 F7 26 16 7C 03 06-1C 7C 03 06 0E 7C A3 3F    |..&.|...|...|.?
080  7C A3 37 7C B8 20 00 F7-26 11 7C 8B 1E 0B 7C 03    |.7|. ..&.|...|.
090  C3 48 F7 F3 01 06 37 7C-BB 00 05 A1 3F 7C E8 9F    .H....7|....?|..
0A0  00 B8 01 02 E8 B3 00 72-19 8B FB B9 0B 00 BE D6    .......r........
0B0  7D F3 A6 75 0D 8D 7F 20-BE E1 7D B9 0B 00 F3 A6    }..u... ..}.....
0C0  74 18 BE 77 7D E8 6A 00-32 E4 CD 16 5E 1F 8F 04    t..w}.j.2...^...
0D0  8F 44 02 CD 19 BE C0 7D-EB EB A1 1C 05 33 D2 F7    .D.....}.....3..
0E0  36 0B 7C FE C0 A2 3C 7C-A1 37 7C A3 3D 7C BB 00    6.|...<|.7|.=|..
0F0  07 A1 37 7C E8 49 00 A1-18 7C 2A 06 3B 7C 40 38    ..7|.I...|*.;|@8
100  06 3C 7C 73 03 A0 3C 7C-50 E8 4E 00 58 72 C6 28    .<|s..<|P.N.Xr.(
110  06 3C 7C 74 0C 01 06 37-7C F7 26 0B 7C 03 D8 EB    .<|t...7|.&.|...
120  D0 8A 2E 15 7C 8A 16 FD-7D 8B 1E 3D 7C EA 00 00    ....|...}.=|...
130  70 00 AC 0A C0 74 22 B4-0E BB 07 00 CD 10 EB F2    p....t".........
140  33 D2 F7 36 18 7C FE C2-88 16 3B 7C 33 D2 F7 36    3..6.|....;|3..6
150  1A 7C 88 16 2A 7C A3 39-7C C3 B4 02 8B 16 39 7C    .|..*|.9|.....9|
160  B1 06 D2 E6 0A 36 3B 7C-8B CA 86 E9 8A 16 FD 7D    .....6;|......}
170  8A 36 2A 7C CD 13 C3 0D-0A 4E 6F 6E 2D 53 79 73    .6*|.....Non-Sys
180  74 65 6D 20 64 69 73 6B-20 6F 72 20 64 69 73 6B    tem disk or disk
190  20 65 72 72 6F 72 0D 0A-52 65 70 6C 61 63 65 20    error..Replace
1A0  61 6E 64 20 73 74 72 69-6B 65 20 61 6E 79 20 6B    and strike any k
1B0  65 79 20 77 68 65 6E 20-72 65 61 64 79 0D 0A 00    ey when ready...
1C0  0D 0A 44 69 73 6B 20 42-6F 6F 74 20 66 61 69 6C    ..Disk Boot fail
1D0  75 72 65 0D 0A 00 49 42-4D 42 49 4F 20 20 43 4F    ure...IBMBIO  CO
1E0  4D 49 42 4D 44 4F 53 20-20 43 4F 4D 00 00 00 00    MIBMDOS  COM....
1F0  00 00 00 00 00 00 00 00-00 00 00 00 00 00 55 AA    ..............U.
```

2-1 Information held in a 1.4 Mb floppy diskette, formatted using MS-DOS 5.0, is shown here.

The boot loader program, at offset 1E hex, would load the DOS routines on a system diskette. However, on this non-system diskette, the loader routine probably will display one of the messages you can see in Fig. 2-1, starting at offset 177 hex.

Immediately following the boot record on the diskette is its File Allocation Table (there are two of them, actually). This table is a special work area reserved for keeping track of the physical location of the various files stored on the disk. This work area is established and initialized during the second, or logical, phase of the formatting procedure.

Adjacent to the File Allocation Table is the diskette's root directory. The root directory is a special file that contains entries for each individual file stored on the disk. As with the File Allocation Table, the directory initially is full of dummy data. The actual entries in the diskette's directory occur as files are added to the diskette.

Although the boot record is always located in the first sector, the size and resulting locations of the File Allocation Table and the directory vary according to the type of format used on the diskette. These two size characteristics (number of tracks and sectors per track) are part of the diskette's format information and are recorded in the boot record. Using this information, DOS can determine where the data portion of the diskette is located. The data portion of the diskette is the area allocated for actual file storage and constitutes most of the diskette's storage space.

Floppy versus hard disk formatting procedures

Unlike floppy diskettes, most hard disks come preformatted. The physical format (i.e., the tracks and sectors) already is established on the disk by technicians at the factory.

The physical format, or *low-level format*, usually is a permanent feature of the disk. For example, the IDE (Integrated Drive Electronics) type of hard drive can be low-level formatted only at the factory; you get all IDE drives preformatted. Other drives might have some method of allowing you to low-level, or physically, format the drive. These methods are covered near the end of this chapter.

Drive designators

To establish a hard disk's logical, or *high-level*, format, you use the same DOS FORMAT command as used with floppy diskettes. DOS is able to distinguish between your computer's hard disk and floppy drive. To understand how DOS recognizes a disk drive as either hard or floppy, you need to be familiar with drive designators.

Most PCs have at least two disk drives, typically a 1.2 Mb 5$1/4$-inch and a 1.4 Mb 3$1/2$-inch drive. (The second drive isn't required.) Each physical drive is assigned a logical device designator, which consists of a letter followed by a colon. These logical drive designators enable DOS to identify which drive a specific command is intended for. The number of logical device designators is limited by DOS to 26, one for each letter of the alphabet (Table 2-2).

Table 2-2 DOS's logical device designators.

Designator	Device
A	First/only floppy drive
B	Second floppy drive/logical second floppy drive
C	First hard drive
D	Second hard drive/logical drive
E	Third hard drive/logical drive
.	.
.	.
.	.
Z	Twenty-third hard drive/logical drive

Traditionally, the designators A: and B: are used for the first two floppy drives, with the remaining alphabetical designators assigned to hard drives, other storage devices, or network drives. You can even assign a drive designator to a portion of your RAM and treat your memory like a disk drive. (You'll learn how to create RAM disks, as they're called, in chapter 20, "Memory optimization.")

On computers with one hard and one floppy drive, the floppy drive is physically drive A:. The hard drive is assigned the C: drive designator. Note that the single floppy drive, although it is physically drive A, can be logically referred to as either A: or B:. When you enter a command for drive B, DOS will ask you to insert a diskette for drive B and press a key to continue. When accessing drive A, the same question is asked, although for drive A. Internally, DOS keeps track of the logical drives B and A, although only one physical drive exists. Whether you have a B drive or not, the first hard drive in your system is always going to be drive C.

When you enter the FORMAT command, you're required to include the letter of the drive containing the disk to be formatted. DOS then checks a table of drive designators for the specific computer you're working on. This table is stored in your computer's ROM BIOS, a special read-only memory chip installed by the computer's manufacturer. This table determines the type of disk to be formatted; DOS proceeds accordingly.

On a hard disk, the DOS FORMAT command dispenses with the physical formatting process and only performs the logical, or high-level, formatting tasks. These include the three following tasks, covered in the previous section:

- Writing the boot record
- Establishing the File Allocation Tables (FATs)
- Installing the root directory

Contrary to floppy diskette formatting, DOS will not initialize the data area of a hard disk during formatting. Data stored on the hard disk is not actually destroyed during reformatting, although access to the data is removed because the directory and File Allocation Tables are rewritten.

Preparing a hard disk

Once you understand the difference between physical and logical formats, you can put the process of hard disk preparation into a sequence of four individual operations:

1. The physical (low-level) format
2. Establishing any partitions
3. The high-level format
4. Copying the operating system, or *sysgening*

The first step in preparing the hard disk is physically formatting the surface of the disk. (Remember from chapter 1 that there might be several platters involved.) The physical format usually is written to the disk at the factory; the disk is said to be preformatted, or low-level formatted (although this might not always be the case).

The next step in hard disk preparation is to partition the drive, which divides the disk up into separate work areas. There are a number of reasons why you might want to partition your hard disk. One reason for hard disk partitions might be to create individual environments for different operating systems. For example, DOS on half the hard drive, then another operating system like UNIX on the other half. Another reason could be to separate networking files from an individual user's files on a hard disk that is acting as a network file server. Another reason might be to divide a single, large hard drive into several smaller and more manageable logical drives. In practice, however, you probably will create only one, large partition, using the entire disk for DOS. (Prior to DOS 4, partitioning was done because DOS couldn't handle a hard drive larger than 32 Mb in size. Larger hard disks had to be partitioned into 32 Mb segments so DOS can access the extra storage.)

Once the hard disk is partitioned, each partition must receive a high-level format. If the entire drive is partitioned as one, huge DOS drive, then you format that drive using the FORMAT command with C: as the drive designator. If you've split the drive into three partitions, then they become logical drives C, D, and E. You must use the FORMAT command with each of those drive designators to format each logical drive.

The final step in preparing a hard disk is transferring a copy of the operating system to the disk. This procedure is sometimes called *sysgening* because it generates a copy of the operating system on the disk. As you'll see, DOS consists of three separate system files, two of which are hidden from view.

The operating system is installed only on drive C, the first hard drive. Once that's done, the computer can be booted from the hard disk. The computer will start up and load the operating system directly from the hard disk without requiring a system disk in Drive A. (Note that this might not be the case for some removable drives; refer to chapter 21.)

Performing a low-level format

Performing a low-level format on a hard disk drive is a fairly drastic action. If there's any data already on the hard disk it will be irrevocably lost. Remember, the low-level formatting process overwrites every data byte on the disk with dummy data. For a hard disk, this statement is true whether the disk was previously formatted or not.

You normally don't need to perform a low-level format on your hard disk, which is why you won't find the instructions for low-level formatting in the DOS manual. (It actually is a function of the hard drive controller's ROM inside your computer, which can differ between computers.) The DOS FORMAT command usually will be sufficient for reformatting your hard disk, should the need arise.

When to perform a low-level format

There are certain instances in which a high-level format will not suffice; you will need to low-level format the hard drive. One situation that requires a low-level format is removing non-DOS partitions. Suppose you have inherited a hard drive and the former user had established one or more non-DOS partitions on this drive. Unless you have access to the operating system software used to establish these partitions, the only way you can remove them and recover the storage areas they isolated is to perform a low-level format.

Another reason for performing a low-level format is if magnetic or physical damage has occurred to your hard disk and this damage is affecting the use of the boot record, the File Allocation Table, or the root directory. If you get many Boot Failure error messages when you attempt to start your computer from your hard disk, or if you get messages like:

    Directory not found

you might need to perform a low-level format. You should always try performing a high-level format first in hopes that this will correct the problem.

A third reason might be to improve the efficiency of the drive. A fast computer, with a fast hard drive, requires a certain type of interleave factor to use the disk at peak efficiency. (The subject of disk interleaves is found in chapter 19, "Storage optimization.")

Yet another reason for low-level formatting is to invigorate some older hard drives. The disk's surface might not have any defects or be on the way out. Somehow, redoing a low-level format on the disk brings some dead sectors or bad tracks back to life.

Because low-level formatting permanently overwrites any data stored on your hard drive, it should be used only as a last resort. If you need to remove non-DOS partitions or if your hard drive is not booting properly, you really have nothing to lose. If at all possible, be sure you back up all the data stored on your hard disk before proceeding. (Backing up is covered in chapter 16.)

Using DEBUG to perform a low-level format

The process of low-level formatting actually is performed by your hard disk controller, which is a special set of circuits, or chips, that are located on the hard disk itself, on a special circuit board known as the *hard disk controller card*, or is integrated into your computer's motherboard. The instructions for operating the hard disk are stored in the hard disk controller ROM chip. The address, or memory location, of this ROM chip typically is in bank C of DOS memory, at about 796 K. (Note that DOS actually can access memory above the 640 K limit, but this memory is normally reserved for video display; special ROM memory, such as the hard disk controller ROM; and the ROM BIOS.)

To access the instructions stored in the hard disk controller ROM, you need to use the special tool, DEBUG. DEBUG actually is an external DOS command, the program file DEBUG.EXE (DEBUG.COM on versions of DOS prior to 5.0). To use this tool, type DEBUG at the DOS prompt.

DEBUG will load and display its own prompt, which is the cryptic hyphen prompt. (Okay, so A> is cryptic too.) To view the contents of the hard disk controller ROM, which is located at hexadecimal address 800 in bank C of memory, type the following command:

```
– DC800:0
```

After pressing ENTER, about half a screen of data is displayed. Off on the right hand of the screen, you might see a description of your hard disk controller or the manufacturer's name (Fig. 2-2). If you don't see the text right away, type D and press Enter. Keep entering D a few times and eventually the ROM copyright message will appear.

```
-dc800:0
C800:0000   55 AA 10 EB 7C E9 28 05-28 43 29 20 43 6F 70 79   U...|.(.(C) Copy
C800:0010   72 69 67 68 74 20 31 39-38 34 20 57 65 73 74 65   right 1984 Weste
C800:0020   72 6E 20 44 69 67 69 74-61 6C 20 43 6F 72 70 6F   rn Digital Corpo
C800:0030   72 61 74 69 6F 6E CF 02-25 02 08 2A FF 50 F6 19   ration..%..*.P..
C800:0040   04 64 02 04 65 02 65 02-0B 05 00 00 00 00 00 00   .d..e.e.........
C800:0050   00 64 02 02 80 00 80 00-0B 05 00 00 00 00 00 00   .d..............
C800:0060   00 64 02 04 65 02 80 00-0B 05 00 00 00 00 00 00   .d..e...........
C800:0070   00 32 01 04 32 01 00 00-0B 05 00 00 00 00 00 00   .2..2...........
```

2-2   A sample screen displaying information pertaining to a hard disk as a result of the DEBUG command **dc800:0**.

From DEBUG, you can instruct your hard disk controller to perform a low-level format. With the Western Digital controller shown in Fig. 2-2, the instructions to do this format are located at offset 5 from address C800. (Other controllers will use different locations, such as C800:CCC.) To tell the hard disk controller to proceed, or go, you would enter the following DEBUG command:

    – G = C800:5

This command produces one of two results: the hard disk controller might go right ahead and reformat your hard disk or it might display a menu offering you a variety of options. The action taken by the hard disk controller depends upon the manufacturer. Actually, a third possible result is that the hard disk controller will do nothing at all. This situation will occur only if you have a non-Western Digital hard disk controller or if your controller doesn't allow low-level formats, such as all IDE controllers.

If your hard disk controller displays a menu or prompts you for input as to the relative disk head number, head count, number of platters, interleave factor, etc., you will have to refer to your hard disk drive owner's manual. These numbers might need to be entered by setting specific microprocessor registers with DEBUG. If this task is too daunting for you to face, you might want to take your computer into the shop and have a professional perform this procedure for you. Otherwise, between the manual and the instructions on the screen, you should be able to go ahead with no problem. Typically, the choices already offered (if there are default values) will be fine.

Remember, the worst you can do at this point is reformat your hard disk, which is exactly what you want to do. You can't do any physical damage to your drive.

A secondary, non-DEBUG possibility also might exist. If the previous procedure doesn't work, you might need to use a special program provided on a diskette that came with the hard drive unit. Typical names for programs that perform a low-level format are HSECT, DTCFMT, and LFORMAT. These programs perform the low-level format either as a convenience to the user or on certain brands of hard drives that require non-standard controllers. In most cases, however, you can use the DEBUG command, G = C800:5 to perform a low-level format.

Partitioning a hard disk

Once the hard disk has been physically formatted, either by you using DEBUG or at the factory, the next thing needed to prepare a new hard disk is the task of partitioning it. Even if you only intend to operate your computer as a stand-alone DOS computer, you still will need to perform this operation. However, you might want to check with your computer dealer, who might have performed this step as a service to you before delivering your computer. If so, you can skip this section and proceed to the section titled "Formatting a hard disk."

Hard disk partitions are created using the FDISK program. FDISK is used to examine or change the partition table on a hard disk. This partition table is written to the first sector of the hard disk and contains information on the number, size, and location of all the partitions. (On a hard disk, the first physical sector is the partition table; the first logical sector of the DOS partition will be the boot sector.)

Although the partition table is created with DOS's FDISK command, the information contained in the table is accessible to other operating systems as well. This accessibility enables you to format separate partitions under different operating systems. You can think of partitioning as dividing your hard disk into several smaller logical hard disks, each with its own operating system and format. Without the partition table created by FDISK, programs or data from one operating system might attempt to read or write over programs and data from another operating system. The result would be chaos, a condition in computing that users assiduously try to avoid.

For whatever purpose you have in mind, FDISK allows you to examine partitions on your hard disk and, optionally, create or remove any DOS partitions. One of the partitions must be chosen as the active partition. This partition is the one under which the computer boots. For DOS, the primary DOS partition is the booting partition, which will become your C drive. Secondary or extended DOS partitions can be used as logical drives D, E, and so forth. However, the primary DOS partition must be the active DOS partition on a DOS computer.

Using FDISK

To use FDISK, type FDISK at the DOS prompt. If you haven't yet set up your hard drive, you'll need a copy of the FDISK program, FDISK.EXE, on a floppy disk. Use it from there.

After DOS loads the FDISK program, the FDISK Options menu appears on your screen, as seen in Fig. 2-3. The menu displays the number of the first fixed drive and four options. If you do have multiple fixed disks (physical hard drives, not logical drives), a fifth option, Change current fixed disk drive, appears. This option allows you to select another physical drive in the system. Note that the first physical drive is numbered one.

```
                        MS-DOS Version 5.00
                       Fixed Disk Setup Program
              (C)Copyright Microsoft Corp. 1983 - 1991

                          FDISK Options

       Currend fixed disk drive: 1

       Choose one of the following:

         1. Create DOS partition or Logical DOS Drive
         2. Set active partition
         3. Delete partition or Logical DOS Drive
         4. Dispaly partition information



       Enter choice: [1]




       Press Esc to exit FDISK
```

2-3 The FDISK Options menu.

As you can see from the Options menu, you can create and delete only DOS partitions. Partitions for other operating systems must be created with their own programs. However, you can make a non-DOS partition active with the FDISK program choice 2. (Choice 3, Delete partition or Logical DOS drive, will be described later.)

To create a new DOS partition, you would use choice 1, Create DOS partition or Logical DOS Drive. A second screen will appear, giving you three options for creating a DOS partition, as seen in Fig. 2-4.

```
                 Create DOS Partition or Logical DOS Drive

        Current fixed disk drive: 1

        Choose one of the following:

        1. Create Primary DOS Partition
        2. Create Extended DOS Partition
        3. Create Logical DOS Drive(s) in Extended DOS Partition



        Enter choice: [1]



        Press Esc to return to FDISK Options
```

2-4 The Create DOS Partition entry screen.

The primary DOS partition is always drive C, the bootable DOS fixed disk. It can occupy some or all of your physical fixed disk. Extended DOS partitions are non-bootable, logical DOS drives. For example, drives D and E on the same physical disk would be logical drives contained in a single extended DOS partition. (The extended DOS partition is divided into logical drives.)

As an example, suppose you're partitioning a 60 Mb hard drive. You need a primary DOS partition, so you would select option 1. The FDISK program then will ask you how much of the total drive you want to use as the primary DOS partition. You can enter a percentage value for the amount of the disk you want to use as drive C. Use 100% for the whole disk, 50% for a 30 Mb drive C, and so on. As a suggestion, never make the primary DOS partition smaller than 10 Mb—minimum. (That would be about 17% of a 60 Mb drive.)

If you're using less than 100% of the drive for the primary DOS partition, the remainder can be partitioned off as an extended DOS partition or used for another operating system. If you're making an extended DOS partition, you can further divide it up into logical drives. The procedure works the same: you assign percentages of available disk space to the extended DOS partition and to the logical drives as well.

Are you insane yet? Don't worry, FDISK normally steps you through all complex operations. The choice you normally want is usually given between the brackets, so pressing Enter will do what you want nine times out of ten.

To see your partition information (even if you haven't created any partitions), you can select option 4 from the FDISK Options menu, Display partition information. You'll see information for the current fixed disk drive, the logical drive letters, partition information, megabytes used, and percentage of physical disk space used.

If you've just finished setting up a hard drive, the FDISK program might reset your computer or request that you do that on your own. The system needs to reboot so that DOS can read and load any partition information. Note that preparing the hard drive isn't complete; you still need to do the high-level format.

Formatting a DOS partition

Each partition on the hard disk, each logical drive you've created, must receive a high-level format. You might recall that the high-level format is only a logical format, not a physical format; it doesn't alter the sector data already stored on the disk. For a fixed disk, the high-level format writes the boot record, the File Allocation Table, and the root directory to each logical disk you've partitioned; the rest of the disk is merely verified.

The logical formatting of a hard disk is done using the same FORMAT command you use to format floppy diskettes. Remember that DOS is able to distinguish between hard drives and floppy drives and will perform the appropriate formatting tasks accordingly.

The primary DOS partition, your C drive, needs to have the operating system on it for you to boot the computer. You can have the computer put the operating system on the disk when you format the disk by adding the /S switch to the FORMAT command. (It also can be done after the diskette was formatted by using the SYS command, which is covered later in this book.) The process has been referred to as sysgening, because it generates a copy of the system on the disk.

The FORMAT C: /S command sysgens the primary DOS partition by copying three files to the hard drive that make the disk bootable: IO.SYS, MSDOS.SYS, and COM-MAND.COM. (The SYS command does the same thing, but without formatting the drive. You can use SYS to transfer the system to an already-formatted drive.)

The files IO.SYS and MSDOS.SYS are hidden and protected, primarily to keep them from being accidentally erased. Because they're hidden, they cannot be seen with the DIR command, although they're present on all bootable hard drives.

How the computer boots

Before discussing the sysgen process any further, it's worth investigating how a DOS computer locates the three boot files. The process essentially is the same whether the computer is set up to boot off a floppy or a hard drive. In this case, assume the computer has one floppy drive and a fixed disk, with the system files installed in a DOS partition on the hard drive.

When the power is turned on, a special program stored in the computer's BIOS ROM is activated. This program directs the computer to check the drive A (the first floppy drive) for a disk. If a disk is present, the boot record is loaded. A program in the boot record then checks the diskette for the presence of the IO.SYS system file. If it's present, IO.SYS is loaded into RAM and control is passed to it. It then seeks out MSDOS.SYS and eventually COMMAND.COM, which completes the booting process.

If there isn't a diskette in drive A, the computer checks for a hard drive. The master boot record on the hard disk is checked to see where the active partition is located. Then, the boot record in the active partition is loaded into memory and the program in the boot record is run. In the case of a bootable disk, the program checks for IO.SYS and the boot process continues along the same lines as for a floppy diskette. Eventually, after a few winks of the eye, you'll end up at the C> prompt, ready to use your computer.

If the computer can't find a boot record on a disk in either the floppy drive or fixed disk, then some sort of message is displayed. For example:

    Unable to locate boot disk

If a non-system DOS diskette is in drive A, then you'll see the following message displayed:

    Non-System disk or disk error
    Replace and press any key when ready

If the hard drive's primary DOS partition lacks the system files, you'll see the same message. If the system files are not present, you can transfer the system files to any formatted disk by using the SYS command, followed by the letter of the drive containing the disk.

The format operation

To format a DOS partition, the FORMAT command is used. FORMAT is a DOS program, located on disk as FORMAT.COM. To format your first hard drive, you'll need a copy of FORMAT.COM on a diskette, which you'll place in drive A. To proceed with the high-level formatting of the hard drive and to install the system files on that disk, the following command is used:

    FORMAT C: /S

If drive C already contains data, you'll see the following message displayed:

    WARNING, ALL DATA ON NON-REMOVABLE DISK
    DRIVE C: WILL BE LOST!
    Proceed with Format (Y/N)?

Type Y only if you truly want to format a drive. If you do, DOS will further prompt you to enter the drive's volume label, which you might have assigned the drive when it was formatted. This prompt is provided as extra security; you don't ever want to accidentally format drive C. (It was all too easy in earlier versions of DOS. The FORMAT command didn't require a drive letter so FORMAT by itself would always format the current drive—even drive C.)

If the drive contains no data, the format will proceed with the warning.

As the format commences, you'll see a percentage indicator, letting you know how much of the disk has been formatted. Remember, this step actually is a verification of the low-level format already performed on the drive. The display looks identical to that of a floppy disk formatting.

Once the entire disk has been formatted, you'll see the following messages displayed:

Format complete.
System transferred

Volume label (11 characters, ENTER for none)?

The *volume label* is an electronic label you apply to the disk. It's a name or description, up to 11 characters long including spaces. DOS will use the volume label when referring to the disk and in various DOS commands. Note that this label is not the same as the sticky label you might apply to a floppy diskette.

Enter a label for your disk, such as DOS DISK or HARD DRIVE or something more clever. Press Enter when you're done or just press Enter if you don't want a label (they're not required).

After pressing Enter, DOS will present a summary of information about the disk you just formatted:

    xxxxxx bytes total disk space
     xxxxx bytes used by system
    xxxxxx bytes available on disk

       xxx bytes in each allocation unit.
      xxxx allocation units available on disk.

    Volume Serial Number is xxxx-xxxx

The disk space and allocation unit information is mere trivia at this point; I'll explain the gory details to you in a later chapter. The serial number will contain both numbers and possibly the letters from *A* to *F*. (Yes, it's a hexadecimal serial number.)

If you're asked if you want to format another disk, respond N for no.

The FORMAT command has several optional switches in addition to the /S switch covered above—a total of 11 switches. These options are discussed in detail in a later chapter. (Don't panic. Out of the 11 possible switches, you only need to know four.)

The LABEL command

The LABEL command can be used to add a volume label to an unlabeled disk or to change or delete an existing label after a disk has been formatted. Remember that the volume label is an electronic label put on the disk, not the sticky label you should put on a floppy diskette's jacket.

To use the LABEL command you must specify the drive you wish to label. For example, to add a label to a previously unlabeled disk, you enter the LABEL command followed by an A:, and the volume label you wish to apply to the diskette in drive A:

    LABEL A: DATA DISK

The label DATA DISK is applied to the diskette in drive A.

To see what a disk's volume label is, you use the VOL command. For example:

    VOL A:

After pressing Enter, you'll see the volume label for the diskette in the specified drive:

```
Volume in drive A is DATA DISK
Volume Serial Number is 414E-1BCB
```

The VOL command tosses in the disk's serial number, just to be nice.

To change or delete an existing volume label, you enter the LABEL command followed by the drive letter and a colon. DOS responds with the disk's current label and prompts you for a new one:

```
Volume in drive A is DATA DISK
Volume Serial Number is 414E-1BCB
Volume label (11 characters, ENTER for none)?
```

You can type in a new volume label or press Enter to delete the existing label. If you press Enter to delete the label, DOS responds with a confirmation message. Press Y to delete the label or N to retain it.

Altering the structure of the hard disk

The number and location of disk partitions, the format of these partitions, and the type and version of operating system installed on the partitions all constitute what might be referred to as the disk's *structure*. This structure is not permanent and can be changed in a variety of ways. For example, DOS 5.0 (and DOS 4 before it) allows for a hard drive partition of virtually unlimited size—or up to 4 Gb (whichever comes first). You might want to take advantage of this and repartition your hard drive to give yourself the larger partitions and to use your disk space more efficiently.

Repartitioning the hard disk

Verily, I say unto you, repartitioning is something you don't want to do. Seriously, consider repartitioning as a major Herculean task. You can live with your older DOS partitions (I do). My advice is to buy a new hard drive and partition that one the way you want it. Why not upgrade and repartition at the same time? It's easier. If you feel the need, however, work through the following instructions.

Refer back to the FDISK Options menu in Fig. 2-3. Item 4 will display your partition information. Take note of your primary and extended DOS partitions on each of your fixed disks. Press Esc to return to the FDISK Options menu.

To repartition the drive, you must first remove all DOS partitions. While you're at it, you can remove non-DOS partitions as well, but you must do so using the operating system under which those partitions were created. Be careful. Removing a partition totally erases all data on that partition. Before proceeding, you must back up your hard drive—totally. This step is the tricky part. DOS's RESTORE command will only put the files back on the same drive from which they were backed up. If you have logical drives D or higher and you want only one, big partition under DOS 5, then you cannot restore drives D or higher to the new, big drive C. Instead, follow these steps:

1. Back up drive C.
2. Delete all the files from drive C. (Don't worry, they're on your backup diskette set.)
3. Copy all files from drive D to drive C.
4. Repeat steps 1 and 2, then repeat step 3 for each additional logical drive in your system.

The only problem you might have is with subdirectories in the root directory. Multiple backups will copy files to directories that already exist, not to unique directories.

It's a hassle, but it can be done. Then again, a new, larger hard drive always sounds so sweet. (I'd go with it instead if I were you.)

When you get the new hard drive or if you're repartitioning, then delete the DOS partitions from the old disk. Use FDISK to recreate your one, big primary DOS partition or to divvy up the disk however you see fit. Remember that you'll need a floppy diskette with the system installed, as well as the FORMAT and FDISK commands. Then, mosey on back to the section titled "Partitioning a Hard Disk" in this chapter and keep reading.

Installing new versions of DOS

Everything changes in the world of personal computers, even operating systems. The developers of DOS continually are adding enhancements and refinements to your computer's basic operating system. While these changes can result in increased ease of use and greater utility, it often means extra work and greater confusion when new versions of DOS are released.

To date, there have been four generations of DOS, coupled with various minor revision numbers within a major version. Such is the case with DOS versions 2.1, 3.0, 3.1, 3.2, 3.3, 4.0, and 5.0 (and beyond).

The original DOS version 1.1 was superseded fairly quickly by version 2.0 and is not used today. However, there still are some DOS 2.1 versions floating around. As of the publication date of this book, DOS 5.0 is fresh on the scene, although version 3.3 still is the most popular, with DOS 4.01 holding a distant second.

The presence of multiple versions of DOS has important ramifications for hard disk users. One important consideration is that, as new versions of DOS are released, you might want to upgrade the version of DOS installed on your hard disk. Then again, after thinking about some of the hassles involved, you might not want to.

As a general rule of thumb, only update DOS when absolutely necessary. This necessity happens under two circumstances:

- The new version fixes bugs present in the version you're using, bugs which prevent you from getting the most out of your system
- The new version offers features that you feel will make you more productive.

Also, bear in mind that you don't need to upgrade DOS incrementally. For example, there's nothing wrong with moving from DOS 3.3 to 5.0. Make the move when you feel it will benefit you the most. However, note that this book is totally based on version 5.0, so it merits the upgrade. (Plus, the benefits of DOS 5 are just too great for a super hard drive user like you to ignore.)

Using the SYS command

Before DOS had a nifty installation program, there were two things you did to upgrade your DOS version:

1. Sysgen your hard drive.
2. Ferret out all your old DOS files and replace them with their newer counterparts.

Step one is accomplished with the SYS command. Using the SYS command to sysgen your hard drive wasn't always possible with DOS versions 3.2 and earlier. The SYS command back then was rather dumb; it couldn't transfer the system files if they wouldn't fit on the drive. Not that any hard drive lacked the space, but the system files insisted on being at the bottom of the totem pole long after the totem pole was hundreds of feet high. To be accommodating, you often had to back up and totally reformat the drive using FOR MAT C: /S and start all over, which was majorly depressing.

With DOS 3.3, you could update by using the SYS command without the benefit of a full backup. The SYS command copies DOS's three basic files to the hard drive or to any formatted diskette. The three files form the core of the operating system, and are absolutely necessary to boot a disk. The files have different names depending on which version of DOS you use (Table 2-3).

**Table 2-3 Different
names for DOS's three basic files.**

PC-DOS	MS-DOS
IBMBIO.COM	IO.SYS
IBMDOS.COM	MSDOS.SYS
COMMAND.COM	COMMAND.COM

The first two files are hidden files and don't show up on your directory. (For more information on these hidden files, see chapter 3.) Because hidden files cannot be copied with the COPY command, the SYS command does the work for you, as well as copying COMMAND.COM:

```
A> SYS C:

System transferred
```

Note that you must use SYS from a drive that already contains the system files.

Step two also was made easier with DOS 3.3. The REPLACE command can be used to compare files from one disk, say the DOS distribution floppy, and another disk, such as your hard drive:

```
REPLACE A: \ *.* C: \ /R /S
```

The REPLACE command would search the hard drive for all matching files on the floppy, replacing those matches it found with their newer versions. Thus, SYS and REPLACE made updating DOS relatively easy for version 3.3. (Personally, I've upgraded to every version of DOS from 2.1 on; version 3.0 was only out for three months, so I didn't use it.)

After SYS and REPLACE, your hard disk will be updated with the latest version of DOS. Just reset the system and you are ready to go.

The DOS 4 INSTALL program

Starting with version 4.0, DOS came with an easy-to-use installation program, INSTALL (Fig. 2-5). It combined FDISK, FORMAT, SYS, COPY, and even builds a few startup files (CONFIG.SYS and AUTOEXEC.BAT), all for you. It was interesting, although mildly confusing due to all the different disk swaps, oddly-named diskettes, and extra hoops you had to jump through. However, it beat the snot out of updating to version 3.3.

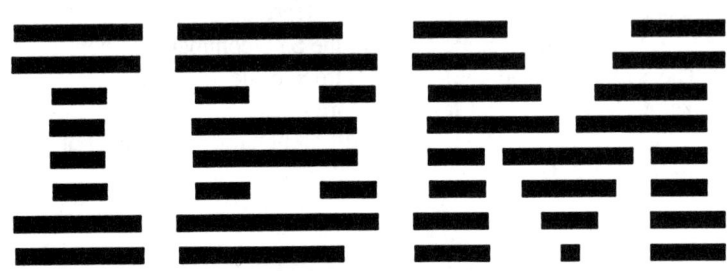

```
┌─────────────────────────────────────────────────┐
│                                                   │
│                   DOS  SELECT                     │
│                   DOS  4.00                       │
│                                                   │
└─────────────────────────────────────────────────┘
```

(C) Copyright IBM Corp. 1988.
All rights reserved.

Press Enter (⏎) to continue or Esc to Cancel

2-5 PC-DOS 4.0's INSTALL program's opening screen.

DOS 4 turned out to be too risky for most DOS users; they stuck with DOS 3.3 for a long time until version 5.0 came out. DOS 4, however, did blaze the trail for easy DOS installation programs.

DOS 5—Nirvana

DOS 5.0's installation program is the best ever. After ten years, DOS finally has an installation program rivaling those of applications put out four years ago. The only problem with the DOS 5 SETUP program (Fig. 2-6) and the DOS 5 Upgrade Kit is that you can install DOS only on a system that already has a version of DOS on it; you cannot start from scratch. If you already have DOS installed, which is the case with most PCs, then sticking your Installation diskette into drive A and typing A:SETUP does the job.

DOS 5 even gives users the option of undoing the installation afterwards. Normally, the installation proceeds as planned. You only have to swap disks a few times, plus supply an UNINSTALL diskette. After a few minutes, the system is updated to DOS 5. No sweat.

```
Microsoft(R) MS-DOS(R) Version 5.00
═══════════════════════════════════

        Welcome to Setup

        Setup upgrades your original DOS files to MS-DOS version 5.0.
        During Setup you need to provide a floppy disk (or disks).
        Setup will use the disk(s) to store your original DOS files.
        Label the disk(s) as follows.

            UNINSTALL #1
            UNINSTALL #2 (if needed)

        The disk(s), which can be unformatted or newly formatted,
        must be used in drive A:.

        Setup copies some files to the Uninstall disk(s), and
        others to a directory on your hard disk called OLD_DOS.x.
        Using these files, you can restore the original DOS on your
        hard disk if you need to.



ENTER=Continue  F1=Help  F3=Exit  F5=Remove Color
```

2-6 DOS 5's SETUP program.

Summary

This concludes the discussion on hard disk preparation. At this point, you are ready to begin using your hard disk system. The first thing you'll need to do is install your application software onto your hard disk. To do so, you will need to understand the concepts of filenames and directories. The following chapter provides a thorough treatment of these two subjects and teaches you the DOS commands you will need to know to set up work areas on your hard disk to store your programs and data.

3
Filenames and directories

By far, the most frequently used DOS command is the directory command, DIR. This command shows you a list of the files stored on a disk as well as other useful information about the disk. You probably already are familiar with this command. However, there's more to the DIR command than meets the eye, as this chapter will reveal.

You can use the directory command to obtain an alphabetically sorted listing of the files on your disk or to obtain a partial listing of just your Lotus spreadsheets. You also can print out your directory listings for reference purposes. These and other handy techniques are explained in this chapter.

Filenames and wildcards

To get the most from the directory command, you need to understand the rules for filenames and wildcards.

A *filename* is the name attached to information on disk. To DOS, the information is merely a collection of clusters, which it finds at various locations on the disk. You could look at the file that way too, but it would drive you nuts. So instead, DOS allows you to assign a name to the file, a handy, though limited, English-like word you can use to identify the file and its contents.

DOS filenames consist of two components. The first part of the filename is used to describe the file's contents and is often referred to as the *descriptive name*. DOS limits descriptive filenames to eight characters, although you can use fewer than eight characters if you wish. Getting descriptive with only eight characters is limiting, but it can be done. Consider all those clever sayings on car license plates and you'll get the idea.

In addition, a filename can include an optional *extension*. Extensions typically are used to classify files according to the type of data or programs they contain. File extensions are separated from the descriptive component of the filename by a period and can contain up to three characters. Certain application programs automatically assign file extensions to the files they create. For example, some word processors tack a .DOC onto the end of a filename. DOS itself uses the file extensions shown in Table 3-1.

Table 3-1 File Extensions for DOS.

Extension	Type of file
COM	A command file (program file)
EXE	An executable file (program file)
BAT	A batch file
SYS	A driver file
CPI	Code Page Information file

Rules for filenames

Not all keyboard characters are allowable in filenames. Acceptable characters include the letters and numbers (0 through 9). Lowercase letters are converted to uppercase when the file is saved. (To avoid confusing filenames with text, filenames will appear in uppercase throughout this book.)

Filenames also can contain any other symbols available on the keyboard, with the exception of the following:

. " / \ [ ] : * | < > + = ; , ?

Filenames can begin with any character (other than those just mentioned) but cannot include any spaces. Including spaces in filenames is probably the most innocent mistake made by novice computer users.

If you use any of the disallowed characters in a filename or if you do not correctly follow the rules for filenames, DOS will display an error message alerting you to the invalid character.

Some valid filenames include:

LETTER
LETTER1
LETTER.NEW
LETTER.OLD
MY__FILE
YOUR-FIL.84
1-18-93

Yes, you can use a letter to start a filename. See how the underline character was used? It works like a space character, separating two words in a filename. (Remember that the space character is illegal in a filename; not that you'll get arrested or anything, DOS just doesn't like it.) Table 3-2 contains examples of improper filenames, along with reasons why they won't work.

Wildcards

Wildcards are special characters that can be substituted for one or more characters in a filename. It's just like the card game Crazy Eights. In that game, the 8 card of any suit can represent any card or suit in the deck. The same thing holds true with special symbols

Table 3-2   Invalid filenames.

Invalid filename	Mistake made
YOUR_FILE	Filename too long
LONG.FILE	Extension too long
01/86.DAT	Filename contains the offending / character
LETR 2.MOM	Filename contains a space
86+87.DAT	Filename contains the offending + character

used by DOS. Those symbols can represent any single or group of characters in a filename før matching purposes.

The two DOS wildcards are the question mark and the asterisk characters. You can think of these two characters as variables.

The question mark wildcard is a variable that represents any single character. For example, the filename:

LESSON?

can be used to refer to:

LESSON1
LESSON2
LESSON3
LESSONA
LESSONB
and so on...

The filename LESSON? actually refers to all of those files at once. In this case, the use of the question mark saves you from typing the separate filenames.

You can include more than one question mark in a filename. For example, suppose you had more than nine lesson files. To include all lesson files, you would need two question marks:

LESSON??

This wildcard example encompasses filenames like LESSON12, as well as the single digit lesson files. It represents them all at once.

The question mark wildcard can be used in file extensions as well. Suppose you had a series of financial statements that were labeled P&L.78 through P&L.99. Imagine that you wanted to refer jointly to all the P&L files from 1980 on. What generic filename would you use? If your answer is P&L.8?, you are correct. (Your gold star is in the mail.)

The asterisk wildcard is more versatile than the question mark wildcard. An asterisk can take the place of multiple question mark wildcards.

In the descriptive filename, an asterisk replaces all characters up to the period. In file extensions, the asterisk replaces the remaining characters in the extension.

To refer to all the lesson files in the previous example, you could use a single *:

LESSON*

You could use:

LES*

In this case, it's unlikely that any non-lesson files will begin with the three letters *LES*.

One use for the asterisk is to save unnecessary keystrokes. Be careful, though, it probably would not be a good idea to use L* to refer to the lesson files.

As with the question mark wildcard, the asterisk wildcard can be used in file extensions. The most common usage of the asterisk in extensions is to refer to any extension. For instance, if you weren't sure what file extension you used, if any, when naming the lesson files, you could refer to them by:

LESSON*.*

In this example, there are two asterisks—one before and one following the period. Although the asterisk wildcard can stand for multiple characters, you must use a separate asterisk in the descriptive filename and the extension.

Another common usage of the asterisk wildcard is to represent any file with a given extension. To include all .COM files, you use:

*.COM

From this example, it's a simple continuation to using two asterisks to refer to all files, as in:

.

This special filename, pronounced star dot star, is very powerful. As you will learn in chapter 4, one important use of this combination is copying files from one disk to another.

Disk directories and File Allocation Tables

A disk directory is itself a file containing information about the other files stored on the disk. There are two types of directories: the main root directory and subdirectories.

Although disks can contain more than one directory, every disk has a *root directory*. The root directory is stored in a specific location on the disk, so DOS always knows where to find it. DOS then uses the information contained in the root directory to locate other files stored on the disk.

The root directory can be linked to other directories, called *subdirectories*. Subdirectories usually are not used with floppy diskettes but are a necessity on hard disks. The subject of subdirectories will be covered in detail in chapter 5, "Subdirectories and paths."

Disk directories consist of file entries containing important information about the files stored on the disk, such as filenames, the sizes of files, dates and times when they were created or last updated, and where the files are physically located on the disk's surface.

Directory entries

Each file on disk has its own directory entry, which consists of 32 bytes of data. A typical directory entry is shown in Fig. 3-1. Table 3-3 describes the information found in the directory entry.

Offset (in hexadecimal)

```
     00 01 02 03 04 05 06 07 08 09 0A 0B 0C 0D 0E 0F

000  43 48 41 50 54 45 52 20-30 30 31 21 00 00 00 00    CHAPTER 001!....
010  00 00 00 00 00 00 75 A9-16 13 BF 00 76 D0 0A 00    ......u.....v...
```

3-1 A typical directory entry as DOS stores it on disk.

Table 3-3   Information for a directory.

Offset (in hex)	Contents
00	Filename
0B	File attribute
0C	Internal information
16	File time
18	File date
1A	Starting cluster (location on disk)
1C	File size

Think of the individual file entries as consisting of records in the directory file, which is very similar to a database. These records contain specific fields of information pertaining to each file in the directory.

The file entry includes the file's eight-character descriptive name as well as its three-character extension. These constitute the first two fields of file information.

Following the file's name is a single-byte field called the *file attribute*. Among other things, the file attribute is used to denote whether the file is hidden or read-only. (You'll learn more about these special file characteristics in chapter 18, "File security.")

Next comes a secret field containing internal information used by DOS. That information is followed by two two-byte fields used to record the file's date and time stamp. These two fields contain the date and time the file was created or last updated. (You'll learn more about the DOS DATE and TIME commands in chapter 4, "The essential DOS commands.")

After the time and date fields in the directory entry comes the location of the beginning of the file, called the *starting cluster address* (at offset 1A hexadecimal). This address tells DOS where the first segment of the file is stored on the disk.

The final field in the directory record contains a four-byte integer value equal to the file's physical size in bytes. Although no file probably will be as large as a four-byte binary integer (several billion bytes), this size is the amount of room set aside in the file entry.

The number of file entries a directory can hold depends upon the size of the directory file itself. Because each directory entry is 32 bytes long, 16 file entries can fit into a single sector (512/32 = 16). In DOS 1.1, four sectors are allocated for the disk directory, which could contain up to 64 file entries. The standard, 360K diskette has seven sectors set aside for the disk directory, resulting in a maximum of 112 file entries. The size of the directory on a hard disk varies. In the case of most hard disks, the root directory consists of 32 sectors, allowing up to 512 directory entries.

Storing files in clusters

Files actually are not stored on a disk sector by sector. Instead, they're stored in *clusters*, or groups of sectors. The size of a cluster varies from one disk format to another. On the standard 360K floppy, one cluster is equal to one sector. On most hard drives, the cluster size is typically four sectors, or 2K (although it all depends on the version of DOS and the actual size of the hard drive).

What does the cluster mean? A cluster actually is the minimum amount of disk space DOS assigns to a file. Each file takes up an absolute number of clusters no matter how big it is. Yes, this does tend to waste disk space for smaller files. For example, a two-byte file will occupy a 2K cluster on your hard drive. That's 2,046 wasted bytes, but it's the way DOS stores files. On the other hand, most files average about 16K in size, which means they neatly fit into eight clusters; little disk space is wasted that way.

While clusters of 2K or more seem inefficient, the opposite actually is true. It would be far more work for DOS to remember and locate files at individual byte offsets, especially on larger hard drives. It's just easier to locate a single 2K cluster than some piddly two-byte file.

File Allocation Tables

Chapter 1 discussed the differences between random and sequential file storage. Whether random or sequential storage is used to write a file to disk, unless the file is smaller than the cluster size, it will occupy multiple clusters on the disk. Note that the clusters might not be adjacent to each other. Piecing this file together again would be extremely difficult without the aid of the File Allocation Table. The File Allocation Table, or FAT as it's known in DOS circles, works in conjunction with the disk directory to keep track of where files are located on the disk.

In the FAT are a series of two-byte addresses, one for each cluster on the disk. (Actually, the first two entries are used by DOS to record information about the disk—the first real cluster reference is found in entry two.) As was mentioned earlier, the directory stores the address of the starting cluster for each file. To find the next cluster, DOS looks up the entry in the FAT for the starting cluster. This entry gives the location for the next cluster (Fig. 3-2).

Following this procedure, DOS is able to locate the subsequent clusters that contain the complete file. When DOS checks the FAT for the reference value of the final cluster, it encounters a special control character indicating the end of the file has been encountered and there are no more clusters to be retrieved.

Essentially, the FAT contains a series of pointers DOS uses to chain together the various clusters into a complete file. Initially, all entries in the FAT are set to zero. The actual pointer values get entered into the FAT as files are written to the disk. A non-zero entry for a given cluster means that the cluster is occupied.

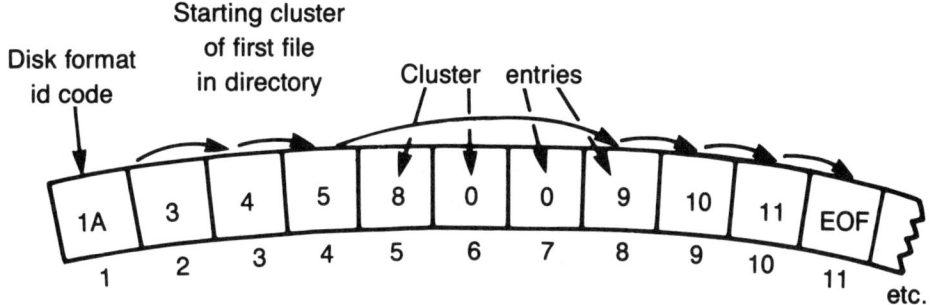

3-2 Organization of the data entries in a sample File Allocation Table.

The FAT also can be used to record the fact that a cluster contains one or more bad sectors. *Bad sectors* are either physically or magnetically damaged and cannot be used to store data (they're picked up by the FORMAT command as the disk's surface is being verified). If a cluster has been identified as containing bad sectors, a special code value is recorded for it in the FAT, which prevents DOS from using that cluster.

As you might imagine, a file's FAT is very important. Without it, the data stored in files on the disk would be unrecoverable. Even if the disk directory becomes damaged, it's possible to rebuild it from the information contained in the FAT. (In chapter 15, "Prevention and cures," you'll learn exactly how that's done.)

The directory command

To see a list of files on disk, you use the directory command as follows:

    DIR

After pressing Enter, DOS retrieves the filenames of all files stored in the root directory and displays them on the screen. In chapter 5, you'll learn about subdirectories and how to display directory listings for them as well. For the sake of simplicity, however, all examples in this chapter assume that the root directory is the only directory on the disk.

Information contained in the directory listing

A sample directory listing is shown in Fig. 3-3. The filenames are listed vertically down the screen in the order they were retrieved from the root directory. Notice that the period between the descriptive filename and the file's extension is not displayed. In its place are spaces, which are used to line up all file extensions in a separate column.

Next to each filename is the size of the file in bytes, along with the date and time the file was created or last updated. The first eight filenames actually are DOS directories—subdirectories—as can be seen by the <DIR> tag in the file size column. The last five filenames are true files stored in the root directory on disk. The total is 13 files.

In addition to information about individual files, the DIR command provides you with three lines of information at the top of the listing. The first gives the volume name for the disk, if any. The next line tells you the volume's serial number. Finally, you'll see the drive designator, where DOS tells you exactly which directory on disk you're looking at. In Fig. 3-3, the letter *C* followed by the colon refers to drive C. The backslash character, \ , refers to the root directory.

At the bottom of the listing, DOS indicates the number of files contained in the directory and the amount of space (in bytes) that they occupy. In Fig. 3-3, the five files listed occupy 117,530 bytes on the hard disk. The final line tells you how many bytes are available for storage on the disk, 17,029,120 or 17 Mb.

That last line can be used as a quick check to determine how much space is available on the disk. Remember, you're limited not only by the amount of physical storage space available, but also by the amount of file entries in the root directory. There still is a lot of room to grow in the disk shown in Fig. 3-3.

```
Volume in drive C is DOS 5
Volume Serial Number is 16CE-9B67
Directory of C:\

123             <DIR>        03-18-91     9:33p
DEV             <DIR>        11-09-90    11:53a
GAMES           <DIR>        09-22-90     5:18p
RAM             <DIR>        03-26-91     2:11p
SYSTEM          <DIR>        09-20-90    10:52p
TEMP            <DIR>        09-20-90    10:54p
WORK            <DIR>        09-21-90     5:54p
WP51            <DIR>        09-21-90     5:12p
AUTOEXEC BAT           488 06-14-91     7:35p
CONFIG   SYS           456 06-18-91     9:11p
COMMAND  COM         47845 04-09-91     5:00a
WINA20   386          9349 04-09-91     5:00a
MIRROR   FIL         59392 06-16-91    12:03p
         13 file(s)       117530 bytes
                        17029120 bytes free
```

3-3 A sample directory listing.

Changing the current drive

The directory command will display a listing of the working or current directory (for now, this means the root directory) on the currently logged disk drive. Most computers containing hard drives are set up to boot off the hard disk. The system will boot off the hard drive and drive C will be the current drive. This is communicated by the fact that the DOS prompt is displayed as a *C* prompt, C>. When you type DIR, DOS assumes you mean the current drive and will show you a directory of it. To obtain a directory listing of a drive other than the current drive you have two options.

The first way to see a list of files on another drive is to include that drive's designator (the drive letter) as part of the DIR command. For example, if the C drive is the current drive and you wanted a listing of the files on the diskette in drive A, you'd enter:

C> DIR A:

A second method for obtaining a directory listing of another drive is to make that drive the current drive. This is just about as easy as the first method, but it requires two separate

DOS commands. The first is to log to the second drive, making that drive the current drive. You log to another drive by typing its drive letter and a colon at the DOS C prompt:

    C> A:

DOS responds by displaying an *A* prompt, indicating that drive A is the working drive. You would then enter the directory command:

    A> DIR

Because a drive designator isn't included, DOS assumes you mean the currently logged drive, A:, and it shows you the files there.

Directory command options

The standard directory command is fine when working with disks containing a limited number of files. However, even with floppy diskettes, the number of files can quickly grow beyond the number that can appear on the screen at one time. With hard disks, the problem can become even more severe as the number of files could expand into the hundreds.

If there are more files in the directory than can be displayed on a single screen, the directory command scrolls off the top of the screen as it continues to list the files in vertical sequence. Unless you're particularly sharp or your computer particularly slow, you're apt to miss a filename that appears in the early part of the listing as it scrolls by.

There are two ways of getting around this problem. The first is to use the wide display option when entering the directory command. The wide display option is activated using the /W switch after the directory command as follows:

    DIR /W

The directory listing (Fig. 3-4) shows filenames displayed across the screen in five columns, allowing up to five times as many files to be displayed on a single screen. There's no such thing as a free lunch. In this case, DOS sacrifices the file size, as well as the date and time information for each file.

```
Volume in drive C is DOS 5
Volume Serial Number is 16CE-9B67
Directory of C:\

[123]          [DEV]          [GAMES]        [RAM]          [SYSTEM]
[TEMP]         [WORK]         [WP51]         AUTOEXEC.BAT   CONFIG.SYS
COMMAND.COM    WINA20.386     MIRROR.FIL
      13 file(s)      117530 bytes
                    17029120 bytes free
```

3-4 A directory listing obtained using the /W option.

If you need to view the complete directory listing or if you have even more files than can be displayed on a single screen with the /W wide display option, you can use the Ctrl−NumLock or Ctrl−S key sequence to temporarily interrupt the scrolling process. If your keyboard has a Pause or Hold key, these keys also have the effect of pausing the display. Pressing a pause key sequence again or the Enter key causes the scrolling to resume.

If your fingers aren't nimble enough to master a pause key sequence, then you can use the directory command with its pause option, /P. The pause option follows the directory command and can be used alone or in combination with the /W wide option. The following are two ways of using the pause option:

DIR /P

DIR /W/P

Whenever you add the pause option to the directory command, DOS displays as many files as will fit on the screen and then displays the message:

Press any key to continue . . .

You can view the contents of the screen as long as you like. When you wish to see the next screenful, just press any key (the Spacebar or Enter key will do nicely). This screen-by-screen display will continue, with you controlling the pace, until the entire directory has been displayed. If you wish, you can halt the directory display by pressing Ctrl−C or Ctrl−Break, which cancels any DOS command and returns you to the system prompt.

Partial directories

The basic DIR command shows you all the files on the disk. However, it can be optionally followed with the name of a specific file you want to locate or a group of files as specified by wildcards. This way, you don't have to tediously scan through multiple screens of file listings to locate the file you want. For example, if you want to see if LESSON1 is stored on the current disk, you would enter:

DIR LESSON1

If it's there, DOS displays the filename and the size of the file, etc. If the file isn't present, DOS responds with the message:

File not found

Maybe LESSON1 is on drive A. If so, you could try the following:

DIR A:LESSON1

Sometimes you might want only a partial listing of the files on disk. Usually, you'll want to view all files satisfying a certain condition, such as all spreadsheet files or all COM files. To obtain a listing of all COM files, you would enter:

DIR *.COM

After pressing Enter, DOS displays a directory listing including only those files with a COM extension (matching *.COM). If there weren't any files satisfying this condition, the File not found message would be displayed.

Partial directory listings are a handy way of limiting the time required to determine the name, size, existence, etc. of a given file when you don't know its exact spelling. Imagine that you are looking for a file you created last week. You're sure you called it something beginning with *INS* because it was an analysis of insurance policies held by your company. Rather than searching through the entire directory, you could enter:

    DIR A:INS*

This command would give you a listing of all files beginning with *INS*. If the file were of a specific type, say a Lotus 1-2-3 worksheet file, you could further narrow the search with:

    DIR A:INS*.WK?

Chances are there will only be a few of them. One word of advice: if several filenames are displayed and you still can't remember which one you want, you can print the output of the directory listing. (This is covered later in this chapter.)

Locating lost files

The directory command also can be used to determine if a given file is anywhere on a given disk. To do this, you need the DIR command's /S switch, added with DOS version 5.0. The /S switch tells DIR to display files in the current directory as well as all subdirectories under the current directory. (Although the concept of subdirectories is covered in chapter 5, read through the following examples and maybe try a few.)

For example, the following DIR command locates every COM file on the hard disk:

    C> DIR *.COM /S

The /S switch sweeps through all your subdirectories, displaying the name of each one and all the COM files contained within. When the listing is complete, you'll see a summary displayed:

    Total files listed:
    xxx file(s)   *xxxxxx* bytes
                    xxxxxxxx bytes free

This is rather inefficient, granted. However, suppose you want to see where that darned LESSON1 file is. Then, you could locate it individually by typing:

    C> DIR LESSON1 /S

If it's on the hard drive, the DIR command will display the subdirectory containing it.

You can combine the /S switch with the /P switch to pause the DIR command's output after every screenful of text. This comes in handy, especially when DIR /S finds a lot of files. For example, the following DIR command will display all files on your hard drive— all of them:

    C> DIR /S /P

Try this on your own and enjoy the listing. If you have several hundred files, however, and you get tired, press Ctrl−C to cancel the DIR command.

Other DIR command options

The DIR command has a wealth of optional switches, each of which controls the output or type of files the DIR command displays. Table 3-4 lists all the switches. Note that you can always see a summary of these by using the /?, help switch, offered with all DOS commands.

Table 3-4
The DIR command's optional switches.

Switch	Function
/W	Displays files in the wide format
/P	Pauses after each screenful of files
/S	Displays matching files in all subdirectories under the current directory
/B	Displays a brief list of filenames only
/L	Displays all files in lowercase
/A	Displays files by their attribute
/O	Displays a sorted list of files

You already are familiar with the /W, /P, and /S switches. The /B switch is used to display a brief directory listing, only the names of the files and nothing else. For example, the following listing is the output of the DIR /B command on the same disk as shown in Fig. 3-3:

```
123
DEV
GAMES
RAM
SYSTEM
TEMP
WORK
WP51
AUTOEXEC.BAT
CONFIG.SYS
COMMAND.COM
WINA20.386
MIRROR.FIL
```

No other information is displayed, not bytes used or free, the name of the disk, nothing.

The /L switch is simply a modifier switch. It doesn't control the display of files in any way, but it does display all filenames in lowercase. You can use /L with any other options. The only thing that changes is the filenames. For example:

```
DIR /L
```

displays all files in the current directory—just like the plain DIR command. The filenames and extensions, however, will be listed in lowercase.

The last two optional DIR command switches are /A and /O. The /A switch displays files by their attributes. Files can have five attributes: *A* for archive files, or those that have been modified recently; *D* for directory files; *H* for hidden files; *R* for read-only files; and *S* for system files. You can use the /A switch with the DIR command to display only those files with specific attributes:

DIR /A

By itself, the /A switch displays all files with any attributes. If you issue the previous command in the root directory of a boot disk, you'll see the hidden files MSDOS.SYS and IO.SYS along with other hidden and system files in the directory. (These normally would not be displayed by the standard DIR command.)

To display only files of a specific type, follow the /A switch with a colon and the letter corresponding to the file attribute you want to see:

DIR /A:H

The previous command displays only hidden files in the current directory.

DIR /A:D

displays only directory files (subdirectories). To display files without a certain attribute, put a minus sign before the switch:

DIR /A: – D

This command displays all files that are not directories. You also can combine switches to display special groups of files:

DIR /A:AR

The previous command displays all files that have both their archive and read-only attributes.

More information on file attributes is presented in chapter 18, "File security." Remember that the /A switch has a slash before it. If you type DIR A:AR, the DIR command will assume you want it to look on drive A for something.

The final switch is the /O, sorting switch (although *O* could be thought of as standing for *order*):

DIR /O

When specified, the /O switch shows you files in the directory in an alphabetically sorted order, by their filenames. You also can follow the /O switch with a colon and five other letters to control the order of the sorting, as seen in Table 3-5.

Table 3-5   The /O switch's sorting keys.

Letter	Sort by
D	Date and time
E	Filename extension
G	Directories (group directories first)
N	Filename (the default)
S	File size

More than one letter can be specified to sort on different levels. Also, a minus (or hyphen) can be used to reverse the sorting order.

    DIR /O

sorts the filenames alphabetically. The /O:N switch would do the same thing. To group the directories first, use the following command:

    DIR /O:GN

To sort the files smallest to largest, use the following command:

    DIR /O:S

To see the files from largest to smallest, use this command:

    DIR /O: – S

The /O switch, as well as all other DIR command switches and options, can be combined, mixed, and matched, to produce the DIR command output you desire. Later, in chapter 9, "AUTOEXEC.BAT," you'll learn how to use your favorite DIR command options over and over without typing them in each time.

Printing directory listings

It often is helpful to have a printed listing of the files stored on a disk. Fortunately, there are several ways to print a hardcopy using DOS, one of which is bound to suit your fancy. The most obvious and handy is the DOS screen dump feature.

There is a special key on most keyboards labeled PrtSc, Print Scrn, or just Print. On some keyboards, this key is a stand-alone one-function key. On other keyboards, notably the early PC/XT keyboards, you have to hold the Shift key down to activate the print screen. This key combination is used to prevent you from inadvertently hitting this key by mistake.

Striking the PrtSc key causes DOS to send a copy of the screen's contents to the printer. (Actually, a copy of the video RAM is sent to the printer, but who wants to get technical?) PrtSc only gives you a copy of what's currently displayed. Also, the PrtSc key will work only if your printer is on, online, and connected to your computer. (You would be amazed at how often people forget this simple fact.) If it is not, your computer might wait (and wait and wait) for the printer. Some smart PCs (depending on their BIOS) will note that the printer isn't on and won't bother waiting. (The only way to really find out is to try it.)

If your directory listings take up multiple screens, there's an alternative to using the PrtSc key to print each screenful of information. Using the Ctrl – PrtSc or Ctrl – P key combination will cause everything displayed on the screen to be sent to the printer—up until a second Ctrl – PrtSc or Ctrl – P is entered. This feature often is referred to as *printer echo*. Everything displayed on the screen will be echoed to the printer after you press the proper key.

To turn off printer echo, press Ctrl – PrtSc or Ctrl – P a second time. You can think of it as a toggle switch. Pressing this key combination once enables the printer; pressing it again disables the printer.

A third method of sending the DIR command's output to the printer will be covered at the end of chapter 4.

Summary

The directory command, DIR, is used to display a list of files stored on disk. The files actually are held in a special directory file that can be considered to be database of sorts. The DIR command displays the information held in the directory file, allowing you to see which files are on disk and examine information about those files.

Using special options on the DIR command, you can view the files on disk either in a wide format or in a special paged mode, one screen at a time. Additionally, you view the files based on their attributes or sort the DIR command's output.

The next chapter continues along the same lines as this one, although the subject is opened up to include all the essential DOS commands, plus a few tricks you probably don't know that will help make DOS—and your PC—more useful to you.

4

The essential DOS commands

Using a hard disk PC requires a number of different skills. Certainly, you need to know how to run the applications programs that let you do useful work. Before you know it, you've added a word processing program, spreadsheet, database management, and maybe graphics or communications software to your repertoire. It's hard enough keeping track of all these programs and their commands. Besides the role of computer user, you wear another hat as well—that of computer operator.

As your system's operator, it's your responsibility to maintain the program and data files stored on your hard disk and to uphold the security. File maintenance is an ongoing chore associated with using a personal computer. There are a number of DOS commands to help you perform the task of file management. These include commands to copy files from one disk to another, delete and rename files, and view and compare the contents of files. Still other DOS commands assist you when working with the operating system.

In this chapter, you'll learn the basic DOS commands you need to manage your files effectively. You probably know some of these commands already. However, the information in this chapter includes some tricks and suggestions you won't find in your DOS manual, so you might want to skim the sections on the commands you already know in search of these special gems. There is nothing quite so gratifying in the field of personal computing as knowing and using some clever little shortcut that the rest of the world hasn't yet heard.

The role of the command processor

In chapter 2, you read about the three system files, IO.SYS, MSDOS.SYS, and COMMAND.COM. These are the basic files needed to start your computer. IO.SYS and MSDOS.SYS are invisible (hidden from view in the DIR command's output) and loaded first when the system boots.

COMMAND.COM is known as the *command processor*. This term refers to its function as an interpreter of the DOS commands you enter from the keyboard. COMMAND .COM intercepts anything you type at the system prompt and attempts to process your command. This processing results in one of three possible outcomes:

- If the command you enter is a DOS command recognized by the command processor, it will execute that command directly.

- If your entry is not one of the basic DOS commands, the command processor will assume it's the name of a program file you wish to run. The command processor then will search the disk directory for the presence of that program and execute it for you.

- If the command processor doesn't recognize your entry as a DOS command and can't find a program file on your disk by that name, it replies with a Bad command or file name error message.

Other command processors exist, notably J.P. Software's 4DOS. It's a direct replacement for COMMAND.COM and offers more advanced and powerful features while still being compatible. This book assumes you're using COMMAND.COM, although it is possible to replace it with something else. The subject of using alternative command processors is covered in chapter 7, "System configuration."

Resident versus external commands

There are two types of commands in DOS, resident and external. *Resident commands* are commands contained within the command processor. These commands include COPY, RENAME, ERASE, and TYPE—all the standard file commands, plus a few simple commands such as CLS, DATE, and TIME. When you're working at the system prompt, you have immediate access to these commands—even if there isn't a disk in any drive.

External commands actually are special DOS program files that perform a DOS-related function. These programs usually are referred to as utilities. The FORMAT.COM program is an example of an external DOS command or utility. Because these commands can't be executed unless the program file with the command filename is present on the disk, they're said to be external, outside the command processor. External commands include FORMAT, FDISK, and SYS, as well as many others.

Your DOS manual identifies commands as either Internal (i.e., resident) or External.

The most commonly used external commands are stored on disk, hopefully in a DOS subdirectory on your hard drive. (The DOS 5 installation program placed them there.) The computer then is set up with a special DOS command, PATH, which will be discussed in chapter 9. The PATH command tells DOS how to find the external commands, so you can use them on any disk without the necessity of the program files having to be on the current disk. (Again, this topic is covered in chapter 9.)

Resident commands

The resident commands you'll use most frequently are COPY, RENAME, and DEL. These commands are used with individual files, although each of them can be made to work with multiple files through the use of the wildcard characters: the question mark and the asterisk. They can be used to affect files stored on the current disk, or on any disk with the addition of a drive designator.

This book follows the conventions of the DOS manual for listing the format of all DOS commands. The rules for languages and operating systems often are specified in terms of a *command format*, which is a shorthand notation describing the rules, or syntax, for the command's use. The command format seems somewhat cryptic if you're a computer novice. Don't let it get in your way. After a few practice rounds in this chapter, you'll have everything down pat.

The COPY command

The COPY command is used to transfer files from one disk to another. The command format is:

COPY *source* [*destination*] [/V]

Both *source* and *destination* represent filenames, with optional extensions and drive letters. The *source* is the original file—the one that the COPY command will duplicate or copy. The *destination* filename is optional (which is why it's enclosed in square brackets). When copying a file from one disk to another, it isn't necessary to include the filename a second time (unless you wish to give the duplicate file a new name).

The /V switch also is optional, as you can see from its square brackets. The use of the /V switch is covered later.

As an example of the COPY command, suppose you wanted to transfer a copy of the file FILE1.DOC from your hard disk to a diskette in drive A. You would enter:

C> COPY FILE1.DOC A:

No drive designator is used in front of FILE1.DOC (the source) because this file is stored on the current drive, C. Also, no filename is specified after the A: because the file is to keep the same name on the destination diskette.

After the file has been copied, DOS responds with a confirmation message:

1 file(s) copied

Be warned: the COPY command will cheerfully copy over an existing file, destroying its contents and replacing it with the file just copied. While this often is what you want to accomplish, as when transferring altered files to a backup disk, it occasionally can result in the loss of important data. Know what's on your target disk before using the COPY command. There is no magic that can recover a file that has been overwritten; I know this from personal experience.

Now, reverse the example. In this case, you want to transfer a copy of FILE1.DOC from the floppy drive to the hard drive. The command is now:

C> COPY A:FILE1.DOC

In this case, the drive designator precedes the source file. There is no need for a second drive designator or even a second filename because the hard disk is the current drive and the file will keep its name when it's copied. The hard disk, or current drive, is always assumed to be the destination.

It would be possible to copy the FILE1.DOC file from drive C to A with a new name, such as FILE2.DOC. The command to accomplish this would be:

    C> COPY FILE1.DOC A:FILE2.DOC

One application of the COPY command is creating a backup of a file on the same disk. This operation can be handy if you are planning to modify a data file but you're not sure you'll like the results and you also are not sure if you'll be able to return the data to its original form. For example:

    C> COPY FILE1.DOC FILE1.BAK

FILE1.BAK is an exact duplicate—a backup—of FILE1.DOC. You'll notice that no drive designators are included in this command. While it isn't necessary to include drive designators with the COPY command, forgetting to include them can lead to the error message:

    File cannot be copied onto itself

This error message would be displayed with either of the following commands:

    C> COPY FILE1.DOC FILE1.DOC
    C> COPY FILE1.DOC

In the first command, the file is being copied from the C drive onto the C drive because no drive designators were specified. Because the source and destination filenames are identical, the command is impossible to execute. Because both the optional drive designator and destination filename are absent in the second command, DOS is being told to copy the file onto itself. (If the COPY command is that smart, why can't it tell you when it's overwriting a file? I haven't the foggiest.)

Using wildcards with the COPY command   In chapter 3, you learned how to use DOS wildcard characters with the directory command to specify groups of files. The wildcard characters also can be used with the COPY command to specify a number of files to be copied at once. For example, you could copy all the files with a DOC extension from drive C to drive A with the following command:

    C> COPY *.DOC A:

The asterisk wildcard also can be used on both sides of the period to copy all files on a diskette onto either another diskette or the hard disk. The following command can be used to copy all files from a diskette in drive A to the hard disk:

    C> COPY A:*.* C:

The question mark wildcard also can be used in combination with the COPY command to substitute for individual characters in source filenames.

Wildcards can be used in destination filenames as well. One practical application of this is for creating backup files. Consider this version of an earlier example:

    C> COPY FILE1.DOC *.BAK

There's no need to specify FILE1 a second time; the wildcard assumes it instead. You periodically could create backups of all your DOC files with the following command:

    C> COPY *.DOC *.BAK

Each DOC file would be duplicated to a file with the same descriptive filename but with the BAK extension. Wildcards can be powerful medicine.

Copying files between devices   When copying files from one disk to another, you actually are copying files between devices. Each disk drive is considered to be a device by DOS. There are a number of different devices in your computer system. These include the disk drives, the screen and keyboard, the printer outputs (called ports), and any communications ports. Each of these devices has a special device name that is recognized by DOS (Table 4-1). The disk drives are named A:, B:, C:, etc. The combination of the keyboard and screen is known as the *console* and has the device name CON:.

Table 4-1   Device names under DOS.

Name	Device
A:	First floppy drive
B:	Second (or logical) floppy drive
C:	First hard drive
D:	Second hard drive (etc.)
CON:	Keyboard and screen
PRN:	Standard printer output, first printer
LPT1:	First printer
LPT2:	Second printer
LPT3:	Third printer
AUX:	Standard serial output, first serial port
COM1:	First serial port
COM2:	Second serial port
COM3:	Third serial port
COM4:	Fourth serial port

Parallel printer ports are given the device names LPT1:, LPT2:, and LPT3:. If you have a printer hooked up to your computer system, it most likely will be a parallel printer attached to LPT1:. This printer output has another commonly used device name, PRN:.

Communications ports use the device names COM1: through COM4:, for the first through fourth serial ports attached to your system. You might not have four, just as you probably don't have three printers hooked up, but four is the maximum number DOS supports out of the box.

With all of these device designators, it's not necessary to include the colon. They have been included in this text for consistency with drive letters, which must always have a colon.

You can copy files (or any information really) to or from any of these devices. Just follow the standard COPY command format, substituting the device name you wish for the source or destination filename.

The most frequent application of copying between devices is to create short text files directly from the keyboard without entering a word processing program. It also is possible to copy files directly to the printer for output, but a better technique is to use the TYPE command to accomplish this (as you'll see later).

To create a text file from the console using the COPY command, you specify the CON device as the source device and the filename you want as the destination. Essentially, you're copying from the keyboard to a file on disk. You then can proceed to type in the text you want to store in the file, ending each line by pressing the Enter key. (Sorry, no word wrap here).

When you're done, you conclude the entry with the special end-of-file marker, Ctrl−Z. You can either enter Ctrl−Z directly (hold the Ctrl key down and type a Z) or press the F6 key. The end-of-file marker also must be followed by Enter.

Why Ctrl−Z? Because you're copying a file from the console device to the disk device. Theoretically, the file could be endless; you could just keep on typing. So, you have to let DOS know when your file is done. That's accomplished with the Ctrl−Z character, which DOS uses to recognize the end of a text file.

To see how easy this really is, try creating a simple text file following these directions. Press Enter at the end of each line:

```
C> COPY CON FLATTERY
HELLO THERE,
YOU HANDSOME DEVIL
```

Press the F6 key on the last line, then press Enter. You'll see ^Z on your screen. By pressing Enter, you're telling DOS that the file input is done. The disk drive light will pop on and you'll see the confirming message:

```
1 file(s) copied
```

You have just successfully created a text file.

To view the results of your handiwork, simply reverse the sequence of the COPY command as follows:

```
COPY FLATTERY CON
```

You'll see the text appear on the screen followed again by the confirmation message telling you that a file has been copied. In this instance, the file was copied from the disk drive device to the console device. The Ctrl−Z stored in the file is what told the COPY command to stop displaying the file on your screen (the CON device).

While the preceding exercise might seem trivial, this technique provides a quick-and-dirty method for creating simple text files. Even the experts will often use the COPY CON text processor to create notes to themselves or even to create special program files called batch files, which you'll read about in chapter 8.

COPY's verify option The COPY command's verify option is /V, which stands for *verify*. This parameter can be added to the COPY command whenever you want to ensure that the destination file matches the source.

Normally, DOS will verify that each sector of the file copied matches the original. There also is some logic in the disk's controller that ensures all information written to disk actually is stored there. By adding /V switch, you activate double-checking, where DOS seriously goes out of its way to check the integrity of each sector written to disk.

The only drawback to the /V switch and a major reason why it's not widely used is that it takes longer to copy a file when /V is specified—sometimes twice as long. With modern-day hardware, the /V switch is almost an anachronism. Yet, if you're unsure about a diskette, /V will provide that extra blanket of insurance for you.

The VERIFY command

If the COPY command's /V switch is appealing to you, then you should know about the VERIFY command, another internal DOS command. What VERIFY does is to turn on a universal verification switch so that all DOS commands that write to disk will double-verify their contents.

To see the current status of the verification switch, type VERIFY at the DOS prompt:

```
C> VERIFY
VERIFY is off
```

If the verification switch is on, you'll see VERIFY is on displayed instead. To turn VERIFY on or off, you simply follow the VERIFY command with either ON or OFF. For example:

```
VERIFY ON
```

Now, double-verification has been turned on. Like the /V switch, however, DOS now will take twice as long to verify information written to disk. Most users keep VERIFY turned off; however, because that's the normal way of things, the VERIFY command is seldom used.

The DEL command

From time to time, it becomes necessary to remove files from your disks, especially from fixed disks. Although 40 Mb might seem like a lot of storage, you might one day encounter the dreaded Insufficient disk space error message. Something has to go.

Normally, you wouldn't wait for that message to occur before removing files from your disk. The DIR command allows you to determine the amount of storage space left on your disk. This lets you plan ahead.

Aside from the perils of a full disk, you also will be removing files as a normal part of file maintenance. This is just what comes natural when you own and use a hard drive. You'll create temporary files, remove duplicate files, and do general housecleaning from time to time. These tasks require a command to help you kill off old and unneeded files.

The DEL command removes files from disk, either singly or in groups by using wildcards. Be careful when using wildcards with the DEL command. You accidentally might remove files you didn't intend to erase.

The format for the DEL command is:

```
DEL filename [/P]
```

The filename is the name of a file you want to delete or a group of filenames to be matched with wildcards. The /P switch is optional.

The rules for using wildcards with the ERASE command are the same as for the

COPY command—with one exception. If you use the global wildcards, *.*, you'll be prompted with the following message:

All files in directory will be deleted!
Are you sure (Y/N)?

The purpose of this confirmation message is to ensure against inadvertently erasing all the files on a disk. Unfortunately, this message can't protect you against forgetting to include the floppy drive designator and deleting all files on the hard disk by mistake. This situation will occur if you enter the following command from drive C:

C> DEL *.*

Type N in response to the message if you don't want to delete all the files; type Y to delete the files. Don't get in the habit of typing DEL *.*, Enter, and then Y. Even if you know it's okay to delete all the files, double check.

Here's something not everyone knows: when you erase a file, the file actually is not removed from the disk. Removing the file would require physically rewriting zeros in all the sectors used to contain the file's data as well as rewriting the directory entry—that's a lot of DOS overhead, which really is unnecessary.

Instead of totally obliterating a file from disk, the directory entry for the file receives a special marker that indicates the file has been erased. The initial cluster entry in the FAT also is replaced with zeros, indicating the area on disk is available. Note that nothing on disk really has changed.

Deleting files under DOS is somewhat like banishment. The file still is physically on the disk, but you can't see it in a directory listing, nor can you read the data stored in it. It is possible to remove this file marker and recover the file. This is exactly what's done by the UNDELETE command, which you'll read about in detail in chapter 15.

Note that the DEL command cannot be used to remove hidden or read-only files from a disk. (Hidden files were discussed in chapter 2.) Two hidden files are IO.SYS and MSDOS.SYS, your system files that you probably will never want to delete. Read-only files have a special file attribute that marks them as available for use, but not for modification or deletion. In chapter 18, you'll learn how to alter file attributes, which will allow you to create your own read-only files that will be protected from accidental deletion.

Incidentally, the DEL command has an identical twin, the ERASE command. Both ERASE and DEL do the same thing. However, the ERASE command is not used often because either it's too long to type or it reminds users too much of the old CP/M operating system.

The RENAME command

The RENAME command is used to change a file's name. You might wonder why you would ever want to change a file's name. After all, what's in a name, right?

Actually, there are several reasons for changing a file's name. One compelling one is that you might have made an error in typing the filename the first time it was created. Another is that you might want to avoid conflicts between too many files with similar (or the same) names on disk. After all, the limited number of characters DOS gives you to name files really can drive you mad.

You also can use the RENAME command to rename program files—but only the descriptive name. If you change the extension, it's no longer a program in DOS's eyes. For example, you can rename your word processor program from WORDPROC.COM to WP.COM. This will save you several keystrokes each time you run the program.

Here is the format of the RENAME command:

RENAME *oldname newname*

Both *oldname* and *newname* are required, although you can use wildcards to rename a group of files—but be careful. (More on that in a second.)

Using the preceding example, here's how you'd rename WORDPROC.COM to WP.COM:

RENAME WORDPROC.COM WP.COM

WORDPROC.COM now has a new name, WP.COM. The RENAME command offers no visual feedback—unless you've erred. That only happens when you try to rename a file with a name already used on disk or when you inadvertently rename a file using an illegal filename character.

You can use wildcards with the RENAME command, but only when renaming groups of similar files. For example:

RENAME *.DOC *.BAK

The previous command changes the file extensions of all DOC files to BAK. The file contents still are the same and the descriptive names remain unchanged. You can even use a wildcard to change a single filename:

RENAME WORDPROC.COM WP.*

The new file is named WP.COM; the COM extension is borrowed from the original filename.

RENAME also can be abbreviated as REN. As with DEL over ERASE, REN is more popular than typing out the full RENAME command.

The TYPE command

The TYPE command is used to view the contents of a file. It types a file out on the screen, allowing you to read it. TYPE really works only with files that contain legible information, such as plain text or ASCII files. Using the TYPE command with program or data files will result in funny-looking characters showing up on the screen, as well as perhaps bells and whistles going off in your computer. (It's nothing bad, just illegible.)

The format of the TYPE command is:

TYPE *filename*

where *filename* represents a single file you want to view. Note that it works on only one file at a time. You cannot specify wildcards with the TYPE command.

The contents of the file will be output to the screen in a continuously scrolling fashion until the entire file is displayed. For example, to view the contents of a file with the filename LETTER.DOC, you would enter:

```
TYPE LETTER.DOC
```

In the preceding section on the COPY command, you learned how to create and view simple text files by designating the CON device as either the source or the destination for the copy. Ordinarily, you would use the TYPE command to view the contents of such text files rather than the COPY command. To view the contents of your FLATTERY file, just enter:

```
TYPE FLATTERY
```

TYPE might not work with some word processing documents. Word processing programs store their documents in non-standard formats, including special control characters to denote things such as centering, underline, and other text formats. The results of using the TYPE command to view the contents of those files are somewhat disappointing. Nonetheless, the TYPE command can give you some idea of the contents of text files.

The DATE and TIME commands

The DATE and TIME commands are used to reset the system date and time. DOS keeps track of the current date and time internally, reading it from a special battery-powered clock inside your PC each time you boot. The system date and time are used to stamp the directory entry of a file when it's created or updated. You can see these dates and times whenever you view the directory in the long form. This information can be quite helpful in determining which version of a file is the most current.

The DATE command allows you to enter the current date in one of several formats, depending on how you've configured your system for use in which country. The *mm-dd-yy* format is standard for the United States. (For more on alternate formats, see chapter 7, "System configuration.")

When you enter the DATE command, you'll be presented with the current date and prompted to enter the new date with a display such as:

```
C> DATE
Current date is Fri 10-08-1993
Enter new date (mm-dd-yy):
```

You can enter the current date separated by hyphens, slashes, or periods. Single-digit months don't have to be preceded by zeros. If you make a mistake in entering the date, you'll receive the message:

```
Invalid date
Enter new date (mm-dd-yy):
```

The TIME command works much like the DATE command. You're given the current time and asked to provide the new time:

```
C> TIME
Current time is 10:03:29:66p
Enter new time:
```

Computers keep the time accurate up to one hundredth of a second (you don't have to enter the time to this level of accuracy). Normally, all you'll do is enter the hours and minutes. The seconds and hundredths of seconds will be set to zero by default. All units of time are separated by colons.

Once the date and time have been set, either at system startup or through the use of the DATE and TIME prompts, the system will increment the time (and date if you work long hours) for you automatically. However, nothing is perfect. Not all PCs—even IBM's own brand—keep the date accurate. From time to time, you'll need to use the DATE and TIME commands to reset the date or time. For example, today is the 27th and I just had to tell the computer that it was no longer the 20th (the system clock was stuck on the 20th for seven days).

The CLS command

A simple yet underutilized command is CLS. CLS stands for *clear the screen*. It does just that. If you enter this internal command at the system prompt, DOS obligingly will clear the screen for you. This command is especially nice if you have just made an error and you don't want your boss scrutinizing from over your shoulder the follow DOS error message:

    File destroyed due to operator incompetence

To quickly wipe that away, type:

    CLS

Then, the screen is cleared.

The VER command

As you probably have gathered by now, there are a number of different DOS versions in existence. In addition to the two distinct versions, MS-DOS and PC-DOS, there are major releases, such as 3.0 and 4.0, plus minor revisions, as in 3.3 versus 4.01. This can be rather confusing, especially as certain DOS commands occur in some versions but not others. Other problems involving differing DOS versions include incompatibilities in disk formats and command processors.

One especially aggravating problem is that DOS versions 2.*xx* cannot recognize disks formatted with DOS versions 3.*xx*. The maxim here is that newer DOS's can read older DOS's, but not vice versa. You also will find that, if you boot the computer with one version of DOS and then replace that disk with another containing a different version of DOS, you'll run into problems whenever you try to execute any DOS commands from the system prompt. Instead, you'll receive the agonizing message:

    Incorrect DOS version

Luckily for you, the DOS command processor includes the VER command, which reports the current version of DOS in use:

    VER

DOS will respond with its version number. For DOS 5.0, it displays:

    MS-DOS Version 5.00

You can and should use the VER command whenever you first use an alien computer. If you suddenly notice one of your favorite DOS commands doesn't work, type VER. If you see some odd DOS version (for example, Wambooli DOS 3.22.44), then you'll know why your DOS 5.0 command doesn't work.

External commands

While the command processor contains many useful DOS commands, there are some DOS commands that come externally in the form of separate programs on disk. Although they aren't a part of COMMAND.COM, they are considered part of your operating system and legitimate DOS commands.

You might wonder why DOS puts some commands in the command processor and makes others external. The reason has to do with the limited amount of memory available on your PC. If all the DOS commands were placed into COMMAND.COM, it would hog up much more memory than your PC has. Because many of these external commands are used infrequently, it makes more sense to place them into separate program files. These programs are loaded into memory as needed, after you type their commands at the system prompt. When they're done, they release the memory, making it available for your applications and data.

There are a number of external DOS utilities. In the remainder of this chapter, you'll learn about three very useful ones: DISKCOPY, MEM, and CHKDSK. To use any of these utilities, you first must have access to them. The file with the utility name and either a .COM or .EXE extension must be present on the hard disk. If you followed the instructions in chapter 2 for setting up your hard disk, then you're ready to roll.

The DISKCOPY utility

The DISKCOPY utility is used to copy the entire contents of one diskette onto another. It can be used to duplicate floppy diskettes only.

The format of the DISKCOPY command is:

DISKCOPY [drive1] [drive2] [/1] [/V]

drive1 and drive2 are optional. They are used to represent the disk drives holding the source and target diskettes, respectively. Both drives must be of the same size and capacity. If not, you can omit drive2 and DOS will prompt you to swap the source and target diskettes into and out of drive1. If both are omitted, DOS assumes the currently logged disk drive, which must be a floppy drive.

The optional /1 switch is used to copy only one side of a diskette. The optional /V switch works exactly like the COPY command's /V switch, turning on verification for all disk sectors copied.

DISKCOPY usually is used to copy the contents of entire disks from one disk drive to another. In the end, you have an exact duplicate of a disk. The second diskette need not even be formatted; DISKCOPY will format it as it's being copied to.

In the era of hard disks, DISKCOPY might seem out of place. It's not. DISKCOPY is the only true way to duplicate a floppy diskette, especially if you have only one drive. To illustrate, if you have a computer with a hard drive and one floppy drive, you would enter:

DISKCOPY A:

The A: indicates the drive you want to use to copy diskettes. In a one-drive disk copy operation, you'll be prompted first to insert the source diskette in drive A. DOS will analyze it and then read from it. After a time, you'll be prompted to insert the target diskette into drive A. This process repeats until the entire diskette is copied.

If you have two floppy drives with your system, you can enter:

DISKCOPY A: B:

You then would be prompted to insert your source diskette in drive A and your target diskette in drive B. The two-drive disk copy operation will proceed without requiring disk swapping. Note that both drives must be of the same physical size and capacity; otherwise, the DISKCOPY operation will be a failure.

Once the disk copy operation is completed, you'll be asked if you want to:

Copy another (Y/N)?

Responding with a Y will allow you to repeat the process with a different set of diskettes. N terminates the DISKCOPY program and returns you to the system prompt.

The MEM utility

The MEM utility is an interesting program that displays the contents of your PC's memory, as well as details of how your system is using memory. The format of the MEM command is as follows:

MEM [/C|/CLASSIFY] [/D|/DEBUG] [/P|/PROGRAM]

The MEM command has three optional switches: /C, /D, and /P (their longer formats are /CLASSIFY, /DEBUG, and /PROGRAM). Only one switch can be used at a time. As expected, most DOS users prefer the single-letter switches.

By itself, the MEM command gives you a summary of your system's memory usage, as seen in Fig. 4-1. The display is divided into several areas, depending on how much and what type of memory you have. The first three lines of the MEM command's output tell you how much conventional or DOS memory you have installed in your system and how much is available. In Fig. 4-1, the full 640 K is installed with about 623 K available for running programs.

The next section details any EMS, or expanded memory, installed in the system. Finally, extended memory and XMS is summarized, along with information on whether or not DOS has been loaded into the High Memory Area (HMA). (These terms are defined and some additional information on DOS memory management is provided in chapter 7.)

If you want to see a list of programs in memory, you can use the /CLASSIFY switch. Type the following:

MEM /CLASSIFY

```
 655360 bytes total conventional memory
 655360 bytes available to MS-DOS
 637616 largest executable program size

3588096 bytes total EMS memory
2260992 bytes free EMS memory

3407872 bytes total contiguous extended memory
      0 bytes available contiguous extended memory
  12288 bytes available XMS memory
        MS-DOS resident in High Memory Area
```

4-1 Sample output of the MEM command.

You'll see a list of programs loaded into memory, then a similar memory summary as seen in Fig. 4-1. If you need to pause the display, press the Ctrl−S key combination.

The /PROGRAM and /DEBUG switches display progressively more detailed information about the contents of memory. Try them if you like, but most of the information displayed is beyond the scope of this book (and beyond the comprehension of 99% of all DOS users).

The CHKDSK utility

The CHKDSK utility is used to find out how much storage space remains on a disk, as well as to check the disk and locate such nasties as bad sectors, any lost chains of files, or missing clusters. These features are invaluable when managing hard disks. As the owner of a hard disk system, you should familiarize yourself with this utility and use it frequently to improve the performance of your system.

The format of the CHKDSK command is:

CHKDSK [*filename*] [/F][/V]

Only the command itself is required; all other elements are optional. I'll hold off on the options for a moment and concentrate on the basic doings of CHKDSK.

In its simplest form, the CHKDSK command reveals the following helpful information:

- Disk volume name
- Date and time the disk was initially formatted
- Total storage space on the disk
- Amount of storage used by and number of hidden files
- Amount of storage used by and number of subdirectories
- Amount of storage used by and number of files
- Number of bytes in any bad sectors on the disk
- Amount of available storage remaining on the disk
- Size of each cluster (called an *allocation unit*)
- Total number of clusters on the disk
- Number of free clusters
- Total amount of RAM
- Amount of RAM available after the system files and any RAM-resident programs are loaded.

To obtain a listing of these statistics, you simply would enter the CHKDSK command and press Enter. To check a disk other than the current disk, follow CHKDSK with the drive designator.

C> CHKDSK

results in output similar to that shown in Fig. 4-2.

An *allocation unit* is a cluster. In Fig 4-2, the cluster size is 2 K, or 2048 bytes. There are 20,687 clusters on the disk, which, when multiplied by 2048, yields a total of 42,366,976 bytes on the disk—the exact amount of the total disk space (40 K).

```
Volume DOS 5        created 09-21-1990 1:26p
Volume Serial Number is 16CE-9B67

42366976 bytes total disk space
   77824 bytes in 4 hidden files
  100352 bytes in 47 directories
25159680 bytes in 841 user files
17029120 bytes available on disk

    2048 bytes in each allocation unit
   20687 total allocation units on disk
    8315 available allocation units on disk

  655360 total bytes memory
  637616 bytes free
```

4-2 A sample status display of a hard disk produced by the DOS CHKDSK utility.

If you wanted to check the status of one of your floppy diskettes, you would follow CHKDSK with the letter of the floppy drive:

CHKDSK A:

CHKDSK all by itself is merely informative. Some naive users attribute a lot of power to CHKDSK. CHKDSK doesn't do anything; it simply reports information DOS already knows—primarily boot sector and FAT table information. However, when used with a filename (or wildcard) or the /F or /V switches features, CHKDSK can do some interesting things.

One important service CHKDSK performs is informing you of the condition of your files. As you'll recall from chapter 2, files can either be stored in contiguous clusters or in fragmented clusters. DOS is smart about allocating disk space. If necessary, it will split up a file to fit it all on disk. The file then is said to be *fragmented*. As more and more files are added to a disk and others are deleted, the fragmentation problem escalates. DOS still keeps track of everything, thanks to the FAT; however, overall disk performance degrades as file fragmentation increases.

The CHKDSK command can tell you if any files are fragmented—either a specific file or a group of files. For example, to check all files for fragmentation, you could enter:

CHKDSK *.*

If the files are all contiguous (stored in adjacent clusters), the following message will be returned:

All specified file(s) are contiguous

However, if the file is stored in two or more non-contiguous clusters, it will be reported to you at the bottom of the CHKDSK output as follows:

A: \ LETTER1.DOC Contains *xx* non-contiguous blocks

The *xx* is the number of non-contiguous clusters involved. At this point, there's little you can do about non-contiguous files. DOS still keeps everything together; however, as you use your drive, the number of non-contiguous blocks in files will increase. There are ways to fix the problem; they're covered in chapter 19, "Storage optimization."

CHKDSK's /V and /F switches

Two optional parameters, /V and /F, can follow the CHKDSK command. The /V switch is used to display all the files on the disk—all of them, no matter where they're located. The purpose of this option will become apparent in the next chapter. For now, you can try the option, type in the following at the DOS prompt:

C> CHKDSK /V

After pressing Enter, you'll see what could end up being several dozen screenfuls of files, all scrolling wildly up the screen. Press Ctrl−C to stop it or keep watching and eventually you'll see the standard CHKDSK output, as shown in Fig. 4-2.

The /F is used to fix some problems that might occur while using your hard disk, particularly if you're one of the naughty people who reset their computer instead of quitting applications. When you do that, and at other times, DOS might create a file and then not close it properly or only part of the file might have been saved to disk. Normally, no data is lost. However, a piece of the file remains on disk. It lacks a directory entry, but it occupies space on disk and in the FAT.

CHKDSK always checks the FAT for file fragments, which it calls lost allocation units (or clusters) or file chains. If they're found, you'll see a message at the bottom of the CHKDSK output, something along the lines of the following:

xxx lost allocation units found in *xx* chains
Convert lost chains to files?

When you see this message, press any key to continue. Even though CHKDSK is asking if you want to rescue the files, it will not do so. You must specify the /F switch to truly convert the lost allocation units to files. Retype the CHKDSK command a second time, adding the /F switch:

CHKDSK /F

After pressing Enter, CHKDSK will locate the lost allocation units and piece them together as files. You'll see the files in the root directory, each of which will be given the name FILE*xxxx*.CHK, where *xxxx* increments from 0000 through 9999, once for each lost chain converted to a file.

If you like, you can examine the files, either using the TYPE command or a disk utility. Chances are, the files contain only garbage and it's safe to delete them all. You can do that with the DEL command, as in:

```
DEL *.CHK
```

The *.CHK filename wildcard matches any and all of the files CHKDSK creates.

You might need to use CHKDSK /F on each of your hard drives (logical or physical) from time to time. It will clean up any sneaky lost chains, converting them to files, which you can quickly erase. Removing these files will improve your disk performance, as well as open up new areas on disk in which you can store files.

Other disk utilities, quite a few of which have some real muscle, are covered in chapter 19, "Storage optimization." CHKDSK is worthy, but don't endow it with any magical powers.

FIND, MORE, and SORT

Three interesting external DOS commands are FIND, MORE, and SORT. These really aren't true commands, but rather input-output filters. They're programs that can be used to modify the output of DOS commands, tweaking it in some convenient way.

For example, the MORE filter can be used to page the output of long DOS commands, inserting an automatic pause between each screenful of text. The SORT filter sorts the output of DOS commands or can be used to sort a file, then save the sorted result to disk. The FIND filter is quite handy at locating tidbits of text hidden in long files.

To use these filters you need a special DOS tool known as the pipe. The *pipe* is the vertical bar character, |, which might or might not have a space in the middle. You use the pipe like a plumber. The output of one DOS command is pumped through the pipe into the filter and then is displayed on the screen. The examples in the following section will show you how it's done with each of DOS's three filters.

The SORT filter

As its name implies, the SORT filter is used to arrange text into either ascending or descending order. Characters are sorted by their ASCII code value, which means the sort order is always alphabetical and for numbers, from lesser to greater. (Refer to appendix C for more information on ASCII code values.)

When used with the directory command, the SORT filter takes the normally unsorted directory listing and sorts it alphabetically. (The DIR command's /O switch does the same thing and does it better, but indulge me.)

```
DIR | SORT
```

pipes the output of the DIR command through the SORT filter. The end result is an alphabetically sorted directory listing.

If you've entered the previous command, notice how SORT sorted the entire directory listing. Not only are the filenames sorted, but other information, such as the number of files, the directory name, and volume information, also were sorted. The SORT filter is not discriminating.

The SORT filter has two optional switches: /R and /+. The /R switch reverses the sorting order, resulting in listings from *Z* to *A*. For example:

```
DIR ¦ SORT /R
```

Now, the SORT command displays the directory in reverse alphabetical order. (Can you recall which DIR command switch did that? Try DIR /O: – N.)

The /+ option allows you to specify which column of text in a given file is to be used as the key for sorted output. Unless /+ is specified and followed by a column number, SORT sorts by the first character in each line of the file.

For example, in a directory listing, the file's size is always shown starting at column 14. You can use this trivia to sort directory listings according to file size by entering the following command:

```
DIR ¦ SORT / + 14
```

Note that the DIR command with the /O:S switch will do the same thing.

The MORE filter

The MORE filter can come in handy with many DOS commands. It works much like the DIR command's /P switch. Information is filtered through the MORE filter a screenful at a time, pausing after each new screen and displaying the message at the bottom of the screen:

```
—More—
```

Pressing the Enter key causes the next screenful of information to be displayed. Because the MORE filter controls the screen display, it's always the last filter to be included in a sequence of DOS commands using filters. To use the MORE filter with SORT and DIR you would enter:

```
DIR ¦ SORT ¦ MORE
```

The result would be a sorted directory listing that would pause after each screenful of text.

The MORE filter comes in extremely handy with the TYPE command. For example, if you're having trouble reading the output from the TYPE command, you can pipe the output through the MORE filter. This causes each screenful of text to remain on the screen until you press any key for the next screen.

```
TYPE LETTER.DOC ¦ MORE
```

allows you to view the file LETTER.DOC one screen at a time. You can cancel the command's output by typing Ctrl–C at any More prompt.

The FIND filter

The FIND filter is used to locate a word, phrase, or group of characters within a specified file. A group of characters is referred to as a *string* in computer terminology. So, to find the string *hello* in the text file LESSON1, you would use the FIND filter as follows:

```
FIND "HELLO" LESSON1
```

Actually, the above command wouldn't locate *hello*, because the FIND command is case sensitive. It would find *HELLO* (all caps) but not *hello* with any lowercase letters. You can direct the FIND filter to ignore the case of the string by including the optional /I switch:

```
FIND /I "HELLO" LESSON1
```

If the text is found, it will be displayed as follows:

```
--------LESSON1
I would like to take this time to say hello to all my students, this year
```

Any lines containing matching text will be displayed by the FIND filter. The filename appears above the lines, preceded by eight hyphens.

Because the directory is a file, it's possible to locate a specific filename within the directory by piping the output from the DIR command through the FIND filter. For example, to verify that the LESSON1 file is located on the diskette in drive A, you would enter:

```
DIR A: | FIND "LESSON1"
```

The /I switch isn't needed here, because the DIR command's output is all uppercase (unless you use the /L switch).

The previous example is rather dumb because DIR LESSON1 will do the same thing (and it's easier to type). A more useful example is to use the FIND filter to locate files with something in common, such as a date or time:

```
DIR A: | FIND "3-15-93"
```

The FIND filter will locate all files created or modified on March 15, 1993. This is the only way to do that under DOS.

Redirecting input and output

The output of all DOS commands normally is sent to the screen. Likewise, DOS expects all input to come from the keyboard. This is why the screen and keyboard—the console (CON:) device—are referred to as the standard output and input devices. This seems only reasonable, right? After all, where else would you want DOS's output to go or input to come from?

DOS is flexible with its use of devices. It's possible to redirect output to a device other than the screen. Likewise, it's possible to provide input for DOS from a device other than the keyboard. DOS allows you to select any device it recognizes for output: the disk drives, the printer, or the serial port. Likewise, input can come from a file on disk or the serial port (the printer doesn't provide input; it's an output-only device). This is what's referred to as *input/output*, or *I/O, redirection*.

As an example, suppose you wanted to save a copy of the directory listing in a data file named DIRLIST.TXT. You would enter:

```
DIR > DIRLIST.TXT
```

The greater-than symbol is DOS's output redirection symbol. The output of the command on the left is redirected from the standard output device to the device named. In the previous example, the device is the current disk drive, on which DOS creates a file DIRLIST .TXT.

After pressing Enter, you won't see a directory displayed. Instead, the DIR command's output now is in the file DIRLIST.TXT. You can verify this by typing the following DOS command:

```
TYPE DIRLIST.TXT
```

After pressing Enter, you'll see the contents of the directory displayed. If you like, you could use your word processor or the DOS text editor to edit the DIRLIST.TXT file, print it, or copy it to a floppy diskette and mail it to Mom (who would probably be amazed at your DOS prowess).

With I/O redirection, the output of any DOS command can be sent to any device. Remember when you printed the DIR command's output using the Ctrl−P toggle? It's much easier to send the directory listing directly to the printer with the following command:

```
DIR > PRN
```

PRN is the name of the printer device. In the previous example, the DIR command's output is sent directly to the printer. (Make sure your printer is up and running before entering any > PRN command; if you don't, you'll get a Device error.)

Any DOS command can be output to the printer:

```
CHKDSK > PRN
```

sends the output of CHKDSK to the printer. If you have any command line options or parameters, they must all appear before the redirection symbol. For example:

```
TYPE GROCERY.LST ¦ SORT > PRN
```

displays the file GROCERY.LST using the TYPE command. Its output is piped through the SORT filter and then is redirected to the printer. The end result is a sorted, printed list.

Output redirection with append

When you redirect a command's output to a disk device, you must name a file. DOS creates that file if it doesn't exist. If the file does exist, it's overwritten. However, it's possible to append the redirected output to a file. This is done using the > > redirection symbol.

```
DIR A: > > DIRLIST.TXT
```

appends the output of the DIR command for drive A to the DIRLIST.TXT file, which already contains the directory for drive C (from a previous example). DIRLIST.TXT isn't overwritten. Instead, the directory of drive A is tacked on to the end of the file.

Redirected input

Redirected input is used to supply input for a DOS command, just as that input would come from the keyboard. This is a tricky thing to do, because the input must exactly match the keystrokes you normally would type. Also, input redirection doesn't work with non-

DOS commands, so it cannot be used to supply input for your word processor, spreadsheet, or any other major application.

The input redirection symbol is the less-than symbol. The input is supplied via the device named after the redirection symbol.

A handy way to try input is with a filter. The following command uses the DIRLIST.TXT file as the input for the SORT filter:

```
SORT < DIRLIST.TXT
```

As DIRLIST.TXT is fed to the SORT filter, the sorted output is displayed on the screen. If you wanted the sorted output to go to a file, you could tack on an output redirection symbol, plus the name of the file to send the output:

```
SORT < DIRLIST.TXT > DIRSORT.TXT
```

The contents of the DIRSORT.TXT file contains the sorted directory listing. It can be viewed on the screen with the TYPE command. If you want to send it to the printer, do the following:

```
TYPE DIRSORT.TXT > PRN
```

Better still, just fix the original SORT command as follows:

```
SORT < DIRLIST.TXT > PRN
```

Summary

This chapter has described some of the most frequently used DOS commands and utilities. The internal commands discussed were COPY, VERIFY, DEL (or ERASE), RENAME (or REN), TYPE, DATE, TIME, CLS, and VER. The external commands were DISK-COPY, MEM, and CHKDSK. Also covered were the three standard DOS filters, SORT, MORE, and FIND, plus using the pipe and I/O redirection to modify the input and output of various DOS commands.

You probably will use these commands on a daily or weekly basis. However, there are a number of other DOS commands and utilities you'll need to be familiar with to manage your hard disk system effectively. These commands and utilities will be introduced throughout the remainder of this book.

The next chapter opens up the door of hard drive discovery all the way. You'll learn how the massive amount of storage on a hard drive can be tamed—brought under control by dividing the drive up into work areas called subdirectories. Organization is the theme, which, next to backing up your data, is the core of all hard disk management.

5

Subdirectories and paths

Hard disk management fundamentally is two things. The first is the repetitive chore of backing up your data. The need to perform periodic backups can be addressed in one of several ways, which I'll gladly postpone until chapter 16.

The second part of hard disk management is organization. This involves creating and maintaining an organized system for storing and retrieving data and program files on your hard disk. Organization on a hard disk is done by dividing the hard disk into separate work areas according to the applications you use or, more generally, how you use your computer.

This chapter covers the concepts of hard disk organization using subdirectories. So far, you've seen disks referenced as absolute storage devices. DOS is more organized than that. Rather than put every single file you have into the disk (which is inherently sloppy and confusing), you can use subdirectories to organize your files, programs, and data. For hard disk users, this is a vital necessity.

Hard disk organization strategies

File organization becomes crucial when working with hard disk systems. The sheer number of files involved can prove overwhelming, especially to novice computer users. When you consider that hard disks provide enough storage to accommodate thousands of files (with over 1,000 being typical on the average hard drive), you begin to realize the complexity of the problem.

For example, the DIR command would become useless on a fully populated hard disk. The listing could easily run to 40 or more screens. Even using the FIND and MORE filters, locating a given file under such circumstances would cross your eyes. Imagine trying to locate an applications program, executing it, and then finding a data file from among several hundred such files. Scenarios such as this occur far too frequently in the world of personal computing. Yet, they don't have to.

If there were only one rule with hard disk organization, that rule would be: keep the root clean. Try to put a minimum number of files in the root directory—as few as possible. How is that done? By dividing your hard drive up into separate work areas.

Work areas

Even if you use your computer for only one thing, you're going to need a separate work area of that one thing. Why? Because, even if you have only one application on your PC, you also have DOS. DOS requires its own work area, as does your single application. Therefore, on the most minimum of computer systems, at least two work areas are necessary. What is a work area?

A *work area* is a separate area of the disk, like a disk within a disk. All the files and programs in that area are separate from the rest of disk. You keep organized by keeping similar programs and data files separate on disk.

There are several distinct advantages to organizing your hard drive into work areas:

- Each work area operates like its own disk, but it's all part of the larger structure of your hard drive. DOS commands, such as the DIR command, operate only on files in a single work area at a time.

- Work areas also can contain their own work areas for additional organization. Under DOS you can have many work areas under other work areas, almost to an unlimited level.

- You can avoid duplicate filenames and other conflicts by keeping files separate, in their own work areas. Also, unlike the root directory, work areas can store an unlimited number of files. Although, in practice, you'll want to keep work areas small. If they grow, then just create more work areas.

- You keep similar files together. For example, all your budget worksheets, document files related to a proposal, client databases, or whatever can all be kept in separate work areas. Even similar program types, such as utility files, can be grouped into their own work areas.

- If more than one person works at the same PC, each can be given their own work area inside the computer. They then can further organize their work area into other work areas as required.

Hard disk organization means work areas. Under DOS, these work areas are referred to as *subdirectories*.

Subdirectories

To divide a hard disk into work areas involves the creation of subdirectories under DOS. There are several specific DOS commands that allow you to work with subdirectories; they'll be discussed in a few pages. Before then, take a moment to concentrate on the subdirectory concept.

Subdirectories are just what the term implies: subgroups of files within a disk's root directory. You can have as many subdirectories as you wish (up to the limit of files in the root directory, 512). Each subdirectory can contain its own subdirectories.

Once created, a subdirectory serves as the organizing structure for a separate work area. You can put files there, more subdirectories, anything you normally can do with files in DOS. The files, however, exist only in that subdirectory, separate from other files on disk.

While there is no limit to the number of subdirectories you can have or to the number of files within a subdirectory, it still is a good idea to give some thought to the location and organization of your programs and data files within your subdirectory scheme. You don't want a cluttered subdirectory, just as a cluttered root directory would go against the keep-the-root-clean maxim. Organization is the destination, subdirectories simply are the route you take.

Organizing a hard drive

To see how subdirectories can organize a hard disk system, consider the typical hard drive system. This chapter will build upon an example, although you should create your own system customized to your needs. (Alternative suggestions are provided later in this chapter.)

The example system presently uses two major applications: the WordPerfect word processor and Quattro Pro, a spreadsheet. Along with those two applications are DOS (which you should never forget; it deserves its own work area), and a few games the user has acquired from a friend. These four items (Fig. 5-1) provide the basis for four work areas on the hard drive.

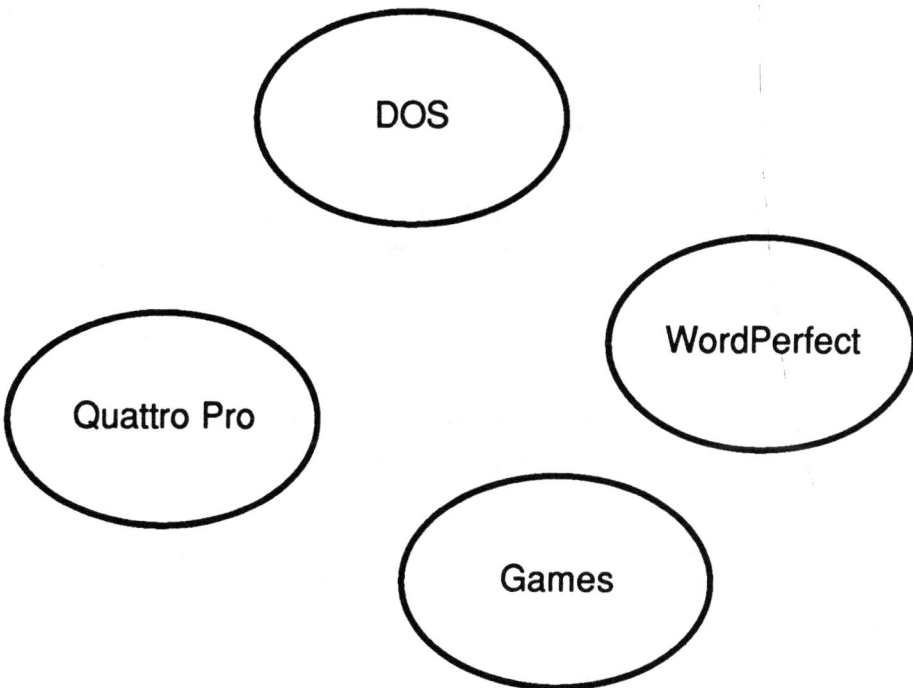

5-1 Applications used on this PC.

Each item should be placed into its own work area, created by special DOS subdirectory commands. You can visualize the subdirectory structure, as seen in Fig. 5-2. DOS, WordPerfect, Quattro, and the games each go into subdirectories on disk.

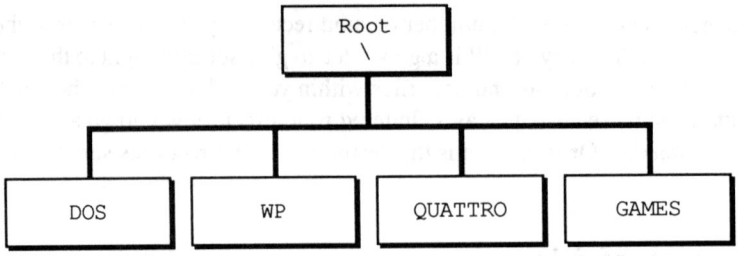

5-2 Each application is given a subdirectory, or work area, on disk.

Suppose that at some point, the user of this example system acquires some disk utilities. They can be put into their own work area, which becomes the UTILITY subdirectory. Further, suppose that the user owns several utilities: The Mace Utilities, a clip art program, plus a memory manager. Each of them could be placed into their own work area under the main UTILITY subdirectory, as shown in Fig. 5-3.

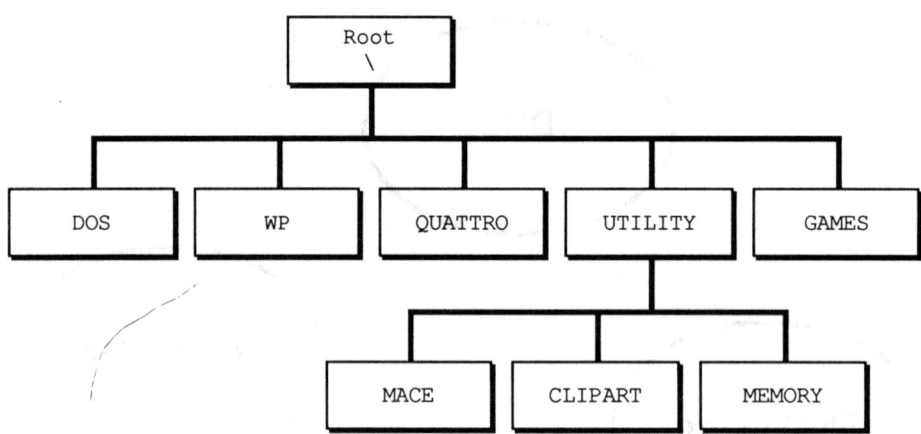

5-3 The UTILITY directory is added, complete with its own subdirectories.

Creating and working with subdirectories under DOS is a snap. Before you start out, it helps to keep an organizational strategy in mind. The one shown in this section is simple. In real life, things get much more complex. This chapter will show you the nuts and bolts, but everything still is easy to do.

Before moving on, there are two terms with which you should familiarize yourself: *tree structure* and *pathnames*.

Trees and pathnames

Notice how the appearance of the subdirectory structure (Fig. 5-3) represents an organizational chart? The root directory is at the top and branching off; the subdirectories are at various levels. A common metaphor for this structure is a tree, albeit an upside down one.

The directory structure shown in Fig. 5-3 is referred to as the *tree structure*. (This terminology might explain why the main directory is the *root*.)

The organization at this level is simple, but I assume your mind is buzzing with all sorts of questions. One question might be how to locate individual files within each subdirectory. That's entirely possible using what's called a pathname.

A *pathname* tells you where a file is on disk. It gives the disk drive and subdirectory in which the file is located. If the file is more than one level deep, then all subdirectories leading to the root are contained in the pathname.

In a sense, the pathname is like a real path, giving you the exact location of a file on disk. A pathname itself can have up to four elements:

- The first element of the pathname is the disk drive letter, followed by a colon. On drive C, all pathnames start with C:.

- The second element is the name of the root directory. Under DOS, the root directory is named using the single backslash character, \ .

- The third element of a pathname is the directory in which the file is located, including all directories that lead to the root (the path to the root). Each of the directory names is separated by a single backslash character.

- The final element of a pathname is the filename and extension.

Consider Fig. 5-3. The file COMMAND.COM typically is found in the root directory. On drive C, it's full pathname would be:

C:\COMMAND.COM

C: is the drive name, the backslash is the root directory, as well as the directory containing the file, and COMMAND.COM is the filename.

Now, suppose a file named LETTER.DOC existed in the WP subdirectory. Its full pathname would be:

C:\WP\LETTER.DOC

C: is the drive name, the first backslash is the root directory, WP is the directory containing the file, the second backslash is the subdirectory separator, and LETTER.DOC is the name of the file.

How about the file XMAS.CLP in the CLIPART subdirectory (refer to Fig. 5-3). Here would be its pathname:

C:\UTILITY\CLIPART\XMAS.CLP

C: is the drive name. The path to the XMAS.CLP file goes from the root, to the UTILITY directory, and to the CLIPART directory (this path is shown as \UTILITY\CLIPART\). Finally, there is the filename.

Pathnames also can be used to locate a directory. For example, this is the full pathname of the GAMES directory:

C:\GAMES

Here is the full pathname of the MACE subdirectory:

C:\UTILITY\MACE

The final backslash separator is only included in a pathname if a file followed the last subdirectory.

Keep in mind that there is a limit to the size of a full pathname, which indirectly limits the number of subdirectories you can have. Under DOS, a full pathname can be no more than 63 characters long (from the drive letter to the filename's extension). Other than that and the subdirectory naming rules that will be covered in the next section, you can do just about anything with subdirectories.

Subdirectory commands

To take advantage of work areas and the organizing power of subdirectories, you need to create them. This is done with special DOS subdirectory commands. All subdirectories are created using these commands, except for a disk's root directory, which automatically is created during the formatting process.

Once a subdirectory has been created, it can be divided further into additional subdirectories. After all the subdirectories have been created, you can move between them and manipulate them using additional DOS subdirectory commands. Files can be copied and stored in subdirectories using the standard DOS file manipulation commands, which are reviewed in relation to subdirectories later in this chapter.

The three commands DOS uses to manipulate and work with subdirectories are listed in Table 5-1.

Table 5-1 DOS's subdirectory commands.

Command	Abbreviation	Function
MKDIR	MD	Create (make) a subdirectory
CHDIR	CD	Change subdirectories/display current directory
RMDIR	RD	Remove a subdirectory

Creating subdirectories with MKDIR

The MKDIR command is used to create or make a new subdirectory on disk. Its format is:

MKDIR *pathname*

An abbreviated and more common version of the command is MD, which uses the same format. *pathname* is the name of a subdirectory you want to create. If a full pathname isn't specified, then the subdirectory is created under the current directory. Otherwise, the subdirectory is created on the drive and in the directory you specify.

The name you give the new subdirectory follows the standard DOS file naming conventions, which were discussed in chapter 3. All subdirectories can be up to eight characters long, followed by an optional dot plus up to three characters for an extension. Note, however, that directories usually are named without an extension.

Logically, you should name a subdirectory to reflect its contents. In Fig. 5-3, note how the subdirectories have names that reflect the applications they contain: WP for WordPerfect, QUATTRO for Quattro Pro, DOS for DOS, and so on.

In a directory listing the subdirectories show up with the rest of the files but have the designator <DIR> where a file size would be listed. Because directories are grouped with files in this manner, note that you cannot give a subdirectory the same name as a file already in that directory, or vice-versa.

As an example of using the MD command, assume you've just brought home your hard disk and PC and you're all ready to set it up. The dealer was nice enough to install DOS into a C: \ DOS subdirectory, but you now want to copy all your games from a floppy disk to a new GAMES subdirectory.

The first task is to create GAMES on the hard drive. The MD command to do that is:

```
MD C: \ GAMES
```

C: \ GAMES is a full pathname, telling DOS to create the GAMES directory off of the root directory on drive C. If you were already on drive C in the root directory, you could just use the following command:

```
MD GAMES
```

Because a full pathname isn't specified, DOS creates the new directory as a subdirectory of the root (the current directory).

In an interesting family-like way, any subdirectory you create is referred to as the *child* of the current directory. The directory immediately above is the *parent*. Note that the root directory has no parent directory.

Becoming mobile with CHDIR

The CHDIR command is used to move between subdirectories. Its format is:

```
CHDIR [pathname]
```

CHDIR can be abbreviated as CD, which is the way you'll see it in this book and the way most DOS users prefer to use it. Note that the pathname is optional. Without it, the CD command displays the current directory:

```
C> CD
C: \
```

The CD command (by itself) causes DOS to display the currently logged directory, the root directory on drive C. The output of this command is always the full pathname of the current directory.

When you first log to a disk drive, you're logged to the root directory. When you want to move to a subdirectory, you log (or change) to it using the CD command with the pathname of the directory you want to log to. For example:

```
CD \ UTILITY \ MACE
```

logs you to the \ UTILITY \ MACE subdirectory on the current drive. That subdirectory then becomes the current directory.

A full pathname to a subdirectory isn't always required. For example, if you're in a parent subdirectory, you need not include the parent's name in the path. In the preceding example, if you already were in the UTILITY subdirectory, all you would have to enter is:

```
CD MACE
```

This command would log you to the C:\UTILITY\MACE subdirectory. (To prove it, just type CD at the DOS prompt to see where you are.)

To log to the root directory on any drive, use the following:

```
CD \
```

Refer to Fig. 5-3. Suppose you're in the C:\UTILITY\MACE directory and you want to log to the \WP directory. You could, if you didn't read this book, type in the following:

```
CD \
CD WP
```

The first command logs you to the root directory, the second logs you to WP. That really is a waste of time. You can log to the C:\WP directory from anywhere on drive C by typing the following command:

```
CD \WP
```

This command avoids what I call climbing the tree—changing from one directory to another to get to someplace else.

Removing subdirectories with RMDIR

Subdirectories are named like files and appear in directory listings like files, but they're not files. You cannot use the COPY, DEL, or RENAME commands with a subdirectory. So, if the day arrives when you need to remove a subdirectory, you need a special DOS command, RMDIR.

The format of the RMDIR command is:

```
RMDIR pathname
```

As with MKDIR and CHDIR, a more popular abbreviated form of the command is available, RD. The pathname isn't optional with RD, just as a filename isn't optional with DEL. There are other rules for using the RD command as well:

- Before a directory can be removed, it must be empty. There can be no files or subdirectories within a directory to be removed. If you attempt to remove a non-empty subdirectory, you'll be greeted with an error message.
- You cannot delete a directory if you're currently logged to it. Log to the parent directory and then use the RD command or log to the root directory and use the RD command with a full pathname.
- You cannot delete the root directory.

The RD command isn't an everyday type of command. Only rarely will you wind up deleting subdirectories, usually only during periods of massive hard drive maintenance.

As long as you start out with a workable hard drive structure, you should never need to delete subdirectories at all.

Organization strategies

You now know about subdirectories, have seen an example of hard disk organization, and know about the DOS commands required to help you build your tree structure. The following sections discuss various hard disk organization strategies, along with examples of tree structures you can create.

A few of these examples might not make sense right away. These will rely upon the powerful concept of batch files to run your system, which is about two or three chapters up the road from here. If you're baffled at this stage, then continue to read ahead and return here after you've learned about running programs with batch files.

Also, feel free to mix and match these strategies as you see fit. There is no recommended or default way to organize a hard disk. For yourself, you'll need to take your brain off the shelf, plug it in, and decide what you want and where you want it.

The no-brain organization

Over the past few years, DOS application programs have come with smarter installation procedures. (I say smarter because they still have a way to go.) These installation programs usually will set up the software in its own subdirectory, which is always in a main subdirectory off of drive C.

This is the *let-it-go method* of installation, where you let your applications create any tree structure necessary. (It can also be called *hands off*, though I feel *no-brain* is more suitable, because it's not the best way to fix up a hard drive.)

There's nothing wrong with keeping all your applications in main subdirectories off of drive C, as shown in Fig. 5-4. The *etc.* under each directory indicates subdirectories that the application might install. Additionally, you might want to create a general-purpose directory for your games or utilities as you see fit.

The only downside to this type of tree structure is that, after a dozen or so applications, the root directory becomes crowded—a situation you should avoid. An organizational solution for this is provided later, in the section "The categorical organization."

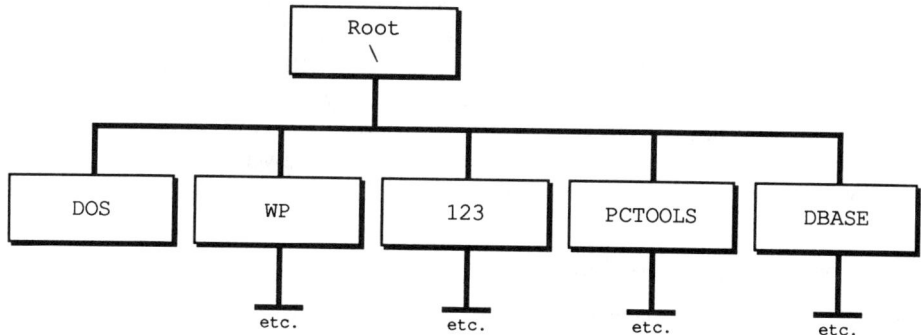

5-4 The hands-off method of hard disk organization.

Data subdirectories

Something that's missing from Fig. 5-4 are data subdirectories. Most applications that set themselves up will put your data files (what you create using the application) in the same subdirectory as the application itself. With most applications occupying more than 1 Mb in their own subdirectories and containing dozens of files, this situation makes for sloppy organization.

A solution is to create a data subdirectory and place it directly under the application subdirectory, as shown in Fig. 5-5. Into that data directory, you'll place files you create using the application. All the files will be the same type; each will belong to the application program in the parent directory.

You can create as many data subdirectories as you need, one for each category of data file. Just use the MD command as described earlier in this chapter. In Fig. 5-5, the data subdirectories are organized along budget, payroll, and planning lines. Note how the budget directory has subdirectories of its own, one for each month of the year. Now that's organization.

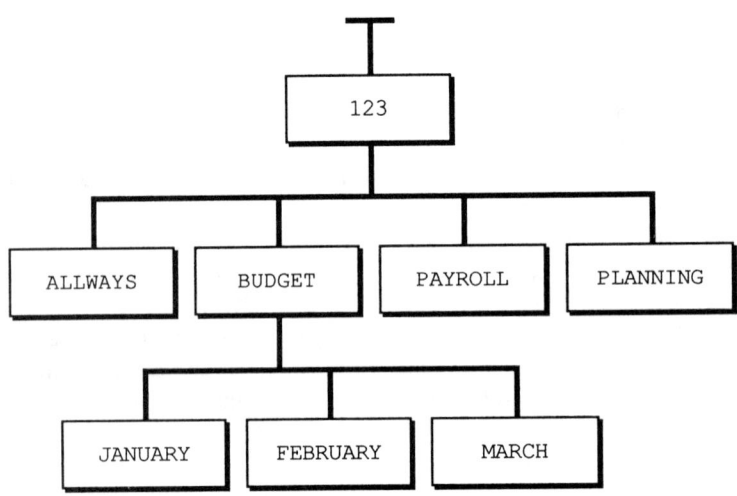

5-5   Data subdirectories.

There also is such a thing as a *general subdirectory*. For example, a PROJECT subdirectory off of the root. Under that directory you could put all your projects—each in its own subdirectory. On my system, the directory is named WORK and contains any projects I happen to be working on, each in their own subdirectory.

Another interesting directory to create off the root is a TEMP subdirectory. Into TEMP, you can place temporary files, files you just-don't-quite-yet want to delete, or miscellaneous files. You can even direct your applications to save files in a TEMP directory.

The categorical organization

After a while, having too many applications installed under the root directory becomes a mess. A good way to avoid that situation is to create general categories of subdirectories and place similar applications into them. This keeps the root directory down to a minimum of files and subdirectories.

Suppose you're using a PC for desktop publishing, plus a little financial stuff on the side. Consider the organization illustrated in Fig. 5-6. See how major applications are grouped into subdirectories at a low level? The DTP branch contains a word processing, graphics, and art library subdirectory. The FINANCE branch contains a spreadsheet and data base program. Further programs could be added, provided they fit into those categories.

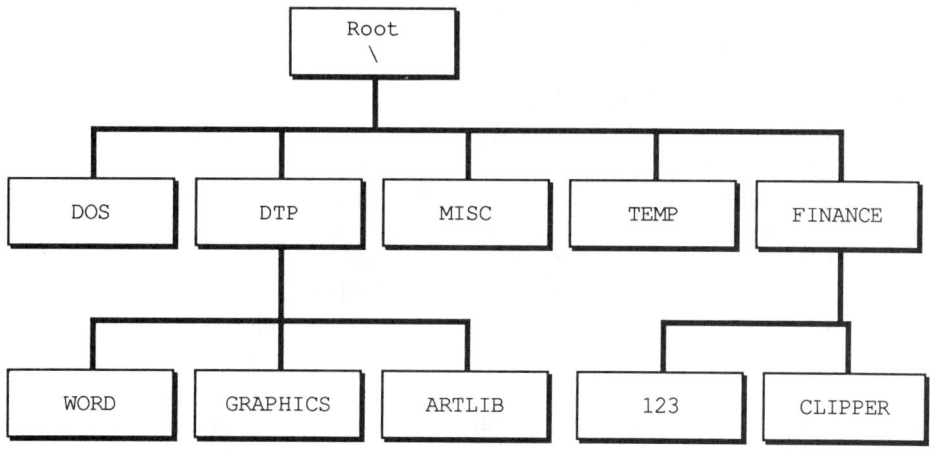

5-6 Categorical organization along application lines.

On my personal systems, I have one main branch used for the system. It's a subdirectory off the root and typically contains from 7 to 15 additional subdirectories. Each subdirectory in the SYSTEM directory contains files related to some system function. Table 5-2 lists the SYSTEM subdirectories on my main computer.

The key here is organization. On any system, each of the subdirectories in the SYSTEM directory could have gone into the root. However, think about how cluttered the root directory would be. By putting everything related to this system in a SYSTEM subdirectory and further organizing things in subdirectories and sub-subdirectories, the disk stays clean and organized.

The SYSTEM or BIN branch organization

So far, the tree structure strategies have centered on organization. That's great because it keeps your system organized and your files separate. However, is everything handy?

To run a program in another directory, you have two options. First, use the CD command to log to that directory, then type in the name of the program to run. Second, type in the full pathname of the program to run. Both of these methods seem cumbersome, especially when you consider that a computer is supposed to make life easier.

The solution is to put all runable files into a single directory for easy access. Better still, you put into that directory batch file programs that, in turn, go out and run the other

Table 5-2 Subdirectories for a SYSTEM directory.

Pathname	Contents
\ SYSTEM \ BATCH	Batch files
\ SYSTEM \ BORLAND	Two subdirectories: SIDEKICK for SideKick II, and SUPERKEY for SuperKey
\ SYSTEM \ DELL	Diagnostics that came with the computer
\ SYSTEM \ DOS	DOS 5.0 and its files
\ SYSTEM \ DV	DESQview and QEMM/386
\ SYSTEM \ FASTBACK	Fastback backup software
\ SYSTEM \ HERCULES	Hercules display utilities
\ SYSTEM \ MACE	The Mace utilities
\ SYSTEM \ MAGELLAN	Lotus' Magellan utility
\ SYSTEM \ MOUSE	The Mouse driver and accompanying files
\ SYSTEM \ NORTON	The Norton Utilities
\ SYSTEM \ PARADISE	Paradise VGA graphics card utilities
\ SYSTEM \ PCTOOLS	Central Point's PC Tools
\ SYSTEM \ UTIL	General utilities, plus subdirectories for PKZIP and PKLITE
\ SYSTEM \ V	Golden Bow's V-series of utilities

programs. This whole concept cannot be fully understood without covering DOS's PATH command, which is introduced in chapter 9. For now, consider the partial hard drive structure shown in Fig. 5-7.

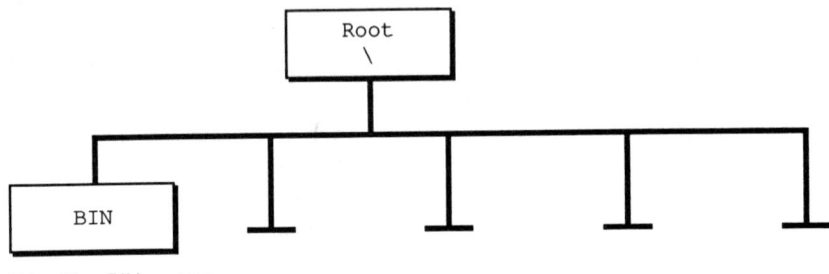

5-7 The BIN system.

The BIN system uses a single subdirectory, one that contains all runable programs on the system. This is a bit hard to do when you're first using a PC, primarily because it's hard to figure out which COM or EXE files to copy there, plus it isn't always a good idea to separate a program file from the support files it needs.

The true and absolute solution is batch files. Batch files, combined with the PATH command, make the BIN system one of the most powerful you can use when organizing a hard drive. If the concept baffles you, keep the thought warm for a few chapters. Especially when you start learning about menu systems, having a single BIN directory will make complete sense.

On my personal system, I use a BATCH subdirectory—actually \ SYSTEM \ BATCH. It contains all the little programs I've written that run the 100 or so other programs located at various places on my hard drive. This concept will be elaborated upon in later chapters.

Using DOS commands with subdirectories

The presence of subdirectories on your hard disk alters the way you use and enter certain DOS commands. Nothing really has changed. All you really could say is that, when I told you about the essential DOS commands in chapter 4, I was kind of fibbing.

Instead of requiring a filename, most commands actually require a pathname. You can substitute a full pathname for any DOS file manipulation command. COPY, DEL, RENAME, and even the DIR command can use a full pathname just as they would a filename. When the path isn't specified, the DOS command simply assumes you mean the current directory and will look for the file there. Otherwise, any DOS command that deals with files can work with files in any subdirectory on any drive. Just specify a full path.

Copying files between subdirectories

Copying files into and between subdirectories requires that you pay particular attention to the paths of both the source and target files. The general format of the COPY command when copying files from or to subdirectories is:

COPY *pathname pathname*

The pathname allows you to be in either the source or the target subdirectory when copying files between two subdirectories on the same disk. You also can be in the root directory of the hard disk when copying files from floppy diskettes into subdirectories on the hard disk. Also, you could be logged onto the floppy disk drive directly and still copy files into or between any subdirectory on the hard disk.

When working with several subdirectories on the hard disk, you might find that you want to transfer files from one subdirectory to another. In such cases, the paths of both the source and the target files need to be considered. However, it isn't always necessary to include both paths in the actual COPY command. Remember, DOS always assumes you mean the current disk and directory unless you tell it otherwise.

If you already are located in the subdirectory you want to copy the file from, you don't need to specify the path to this file. For example:

COPY LETTER.DOC \ WP \ STUFF

LETTER.DOS is assumed to be in the current directory. It will be copied to the subdirectory \ WP \ STUFF on the same drive.

If you already are in the subdirectory that you want to copy the file to, you don't need to include its path in the COPY command. For example:

COPY \ 123 \ JULY \ INCOME.WK2

The file INCOME.WK2 is copied from the \ 123 \ JULY subdirectory to the current directory.

You can always copy a file from any two subdirectories anywhere on disk, even when you're not in either one of them. For example:

```
COPY \WP\LETTER.DOC \PROJECT
```

The file LETTER.DOC is copied from the \WP directory to the \PROJECT directory. The initial backslash tells you that these are subdirectories of the root. However, if you're currently logged to the root, you don't need to specify them:

```
COPY WP\LETTER.DOC PROJECT
```

DOS assumes everything. In this command, DOS has assumed that the subdirectories mentioned are off the current directory, the root. (Remember PROJECT is the name of a directory, not a file. DOS knows this and copies the file to the PROJECT subdirectory, not to a new file named PROJECT.)

Using the DIR command with subdirectories

The DIR command works within subdirectories just as it does with the root directory. You can use any of the directory options or filters described in chapter 3. However, when you view a directory listing of a subdirectory, you'll see two additional entries at the top of the listing:

```
.
..
```

(These are called *dot* and *dot-dot*.) For example, Fig. 5-8 shows a sample subdirectory listing. Take a look at the third line at the top of the listing. See how it says Directory of C:\GAMES? That line tells you which directory on which disk you're looking at. C:\GAMES is exactly what you'd see if you used the CD command to display the current directory.

Take a look at the first two entries in the directory listing. Each are followed by the <DIR> notation, so you know they refer to subdirectories. The dot and dot-dot entries are unusual—and illegal names. What are they?

```
Volume in drive C is DOS 5
Volume Serial Number is 16CE-9B67
Directory of C:\GAMES

.               <DIR>       09-22-90    5:18p
..              <DIR>       09-22-90    5:18p
CASINO    DOC      10309 01-26-88    5:21p
CASINO    EXE      98243 01-26-88    5:01p
CLONINV   DOC       3518 01-29-89   10:28a
CLONINV   EXE     138076 11-24-90    6:44a
MAHJONGG  DOC      21599 12-30-88   10:11a
MAHJONGG  EXE     111298 12-30-88    2:50p
MAHJONGG  TXT       3359 12-30-88   10:59a
SI        BAT         10 05-18-89   12:23a
VGABOMB   DOC      10687 09-15-89   11:18p
VGABOMB   EXE      55873 09-15-89   11:35p
       12 file(s)        452972 bytes
                       17027072 bytes free
```

5-8 A directory listing of a subdirectory.

It's nothing to lose any sleep over. The dot entry indicates the current directory; the dot-dot entry refers to the parent directory. You can prove this by using the DIR command:

```
DIR .
```

This DIR command uses the dot as a shorthand for displaying the current directory. Consider this command:

```
DEL .
```

Here, the dot means *.* or all files in the current directory. (Type N if you don't want to delete them.)

Dot-dot means the parent directory.

```
DIR ..
```

lists files in the parent directory. How about this one:

```
CD ..
```

This CD command is used to log to the parent directory. This is a great shortcut to avoid typing out the directory's full pathname.

Note that DIR command also has some special switches to deal with directory entries. For example, the /A (attribute) switch can be used with its D option to force the DIR command to display only subdirectories:

```
DIR /A:D
```

If you want to display all files but subdirectories, try the following:

```
DIR /A: – D
```

(Remember to put the slash before the /A: switch. Without it, DOS lists the files on drive A.)

The DIR command's sorting switch, /O, can be used with its G option to list subdirectories first in a directory listing:

```
DIR /O:G
```

If you want to list the subdirectories last, try the following:

```
DIR /O: – G
```

Additionally, to sort the subdirectories by name, add the N option:

```
DIR /O:GN
```

To sort them in reverse alphabetical order, use this command:

```
DIR /O:G – N
```

Also, note that the DIR command's /S switch forces the DIR command to look in all subdirectories under the current directory for matching files. This command makes it easy to locate lost files on a hard drive. For example:

```
DIR \ LETTER.DOC /S
```

will locate the file LETTER.DOC anywhere on the hard drive C. If it's found, you'll see output such as shown in Fig. 5-9, where the file was found in the \ WORD \ LETTERS subdirectory. Additional finds would be listed as well (because you can have duplicate filenames in different directories). If the file wasn't found, you'd see the classic File not found error message.

```
        Volume in drive C is DOS 5
        Volume Serial Number is 16CE-9B67

     Directory of C:\WORD\LETTERS

     LETTER    DOC       256 10-30-89    2:48p
              1 file(s)           256 bytes

     Total files listed:
              1 file(s)           256 bytes
                        17027072 bytes free
```

5-9   The DIR command locates a long-lost file.

The TREE command

The structure of a hard drive can be pictured as shown in the various figures in this chapter; however, it's a mental picture only. The actual structure on disk is merely a bunch of bytes and sectors—nothing impressive. Yet, if you long for the visual, DOS has a TREE command that can help you see your hard drive's structure.

The format for the TREE command is as follows:

TREE [*pathname*] [/f] [/a]

By itself, the TREE command displays a graphical tree, representing your hard drive's structure. A sample of the TREE command's output is shown in Fig. 5-10. You might want to pipe this output through the MORE filter, because it tends to be long:

TREE ¦ MORE

At the top of the listing (Fig. 5-10), you see the drive letter followed by a period. The period indicates the current directory, which is what the TREE command assumes you mean when you enter TREE without any options. The TREE command will display the drive's tree structure from the current directory down through all subdirectories.

If you want to specify a directory for the TREE command to start its display, then the optional pathname is specified. For example:

TREE C:\

displays the tree structure for drive C, starting at the root directory. At the top of the listing, you'll see C:\ displayed.

TREE C:\TC

will display only the branches below the C:\TC directory, as seen in Fig. 5-10.

The optional /F switch tells the TREE command to list all files found in any directories. As the tree structure is displayed, you'll see a list of files in each directory, listed

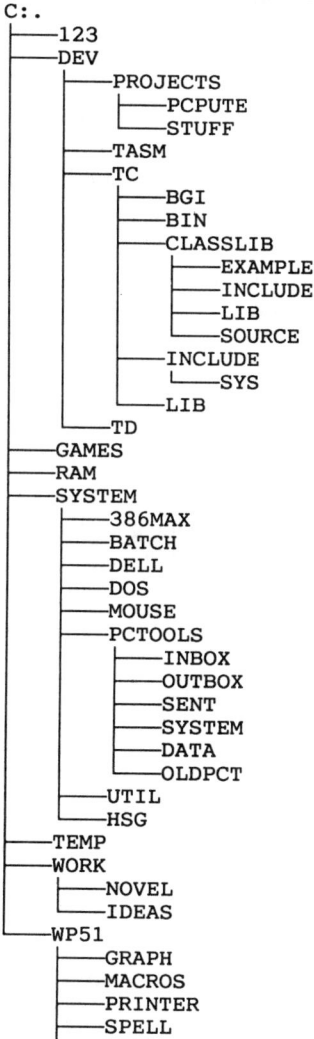

```
Directory PATH listing for Volume DOS 5
Volume Serial Number is 16CE-9B67
C:.
├────123
├────DEV
│        ├────PROJECTS
│        │        ├────PCPUTE
│        │        └────STUFF
│        ├────TASM
│        ├────TC
│        │        ├────BGI
│        │        ├────BIN
│        │        ├────CLASSLIB
│        │        │        ├────EXAMPLES
│        │        │        ├────INCLUDE
│        │        │        ├────LIB
│        │        │        └────SOURCE
│        │        ├────INCLUDE
│        │        │        └────SYS
│        │        └────LIB
│        └────TD
├────GAMES
├────RAM
├────SYSTEM
│        ├────386MAX
│        ├────BATCH
│        ├────DELL
│        ├────DOS
│        ├────MOUSE
│        ├────PCTOOLS
│        │        ├────INBOX
│        │        ├────OUTBOX
│        │        ├────SENT
│        │        ├────SYSTEM
│        │        ├────DATA
│        │        └────OLDPCT
│        ├────UTIL
│        └────HSG
├────TEMP
├────WORK
│        ├────NOVEL
│        └────IDEAS
└────WP51
         ├────GRAPH
         ├────MACROS
         ├────PRINTER
         ├────SPELL
         └────UTIL
```

5-10 The TREE command shows a graphic representation of your hard drive's structure.

under the directory's name. The display still uses graphics characters and, as you can guess, can be quite long. (Pull out that MORE filter or redirect the output to your printer if need be.)

The /A switch controls the TREE command's graphic output. Normally, the TREE command displays the branches using extended ASCII line drawing characters. However, if you specify the /A switch, the TREE command will use ASCII characters: the hyphen, the pipe, the plus sign, and the slash.

The /A switch helps you to redirect the TREE command's output to a printer that might not properly render the extended ASCII character set. If you're redirecting to a file,

Using DOS commands with subdirectories **93**

you can freely edit the ASCII characters, where some word processors totally choke on the extended ASCII characters.

The XCOPY program

Starting with DOS 3.2, the XCOPY program has provided a unique hybrid of the BACKUP and COPY programs. XCOPY has many of the advantages of BACKUP (covered in chapter 16) but acts more like COPY in that the files are not stored in the special archived format. For subdirectories, XCOPY can be directed to copy entire subdirectories or part of a tree structure, from one place to another. Finally, XCOPY makes the best use of the memory in your computer. Rather than copy one file at a time, XCOPY loads as many files as it can into memory before actually copying them. This makes XCOPY much faster than a simple COPY.

The format of the XCOPY command is:

XCOPY filename [filename] [/A][/D][/E][/M][/P][/S][/V][/W]

The first item after XCOPY is the source filename, the second is the target filename—just like the COPY command. You can use XCOPY to totally replace COPY. Where XCOPY differs from COPY is in its optional switches. For example, the following is a simple example of using XCOPY instead of COPY:

XCOPY C:\WP\POEM*.* A:

XCOPY copies the files POEM*.* from the hard disk to drive A. After typing XCOPY, DOS displays:

Reading source file(s) ...

Here, XCOPY reads as many files as it can into memory. Then, it copies the files from memory to the target diskette A, displaying the name of each file as it's copied. As with COPY, the names of the files are not changed (unless specified).

Many of XCOPY's optional switches are similar to those used by BACKUP and RESTORE (see chapter 16). Some of the switches can be used in conjunction with others to vary the preciseness of the files XCOPY copies.

The /S switch directs XCOPY to copy all files in all subdirectories under the current subdirectory. If the subdirectories do not exist on the target disk, they are created. (Nifty, eh?)

XCOPY \123\PROJECTS*.* \WORK /S

copies the tree structure under \123\PROJECTS to the \WORK branch of the disk. Any and all subdirectories under \123\PROJECTS and all their files will be copied there.

The /E switch can be used with the /S switch. /E creates subdirectories on the target disk even if the subdirectory is empty on the source disk. The /S switch alone will not copy empty subdirectories.

XCOPY C:\WP\DATA*.* C:\WRITING /S /E

copies all files and subdirectories in and under the \WP\DATA directory to the subdirectory \WRITING. The subdirectory structure under \WP\DATA will be duplicated in \WRITING—even empty subdirectories will be copied by XCOPY.

The /M switch directs XCOPY to copy on those files that have been modified or changed since the last backup. After XCOPY /M is performed, those files are considered by DOS to be backed up (their modify bit is reset, as is done by the BACKUP program).

The /A switch works exactly like the /M switch with only one difference: /A does not reset the file's modify bit. According to DOS, the files copied still have been modified or changed since the last backup. (Technically, this is a differential backup; the files' modify attributes aren't changed.)

The /D switch is followed by a date. When specified, XCOPY copies only those files that have been created or updated since that date. The date XCOPY checks is the same date that appears in the directory listing.

```
XCOPY \ADMIN\LOTUS\*.* A: /S /D:5-6-92
```

XCOPY copies to drive A all files and subdirectories under \ADMIN\LOTUS that have a date of May 6, 1992 or later.

When the /P switch is specified, XCOPY prompts (Y/N)? for each file listed. Pressing Y directs XCOPY to copy the program. If N is pressed, the file is not copied.

```
XCOPY D:\WP\NOVEL\*.* A: /P
```

copies the files in the directory D:\WP\NOVEL to drive A. As XCOPY displays the name of each file, you're asked whether or not you want that file copied by pressing Y or N:

```
CHAPT1 (Y/N)? y
CHAPT1.BAK (Y/N)? n
CHAPT2 (Y/N)? Y
CHAPT2.BAK (Y/N)? n
OUTLINE (Y/N)? y
    5 file(s) copied
```

When the /W switch is specified, XCOPY displays the following message before it begins copying:

```
Press any key to begin copying file(s)
```

After any key is pressed, XCOPY proceeds with the copy operation.

The /V switch turns on the verify option. This is the same for COPY /V and when DOS's VERIFY command is turned on. When specified, XCOPY verifies (double checks) that the information copied is the same as the original. Because of this extra checking, XCOPY with the /V switch operates slower than a normal XCOPY.

Summary

In this chapter, you've learned how to create and work with subdirectories on your hard disk, which involves a new set of DOS commands and special techniques. Some of these commands, such as MKDIR and TREE, will be used only periodically. However, other commands, such as CHDIR and the commands you'll use to run the programs scattered all over your hard drive, must be used every time you operate your computer. Because these commands can be quite lengthy to enter, especially on a repetitive basis, it would be nice if there were some way to retain them for reuse each time the computer is turned on.

There is a technique for entering repetitive commands without having to type them in each time you need them. This technique involves creating special DOS command files called batch files. A workable DOS solution just isn't possible without them. There still are other items to learn, one of which is how to use the DOS text editor.

The next chapter covers the MS-DOS Editor, a handy little program you can use to create interesting little text files (maybe not the Great American Novel, but possibly the Great American Short Story). This tool will come in handy throughout the rest of the book as you create batch files, as well as your own private DOS menu system.

6

The MS-DOS Editor

Much better than the cryptic old line editor, EDLIN, the MS-DOS Editor is a full-screen mouse-driven text editor, complete with all the power and features DOS users need (and eventually crave). The Editor offers advanced editing functions and provides access to the special graphics characters that you can use to enhance your text files (and eventually create DOS menus).

This chapter is about the MS-DOS Editor, EDIT. It's a text editor, which means it's not as fancy as a word processor. However, it still allows you to create and edit files containing text, plus pull a few simple word processing tricks like search and replace and move blocks of text. This chapter will get you up and running with the Editor and show you how to use the Editor for later chapters in this book.

What is the Editor?

The MS-DOS Editor is a DOS utility. It's a text editor you can use to create ASCII or text files. The filename is EDIT.COM, which was installed in your DOS directory when you upgraded to DOS 5. (Prior to DOS 5, the DOS editor was the old EDLIN utility, which is discussed briefly in appendix B.)

EDIT.COM is a tiny program, only some 400-odd bytes. The real muscle behind EDIT is the file QBASIC.EXE, the QuickBASIC interpreter. To run the MS-DOS Editor, you need to have the file QBASIC.EXE in your DOS directory, just as the SETUP program installed it. If ever you run the Editor and see the message Cannot find file QBASIC .EXE, you've either deleted QBASIC.EXE, or placed it in a directory not on the path. (The subject of paths and directories is covered in chapter 9.)

You'll be using the Editor in this chapter and throughout the rest of this book to create text files. If you have a word processor and you're very fond of it, you can use it instead. However, you should save all the text files in the text-only mode—not the document mode. Also, you should turn off the word wrap feature in your word processor (if that can't be done, set the line length to 255, or just remember to press Enter at the end of a line as opposed to the end of a paragraph). These are extra steps that make using a word processor a wee bit cumbersome for creating modest text files. However, it can be done. Likewise, if you have your own favorite text editor, such as QEdit or VDE, feel free to use them instead.

Working with the Editor

To use the MS-DOS Editor, you enter the following:

EDIT [*filename*]

The filename is optional. If you don't include it, the Editor just pops up with a blank screen—a blank sheet of paper—on which you can start jotting down your prophetic prose. If you do include a filename, the Editor will load the file from disk and it will be ready for editing.

To try out the Editor and learn how it works, you can work through the tutorial in this chapter. If you have a grip on things, feel free to skim through this chapter. Otherwise, power up your computer (if it's not on already), crack your knuckles, and get ready to type.

Creating a new file

Start the Editor by entering the EDIT command at the DOS prompt, and press Enter:

EDIT

You'll see the Editor's startup screen, as shown in Fig. 6-1. This screen always appears, giving you a chance to use the Editor's Survival Guide by pressing Enter. You can just press Esc to go right into the Editor. For now, press Esc to go directly into the Editor.

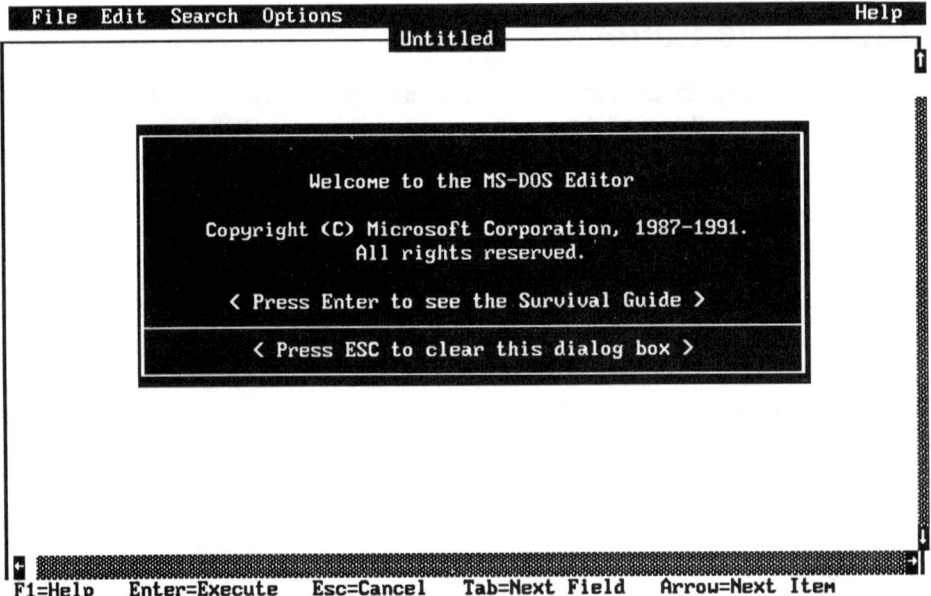

6-1   The Editor's startup screen.

To create a new file, just start typing. Note the cursor (a flashing underline) at the upper left corner of the text entry window. Any text you type at the keyboard appears on the screen at the cursor's position—just like any other word processor or text editor. For example, type the following:

This is a text file I'm creating using the Editor.

You can type a line of text up to 255 characters long. Most of the time, you'll want a line shorter than that, so when the cursor nears the edge of the screen, press Enter to end the line and start a new one. (The screen will scroll to the left as you enter long lines of text.) Note the line-column indicator at the lower right of the screen. The first number tells you which line of text you're on, with 0001 representing the first line in the file. The second number tells you which column you're on, ranging from 001 for the first (left-most) column through 255. Enter the following text, pressing Enter at the end of each line:

This sure beats the heck out of EDLIN, in fact,
this Editor is yet another good reason why I'm a
DOS 5 user.

Your sample text file now is complete (feel free to type some more if you want). When you're done entering text in the Editor, you just stop typing. You'll want to save your text to disk and then quit back to DOS. To do that, you need to learn how to use the Editor's menus.

Using the Editor's menus

The Editor's commands are held in drop-down menus along the top of the screen. There are five menus: File, Edit, Search, Options, and the Help menu off to the right. Each menu contains a list of commands, each categorized by the menu title.

To access a menu, you press the Alt key plus the first letter of the menu you want: F, E, S, O, or H. That drops down the respective menu and lets you see the menu items, or actual commands, grouped under each menu. You select an item by pressing it's key letter, which is highlighted on the screen (Fig. 6-2). You also can use the up and down arrow keys to highlight an item, then press Enter to select it. The general key commands for using the menus are listed in Table 6-1.

The left and right arrow keys will move you between the menus while they're dropped down. To cancel the menu selection, press Esc. You'll be returned to the text editing window.

If you have a mouse, you can hover the mouse cursor over a menu and click the mouse once to drop down the menu. Select a menu item by clicking on it with the mouse or click in the text editing area to cancel the menu.

To save a file in the Editor, you must drop down the File menu and select the Save option. Press the Alt−F key combination to drop down the File menu, then press S to select the Save menu item. If you have a mouse, click on the File menu, then on the Save menu item. Either way, the Save dialog box will appear, as shown in Fig. 6-3.

Dialog boxes in the Editor work by using the Tab key, arrow keys, Enter, and Esc. Tab moves you around the various areas of the dialog box; the arrow keys move you around within various areas; Enter accepts the dialog box's settings; and Esc is used to cancel.

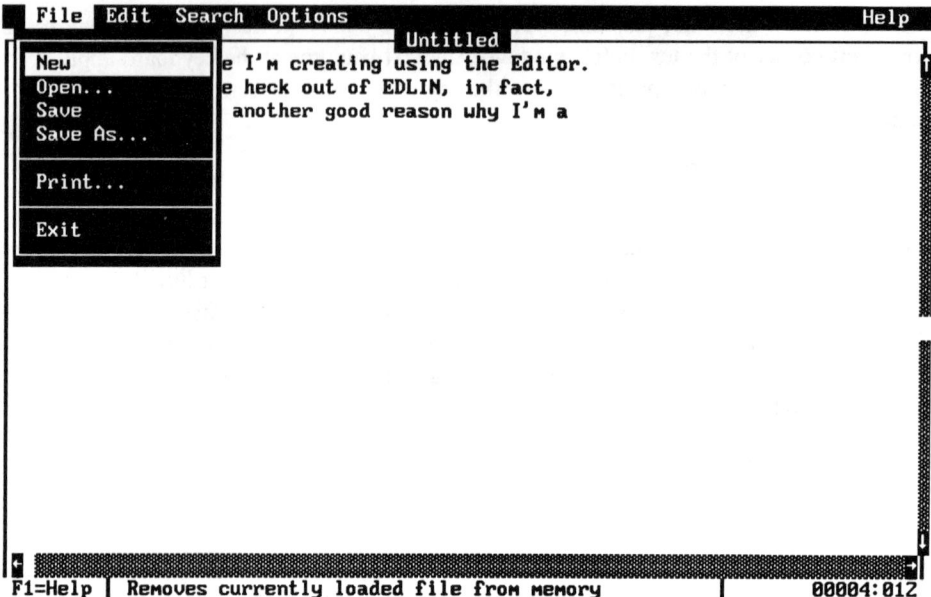

6-2 The File menu.

Table 6-1 Key commands for using the menus.

Key command	Function
Alt	Activate the menu bar
Alt−letter	Activate the menu beginning with "letter"
→	Drop down the next menu on the right
←	Drop down the next menu to the left
↓/Enter	Drop down a menu
↓	Move down through the menu items
↑	Move up through the menu items
Enter	Select the highlighted menu item
Esc	Cancel the menu; return to the Editor

Highlighted keys, such as N and D in the Save dialog box (Fig. 6-3), control the dialog box as well. Use the Alt key in conjunction with those keys to access their features. (More information on using a dialog box can be found in the Editor's Survival Guide, refer to the section titled "Using help" later in this chapter.)

To save the file to disk, you must enter its name in the box by the File Name prompt. The cursor already should be flashing there, awaiting your input. Type the filename SAMPLE and press Enter. This saves the Editor's contents to disk in a file named SAMPLE.

After the file is saved, the Save dialog box disappears and you're returned to the edit-

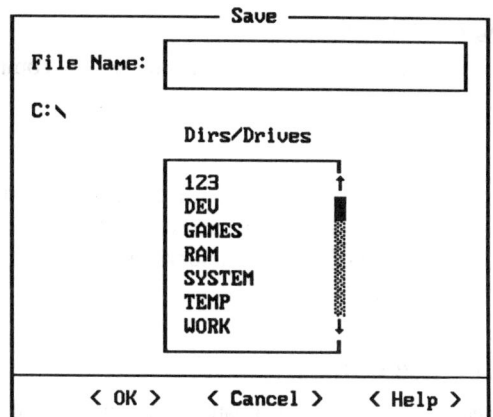

6-3 The Save dialog box.

ing window. Note that the top of the window has changed. Where it used to say Untitled it now gives the name of the file, SAMPLE.

To quit to DOS, you must select the Exit menu item in the File menu. (Because the file is saved, it now is okay to quit.) Drop down the File menu by pressing Alt−F. Select the Exit item—the last item in the menu—by pressing X. The screen will clear and you'll be back at the DOS prompt.

To verify that your file is on disk, you can use the DIR command. Enter the following:

    DIR SAMPLE

You'll see something along the lines of the following:

    Volume in drive C is DOS 5
    Volume Serial Number is 16CE-9B67
    Directory of C: \

    SAMPLE 166 06-28-91 12:06p
      1 file(s) 166 bytes
        17027072 bytes free

You can further verify the file's contents using the TYPE command:

    TYPE SAMPLE

After pressing Enter, the contents of the text file will be displayed on the screen. If you want to print the file, you have two options:

    COPY SAMPLE PRN

copies the file SAMPLE to your printer. If you like I/O redirection, you can do the following:

    TYPE SAMPLE < PRN

Either way, your literary masterpiece will be in hard copy for the world to see and marvel at.

Editing an existing file

To edit a file already on disk, you use the EDIT command followed by that file's name. Type in the following:

    EDIT SAMPLE

The Editor locates the file you've named and loads it into memory. When the Editor starts, you'll see your file on the screen ready for editing. Note that the initial dialog box (which gives you the option of seeing the Survival Guide) isn't presented when you start the Editor with a filename.

Changing the text

To change text in the editor, position the cursor at the location where you want to start editing. You can move the cursor using the keyboard commands listed in Table 6-2. If you're familiar with the old WordStar keyboard commands, the Editor uses them as well. They're shown in Table 6-3.

   Once the cursor is positioned in a new location, you just start typing to insert text. If you want the new text to overwrite the old text, then press the Ins (Insert) key once. The cursor changes to a full block, indicating you're in the overwrite mode. Press Ins again to return to the insert mode. (The Ctrl−V key combination also toggles the insert/overwrite modes.)

   As an example, suppose you wanted to insert a new line after the first line. To do this, position the cursor at the end of the first line. Use the up arrow key to move the cursor to

Table 6-2   The Editor's cursor movement commands.

Keystroke	Function
→	Move cursor right one character
←	Move the cursor left one character
↑	Move the cursor up one line
↓	Move the cursor down one line
Ctrl−→	Move the cursor right one word
Ctrl−←	Move the cursor left one word
Home	Move the cursor to the start of the line
End	Move the cursor to the end of the line
Ctrl−Enter	Move the cursor to the first character on the next line
PgDn	Move down one screenful of text
PgUp	Move up one screenful of text
Ctrl−Home	Move to the start of the file
Ctrl−End	Move to the end of the file
Ctrl−↑	Scroll the text up one line
Ctrl−↓	Scroll the text down one line
Ctrl−PgUp	Scroll the text left one screen
Ctrl−PgDn	Scroll the text right one screen

**Table 6-3   The Editor's
WordStar-compatible cursor movement commands.**

Keystroke	Function
Ctrl−D	Move cursor right one character
Ctrl−S	Move the cursor left one character
Ctrl−E	Move the cursor up one line
Ctrl−X	Move the cursor down one line
Ctrl−A	Move the cursor left one word
Ctrl−F	Move the cursor right one word
Ctrl−Q,S	Move the cursor to the start of the line
Ctrl−Q,D	Move the cursor to the end of the line
Ctrl−J	Move the cursor to the first character on the next line
Ctrl−Q,E	Move the cursor to the first line in the window
Ctrl−Q,X	Move the cursor to the last line in the window
Ctrl−C	Move down one screenful of text
Ctrl−R	Move up one screenful of text
Ctrl−Q,R	Move to the start of the file
Ctrl−Q,C	Move to the end of the file
Ctrl−W	Scroll the text up one line
Ctrl−Z	Scroll the text down one line

Note: For Ctrl−Q,S (and other two-key combinations), press the
Ctrl−Q combination first, then type an S.

the first line (if it's not already there), then press the End key to move to the end of the line. Press Enter and you'll have your new line.

As you type text, you can use the Backspace key to erase the previous character. The Del (Delete) key is used to erase the character the cursor is under. Type in the following line:

I'm finding this extremely frustrating.

You really don't find the Editor extremely frustrating. It would be nice to change the word frustrating to *fun* or some other positive word. To do that, you can delete the word *frustrating* and replace it with your own optimistic word. The keyboard commands to delete something are shown in Table 6-4. Position the cursor under the *f* in *frustrating* and choose your weapon to delete it.

If you accidentally type Ctrl−Y, the entire line is erased. Unfortunately, the Editor has no undo feature, so you'll have to type the line over again. Be careful with Ctrl−Y.

Inserting special characters

You can use the Editor to create all sorts of interesting text files, which can include even special characters. For example, move the cursor to the end of the document by pressing

Table 6-4
The Editor's text deleting commands.

Keystroke	Deletes
Del	The character at the cursor
Ctrl−G	The character at the cursor
Ctrl−Backspace	The character at the cursor
Backspace	The character left of the cursor
Ctrl−H	The character left of the cursor
Ctrl−T	The word at the right of the cursor
Ctrl−Y	The current line
Ctrl−Q,Y	From the cursor to the end of the line
Shift−Tab	Spaces from the start of a line

the down arrow key repeatedly. Then press Enter a few times. Now, enter the following line:

It was cold out, some say nearly 20° below zero.

What? You can't find the degree symbol on your keyboard? Of course not. Only standard ASCII keys are on the keyboard. The degree symbol is an extended ASCII character, which you can produce using the Alt key and your keyboard's numeric keypad.

To enter an extended ASCII character, you must know it's code number. A full list of characters and codes is provided in appendix C. If you look there, you'll find that the degree symbol is code 248. To enter that character, you must press and hold your Alt key, then type 248 on the numeric keypad. Release the Alt key and the degree symbol appears in the Editor.

You can enter any of the special extended ASCII characters into the Editor this way. Some of the more popular codes include those for creating boxes and lines. These are shown in Fig. 6-4, along with their code values.

Sometimes, you might want to insert special character codes into a document as well. For example, the escape character will be used throughout this book to enter special codes, called *ASCII codes*, into files. Normally, nothing happens when you press the Esc key in the Editor; the escape character isn't inserted into the text. To insert escape and other special characters, you must first type a Ctrl−P, the prefix key.

For example, type Ctrl−P then press the Esc key. You'll see a left-pointing arrow inserted into the text. That's the escape character. The use of this special character will be discussed fully, starting in chapter 12.

Working with text blocks

Part of the drudgery computers help ease is the ability to do things over and over. For example, suppose you were creating a simple form using the Editor. On that form, you had to produce six lines of blanks to be filled in with information (such as items to declare for customs, a list of funny things your kid says, or reasons why you can't stop eating ice

┌	218	┬	194	┐	191
├	185	┼	197	┤	180
└	192	┴	193	┘	217
│	179	─	196		
╔	201	╦	203	╗	187
╠	204	╬	206	╣	185
╚	200	╩	202	╝	188
║	186	═	205		

6-4   The extended ASCII line drawing characters and their codes.

cream). You could just sit there and press the underline key 1000 times. Better still, create one line and duplicate it using the power of the Editor.

The Editor lets you define a block of text. You mark the start and end of the block. All text between is highlighted and becomes the block of text. Once that's done, you can copy, move, or delete the block of text, handling all the text like one single unit. Here are the steps summarized:

1. Mark the block, define the start and end
2. Copy, move, or delete the block

Rather than create a new form document, continue using the SAMPLE document currently in the editor. In that document, you'll be marking a block containing the words *This sure beats* up though *EDLIN*. That's only one line, but keep in mind that a block can be any length of text, from one character up through the entire document.

To mark text, you select it using either the keyboard or the mouse (if you have one). Using the keyboard, position the cursor at the start of the block and move the cursor to the end of the block, keeping the Shift key down the entire time. For example, position the cursor under the *T* at the start of *This sure beats* and press either Shift key. Then, use your keyboard cursor commands to move the cursor under the *N* in *EDLIN*. Keep the Shift key down the entire time to mark the block. Once the block is highlighted, you can release the Shift key.

Using a mouse, simply select the text by dragging the mouse over it. Position the mouse cursor over the *T* at the start of *This sure beats* and drag the mouse (hold its right button down while moving the mouse cursor) over to the *N* in *EDLIN*. Release the mouse button.

With the text selected, your screen should look similar to that shown in Fig. 6-5. If not, select the text again, following the instructions in either of the two previous paragraphs.

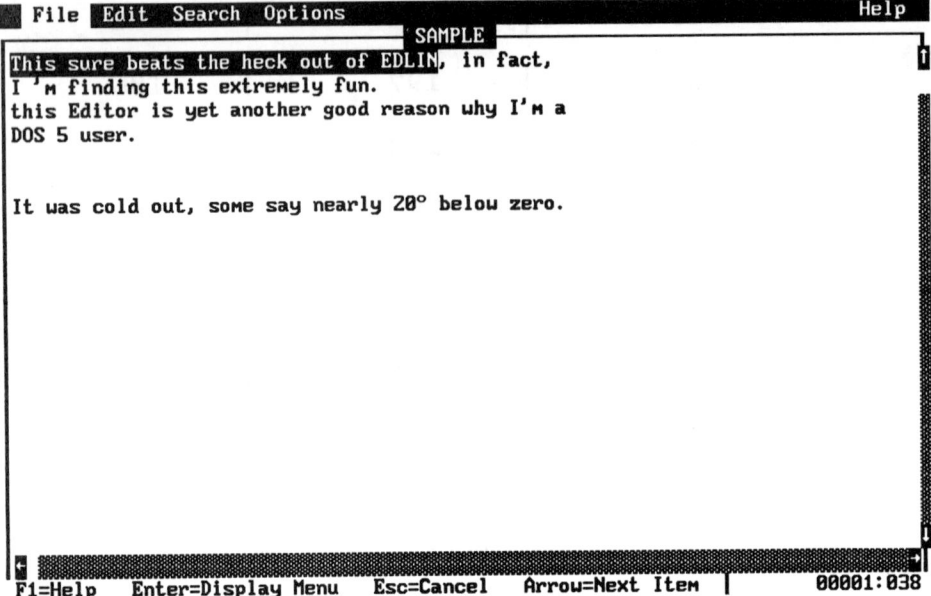

```
 ▪ File  Edit  Search  Options                              Help
 ┌─────────────────────── SAMPLE ────────────────────────────────┐
 │This sure beats the heck out of EDLIN, in fact,                ▓│
 │I 'm finding this extremely fun.                               ║│
 │this Editor is yet another good reason why I'm a               ║│
 │DOS 5 user.                                                    ║│
 │                                                               ║│
 │                                                               ║│
 │It was cold out, some say nearly 20° below zero.               ║│
 │                                                               ║│
 │                                                               ║│
 │                                                               ║│
 │                                                               ▼│
 │◄▒▒▒▒▒▒▒▒▒▒▒▒▒▒▒▒▒▒▒▒▒▒▒▒▒▒▒▒▒▒▒▒▒▒▒▒▒▒▒▒▒▒▒▒▒▒▒▒▒▒▒▒▒▒▒▒▒▒►    │
 │ F1=Help  Enter=Display Menu  Esc=Cancel  Arrow=Next Item │ 00001:038│
 └────────────────────────────────────────────────────────────────┘
```

6-5 Text is selected in the Editor.

After you've defined a block, you can copy, move, or delete it. These commands can be carried out using the keyboard or the commands listed in the Edit menu. Pull down the Edit menu by typing Alt−E or click on the word *Edit* using the mouse. Figure 6-6 shows what the Edit menu will look like. Take a second to look at the keyboard equivalents to the block-editing commands.

```
 ▪ Edit
┌──────────────────┐
│ Cut    Shift+Del │
│ Copy    Ctrl+Ins │
│ Paste  Shift+Ins │
│ Clear        Del │
└──────────────────┘
```

6-6 The Edit menu.

Copy takes the block and makes a duplicate of it in a memory storage area called the *clipboard*. The Cut command makes a duplicate of the block, but then deletes the original. The Paste command takes the block stored in the clipboard and pastes it back into the text at the cursor's position. The Clear command deletes the block.

To copy a block, you select the Copy command or press Ctrl−Ins. Then, position the cursor to a new location in the text and select Paste from the Edit menu or press Shift −Ins. To move a block, you select the Cut command or press Shift−Del. Then, position the cursor to the block's new location and select Paste from the Edit menu, or press Shift −Ins. Deleting a block is done by selecting the Clear menu item or by pressing the Del.

If you delete a line of text with Ctrl−Y, that line is quick-cut into the clipboard. To recover or move the line, press Shift−Ins.

Copy your highlighted block by selecting the Copy command in the Edit menu or pressing Ctrl—Ins. Then, move the cursor down to the end of the file.

Paste the line at the end of the file by selecting the Paste command from the Edit menu or by pressing Shift—Ins. The block is copied from the clipboard to the screen.

You can paste a second block by selecting the Paste command or pressing Shift—Ins again. Note how the second block is inserted before the first block, on the same line. That's because an Enter character wasn't included in the block.

Searching and replacing

Another way you can use the power of the computer in the Editor is by searching and replacing instances of text. *Search and replace* actually refers to two separate items. The first is the search, or locating instances of text in a document. The second is search and replace, where instances of text are replaced with other text or are just deleted.

Move to the top of your SAMPLE document by pressing Ctrl—Home. To search or replace text throughout your document, the Search menu is used. Pull down that menu by pressing Alt—S or by using the mouse. The Search menu is shown in Fig. 6-7. The three commands in that menu are: Find, which is used to locate text; Repeat Last Find, which locates the next occurrence of text originally found with the Find command; and Change, which replaces found text with new text you specify.

6-7 The Search menu.

The menu items in the Search menu also have keyboard equivalents—shortcuts you can use if you find menus too cumbersome. The keyboard equivalents are listed in Table 6-5.

Say you wanted to find the word *This*. Select the Find command in the Search menu or press Ctrl—Q, F. A dialog box appears, which is similar to the one shown in Fig. 6-8. Note that the word *This* already is present for you to search for. Why? Because the cursor was on the word *This* when you activated the Find command. (If not, the word the cursor was under will be in the box; type the word *This* instead.)

Press Enter to look for the word *This* in your text. It will be highlighted, selected as a block, on your screen. To find the next occurrence of *This*, you can select the Repeat Last

Table 6-5   The Search menu's keyboard equivalents.

Menu Item	Keyboard equivalent
Find . . .	Ctrl—Q,F
Repeat Last Find	F3 or Ctrl—L
Change . . .	Ctrl—Q,A

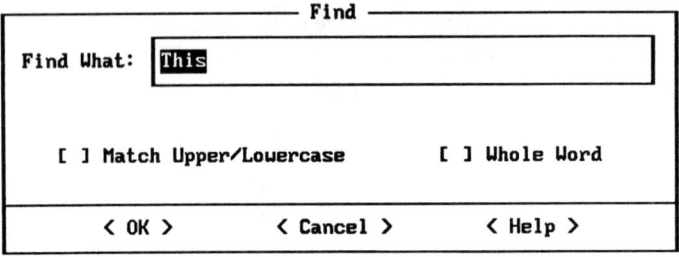

┌─────────────────────── Find ───────────────────────┐
│   │
│ Find What: ▐This▌   │
│   │
│   │
│   [ ] Match Upper/Lowercase   [ ] Whole Word │
│   │
├───┤
│   < OK >   < Cancel >   < Help >   │
└───┘

6-8   The Find dialog box.

Find item from the Search menu or press the F3 key or Ctrl−L. The Editor will locate the next occurrence of the text throughout your document. When it reaches the end of the document, it will start over again at the top.

To replace text, select the Change menu item in the Search menu or press Ctrl−Q, A. The Change dialog box appears, as shown in Fig. 6-9. What you'll want to change is *Editor* to read *fancy new MS-DOS Editor*. Type the word *Editor* in the top box. Press the Tab key to move to the next box, then type in *fancy new MS-DOS Editor* and press Enter.

┌───────────────────────── Change ─────────────────────────┐
│   │
│ Find What: │Editor   │   │
│   │
│ Change To: │fancy new MS-DOS Editor   │   │
│   │
│   [ ] Match Upper/Lowercase   [ ] Whole Word   │
│   │
├───┤
│ < Find and Verify > < Change All > < Cancel > < Help >   │
└───┘

6-9   The Change dialog box.

As the Editor finds each occurrence of text, you'll see a box on the bottom of the screen with four choices: Change, Skip, Cancel, and Help. Change changes the text; Skip skips that instance and moves to the next instance of text to change; Cancel or Esc backs out of the search and replace; and Help or F1 gets more information.

Press Enter to make the change. See how the new text is inserted? Once the Editor reaches the end of the document, it will start searching again at the top. If it cannot find any more occurrences of text, you'll see a dialog box with the message Change complete displayed. Press Enter. (Remember that you can press Esc at any time to stop the search and replace option.)

You can quit the Editor now if you like. Select the Exit menu item from the File menu. This time, the Editor will ask if you want to save your document (because changes were made). Type Y to save the changes, N if you don't want to, or Esc to cancel and return to the Editor.

Using help

Wherever you are in the Editor, pressing the F1 key will get you help. More keenly than that, F1 always displays help about the specific area of the Editor you happen to be using.

For general help, press the F1 key twice. This presents you with the short list of help topics. To see the Survival Guide, press F1 once when you're in the text editing window.

The help system and Survival Guide are menu-driven programs that allow you to see a command summary plus descriptions of how everything in the Editor works. The help is on-line and is always available and ready for you (unless you delete the EDIT.HLP file on disk).

Figure 6-10 shows the Survival Guide's opening screen. To work with the help system, you can use the keyboard commands listed in Table 6-6. Additional information will be shown on your screen as you work your way through the help system.

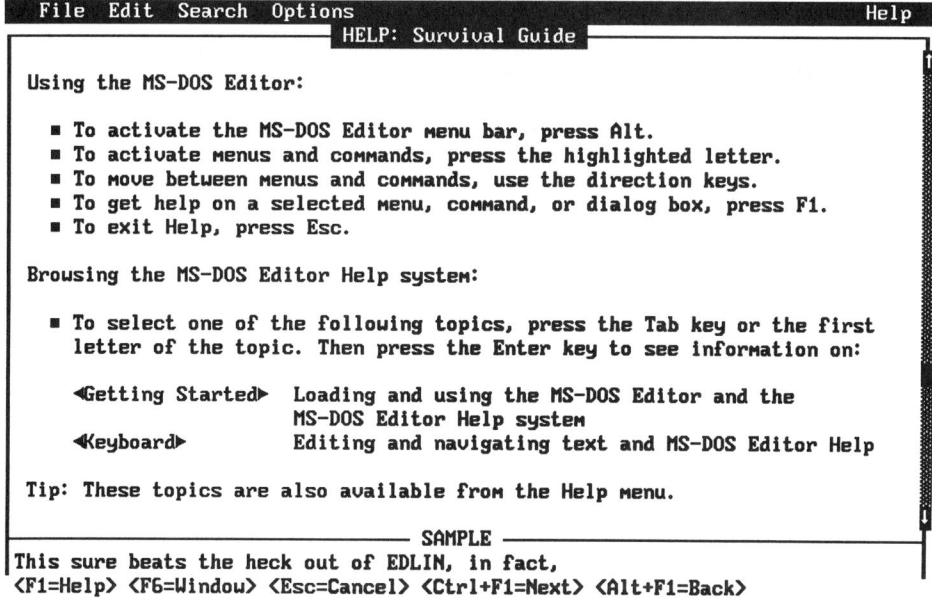

6-10 The Editor's Survival Guide.

Table 6-6   The key commands used in the help system.

Key	Function
Enter	Select the highlighted topic
Esc	Quit the help system
Tab	Move to the next highlighted topic
Shift – Tab	Move to the previous highlighted topic
Letter	Move to the topic beginning with "letter"
Shift – letter	Move to the previous topic beginning with "letter"
Alt – F1	Re-display the previous help screen
Ctrl – F1	Move on to the next help topic
Shift – Ctrl – F1	Move back to the previous help topic

Summary

This chapter was a brief but deep dive into the world of the MS-DOS Editor, DOS's text editing program. While the Editor might not be the ultimate, it is common ground as a free (with DOS) text editor. It's much better than EDLIN and offers features and powers that will serve you well throughout the coming chapters.

So, now that you know how to use the Editor, the next chapter will put your knowledge to practical use. The subject is the DOS configuration file, CONFIG.SYS. That's a text file on disk, one you can edit using the Editor and one of the most important files you have direct control over. A well-written CONFIG.SYS means a top-performing computer.

7

System configuration

DOS is good at making assumptions. When your computer starts, DOS will go left and right making assumptions about the way you want to run your computer. That's okay, but DOS makes very conservative assumptions. You'll want more than that. For example. you'll want a system customized to the way you work, a top-performance computer that you can create by telling DOS exactly how to set up your system. That information is conveyed to DOS via the CONFIG.SYS file located in the root directory of your boot disk.

This chapter is about system configuration, which takes place in a text file named CONFIG.SYS. In your CONFIG.SYS file you tell DOS how you want it to work with files and disks, how much memory to use and how to use it, as well as loading programs called *device drivers*, which control special PC hardware. CONFIG.SYS is a vital part of DOS's boot process, made even more so because you can control its contents.

About CONFIG.SYS

The CONFIG.SYS file on your system is a text file you create and can change as your system's hardware is upgraded or as your needs change. To understand CONFIG.SYS and to get the most from it, you need to know two things: how DOS boots and how CONFIG.SYS fits into the Big Picture.

How DOS boots

When you turn on your PC, the microprocessor jumps into action. By instinct, it starts looking for instructions at a specific memory location inside the computer. In all PCs, that memory location is in a special ROM chip called the *BIOS*.

A ROM chip is like a RAM chip; however, although it's read like RAM, ROM cannot be written to or altered. In microcomputers, ROM chips contain instructions for the microprocessor. The BIOS (Basic Input/Output System) is a set of simple hardware instructions for the microprocessor, all contained on a ROM chip in your PC. Basic keyboard, screen, and disk operations are handled by the BIOS. At this point, it's important to note that the BIOS handles how a PC boots.

The microprocessor starts its day by jumping right to the BIOS and executing special startup instructions. The first part of these instructions is the *Power-On Self Test*, or *POST*. This is a battery of tests the computer puts itself through to size up how much memory it has, the number of disk drives, and other inventory, as well as testing each device to make sure it's working properly. The POST also checks each of the computer's expansion slots, looking to see what's there, as well as testing each component it finds.

The final act of the POST is to lunge out toward the disk drives, looking for a floppy diskette in drive A and, if that's not found, a hard drive.

As was discussed in chapter 2, from either disk, the BIOS—in its last act—will load the boot sector of the first disk it finds and execute the program located therein. Supposing the disk is a bootable one, the boot sector program next looks for the file IO.SYS on disk and loads it. (On PC-DOS diskettes, the file is named IBMBIO.COM.)

The IO.SYS file is what integrates DOS with your PC's hardware, the BIOS. It also starts and runs the system initialization, or sysinit, process, as shown in Fig. 7-1. The sysinit process continues booting DOS by looking for and loading the MSDOS.SYS file (called IBMDOS.COM under PC-DOS).

MSDOS.SYS is the DOS kernel, or the core routines that make up DOS. This core includes DOS's time keeping functions, disk drive routines, and all the procedures that allow interaction between the computer's devices.

Sysinit's last duty is to look for a file named CONFIG.SYS in the root directory of the boot disk. If found, CONFIG.SYS is loaded and the instructions contained within it are read and executed. If CONFIG.SYS isn't found, DOS makes some assumptions and sets up your system accordingly.

The next step is for DOS to load the command interpreter, COMMAND.COM. COMMAND.COM is the DOS shell, or the program the computer operator (that's you) uses to tell DOS what to do. The shell passes instructions to the kernel (MSDOS.SYS, now in memory), and the kernel carries out those orders.

COMMAND.COM is the standard shell that comes with DOS. You can use other shells, which must be specified in CONFIG.SYS using the SHELL configuration command, which is covered later in this chapter. This is why CONFIG.SYS comes before COMMAND.COM in the boot process.

After COMMAND.COM loads, it looks for a file named AUTOEXEC.BAT in the root directory of the boot disk. If found, the instructions in that batch file are executed. (AUTOEXEC.BAT and it's functions are covered in chapter 9; general information about batch files is discussed starting in chapter 8.)

The optional files in the boot process (Fig. 7-1) are CONFIG.SYS and AUTOEXEC .BAT. DOS will start just fine without them, but it won't be perfect—which is why creating a CONFIG.SYS (and AUTOEXEC.BAT) file is important to good hard disk management.

Note that CONFIG.SYS does control the boot process in that it lets you select your command interpreter (the shell), which intern controls AUTOEXEC.BAT. This option is covered later in this chapter under the SHELL configuration command. Normally (and this is assumed throughout this book), you'll use COMMAND.COM as you shell.

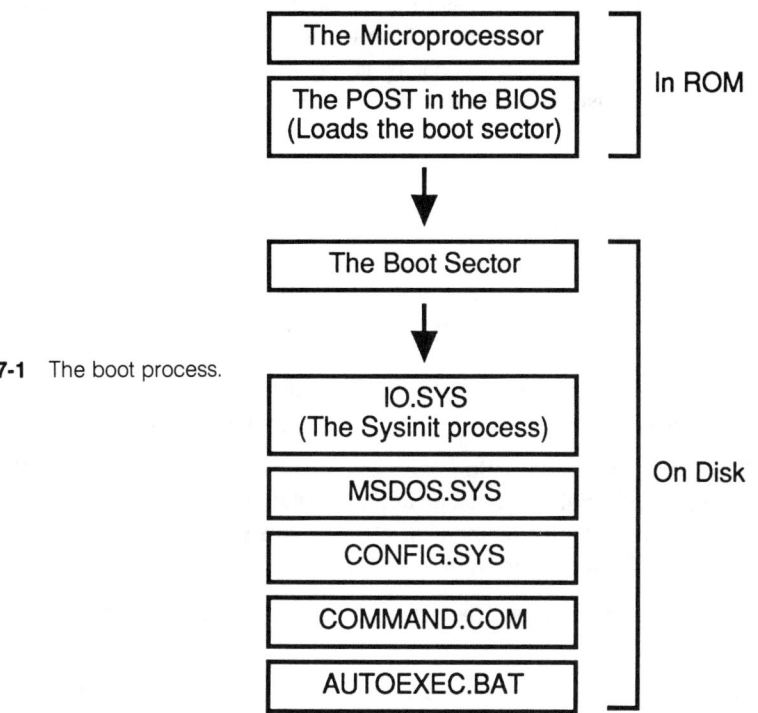

7-1 The boot process.

The Microprocessor	In ROM
The POST in the BIOS (Loads the boot sector)	
The Boot Sector	On Disk
IO.SYS (The Sysinit process)	
MSDOS.SYS	
CONFIG.SYS	
COMMAND.COM	
AUTOEXEC.BAT	

Take a look at your CONFIG.SYS file

All computers running DOS 5.0 should have a CONFIG.SYS file. If you didn't have a CONFIG.SYS file already under your previous version of DOS, then the DOS 5 SETUP program will have created one for you.

To look at your CONFIG.SYS file, use the TYPE command. On your hard drive, enter the TYPE CONFIG.SYS command:

    C > TYPE CONFIG.SYS

You'll see several lines of text displayed, usually less than a screenful. (If you see more, you can use the MORE filter to help pause the display a screenful at a time. Use the command TYPE CONFIG.SYS ¦ MORE or refer to chapter 4, "The MORE filter.")

You can get a hard copy of your CONFIG.SYS file by copying it to the printer. Try the following command:

    COPY CONFIG.SYS PRN

Make sure your printer is ready to print before pressing Enter. If you prefer to use I/O redirection, try this command:

    TYPE CONFIG.SYS > PRN

(Again, refer to chapter 4 if you need to brush up on using devices or I/O redirection.)

On some laser printers, you might have to eject the page from the printer manually before you see it print. This can be done by taking the printer offline (press the Online or Select button), then pushing the Form Feed or Page Eject button. From DOS, you can use the following handy command to eject a page from the printer:

```
ECHO ^L > PRN
```

The ^L is the Ctrl−L character, which you produce by typing Ctrl−L (don't type ^L, the caret and the *L* character).

Your CONFIG.SYS file contains system configuration commands and directives for DOS. Everything in there configures your system. Thankfully, it's all English text (although it might appear like gibberish at this point).

To help ease you into the concepts behind your CONFIG.SYS file, look for the following commands on your screen or on the hard copy you might have just made.

DEVICE   These are configuration commands that load a device driver into memory. Device drivers are special programs that control DOS devices as well as external devices you can add to your system. Common DEVICE drivers you might see are SETVER.EXE, HIMEM.SYS, ANSI.SYS, and MOUSE.SYS.

FILES   FILES is an important part of CONFIG.SYS, especially when dealing with a hard drive.

BUFFERS   BUFFERS is a counterpart to FILES; typically, both are set to the same value.

DOS   The DOS configuration command is used on 80286 and 386 systems to help free up memory, by giving more memory to your programs by hiding DOS in a special reserved area of memory.

SHELL   The SHELL configuration command tells DOS where to find the command interpreter, COMMAND.COM. Unless SHELL is specified, DOS assumes you want COMMAND.COM to be your command interpreter and that it's located in the root directory of your boot disk.

REM   The REM configuration command is used to include comments in your CONFIG.SYS file. Any text following REM on the same line is a comment or remark.

DOS 5's standard CONFIG.SYS file is shown in Fig. 7-2. This is the CONFIG.SYS file DOS 5 would create on an 80286 or later PC if the PC didn't have a CONFIG.SYS file already. Some elements of this CONFIG.SYS file might have wound their way into your own CONFIG.SYS file.

```
DEVICE=C:\DOS\SETVER.EXE
DEVICE=C:\DOS\HIMEM.SYS
DOS=HIGH
FILES=10
SHELL=C:\DOS\COMMAND.COM C:\DOS\ /p
STACKS=0,0
```

7-2   DOS 5's standard CONFIG.SYS file.

Figure 7-2 shows a smart CONFIG.SYS file, but one that still makes assumptions. The commands won't harm the system, but the system won't run as well as if a human had designed the file and placed into it commands that reflect how the PC is used.

Editing the CONFIG.SYS file

Because CONFIG.SYS is a text file, you can edit it using any text editor, including the DOS Editor, which was discussed in chapter 6. (You can even use old EDLIN to make changes, providing you have a high tolerance for pain.)

For example, suppose you needed to edit CONFIG.SYS to change the number of FILES from 10 up to 25. You first would edit CONFIG.SYS using the MS-DOS editor (or the editor of your choice):

    EDIT CONFIG.SYS

With CONFIG.SYS in the Editor, you would move the cursor to the FILES command, delete the 10, and replace it with 25. If you were adding a new command, you would place it somewhere into CONFIG.SYS on a line by itself.

The positioning of commands in CONFIG.SYS isn't crucial. Some commands require other commands to be present. Some commands have a definite pecking order. When that's the case, you'll be alerted to the order by the command's instructions. Otherwise, a command can just about go anywhere in CONFIG.SYS, although you should know that DOS reads the commands from the top of the file to the bottom.

When you're done making changes, save CONFIG.SYS back to disk. In the Editor, that's done by selecting the Save command from the File menu. Press Alt−F, then S. You then can quit the Editor and return to DOS.

There's only one important point to remember when editing your CONFIG.SYS file: any changes made will not take effect until after you've saved CONFIG.SYS back to disk, then reset your computer. Because CONFIG.SYS is read only when the system boots, you must always save and reset to try your modifications.

Another, minor point is that CONFIG.SYS is edited with a purpose in mind. It's not like writing a batch file, which is akin to programming. With programming, you make minor changes frequently. With CONFIG.SYS, you'll edit or change it only under one of the following circumstances:

- When something already in CONFIG.SYS doesn't work
- When adding a new device to your system, one that requires a device driver
- When making a change to your system that requires an update to CONFIG.SYS
- When you need to remove a device driver

This isn't an exhaustive list, but the point here should be obvious: you'll change CONFIG.SYS only once in a blue moon. (On my desktop system, I've had the same CONFIG.SYS file for three months, which would have been longer but I updated a device driver a while back.) Once you get CONFIG.SYS right, keep it that way.

System configuration commands

To make CONFIG.SYS work and to tell DOS how to configure your system, you use special system configuration commands. With DOS version 5.0, there are 15 commands, as shown in Table 7-1. Note that of the 15, you probably will use only five or six in your own CONFIG.SYS file. The most popular command is the DEVICE command, followed by FILES, BUFFERS, REM, SHELL, and DOS.

The following sections briefly describe each of the configuration commands, along with an example of each. Read each command's description, then use that command only if it applies to your PC's situation. The final section in this book describes how to create a CONFIG.SYS file, then you can use each of the following descriptions as a reference.

Note that all configuration commands appear in CONFIG.SYS on a line by themselves. Each line in CONFIG.SYS can be only 127 characters in length or less.

Table 7-1 DOS 5's configuration commands.

Command	Function
Break	Monitors Ctrl−C/Ctrl−Break key
Buffers	Reserves memory for reading and writing files
Country	Sets country and language rules for DOS
Device	Loads a device driver program
Devicehigh	Loads a device driver program into upper memory blocks
Dos	Loads DOS "high" and creates upper memory blocks
Drivparm	Configures disk drives
FCBS	Reserves file control block (for older DOS programs)
Files	Controls the number of files DOS can open
Install	Loads memory-resident software
Lastdrive	Sets the highest drive letter
Rem	Used for comments
Shell	Assigns the command interpreter
Stacks	Allocates memory for DOS's internal stacks
Switches	Controls the enhanced keyboard and other miscellany

BREAK

The BREAK configuration command is used to activate extended monitoring of the Ctrl−C or Ctrl−Break key press. Normally, Ctrl−C cancels all DOS commands. If you turn on extended monitoring with the Break command, DOS will double check for the Ctrl−C key press, which might cancel some commands quicker. On the downside, turning extended monitoring on will slow down your system somewhat.

To turn on extended monitoring, put the following BREAK configuration command into your CONFIG.SYS file:

BREAK = ON

Normally, DOS keeps extended Ctrl−C checking off, which is the same as the following BREAK configuration command:

BREAK = OFF

BUFFERS

The BUFFERS configuration command is one of the more important ones. It sets aside memory for DOS to use when reading and writing to disk. Each buffer holds 512 bytes that DOS will write to disk.

Having enough buffers is crucial to hard disk performance, especially for disk-intensive programs, such as data bases and accounting software. They usually require a great number of buffers in order to function properly.

The format of the BUFFERS command is:

BUFFERS = n[,m]

The value of n indicates the number of buffers you want DOS to use. Possible values range from 1 through 99, with 15 being about the minimum number. If you're using the SMARTDrive disk cache (covered in chapter 20), don't specify a value greater than 20 for n; otherwise, I recommend 32.

The m value is optional and is separated from the n value by a comma. m controls what's called a *secondary buffer cache*, or a special read-ahead storage area. Values for m range from 1 through 8. Specifying a read-ahead cache can speed up disk operations (although, personally, I recommend using a disk cache, as discussed in chapter 20).

A good all-purpose BUFFERS command to put into your CONFIG.SYS file is as follows:

BUFFERS = 20

If you're using a data base that recommends a higher value or if the BUFFERS configuration command already in your CONFIG.SYS file has a larger value, then go with that instead. For example:

BUFFERS = 32

COUNTRY

The COUNTRY configuration command is used to customize DOS for international use. If you're in the United States, this command isn't necessary. However, if you use a PC overseas or if you use it in the U.S. and want to access some foreign language characters or just play with a differently configured computer, you can use the COUNTRY configuration command to make your PC go international.

What the COUNTRY configuration command does is to set the following for DOS:

- The date and time format
- The currency symbol and the dollars and cents separator
- Numeric separators and number formats
- Alphabetical sorting order

When you open the door to international PC computing, a few new and unusual terms rear their ugly heads. The most common (and annoying) is code page. A *code page* is a list of extended ASCII characters and code numbers. All PCs come with the standard U.S. code page (which you can see in appendix C). Other code pages are customized to include special characters and accented characters for foreign languages.

The format of the COUNTRY configuration command is:

COUNTRY = xxx[,[yyy][,filename]

The *xxx* is a value representing a code for the country; *yyy* is optional and specifies a code page to be used; and the optional *filename* indicates the name of a country information file.

Values for *xxx* and *yyy* are listed in appendix F. The filename usually is the COUNTRY.SYS file that comes with DOS. As an example of a COUNTRY command in CONFIG.SYS, the following will change your computer to work in an Italian mode of thinking:

COUNTRY = 039,850,C: \ DOS \ COUNTRY.SYS

Code 039 is the code for Italy (actually, it's the international phone access code for Italy); 850 is the Latin I code page, which contains come characters that might come in handy in Italian; and COUNTRY.SYS is the standard DOS country configuration file.

DEVICE

The DEVICE configuration command is the most popular and common command found in CONFIG.SYS. It loads a device driver, which is special software designed to control a DOS device or an external device outside what DOS normally knows about.

For example, a device driver is required to add a mouse to your system. The basic PC doesn't know squat about a mouse, so, by loading a MOUSE.SYS device driver in your CONFIG.SYS file, DOS and other applications can take advantage of the rodent-like pointing device.

The format of the DEVICE configuration command is:

DEVICE = filename options

The *filename* is the full pathname for the device driver, which includes the file's extension as well. If the device driver requires additional switches or parameters, they're specified after the filename, as *options*.

DOS comes with ten device drivers, which are listed in Table 7-2. Other device drivers might come with external hardware devices you buy or with DOS enhancement software. All device drivers are installed using the DEVICE configuration command in the previous format. Many of these device drivers are covered later in this book, each in a different chapter.

The common (and quite interesting) ANSI.SYS driver would be installed using the following command:

DEVICE = C: \ DOS \ ANSI.SYS

Note how a full pathname is specified with the DEVICE command.

For memory management on an 80286 or later system with at least 350K of extended memory, the following configuration command is used:

DEVICE = C: \ DOS \ HIMEM.SYS

What the HIMEM.SYS device driver does, as well as the broader topic of DOS memory management, is covered in part IV of this book.

Table 7-2   DOS's 10 device drivers.

Device driver	Device controlled and function
ANSI.SYS	The screen; provides additional control over the screen, cursor, color, and keyboard functions
DISPLAY.SYS	The screen; provides code page support
DRIVER.SYS	Disk drives; allows for the addition of external and non-standard disk drives
EGA.SYS	The screen (EGA monitors only); allows EGA systems to recover their graphics display when using the DOS Shell or Windows applications
EMM386.EXE	Memory on a 386; converts extended memory into expanded memory, creates upper memory blocks
HIMEM.SYS	Memory on an 80286 and 386 system; controls all extended memory
PRINTER.SYS	The printer; provides code page support
RAMDRIVE.SYS	Memory; allows you to set aside RAM for use as an electronic disk drive
SETVER.EXE	DOS itself; the DOS version-fooling utility
SMARTDRV.SYS	Memory; allows you to set aside RAM for use as a disk cache

Note that most device drivers end with the SYS filename extension. Two exceptions under DOS are SETVER.EXE and EMM386.EXE, which also are command line programs in addition to being device drivers (they're dual-purpose). You should note that not all files ending in SYS are device drivers. COUNTRY.SYS and KEYBOARD.SYS are not device drivers and shouldn't be used with the DEVICE configuration command.

DEVICEHIGH

The DEVICEHIGH configuration command works just like the DEVICE command, but only on specially-configured 386 systems with extended memory. The difference between DEVICE and DEVICEHIGH is that the latter will load a device driver into an upper memory block, which gives DOS and your applications more of main memory in which to run.

Upper memory blocks (UMBs) are created on a 386 PC by using the following three commands in your CONFIG.SYS file:

```
DEVICE = C: \ DOS \ HIMEM.SYS
DOS = UMB
DEVICE = C: \ DOS \ EMM386.EXE /RAM
```

The function of each of these commands is detailed in chapter 20. Note that the C: \ DOS subdirectory is assumed to be the location of your DOS files. On your system the proper full pathname should be specified.

Once you've created upper memory blocks, you can substitute the DEVICEHIGH command for DEVICE in your CONFIG.SYS file. The format is similar:

DEVICEHIGH [size = hex] *filename options*

Both the *filename* and *options* items are identical to the DEVICE command's format. The optional size = *hex* item is used for some expanding device drivers. The word size is followed by the resident size of the device driver, as obtained from the MEM /C command. (This entire procedure is covered in detail in chapter 20.)

As an example, the following DEVICEHIGH configuration command loads the MOUSE.SYS device driver into a UMB:

DEVICEHIGH = C: \ MOUSE \ MOUSE.SYS

(The size = *hex* option isn't necessary for the MOUSE.SYS driver.)

You can use the DEVICEHIGH configuration command with all of DOS's device drivers, except for HIMEM.SYS and EMM386.EXE.

DOS

The DOS configuration command is used on 80286 and 386 systems with at least 350 K of extended memory. What it does is to take DOS and load it into a special area of memory called the High Memory Area (HMA), instead of in low memory. The end result is that you have some 50 K of additional memory that your programs can use.

Additionally, the DOS command is used in conjunction with the EMM386.EXE device driver to create upper memory blocks. This subject, as well as all of memory management (and HMA, UMB, etc.), is covered in part IV of this book, in chapter 20, "Memory optimization."

The format for the DOS configuration command is:

DOS = [LOW | HIGH][,UMB | NOUMB]

The first item is either LOW or HIGH. That indicates whether DOS is to be loaded in low memory or into the HMA. For example:

DOS = HIGH

loads DOS high, freeing up some 50 K of memory for your applications. The command DOS = LOW loads DOS low—the same as it would if you didn't use the DOS configuration command.

The second item is either UMB or NOUMB. It tells DOS to either open up links to the Upper Memory Blocks or to ignore them. The UMB option opens the links, NOUMB does not.

DOS = UMB

is required if you want to use the DEVICEHIGH command (and later, the LOADHIGH command, which is covered in chapter 20).

Both options can be combined in a single DOS configuration command on one line in your CONFIG.SYS file:

DOS = HIGH,UMB

Note that the HIMEM.SYS device driver must be installed for you to use the DOS configuration command. The location is not important, although most users place the HIMEM .SYS device driver at the top of their CONFIG.SYS files.

DRIVPARM

The DRIVPARM configuration command is used to configure an external drive or to tell DOS about a high capacity drive you've installed on an older type of PC.

The format for DRIVPARM is rather long. Here is a brief rendition of it:

```
DRIVPARM = /d:number
[/c][/f:factor][/h:heads][/i][/n][/s:sectors][/t:tracks]
```

As an example of using DRIVPARM, suppose you've added an external 3^1/$_2$-inch 1.4 Mb floppy drive. The commands in CONFIG.SYS required to configure DOS to accept the drive are as follows:

```
DEVICE = C: \ DOS \ DRIVER.SYS /d:2 /f:7
DRIVPARM = /d:2 /f:7
```

The /d:2 switch tells DOS the drive is an external drive, D. The /f:7 switch species the form factor of a 3^1/$_2$-inch 1.4 Mb floppy drive. (A *form factor* is the physical characteristics of something—its size and capacity in this case.)

FCBS

The FCBS configuration command was used in DOS version 1.*x* to set aside space for file control blocks. Under that version of DOS, all files were opened using file control blocks and if you planned on opening a lot of them, you needed a big FCBS value.

The format for the FCBS configuration command is:

```
FCBS = n
```

The value of *n* ranges from 1 through 255.

Only use this configuration command if the software you run requires it. Otherwise, use the FILES configuration command instead.

FILES

The FILES configuration command is used to set the maximum number of files DOS can open at once. While this seems trivial, setting a proper value for FILES is as important as setting a high enough value for BUFFERS. It can either make or break your system.

The format for the FILES configuration command is:

```
FILES = n
```

The value of *n* ranges from 8 through 255 and indicates the maximum number of files DOS can have open at once. If you use a lot of disk-happy programs, such as data bases, then a high value for FILES is in order. For example:

```
FILES = 20
```

INSTALL

The INSTALL configuration command is used to load memory-resident software in CON-FIG.SYS. Normally, such software would be loaded at the DOS prompt or in the special startup batch file, AUTOEXEC.BAT. By using the INSTALL configuration command, however, you can load memory-resident software low in memory, as well as avoid some memory overhead that's otherwise required.

The format of the INSTALL configuration command is:

INSTALL = *filename options*

The *filename* indicates the full pathname (including the filename extension) of the program to load. Any switches or parameters follow the filename as *options*.

I have two opinions about the INSTALL command. First, if you're using DOS 5.0's memory management abilities, don't bother with it; use the LOADHIGH command instead. Second, some programs just don't like the INSTALL command. Only if it mentions in the manual that it's okay to use INSTALL should you go ahead and try it. For example:

INSTALL = C: \ DOS \ GRAPHICS.COM

loads DOS's memory-resident GRAPHICS.COM program using the INSTALL configuration command. (Other DOS commands that can be used with the INSTALL configuration command include: APPEND.EXE, DOSKEY.COM, FASTOPEN.EXE, GRAFTABL.COM, KEYB.COM, NLSFUNC.EXE, and SHARE.EXE.)

LASTDRIVE

The LASTDRIVE configuration command is used to set the highest allowable drive letter DOS can assign to a hard drive, external floppy drive, network drive, RAM drive, or drive created using the SUBST command.

Normally, DOS only gives you up through drive E. That gives you two floppy drives, A and B, plus up to three hard drives or logical drives, C, D, and E. If you need any more drives, you must use the LASTDRIVE configuration command to tell DOS you want more drive letters.

The format for the LASTDRIVE configuration command is:

LASTDRIVE – *drive*

where *drive* is a letter from *A* through *Z*, although, practically speaking, it ranges from the highest-lettered drive in your system up through *Z*. You'll want to specify a letter that includes all of your logical hard drives, any RAM drives you create (covered in chapter 20), plus any network drives you might be connected to. For example:

LASTDRIVE = H

tells DOS that it's okay to have up to *H* (8) drives in the system, including the two floppies, a hard drive, plus any logical, RAM, or network drives. On my system, I just set LASTDRIVE to the highest possible value:

LASTDRIVE = Z

This command uses up a tad more memory than a conservative LASTDRIVE command. On the other hand, I'll never get an Invalid drive letter error message.

REM

The REM configuration command really doesn't do anything. Instead, REM allows you to insert comments into your batch file.

The format of the REM configuration command is:

REM comments

comments is optional text that follows the REM command (and at least one space character). For example:

REM This is my CONFIG.SYS file

The text This is my CONFIG.SYS file is considered a comment; DOS will not try to execute it as a command. By using the REM command in this way, you can include comments and notes to yourself in the CONFIG.SYS file.

The REM configuration command also can be used to remove a configuration command temporarily without actually deleting it. For example:

REM DEVICE = C: \ DOS \ HIMEM.SYS

Above, the REM command was inserted in front of the DEVICE configuration command that loads the HIMEM.SYS driver. Because REM is there, DOS will ignore the DEVICE command. This is a good way to suspend a configuration command temporarily without actually deleting that line. As you'll soon discover, this might be necessary when tweaking a CONFIG.SYS file. (It's handy because, to restore the command, you simply delete the word *REM*.)

SHELL

The SHELL configuration command tells the sysinit process where to look for the command interpreter and which command interpreter to use. The format is:

SHELL filename options

where filename is the name of the command interpreter, the DOS shell. options are any options that would follow.

The great majority of the time, the filename will be COMMAND.COM—which is what DOS looks for anyway. That makes the SHELL command seem rather redundant, unless you're planning on using another shell (like J.P. Software's 4DOS). However, it's possible to use the SHELL configuration command to force DOS to look elsewhere for COMMAND.COM. For example:

SHELL C: \ DOS \ COMMAND.COM

tells sysinit to use the copy of COMMAND.COM found in the DOS subdirectory on drive C. This method is the only way to move COMMAND.COM from the root directory of your boot disk. Without the SHELL command, DOS always assumes COMMAND.COM to be in the root directory.

As long as COMMAND.COM is the command interpreter of choice, here are its options and command format for use with the SHELL configuration command:

COMMAND.COM [*path*] [*device*] /e:*nnnn* /p

where *path* specifies the location of COMMAND.COM (in addition to the full pathname for COMMAND.COM required by the SHELL command). This parameter is required so that DOS knows where to locate COMMAND.COM after a program has run.

device is optional and usually is omitted. It specifies the I/O device DOS is to use for its standard input and output. Normally, the CON: device is used, although it's possible to specify another device, such as AUX. The practical purposes for doing so are limited.

The /e switch is used to set the size of DOS's environment, using the value *nnnn*. The environment can be from 160 through 32,768 bytes. The default value of 256 bytes usually is enough.

The /p switch is the permanent switch, which makes a copy of COMMAND.COM resident in memory. Also, the /p switch directs COMMAND.COM to load and execute the AUTOEXEC.BAT file in the root directory of the boot disk, which probably is what you want.

Keeping all this in mind, the following is a sample SHELL configuration command you can use in your computer:

SHELL = C: \ DOS \ COMMAND.COM C: \ DOS \ E:/512 /P

COMMAND.COM is assumed to be in the DOS directory on drive C, the size of the environment is set to 512 bytes, and the /p switch tells COMMAND.COM to hunt for and run the AUTOEXEC.BAT file.

STACKS

The STACKS configuration command sets aside memory for DOS's internal interrupt stacks, which are special memory locations used by DOS's own programming. The format of the STACKS configuration command is:

STACKS = *n,s*

The value of *n* is the number of stacks, which can be zero or any number in the range of 8 through 64. The value of *s* is the size of each stack, which can be zero or any number in the range of 32 through 512.

The STACKS command is a major memory hog. To find out how much memory it uses, multiply the *n* value by *s*. For example, consider the following command in CONFIG.SYS:

STACKS = 8,32

Multiply 8 times 32 to get 256 bytes—not a lot, but it turns out the STACKS command really shouldn't be used this way under DOS 5. The best way to use it, and to save on memory, is to insert the following into your CONFIG.SYS file:

STACKS = 0,0

This saves memory—especially compared to using no STACKS command at all. (When you omit the STACKS command, DOS goes ahead and assumes you want 9 stacks at 128 bytes, which is a little over 1 K of memory wasted.)

SWITCHES

The SWITCHES configuration command is dual-purpose, with neither of the two purposes related to each other. The first function of the SWITCHES configuration command is to suppress the interpretation of the enhanced 101-keyboard's extra keys, especially the F11 and F12 keys. The format is:

```
SWITCHES = /K
```

This command is used in conjunction with the DEVICE command that loads the ANSI .SYS driver. For example, if you have an older program that misreads the stand-alone cursor keys or the F11 or F12 key, put the following two commands into your CONFIG.SYS file:

```
DEVICE = C: \ DOS \ ANSI.SYS /K
SWITCHES = /K
```

Note that C: \ DOS is assumed to be the location of the ANSI.SYS device driver; be sure to specify a proper location on your own PC.

The second function of the SWITCHES configuration command comes into play on 386 systems that run Windows. When you do so, the WINA20.386 file is required to be in the root directory of your boot disk. (WINA20.386 tells Windows that it's okay to run under DOS 5.0.) To move WINA20.386 out of the root directory, you use the SWITCHES configuration command as follows:

```
SWITCHES = /W
```

After making that change in CONFIG.SYS, you must further modify your Windows SYSTEM.INI file. Under the section titled [386Enh], you need to add a line reflecting the proper location of the WINA20.386 file. For example:

```
DEVICE = C: \ WINDOWS \ WINA20.386
```

Save that change to your SYSTEM.INI file, then it's okay to move the WINA20.386 file out of the root directory and into the directory specified (C: \ WINDOWS, in the previous example). Reset your system and you have a cleaner root.

Creating and updating CONFIG.SYS

If you don't have a CONFIG.SYS file already, make one right now. For the following examples, it's assumed all DOS files are in the DOS subdirectory on drive C. Make any modifications necessary to reflect their correct location on your system. Also, keep in mind that these are general examples and are not intended for any individual computer.

8088/8086 example

The following CONFIG.SYS file would do great on any system; the 8088/8086 system is highlighted here because there are no DOS 5 memory management commands included.

(Line numbers have been added here for reference purposes only; do not put line numbers into your CONFIG.SYS file.)

```
1: REM CONFIG.SYS for an 8088/8086
2:
3: FILES = 20
4: BUFFERS = 20
5: SHELL = C:\DOS\COMMAND.COM C:\DOS\ /P
6: DEVICE = C:\DOS\ANSI.SYS
7: DEVICE = C:\DOS\SETVER.EXE
8: DEVICE = C:\MOUSE\MOUSE.SYS /C1
```

Line 1 is a REM statement, telling you about this CONFIG.SYS file. Line 2 is blank, which is okay in a CONFIG.SYS file; blank lines can be used to clean up the listing a bit. Lines 3 and 4 set the FILES and BUFFERS commands to 20—a good value.

Line 5 tells DOS to find COMMAND.COM in the C:\DOS subdirectory. The /E switch isn't included, meaning DOS sets the environment size to 256 bytes. The /P switch is added, which makes COMMAND.COM permanent and also runs the AUTOEXEC .BAT file.

Lines 6 through 8 load three device drivers: ANSI.SYS, which provides extended screen and keyboard control; the SETVER.EXE device driver; and the MOUSE.SYS device driver for controlling a mouse. Note how the /C1 switch is specified after the MOUSE.SYS device driver is installed.

80286 example

Here is an example that could be used on an 80286 system. It's assumed this system has enough extended memory to support the RAM drives created in lines 13 and 14.

```
1: REM 80286 system example
2:
3: DEVICE = C:\DOS\HIMEM.SYS
4: DOS = HIGH
5:
6: FILES = 10
7: BUFFERS = 20
8: SHELL = C:\DOS\COMMAND.COM C:\DOS\ /p
9: STACKS = 0,0
10: DEVICE = C:\DOS\SETVER.EXE
11:
12: LASTDRIVE = Z
13: DEVICE = C:\DOS\RAMDRIVE.SYS 512
14: DEVICE = C:\DOS\RAMDRIVE.SYS 512
```

Lines 3 and 4 are DOS 5 memory management tricks, as discussed in chapter 20. DOS is loaded high, freeing up some 50 K of memory.

Lines 6 through 10 are standard CONFIG.SYS commands. First are FILES and

BUFFERS, then the SHELL configuration command, followed by a STACKS command and the DEVICE command that loads the SETVER.EXE utility.

Lines 12 through 14 are used to set up two RAM drives in the system, uses DOS's RAMDRIVE.SYS device driver. Note how LASTDRIVE is set to drive Z, to allow for many RAM drives, yet only two are created, each only 512 K in size. (The subject of RAM drives is discussed in chapter 20).

386 example

Here is a CONFIG.SYS file for a 386 system that runs Windows:

```
 1: REM 386 Windows system CONFIG.SYS file
 2:
 3: DEVICE = C: \ DOS \ HIMEM.SYS
 4: DOS = HIGH,UMB
 5: DEVICE = C: \ DOS \ EMM386.EXE /NOEMS
 6:
 7: REM DEVICEHIGH = C: \ DOS \ SETVER.EXE
 8: DEVICEHIGH = C: \ DOS \ ANSI.SYS
 9: DEVICEHIGH = C: \ DOS \ SMARTDRV.SYS 512
10:
11: FILES = 32
12: BUFFERS = 32
13: STACKS = 0,0
14:
15: SWITCHES = /W
```

Lines 3, 4, and 5 activate DOS 5's 386 memory management tools. First comes HIMEM .SYS, then the DOS command, and finally the EMM386.EXE device driver, which creates upper memory blocks. (This is all detailed in chapter 20.)

Lines 7, 8, and 9 load device drivers using the DEVICEHIGH command. Note how the SETVER.EXE device driver has been deactivated in line 7 using the REM command.

Lines 11, 12, and 13 are standard CONFIG.SYS configuration commands. The SWITCHES configuration command in line 15 is used, supposedly, to relocate the WINA20.386 file.

Because not all 386 systems run Windows, here is a non-Windows 386 system CONFIG.SYS file. This CONFIG.SYS file also uses a non-DOS memory manager, QEMM/386:

```
1: DEVICE = C: \ DV \ QEMM386.SYS RAM EXTMEM = 2288
2: DOS = HIGH
3:
4: BUFFERS = 20
5: FILES  = 20
6: LASTDRIVE  = L
7: STACKS = 0,0
```

```
 8:
 9: SHELL = C:\DOS\COMMAND.COM C:\DOS\ /E:512 /P
10:
11: DEVICE = C:\DV\LOADHI.SYS /R:1 C:\MOUSE\MOUSE.SYS
12: DEVICE = C:\DV\LOADHI.SYS /R:3 C:\DOS\ANSI.SYS
13: DEVICE = C:\DV\LOADHI.SYS /R:1 C:\DOS\RAMDRIVE.SYS 32 /E
14: DEVICE = C:\DV\LOADHI.SYS /R:1 C:\DOS\RAMDRIVE.SYS 512 /E
15: DEVICE = C:\DV\LOADHI.SYS /R:1 C:\DOS\RAMDRIVE.SYS 720 /E
```

The QEMM/386 device driver is loaded in line 1. It takes the place of both the HIMEM .SYS and EMM386.EXE device drivers DOS provides. DOS is set to HIGH in line 2, which is allowable under DOS 5.0 using QEMM/386.

Lines 4 through 7 are standard CONFIG.SYS commands, setting FILES, BUFFERS, LASTDRIVE, and the STACKS configuration commands. Line 9 specifies a new location for COMMAND.COM using the SHELL configuration command, plus creates a 512 byte environment.

Lines 11 and 12 load the MOUSE.SYS and ANSI.SYS device drivers. They're loaded high using QEMM's LOADHI.SYS command, which is why there are many more switches on each line than had DOS's DEVICEHIGH command been used.

Lines 13 through 15 are used to create three RAM drives. The first is 32 K, the second 512 K, and the third 720 K. The reasons for doing this, and how it can improve your system's performance, will be divulged in chapter 20.

Updating and experimenting

The previous examples are suggestions only. Each PC is different and, sooner or later, you'll be adding new devices that require device drivers or using commands that require a change to your CONFIG.SYS file. When that day comes, make the change, save CONFIG.SYS to disk, and reset your computer to test the changes. If it doesn't work, you'll see one of the following error messages:

Error in CONFIG.SYS line xx

Line xx will be a line number in CONFIG.SYS that either contains a typo or some other incorrect parameter for a configuration command.

Unrecognized command in CONFIG.SYS

Usually, this is a typo. Sometimes, this happens if you forget to put a space after the REM command.

Device driver not found

Check the path for the device drivers, as well as its spelling. Remember that some device drivers end in EXE, not SYS.

Other specific errors can occur with individual device drivers, such as specifying incorrect parameters or missing devices (such as an unplugged mouse). These error messages vary with the device driver itself.

Remember that you can use the REM command to suspend certain CONFIG.SYS commands temporarily. It also is a good idea to save your old CONFIG.SYS file; use the COPY command to create a backup:

```
COPY CONFIG.SYS CONFIG.BAK
```

Do this before you edit the file, especially if your text editor doesn't create a backup file automatically.

Summary

CONFIG.SYS is an important file in the DOS boot process and is used to configure your system. It's important in that you control CONFIG.SYS's contents. A well-written CONFIG.SYS file means a well-performing PC.

You edit CONFIG.SYS like any text file. Into CONFIG.SYS, you put special configuration commands, which direct DOS to do certain things. The most popular configuration commands are DEVICE, FILES, BUFFERS, SHELL, and REM, although there are a total of 15 possible configuration commands you can use.

The next chapter starts off on a new foot—batch file programming. These are program files that you can create using a text editor. They form the basis of some amazing things you can do with your hard drive. This leads up to a later chapter on AUTOEXEC.BAT, which is the second system configuration file over which you have direct control.

8
An introduction to batch files

In chapter 5, you learned how to place program and data files into separate subdirectories and how to move into these subdirectories to access these files when needed. While that's useful, it requires you to enter a series of simple, yet repetitive commands every time you want to use your software. Isn't a computer supposed to make life easier? Why should you have to do all the work?

Fortunately, DOS provides you with a way to automate these repetitive commands by placing them into special program files called *batch files*. This chapter provides you with an introduction to batch files: what they are, how to create them, and what types of things you can do with them. As you soon will learn, batch files are the power behind good hard disk organization.

What are batch files?

Batch files basically are text files. They contain readable, ASCII text and can be created or edited using any word processor or text editor, such as the MS-DOS Editor (covered in chapter 6). Batch files also are program files, as identified by the special extension, BAT. DOS will run a batch file, just as it does a COM or EXE file—with one major exception: anyone who knows DOS can write a batch file. This is because each line of text in a batch file is simply a DOS command line or a special batch file instruction. That's the power behind batch files.

When the command processor, COMMAND.COM, runs a batch file, it executes the individual lines in the file as DOS commands, almost as if you'd typed those commands at the DOS prompt yourself.

Batch files can be quite simple or very elaborate. Most simple batch files are used to automate repetitive processes, such as setting changing directories to run your word processor or executing a whole slew of commands you might type to configure your printer.

Advanced batch files can be written as well. They can be used to drive complete menu-driven hard disk management systems. Such files can display specially designed menu screens, accept user input, and perform complex programming tasks involving decision-making and looping. These sophisticated batch files literally are computer programs. The techniques for creating them are covered in chapter 10, "Batch file programming."

How batch files work

When you type something at the DOS prompt, the command processor interprets what you've typed. First, it checks to see if what you've entered is an internal DOS command, such as COPY or CLS. If not, DOS checks the current directory to see if there is a COM, EXE, or BAT file corresponding to the command you entered. If this isn't the case, the command processor then checks DOS's file search path, to look for the command in another directory. (The search path is covered in chapter 9.) If the command isn't found after all that, you'll see the Bad command or filename error message.

In the case of a COM or EXE file, that program is loaded into memory and the instructions then are executed by the PC's microprocessor. For a BAT file, DOS opens the file and reads in the first line. It then executes that line as if you've typed it at the DOS prompt. Subsequent lines in the batch files also are executed, one at a time.

You should note that there is a definite pecking order here: COM files come first, followed by EXE files, then BAT files. For this reason, you should be careful what you name your batch files. For example, a batch file that copies files shouldn't be called COPY.BAT. Why? Because COPY is an internal DOS command. When you type COPY, DOS will first check for the internal COPY command; COPY.BAT will never be executed.

Creating batch files

Anyone can learn how to create and execute simple batch files. For example, you might want to set up a special batch file that displays a sorted directory listing in lowercase. You could name the batch file D.BAT. To see a sorted directory you only need press D and Enter at the DOS prompt. This saves you from memorizing the DIR command's switches and cuts down on extra typing. In this instance, the batch file would be a simple shortcut, nothing fancy.

The DIR command you want to use is:

```
DIR /O /L
```

This command displays a sorted directory and the /L switch adds the interesting touch of displaying the filenames using lowercase letters.

To create this simple batch file, you can use the COPY CON command, as discussed in chapter 4. For example:

```
C> COPY CON D.BAT
DIR /O /L
^Z
```

```
1 file(s) copied
```

From the CON: device, you create the batch file D.BAT. It contains only one line, which DOS will execute whenever you type D at the DOS prompt. Remember that ^Z is the Ctrl−Z character, which can be produced by pressing the F6 key.

To test run this batch file, type its name at the DOS prompt:

```
C> D
```

The command processor will search the current directory and will find and execute the commands contained within the D.BAT file for you. That really cuts down on your typing.

Batch files such as this serve a useful though limited function. They allow you to store either single or multiple DOS commands in a file for execution at a later time. To execute the stored commands, all you have to do is enter the name of the batch file.

The batch file directory

As you discover new uses for batch files, it helps to keep them all in a single place. Some will recommend the root directory. I don't. That sends up the red flag of *Keep the root clean!* Instead, you should create a special BATCH subdirectory somewhere on disk, either off the root directly or in a SYSTEM or BIN directory.

For example, if you have a SYSTEM directory, you can create a batch subdirectory with the following command:

    C> MD \SYSTEM\BATCH

If you're working on a simple hard disk structure, make your BATCH directory a sub-directory of the root:

    C> MD \BATCH

Into your BATCH directory, you should place all your useful batch file programs. For example, the D.BAT file could go there. Copy it from its current location to the BATCH subdirectory:

    C> COPY D.BAT \BATCH

Then, remove the original batch file, keeping the root directory clean:

    C> DEL D.BAT

Feel free to create other useful batch files as you see fit. If you can't think of any, just keep a lazy eye on what you type as you use your computer. If you're ever typing two or three commands consistently to get things done, consider putting them into a batch file. (Remember to create the batch file in your BATCH directory.)

Also, while COPY CON is great for creating quick and dirty batch files, you might consider using the Editor for longer batch files. Additionally, the Editor is your only method for editing an already-created batch file; COPY CON always overwrites existing files.

If you're using a word processor to create a batch file, remember to save it in the plain text or ASCII format. Also, note that each line in a batch file can be no more than 127 characters long.

Batch files that load application programs

The most popular type of batch files and the most useful for hard disk management and directory structure are those that run your applications. This solves the problem of a complicated tree structure. By using batch files to run applications, you don't have to CD all over to run a program—and you don't have to remember where the program is. The batch file handles all the overhead for you.

As an example, suppose you use WordPerfect as your word processor. Each time you want to create a document, you must execute the following sequence of commands:

```
C> CD \WP51
C> WP
```

These are consistent commands you always type each time you want to process words. Would it be simpler to place this sequence of commands into a batch file? Name the batch file WP.BAT and stick it into your batch subdirectory. Consider the following for its contents (line numbers have been added only for reference):

```
1: CD \WP
2: WP
3: CD \BATCH
```

Line 1 CDs to the WordPerfect subdirectory; line 2 runs WordPerfect; and, finally, line 3 returns you back to the batch file subdirectory. Once there, you can run other batch files or applications run by batch files.

Note that the batch file will continue to run, even after WordPerfect—or any DOS program—is run. DOS knows when it's running a batch file and will continue to read lines from that batch file until it's done. (There are a few limited exceptions to this rule; they're covered in chapter 10.)

The WP batch file runs WordPerfect. You don't need to remember where it's located every time you run it. Also, you only need to type two characters instead of three lines of DOS commands.

Similar batch files could be created for all of your applications. They don't need to be anything fancy. For example, the following batch file could run Lotus 1-2-3:

```
1: CD \123
2: 123
3: CD \BATCH
```

No sweat. Any application, anywhere on your hard drive, in any subdirectory, can be run using batch files. Consider the following:

```
1: D:
2: CD \WINDOWS
3: WIN
4: C:
5: CD \BATCH
```

Above, the batch files has been modified to run a program on drive D. Note how the drive is changed in line 1 and again in line 4 after the program (WIN or Windows) has been run. If you type it at the DOS prompt, you can put it into a batch file.

Terminating a batch file

For whatever reason, you can terminate a batch file in the middle of execution by pressing Ctrl−C or Ctrl−Break. Pressing either key combination causes the following message to appear on the screen:

Terminate batch file (Y/N)?

Respond by typing Y to stop the batch file and return to the DOS prompt or by pressing N to continue the batch file.

Messages, prompts, and variables

Simple batch files, such as D.BAT or WP.BAT, automate repetitive tasks and make using DOS easier. Yet, they're quite limited. All they can do is perform a series of predetermined DOS commands, which could have been entered directly from the system prompt.

It's possible to create batch files that can accomplish far more than the simple examples illustrated so far. To do this, you need to learn about DOS's special batch file commands. Three of these commands, ECHO, REM, and PAUSE, are covered in this chapter, as well as the batch file concept of command line variables. (The rest of the batch file commands are covered in chapter 10.)

Including messages in batch files

One problem with the batch files described so far in this chapter is that they're ugly. Consider the following output from the batch file used to run Windows:

C> D:

D> CD \ WINDOWS

D> WIN

(Windows is run here.)

C> C:

C> CD \ BATCH

Sure, it looks just as the screen would have had you been entering in all the commands. Doesn't that take away some of the magic? Wouldn't it be nicer if the display were silent while the batch file runs?

The ECHO command

The first and most popular batch file command is ECHO. ECHO controls the echoing of DOS commands to the screen while it runs. For example, by putting the command ECHO OFF at the start of your batch file, you can make it run without displaying anything. (Unfortunately, the ECHO OFF command itself still is echoed, but you'll learn how to fix that in a jiffy.)

For example, create the following batch file, DEMO.BAT, using COPY CON or the MS-DOS Editor. Name the batch file DEMO.BAT and place it into your BATCH subdirectory:

1: CD

```
2: VOL
3: VER
```

It's a silly batch file, granted, But run it. You'll see something like:

```
C> CD
C:\BATCH

C> VOL

Volume in drive C is DOS 5
Volume Serial Number is 16CE-9B67

C> VER

MS-DOS Version 5.00

C>
```

Now, use the Editor to edit the file again:

```
C> EDIT DEMO.BAT
```

Insert the following line at the top of the batch file:

```
ECHO OFF
```

The entire batch file should read like this:

```
ECHO OFF
CD
VOL
VER
```

Save the batch file to disk, then run it again. It's a little cleaner, but that initial ECHO OFF still gets in the way. For now, that's livable.

ECHO OFF turns off the display of all DOS commands while the batch file runs. The output of those commands still is displayed. However, if you want to turn off the display of any DOS command, you can do it by using I/O redirection and the NUL device. For example:

```
COPY *.DOC A:
```

would display the name of each file copied, then a summary such as 10 file(s) copied. You can suppress those messages and the message of any DOS command with > NUL, redirecting output to the NUL: device:

```
COPY *.DOC A: > NUL
```

The output of the COPY command now is redirected to the NUL device. If ECHO is turned off, the command will run without displaying anything at all. Echoing can be turned back on again with the ECHO ON command, although it's rarely used.

The ECHO command also can be used to display messages on the screen, even after issuing ECHO OFF. To do so, place the text you want echoed after the ECHO command.

The ECHO command doesn't need to be used in a batch file. For example, to echo the phrase, *Happy computing!*, you could type the following at the DOS prompt:

ECHO Happy computing!

Try this one to wake up the dog:

ECHO ^G

Reload the DEMO.BAT file into the Editor and sprinkle in some ECHO commands as follows (the line numbers are for reference):

```
1: ECHO OFF
2: REM This is a demonstration batch file
3: ECHO Here is the current directory:
4: CD
5: ECHO Here is the volume information:
6: VOL
7: ECHO Here is the DOS version:
8: VER
```

The new lines are 2, 3, 5, and 7. Note the REM comment in line 2. REM works in batch files just as it does in CONFIG.SYS (covered in chapter 7).

Save the file back to disk, then run it. See how the ECHO command displays the text? ECHO can be used to display any text. You'll see some interesting and exciting examples in the next part of this book.

Generally ECHO displays any text that follows it—except for a blank line. If you type ECHO alone, DOS tells you the ECHO state. For example:

C> ECHO
ECHO is on

If you've turned ECHO OFF in a batch file, ECHO on a line by itself displays ECHO is off.

To echo a blank line in a batch file, immediately follow the ECHO command with a period:

ECHO.

You can use the blank lines to pad out the display. Also, don't forget the CLS command, which clears the screen.

Using the @ prefix

Just like ECHO OFF, the @, or at, symbol can be using in batch files to prevent a batch file command from being displayed. This works whether or not ECHO is on or off. You can even use the @ to suppress the initial ECHO OFF.

For example, to suppress the first ECHO OFF in the DEMO.BAT file, edit the first line in the file to read:

@ECHO OFF

Save the file to disk, then run it again. The initial ECHO OFF won't be displayed. Ta-da! After all this time, you finally have a completely silent batch file. Congratulations. (Now the DOS-oblivious won't know if they're running a batch file or a real program.)

You also can use @ to suppress every line in a batch file from being displayed, neglecting the need for having an initial ECHO OFF at all. For example:

```
1: @REM This is a demonstration batch file
2: @ECHO Here is the current directory:
3: @CD
4: @ECHO Here is the volume information:
5: @VOL
6: @ECHO Here is the DOS version:
7: @VER
```

There's no initial ECHO OFF or @ECHO OFF command needed here. Not a single line in the previous batch file will be displayed on the screen; the @ command suppresses each of them.

The PAUSE command

It's possible to suspend the execution of a batch file temporarily using the PAUSE command. This command allows the user to read the screen, make a decision, or perform some task.

The PAUSE command is simply put on a line by itself. In the DOS manual, it states that the PAUSE command can be followed with optional text. However, when you turn ECHO OFF, as is the case with most batch files, any text you include after the PAUSE command will never be displayed.

The PAUSE command displays the following prompt:

```
Press any key to continue . . .
```

(Earlier versions of DOS might display Strike a key when ready . . .)

There DOS sits and waits for you to press any key, such as Enter or the Spacebar. (If you press Ctrl−Break here, you can terminate the batch file.)

As an example, suppose you have a batch file to back up your word processing documents automatically onto a floppy diskette. This special batch file, DOCBACK.BAT, looks something like this:

```
1: @ECHO OFF
2: CD \WP\DATA
3: ECHO Place the document diskette in Drive A and
4: PAUSE
5: COPY *.DOC A:
```

The batch file echoes the following message to the screen:

```
Place the document diskette in Drive A and
Press any key to continue . . .
```

See how the ECHO command in line 3 blends with the PAUSE command's output in line

4? The *and* at the end of line 3 provides the conjunction. There DOS will sit, waiting for you to put the diskette into drive A. Once that's done, the batch file continues with line 5 and copies the files.

Replaceable parameters

You can customize the execution of DOS commands by including your own messages and prompts. Still, all the commands contained in the batch files introduced so far have been static. This means that each batch file only performs a specific inflexible function.

Suppose you had several different but related tasks that you wanted to automate. Rather than creating a separate batch file for each of them, wouldn't it be nice if you could develop a general purpose batch file, then identify the specific task you wanted performed at the time of execution? DOS gives you this flexibility by allowing you to include replaceable parameters or command line variables in your batch files.

How they work

Replaceable parameters serve as variables and are included with the individual commands in a batch file. They can take the place of filenames, paths, and even DOS commands. The actual filename, path, or command is typed at the command line by the user when the batch file is executed.

The command line variables are the symbols %1, %2, on up through %9. These variables represent the first through ninth items typed after the batch file name at the DOS prompt. (A tenth variable, %0, is always equal to the batch file name itself.)

For example, consider the following command:

COPY LETTER.DOC A:

The command, COPY, is assigned to the variable %0. The filename, LETTER.DOC, is assigned variable %1. Finally, A: is assigned to variable %2.

When you run a batch file, DOS remembers the replaceable parameter assignments until the batch file is through executing. If the value A: is assigned to %2 (as previously), it will stand for A: throughout the entire batch file.

To see how this works, create the following batch file named SHOW.BAT:

```
 1: @ECHO OFF
 2: ECHO Here are the replaceable parameters:
 3: ECHO The name of the batch file is %0
 4: ECHO The first parameter is %1
 5: ECHO The second parameter is %2
 6: ECHO The third parameter is %3
 7: ECHO The fourth parameter is %4
 8: ECHO The fifth parameter is %5
 9: ECHO The sixth parameter is %6
10: ECHO The seventh parameter is %7
11: ECHO The eighth parameter is %8
12: ECHO The ninth parameter is %9
```

Run the batch file, but type a few items after SHOW on the command line. Below is a sample run for the batch file:

```
C> SHOW THIS IS A TEST
Here are the replaceable parameters:
The name of the batch file is SHOW
The first parameter is THIS
The second parameter is IS
The third parameter is A
The fourth parameter is TEST
The fifth parameter is
The sixth parameter is
The seventh parameter is
The eighth parameter is
The ninth parameter is
```

As the batch file runs, it replaces the parameters %0 through %9 with the items on the command line. Parameters without an item assigned to them display as nothing.

A practical example

Most applications allow you to load a file by specifying that file's name after the application. For example, if you want to edit the file LETTER.DOC in WordPerfect, you can start WordPerfect with the following:

```
WP LETTER.DOC
```

WordPerfect loads itself into memory, then looks for and loads the file LETTER.DOC for editing.

If you're running WordPerfect using a batch file, then you can use a replaceable parameter to pass along a filename just as above. For example:

```
1: @ECHO OFF
2: C:
3: CD \WP51
4: WP %1
```

The previous batch file runs WordPerfect on my computer. Line 1 turns the echo off; line 2 logs to drive C; line 3 changes to the WordPerfect subdirectory; and line 4 loads WordPerfect—plus the %1 command line variable is used to load any file I've specified.

If a filename isn't specified after WP.BAT is run, then no file is loaded into WordPerfect. However, with the command line variable in place, I can run WordPerfect and load any file, just as if it were WP.EXE and not WP.BAT I was running. Again, this example shows the power of batch files on a well-integrated hard disk system.

Summary

This chapter has shown you how to create batch files for simplifying repetitive DOS commands, as well as showing you how batch files in a BATCH directory can be used to run your system. In chapter 10, you'll learn how to use more powerful batch file commands. These commands bring batch files up to the level of a mini-programming language. Yet, with all that power, they still are easy to use and simple to write.

The next chapter takes a look at one batch file in particular, the most important batch file on your system. It's the AUTOEXEC.BAT. What CONFIG.SYS is to the computer, AUTOEXEC.BAT is to the computer operator. Using AUTOEXEC.BAT, you can further configure DOS to the way you like it. Because it's a batch file, it removes a lot of the drudgery you might be going through each time you start your PC.

9

AUTOEXEC.BAT

Every time you start your computer, there are certain commands you regularly type. Over and over, you enter these commands each time the computer boots. Batch files are the solution for repeated strings of DOS commands; simply put the commands into a batch file and type the batch file name. Simple, yet you still would have to type that batch file's name each time you start your computer.

You really don't have to. If you name the batch file AUTOEXEC.BAT, it will always be run every time you boot your system. When COMMAND.COM first runs, it looks for and executes a file named AUTOEXEC.BAT in the root directory of your boot disk. This file opens the door to many possibilities. Not only can AUTOEXEC.BAT type commands you normally would enter, but it can configure DOS, prep some applications, load memory-resident programs, even pass control right over to a menu system or application—all automatically.

This chapter is about your AUTOEXEC.BAT file. Also introduced here are three DOS commands, PATH, PROMPT, and SET, each of which can play powerful roles in your hard disk system. Thanks to the potential of AUTOEXEC.BAT, you're about to ease a lot of drudgery—some of which you might not even know you have.

The automatic startup file

CONFIG.SYS is your system configuration file, but it just doesn't do enough. Sure, it tells DOS how much memory to use for certain things, loads device drivers, and other miscellany. However, your system just isn't fully configured after CONFIG.SYS is done. You need more.

The rest of your computer's setup is handled by AUTOEXEC.BAT, a text file you can control just like CONFIG.SYS. Where you can say CONFIG.SYS configures the system, AUTOEXEC.BAT is used to configure DOS.

How AUTOEXEC.BAT works

AUTOEXEC.BAT is part of your PC's boot process, which was covered in chapter 7 (in the section titled "How DOS boots"). It actually is the last step in the process, but the only step that allows you to store and execute DOS commands.

After COMMAND.COM loads, it looks for AUTOEXEC.BAT in the root directory of your boot disk. DOS won't look for it elsewhere. Also, the file must be named AUTOEXEC.BAT. Note that, if you're using the SHELL configuration command to relocate COMMAND.COM, you must specify the /P switch so that AUTOEXEC.BAT will run.

AUTOEXEC.BAT is loaded and run just like any other batch file. Into AUTOEXEC .BAT you can place a whole stack of commands that you'd normally type to set up your PC. DOS reads in each line as if you've typed it at the DOS prompt. This is nice because it's done automatically; you never need to type AUTOEXEC.BAT—just sit back and watch your computer set itself up the way you like.

What if AUTOEXEC.BAT isn't found? Then, DOS, being cautious, goes ahead and makes assumptions. If your PC has an 80286 or later microprocessor with a working internal battery, then you'll see only the DOS copyright notice and the system prompt when the system starts. If you have an older system, you'll be prompted to enter the date and time when the system starts. After that, you'll see the DOS copyright notice and the system prompt. However, it's much better to create AUTOEXEC.BAT—if nothing else, to avoid the droll date and time prompts.

Checking your AUTOEXEC.BAT file

Chances are good that your hard disk already has an AUTOEXEC.BAT file. This AUTOEXEC file was either placed on your disk by your dealer, the office computer person, your favorite PC guru, or by the DOS 5 installation program. If it's there, why not take a look at it—just to get warmed up for this chapter. Use the TYPE command:

```
C> TYPE AUTOEXEC.BAT
```

If it scrolls and scrolls, you can try to pause it by typing Ctrl−S or pressing your Pause key. Better still, use the MORE filter:

```
C> TYPE AUTOEXEC.BAT ¦ MORE
```

Here's an interesting trick you can use with the MORE filter and a text file:

```
C> MORE < AUTOEXEC.BAT
```

Your AUTOEXEC.BAT file is spoon fed into the MORE filter using input redirection. Neat, eh?

As one final diversion from the topic at hand, you can get a hard copy of your AUTOEXEC.BAT file with the following:

```
C> COPY AUTOEXEC.BAT PRN
```

(I'll leave it to you to figure out how to use I/O redirection to do the same thing.)

The sample AUTOEXEC.BAT file that DOS 5 installs is shown in Fig. 9-1. It really is not that bad. If you've run the SETUP program properly, all the settings might be

9-1   DOS 5's standard no-frills AUTOEXEC.BAT file.

```
@ECHO OFF
PROMPT $p$g
PATH C:\DOS
SET TEMP=C:\DOS
```

exactly what you need. At this stage in the game, however, you might be unfamiliar with some of the commands you see in that batch file. The following sections should clear that up for you.

You might recognize a few of the lines in AUTOEXEC.BAT, such as DOS commands, batch file commands (ECHO, PAUSE, or REM), or the names of programs on your system. Some commands are new, such as PATH and PROMPT. These are DOS commands, yet their role in AUTOEXEC.BAT is crucial.

Special AUTOEXEC.BAT commands

AUTOEXEC.BAT is about configuring DOS. You would think CONFIG.SYS would do that (it does do that under OS/2). However, there's a lot of configuring left to do, plus a few DOS commands, utilities, and application programs you might want to run when you start your computer. That just can't be done in CONFIG.SYS.

To augment the power of AUTOEXEC.BAT, there are two major things you can do in it, plus one incidental thing. The major things are setting DOS's program search path and changing the DOS prompt to something more lively than the boring C> prompt. The incidental thing involves DOS's storage area, the environment. These things are handled by three DOS commands, PATH, PROMPT, and SET.

The PATH command

In chapter 8, you saw how DOS looks for a command in three places when you type something at the DOS prompt. First, DOS checks for the command internally. Second, DOS checks for a COM, EXE, or BAT file in the current directory. Third, DOS checks for a COM, EXE, or BAT file in all subdirectories listed on the search path. However, what is a search path?

The search path is a list of subdirectories in which DOS can look for program files. Without a search path, DOS stops looking for commands after the current directory. However, you can create a search path to help DOS locate commands and programs elsewhere on disk.

This is powerful stuff. For example, consider putting your DOS subdirectory on the search path. That means you can access all of the DOS commands, the COM or EXE files, from any other drive or directory on your system. DOS will always find the programs because its subdirectory is named on the search path.

Any subdirectories that contain lots of runable files, such as a BATCH subdirectory, work great on the search path. However, it's important not to get carried away. For example, while putting every subdirectory in your system on the search path sounds neat, it's counterproductive. Such a setup would cause DOS to take way too long to search for a program.

To create a search path you use the PATH command. The format of the PATH command is:

PATH [*subdirectory*][*;subdirectory;*...]

By itself, the PATH command displays the current search path. If you type PATH at the DOS prompt, you'll see something like the following:

```
C> PATH
PATH = C:\DOS;C:\BATCH
```

In this example, two subdirectories are on the search path, C:\DOS and C:\BATCH, each separated by semicolons. On your screen, you might see several subdirectories, each of which is separated by a semicolon. It also is possible that your system might not have a search path defined. In that case, you'll see the message No Path displayed.

To create a path, you follow the PATH command with the names of one or more subdirectories, each of which is separated by a semicolon. If you only specify one subdirectory, then the semicolon isn't needed. Likewise, don't follow the last subdirectory with a semicolon.

Each subdirectory listed on the search path should identify a valid directory to be searched for programs. Remember to specify a drive letter as well; DOS otherwise will assume you mean a subdirectory on the current drive, not the specific drive where the subdirectory is located.

When working with the search path, here's a handy rule, right up there with *Keep the root clean*:

Don't put too many subdirectories on the path!

There is a tendency to go overboard here. For example, you might love your word processor and always want access to it. If so, put its directory on the path. Yet, your word processor probably is the only program you'll be running in that directory. In that case, DOS really is wasting its time searching that directory whenever you type in a command at the DOS prompt. This isn't bad if your path looks like this:

```
PATH = C:\DOS;C:\WP
```

However, if you add on your spreadsheet, games directory, utility directory, and on and on, you get a cluttered search path that actually will slow down your system:

```
PATH = C:\DOS;C:\WP;C:\QUATTRO;C:\GAMES;C:\UTILITY;
C:\SIDEKICK
```

The previous search path is way too long. I'd say any search path listing over four subdirectories is too long. A better idea is to create a batch file to run your word processor. Create similar batch files for other applications that sit in their own directories. Then, you can put those batch files in a subdirectory already on the path:

```
PATH = C:\DOS;C:\BATCH
```

The previous PATH command defines a search path that looks in only two directories, C:\DOS and C:\BATCH. If there are batch files in C:\BATCH to run your other applications, you don't need to put their directories on the path.

Although the PATH command is a handy trick, keep in mind that DOS only looks for program files (COM, EXE or BAT) in the subdirectories listed. You still must use full pathnames for data files or log to the proper drive and directory, then access the data files directly.

To remove all subdirectories from the PATH—to wipe it clean—enter the PATH command with only a semicolon:

```
PATH;
```

Now, the path is gone. There's no real reason to do this, although it does point out that each time you use the PATH command to create a new path, the old path is gone. Yes, this means, if you want to add one more subdirectory to the path, you must retype the entire path again. For example, consider the following output from the PATH command:

```
C> PATH
PATH = C:\DOS;C:\BATCH
```

Now, suppose you want to add the C:\UTIL directory to that path. If so, you must retype the entire path as follows:

```
C> PATH C:\DOS;C:\BATCH;C:\UTIL
```

That's the only way it can be done. A shortcut is possible using the SET command, which is covered later in this chapter. The shortcut, however, only works in batch files; at the DOS prompt you still have to type in the complete search path.

The search path you create for your system depends on your hard disk's structure. For example, if you have a simple no-brain structure, you probably can get by with putting each directory on the path, as in the following PATH command:

```
PATH C:\DOS;C:\WP;C:\123
```

However, be wary of the no-brain scenario. Installation programs that like to set their applications up in subdirectories off the root also can modify your PATH. They usually will place their directory in the search path, usually as the first item. After installing a few applications, your PATH might look like this:

```
PATH C:\DBASE;C:\GV;C:\PCTOOLS;C:\DOS;C:\WP;C:\123
```

This path is not what you want. Instead, you'll need to switch over to the BATCH file subdirectory strategy and run things from there:

```
PATH C:\DOS;C:\BATCH
```

As you probably can guess, the best place to set the search path is in your AUTOEXEC .BAT file. That way, you'll have the path and immediate access to all your important programs each time you start your system. Keep in mind, however, that you can change the search path at any time, either at the DOS prompt or in another batch file. For example, the following is a batch file to run Windows:

```
1: @ECHO OFF
2: PATH = C:\WINDOWS;C:\DOS;C:\BATCH
3: C:
```

```
4: CD \WINDOWS
5: WIN
6: PATH = C:\DOS;C:\BATCH
```

Windows wants its own directory on the path. In line 2, the search path is reset to reflect the C:\WINDOWS subdirectory. After Windows runs (in line 5), however, its subdirectory no longer needs to be on the path. The path is reset back to normal in line 6.

Later in this chapter, you'll learn some quick-and-dirty tricks for using the PATH command. However, the search path you set on your computer always depends on your own hard drive structure and where all your programs are located.

The PROMPT command

What's the most boring thing about DOS? If anything makes DOS uninteresting it has to be the DOS prompt. Look at it:

```
C >
```

So far in this book, you've seen nothing but the standard droll DOS prompt. It shows the currently logged disk drive and the greater-than symbol. Yawn. Things don't have to be that way, however. DOS's PROMPT command allows you to insert your own text messages at the system prompt, as well as include the date, time, current drive, and other interesting information. The days of the boring DOS prompt are gone!

The format of the PROMPT command is as follows:

```
PROMPT [string]
```

The optional *string* contains characters and special symbols you can use to create a new system prompt.

As an example, suppose you wanted the system prompt to read Enter your command:. You would create this prompt by entering the following:

```
PROMPT Enter your command:
```

After the previous command, the new system prompt would be:

```
Enter your command:
```

This prompt would remain in effect until you change it again using the PROMPT command.

To reset the PROMPT back to the sad standard DOS prompt, use the PROMPT command by itself:

```
Enter your command:PROMPT
```

```
C >
```

Besides letting you change the prompt to a text message, the PROMPT command also lets you include special information, such as the date and time, the current drive letter, the current path, plus special symbols and other interesting tricks. This is done by including the special PROMPT command meta characters in the prompting string. The meta characters are each two characters long and all start with a dollar sign, as shown in Table 9-1.

Table 9-1 The PROMPT
command's meta characters.

Meta Character	Displays
$$	The $ character
$_	A new line
$b	The ¦ character
$d	The date
$e	The Escape character
$g	The > character
$h	The backspace character
$l	The < character
$n	The current drive letter
$p	The current directory
$q	The = character
$t	The time
$v	The current DOS version number

Any of these meta characters can be included in the PROMPT command string. Be careful to note the special characters: $b for the pipe, $g for greater-than, and $l for less-than. Because those characters are I/O redirection symbols, they can be included in a PROMPT string only via their meta characters. Also, the dollar sign must be listed twice.

Note that any meta character can be specified in upper- or lowercase.

The most popular PROMPT command, and the one DOS 5's SETUP program automatically creates for you is the following:

```
PROMPT $p$g
```

This command changes the prompt to reflect the currently logged drive and directory, plus the greater than symbol:

```
C:\>
```

In this case, the prompt tells you that you're logged to the root directory of drive C. This prompt is much more informative than the plain C> prompt. (From this point onward, this book will use the pg style prompt.)

Another popular prompt includes the date and time, as well as the currently logged path:

```
Sun 7-04-1991
11:54:35.22
C:\DOS>
```

This prompt shows the current date, time, and path. Note that the time is updated each time you see a new DOS prompt; it doesn't update in real time. To create this prompt, the following **PROMPT** command is used:

PROMPT d_t_pg

This breaks down as follows:

$d   The current date
$_   A new line
$t   The current time
$_   A new line
$p   The current directory
$g   The greater-than symbol

One downside to this prompt is that the time is displayed to the seconds and hundredths of a second. That's not a drawback, but the display would look cleaner without them.

To erase part of the time display, you can use the backspace meta character, $h. Consider the following **PROMPT** command:

PROMPT d_thhhhhh_pg

This command is identical to the previous **PROMPT** command, but contains six backspaces ($h). That will erase the hundredths and seconds output of the $t (time) meta character, plus the two separator characters. Your prompt would look something like this:

Sun 7-04-1991
11:54
C:\ DOS>

You can even add text to the prompt, in addition to the meta characters:

PROMPT d_Time is thhhhhh_pg

This command displays the following:

Sun 7-04-1991
Time is 11:54
C:\ DOS>

Creating your own customized system prompts is both fun and helpful. It also can be a great source of entertainment as you sneak around changing the prompts behind your co-workers' backs. (I shouldn't be telling you this.) For example:

PROMPT Error reading drive N_Abort, Retry, Ignore?

That's a nasty prompt.

Even more creative prompts can be built using $e, the meta character for the Escape character. Later, when you read about ANSI.SYS in chapter 12, you'll learn how to incorporate ANSI commands into your PROMPT. This allows you to create colorful prompts, move the cursor about, and play with interesting text effects.

Back to the subject at hand, the best place to set up your system prompt is in AUTOEXEC.BAT. Now that you know about the PROMPT command, you probably will spend some time experimenting with various prompts. Go ahead. Try each of the meta commands, create interesting prompts. However, when you've settled on one you like (something practical), then stick it into your AUTOEXEC.BAT file; you'll have it each time you start your PC.

As with the PATH command, remember that you can reset the PROMPT at any time, either at the DOS prompt or in a batch file.

The environment

You can't discuss the PATH and PROMPT commands without touching upon the environment. The *environment* is a special area in memory where DOS stores information—like a scratch pad. When you create a PATH, DOS stores the path you've defined in the environment. Likewise, the PROMPT definition is held in the environment. DOS also uses the environment for other temporary storage. Also, your applications might be able to take advantage of the environment as well.

You view the contents of the environment using the SET command, which will be discussed in a moment. However, you should know that the environment is of a limited size. Normally, DOS gives you 256 bytes for the environment. With a byte equal to one character, this could limit the amount of information you can store in the environment. (This normally isn't a problem, however.)

The environment size can be changed by using the SHELL configuration command in CONFIG.SYS. One of COMMAND.COM's optional startup switches is /E:*nnnn*. The value of *nnnn* indicates the size of the environment, from 160 through 32,768 characters (or bytes). You can change the size of the environment to any value within that range. For example:

```
SHELL = C: \ COMMAND.COM C: \ /E:512 /P
```

sets the size of the environment to 512 bytes. Refer to chapter 7, "Shell," for more information.

The SET command

You view, change, or edit the environment's contents using the SET command. The format of the SET command is:

```
SET [variable = [string]]
```

By itself, the SET command displays the contents of your environment. Type the SET command at your DOS prompt. You'll see something like the following:

```
C: \ > SET
COMSPEC = C: \ DOS \ COMMAND.COM
PATH = C: \ DOS;C: \ BATCH
PROMPT = $p$g
TEMP = C: \ DOS
```

What you see will doubtlessly be different. However, look at the format of the SET command's output. Each line contains two elements. The first is the environment variable, which is followed by an equal sign. Then comes the string to which the variable is assigned. Note that the variable is always uppercase in the environment; the string can be any case.

The way the environment works, DOS and other applications look for specific variable names. Internally, they then replace those variable names with the variable's string. For example, when DOS displays the prompt, it looks for the PROMPT variable's string and uses that as the definition for the system prompt. You might run a program, such as Central Point's PC Tools, that relies upon a variable. With PC Tools, it looks for the variable PCTOOLS, which is set to a special data directory.

Standard variables   There are two items you'll always find in the environment: COMSPEC and PATH. DOS creates COMSPEC when it boots. COMSPEC is set equal to the location of the command interpreter, COMMAND.COM. By default, that's the root directory of the boot disk. However, if you use the SHELL configuration command, you can tell DOS where COMMAND.COM is located by specifying its subdirectory. (Refer to chapter 7 for the format.) That location then will be reflected in the environment, by the COMSPEC variable:

```
COMSPEC = C: \ DOS \ COMMAND.COM
```

This statement sets the COMSPEC variable equal to COMMAND.COM, located in the DOS subdirectory of drive C.

Additionally, the PATH variable is always present and indicates DOS's search path. Even if a search path isn't defined, PATH still will sit in the environment:

```
PATH =
```

If you've created a path using the PATH command, then those subdirectories you've defined will appear next to PATH = in the environment.

Using the SET command to create variables   The SET command's second purpose is to place items into the environment. To do so, you follow SET with the name of the environment variable, an equal sign, and the variable's contents.

For example, DOS can use a TEMP environment variable. TEMP is set to the location of a temporary files directory on disk. DOS uses that directory to store temporary files. The TEMP variable is required under DOS 5 if you're using the pipe character to filter command output.

To set the TEMP variable you would use the following command:

```
SET TEMP = C: \ DOS
```

This command sets the TEMP variable to the DOS subdirectory on drive C.

Say, for example, that a program you're using requires you to set a variable named FRUIT. You're to set that variable to equal your favorite fruit, which for this example just happens to be bananas. The following command will do it:

```
SET FRUIT = BANANAS
```

In the environment, you now will see the string FRUIT = BANANAS somewhere. Note that the SET command will always capitalize the variable name when it's placed into the environment. The string will remain the same case.

```
SET fruit = bananas
```

places the string FRUIT = bananas into the environment.

You can place anything into the environment using the SET command in this manner. Due to the limited size of the environment, you shouldn't be frivolous with it. As far as the variable name is concerned, it can be any length and can contain any characters, save for an equal sign. Keep in mind that short, descriptive variable names are best. The string also can be any length and contain any characters save for an equal sign. Note that the length of both the variable and string cannot be more than 127 characters, which is the size of the longest command line you can type.

You also can use the SET command to change the PROMPT or PATH. You could look at the PROMPT and PATH commands as simply specialized forms of the SET command:

```
SET PROMPT = $p$g
SET PATH = C:\DOS;C:\BATCH
```

Note how the PROMPT and PATH commands are created using SET. Carefully notice that there is never a space on either side of the equal sign. If so, the space would become part of the variable name or the string. That's not what you want.

Other special DOS environment variables   In addition to PATH, PROMPT, COM-SPEC, and TEMP, DOS has two more environment variables you might want to use: DIRCMD and DOSSHELL.

You might find the DIRCMD variable handy, especially if you're enamored with one or more of the DIR command's optional switches. (Refer to chapter 3 for a full description of the DIR command's switches.) Using the SET command, you can assign the DIRCMD variable to any DIR command switches you always want to use.

For example, suppose you like a sorted directory in lowercase. To produce that you use the /O and /L switches. Use the SET command as follows:

```
SET DIRCMD = /O:N /L
```

This command sets DIRCMD equal to /O:N /L (the space between them is optional; it just uses one extra character in the environment). When you enter the DIR command, DOS will check for the DIRCMD variable in the environment. When it's found, DOS then will tack on those switches to the DIR command, always giving you a sorted directory in low-ercase. (You can override the switches by using /O: – N and / – L with the DIR command at the DOS prompt.)

The DOSSHELL variable is used with the DOS Shell menu program, which is cov-ered in chapter 13 of this book. Basically, DOSSHELL tells the DOS Shell program where it can find its DOSSHELL.INI file (a program initialization file). This is required only if, for some reason, you stick DOSSHELL.INI into a subdirectory other than the DOS-SHELL.COM file, which starts the DOS Shell.

For example, if you wanted to put DOSSHELL.INI in your C:\MISC\JUNK direc-tory (for who knows what reason), you could use the following SET command:

```
SET DOSSHELL = C:\MISC\JUNK\
```

This, as with the DIRCMD variable, is best set when you start the computer, which makes them ideal candidates for your AUTOEXEC.BAT file.

Removing variables with the SET command   The SET command also can be used to remove variables from the environment. In this format, the SET command is used without the string parameter. For example, to remove the DIRCMD variable, you would enter the following:

```
SET DIRCMD =
```

With DIRCMD set equal to nothing, DOS simply removes that variable from the environment and frees up the space it uses.

Why do this? Because the environment is of a limited size. If you place too many items into the environment, you'll see the following error message displayed:

```
Out of environment space.
```

The SET command produces this error message. Typically, the last item you placed into the environment didn't make it or will have been placed into the environment but in a truncated state.

To increase the environment's size, use the SHELL command in CONFIG.SYS, as described in chapter 7. Also, you can delete no-longer-needed environment variables using the SET command.

Using environment variables in batch files To create an environment variable in a batch file, you use the SET command. Likewise, you can destroy a variable using SET or even use SET alone to list the environment's contents. Otherwise, environment variables work in batch files similarly to command line variables.

As a review, there are 10 command line variables, %0 through %9, each representing items typed at the DOS prompt. When you refer to one of those variables in a batch file, it is expanded to equal the text item it represents at the DOS prompt. (Refer to chapter 8 if you need brushing up on the concept.)

You use an environment variable in a batch file in much the same way. The difference is that the variable name is surrounded by percent signs and the variable expands out into its string value when the batch file runs.

For example, the following is a batch file named SHOWENV.BAT. It displays the contents of DOS's standard environment variables. Enter it using the MS-DOS editor and save it to disk as SHOWENV.BAT:

```
1: @ECHO OFF
2: ECHO The COMSPEC variable is equal to: %COMSPEC%
3: ECHO The PATH variable is equal to: %PATH%
4: ECHO The PROMPT variable is equal to: %PROMPT%
5: ECHO The TEMP variable is equal to: %TEMP%
6: ECHO The DIRCMD variable is equal to: %DIRCMD%
7: ECHO The DOSSHELL variable is equal to: %DOSSHELL%
```

Run this batch file. You'll see something similar to the following:

```
The COMSPEC variable is equal to: C:\DOS\COMMAND.COM
The PATH variable is equal to: C:\DOS;C:\BATCH
The PROMPT variable is equal to: $p$g
The TEMP variable is equal to: C:\DOS
```

The DIRCMD variable is equal to:
The DOSSHELL variable is equal to:

If a variable isn't assigned to anything, nothing is displayed, as is the case for DIRCMD and DOSSHELL (and probably other items on your own system).

The key to remembering how this works is this: as the batch file runs, it takes an environment variable, %VARIABLE%, and expands it out into its assigned contents. You can see this in the previous sample batch file if you remove the initial ECHO OFF. (Stick REM in front of it.)

One sad note, however, is that the expansion of environment variables only takes place in a batch file. If you try something like ECHO %COMSPEC% at the DOS prompt, it won't work.

A handy use for environment variables in batch files is to save certain items that might be changed as a batch file runs. For example, if you reset the path while running a batch file, you can save the original path—no matter what it is—in a temporary environment variable. Here's another look at an earlier batch file that illustrated how to run Windows:

```
1:  @ECHO OFF
2:  SET TEMPATH = %PATH%
3:  PATH = C: \ WINDOWS;%PATH%
4:  C:
5:  CD \ WINDOWS
6:  WIN
7:  PATH %TEMPATH%
8:  SET TEMPATH =
```

The SET command in line 2 creates the variable TEMPATH, which temporarily stores the contents of the path. In that line, %PATH% is expanded to equal the current search path as the batch file runs.

The new path, set in line 3, is equal to the old path plus C: \ WINDOWS. Again, the %PATH% variable is used to represent the current search path.

After Windows is run, the original PATH is restored in line 7. This time, the PATH command is used and is set equal to the value of TEMPATH. In line 8, the TEMPATH variable is destroyed, which frees up space in the environment.

Building a proper AUTOEXEC.BAT file

As with CONFIG.SYS, the AUTOEXEC.BAT file you create for your system will be unique, reflecting your personal tastes as well as the work you do on your computer. Unlike CONFIG.SYS, your AUTOEXEC.BAT won't remain static. As you update software and add new applications to your system, you might have to modify AUTOEXEC.BAT. Remember to test it first. Like any program you create, there's a bit of getting the bugs out as required.

The following sections should give you some idea of what to put into your AUTOEXEC.BAT file, as well as show you some examples you can steal from and improve upon.

Standard items worth doing in AUTOEXEC.BAT

Here is a list of some things you might consider placing into your AUTOEXEC.BAT file. The order here is important only for the last few items. If some utility or program requests to be first or last in your AUTOEXEC.BAT file, then you should consider moving it there.

Set the system clock   Setting the system clock can be done with the DATE and TIME commands—what DOS normally would ask you if an AUTOEXEC.BAT file weren't present. Using DATE and TIME on an 80286 or later system with an internal clock isn't needed. On some older system, you might want to run some utility program that reads the date and time from some special hardware.

Set the search path   Setting the search path is done via the PATH command, as described in this chapter. Remember to place as few subdirectories as possible on the path, keeping only those that contain lots of files to run (such as batch files—hint, hint).

Set a system prompt   Setting a system prompt is done with the PROMPT command described in this chapter. You can be as creative or absurd as you like, although I'd put off doing a prompt-for-life until you've read chapter 12 on ANSI.SYS.

Set up the screen   Your PC's graphics card might have come with special screen driving software. You might want to load a special font, you might want to add more lines to the display using the MODE command, or you might want to change the screen's colors. These items can be handled in AUTOEXEC.BAT using the proper DOS commands or utilities.

Set up the printer   If your printer requires any initialization or setup, the time to do it is in AUTOEXEC.BAT. You want to include a prompting command to remind yourself to turn on the printer:

```
ECHO Turn on the printer for initialization
PAUSE
```

Also, you can use I/O redirection to send the printer special commands, use the MODE command to set up the printer, download fonts, or run special printer control software.

Substitute or join drives and subdirectories   Substituting or joining drives and subdirectories is done using the SUBST and JOIN commands.

Set environment variables   Setting environment variables is done as required by your applications or DOS. For example, you can use the SET command to create a DIRCMD variable, the TEMP variable, and so on.

Run startup programs   Startup programs include memory-resident programs, such as DOS's MIRROR (covered in chapter 15) and DOSKEY, plus any other memory-resident programs you might use. If you're using a 386 system under DOS 5, you should consider loading these programs high, which is covered in chapter 20 (the LOADHIGH command).

This category also includes other startup programs. For example, a program to dial up MCI Mail and get your morning's mail, display your daily schedule, and so on. This can all be done automatically by AUTOEXEC.BAT. (Remember, AUTOEXEC.BAT can do anything you normally would do when you start your PC.)

Run applications programs, menus, or shells   Finally, you can end AUTOEXEC.BAT by running whatever program you normally first run when you start your PC. For example, if you immediately (and almost unconsciously) type WP and Enter each time you start your PC, just put WP as the last line in AUTOEXEC.BAT. If you use a menu or shell program, put the command to start it at the end of AUTOEXEC.BAT.

A sample AUTOEXEC.BAT file

The AUTOEXEC.BAT file from one of my personal systems is shown in Fig. 9-2. It does several of the items covered in the previous section: sets up the screen (3), sets the prompt (6), sets the path (7), sets environment variables (8 and 9), loads a memory-resident program (12), and runs a startup shell (17). Take a good look at the figure. Although it's several lines long, what it does is fairly straightforward.

```
 1: @ECHO OFF
 2:
 3: \SYSTEM\DELL\SEMISTRT
 4:
 5: REM Set system variables...
 6: PROMPT $p$g
 7: PATH C:\SYSTEM\DOS;C:\SYSTEM\BATCH;C:\SYSTEM\UTIL
 8: SET PCTOOLS=C:\SYSTEM\PCTOOLS\DATA
 9: SET TEMP=C:\TEMP
10:
11: REM Set your DOSKEY macros
12: LOADHIGH DOSKEY /INSERT
13: C:\SYSTEM\DOS\DOSKEY D=DIR /W
14: C:\SYSTEM\DOS\DOSKEY H=DOSKEY /HISTORY
15:
16:
17: PCSHELL
```

9-2   A sample AUTOEXEC.BAT file.

Construct your own AUTOEXEC.BAT file depending on your own needs. It's okay to start out simple. For example:

```
@ECHO OFF
PATH = C:\DOS
PROMPT $p$g
```

Three lines really is all you need for the barest of minimum systems. Later, you can expand as necessary. Keep in mind the points mentioned in this chapter and review your AUTOEXEC.BAT file from time to time, especially as you learn more about DOS.

Summary

AUTOEXEC.BAT is the final file in the DOS boot process and a file over which you have direct control. You can use AUTOEXEC.BAT to further configure DOS, run startup programs, set a search path and prompt, or automatically run your first program of the day. Anything you normally type at the DOS prompt when you first start your computer can safely and handily go into AUTOEXEC.BAT.

This wraps up the first part of this book, on hard disk organization. Part II deals with DOS menu systems and shells, which ties in nicely to this chapter because creating menu systems and shells probably is the last step you'll take in your AUTOEXEC.BAT file. Using DOS and the power of batch files, you can even create your own customized DOS shell. That's the subject of the next chapter, as well as the great majority of the next part of this book.

Part II

Menu systems and shells

The DOS command line is power. Armed with the right knowledge, a command line is the fastest and most powerful way to run a PC. Without a doubt, it really can drive some users nuts. To alleviate the problem, you can use such a thing as a DOS shell or a menu system. These methods provide a handy one-keystroke/one-function approach to using a PC for the DOS timid. For the DOS master, they give you quick access to your applications and utilities.

Making DOS more convenient to use is the subject of this part of the book. Chapter 10 explores batch file programming, which preps you for creating your own smart DOS commands, as well as custom-designed menu systems. Chapter 11 introduces you to batch file menu systems that you create yourself. Chapter 12 continues the menu system—this time, by adding the color and flash of ANSI.SYS. Chapter 13 is on the DOS Shell system that comes with DOS 5. Chapter 14 wraps up the discussion of DOS shells and menu systems with a rundown of popular shells and menus available at your local software dealer.

———10———
Batch file programming

Before you can start building a menu system using batch files, you need to hone your batch file skills. Basically, batch files allow you to execute a series of DOS commands without having to enter them individually. The batch file essentially stores them up for later execution.

The batch file techniques you know thus far can help you extend the power of your system significantly. However, ECHO, REM, and PAUSE don't offer much robust programming potential. To gain further control over the operation of your hard disk, you'll need batch files that can perform repetitive tasks, make decisions, and call upon the functions of other batch files.

This chapter covers the rest of DOS's special batch file commands. These include GOTO, FOR, IF, and CALL. Before discussing each of these commands in turn, it will be useful to consider the basic concepts involved in programming so you can better understand how each is used.

Programming techniques

Programming in any computer language is nothing more than the collection of individual commands put into an executable file. While some commands included in a computer program can be executed directly, such as a command to print out the results of a computation, others are used to control the execution of the program itself.

There are four ways that commands in a program can be executed:

- Sequentially
- Looping
- Conditionally
- Chaining

The simplest way to execute commands in a program is sequentially. In *sequential execution*, program commands are executed one after the other from beginning to end. This is how all the batch files covered so far in this book have operated. Sequential execution of commands is the simplest programming technique.

Not all programming tasks can be accomplished sequentially, however. Certain repetitive processes are best handled by a technique known as looping.

Looping applies a sequence of commands to a series of different values. It's accomplished through the use of variables, or, in the case of batch files, replaceable parameters. The variables are used in the commands within the loop and are replaced with actual values each time the loop is executed. Program loops must be controlled properly or they might continue indefinitely, forming an *infinite loop*. The following spurious dictionary entry is an example of an infinite loop:

REDUNDANT: *See* REDUNDANT

Sequential execution and looping are two important programming techniques. However, in each case, the execution of the commands involved is predetermined and, therefore, limited. It's possible to select one command from a number of options through the use of conditional statements.

Conditional statements typically begin with the word *if*. You deal with conditional situations every day. If the traffic light is green, you keep driving; if it's red, you stop; if it's yellow, you drive faster (if you drive like I do) because the light is about to turn red.

Similar conditional situations can occur in programming. If you have ever used a menu-driven program, you're familiar with the results of conditional programming. If you select 1, you get option one; if you select 2, you get option two; etc.

Another way to execute program commands is through chaining. *Chaining* is a technique that involves linking various groups of commands together. These individual groups of commands are each designed to perform some specific task. In the BASIC programming language, these groups are referred to as *subroutines*, other languages might call them *modules* or *functions*.

A number of different subroutines can be chained together within a single batch file by using the special IF and GOTO batch file commands. In addition, separate batch files can be chained together to form a complex and sophisticated network of batch files, which would be capable of monitoring and controlling your computer. The goal of this book is to teach you how to develop just such a system of batch files specifically designed to meet the needs of your system.

Looping in batch files

Certain tasks in computing are repetitive. Rather than re-issue the same sequence of commands over and over again, they can be included in a loop.

For example, consider the need to perform the same type of processing on all the records in a database file. Suppose that you wanted to print mailing labels for each of over 1000 names and addresses stored in the file.

The application (which I'm just making up here) uses a programming language to print the labels. Using that language, you could create the sequence of commands necessary to print a single label. For example, suppose the commands to print the first label are:

```
GO TO RECORD 1
PRINT LABEL
```

These commands could be placed into a loop. The loop commands would cause the computer to move to the next record in the data file, print out the mailing label, and proceed until all the records were completed. For example:

```
GO TO RECORD 1
REPEAT 1000 TIMES:
  PRINT LABEL
  GO TO THE NEXT RECORD
ALL DONE
```

PRINT LABEL and GO TO THE NEXT RECORD are in the loop. The loop is defined by the REPEAT 1000 TIMES command.

The batch file GOTO command Simple looping in batch files is accomplished through the use of the GOTO command. This is similar to the way looping is performed in the BASIC programming language. The GOTO command redirects the flow of commands in a batch file, skipping all subsequent commands until the specified point in the batch file is reached.

GOTO alone, however, is insufficient, because DOS won't know where to go to unless you tell it. Imagine responding to a lost tourist's request for directions with the single phrase, "Go to." Pretty uninformative (although, for some reason, Shakespeare could get away with it).

The label For the GOTO command to work, it must be used in conjunction with a label. Labels in batch files act like place markers or street signs. Just as you might say to the traveler, "Go to Maple Street and turn left," you can include a GOTO command, such as GOTO DONE, in a batch file.

Labels are preceded by a colon and are placed on a line by themselves. For example:

```
:MAPLESTREET
```

Labels can be as long as you like, but only the first eight characters are recognized by DOS. Once labels have been inserted into a batch file at appropriate locations, they can be used with GOTO commands to alter the order that the batch file commands are executed.

To see how the GOTO command works and how it can redirect the flow of statements in a batch file, consider the following nonsensical batch file, NONSENSE.BAT:

```
1: @ECHO OFF
2: ECHO This batch file is
3: GOTO WORTHLESS
4: ECHO a wonderful batch file
5: ECHO full of useful commands.
6: :WORTHLESS
7: ECHO worthless!
8: PAUSE
```

When executed, this batch file displays the following text on the screen:

```
This batch file is
worthless!
Press any key to continue . . .
```

Did you see the lines, a wonderful batch file and full of useful commands? Instead of being executed, these two ECHO commands are skipped over by the GOTO command. The next line to be executed after ECHO This batch file is ECHO worthless! (line 7). Note that the :WORTHLESS label itself is ignored. Anything after a colon in a batch file is ignored, so you can use the colon as well as the REM command to add a comment.

GOTO backwards The preceding example illustrated the use of the GOTO command to execute a forward jump in the batch file. You also can use GOTO to jump backward as well. However, once you go backward, you must proceed forward through commands already executed. This will continue until the backward GOTO command is encountered, then the process will repeat itself. For this reason, a backward GOTO can be used to create a circle of commands, or loop, within a batch file.

Consider the situation of an individual who must create multiple copies of a series of worksheet files for distribution within a large organization. Suppose that these files already have been placed into a special subdirectory on the hard disk and that the path to this subdirectory is C: \ LOTUS \ DISTRIB.

A batch file, DISTRIB.BAT, could be created to repeatedly transfer all the files stored in this subdirectory onto separate floppy disks. This will happen until the individual running the batch file halts it with a Ctrl−C. A batch file to accomplish this task is shown here:

```
 1:  @ECHO OFF
 2:  C:
 3:  CD \LOTUS\DISTRIB
 4:  :AGAIN
 5:    CLS
 6:    ECHO Place the target diskette in drive A.
 7:    PAUSE
 8:    COPY *.* A:
 9:    ECHO Copying completed.
10:    ECHO When you're done, press Ctrl−C, or
11:    PAUSE
12:  GOTO AGAIN
```

This batch file turns off the echo feature (line 1) and moves into the \ LOTUS \ DISTRIB subdirectory on drive C (lines 2 and 3). The :AGAIN label is ignored (line 4) and the loop processing commences by clearing the screen (line 5). Note that the actual loop itself is indented. This spacing cleans up the listing and tells you immediately which part of the program is being repeatedly executed. (Batch files can contain blank lines as well as have their lines indented.)

The user next is instructed to place a diskette into the A drive (line 6) and press any key when ready (line 7). Once this is done, the batch file transfers all files stored in the \ LOTUS \ DISTRIB subdirectory onto the diskette in drive A (line 8).

When the copying is completed, a confirmation message is displayed (line 9) and the user is instructed to enter a Ctrl−C to conclude the operation (line 10) or to press any key to proceed (line 11). Unless a Ctrl−C is entered at this point, the control of the batch file is transferred, via the GOTO command (line 12), back to the :AGAIN label (line 4). Then, everything repeats itself.

The DISTRIB.BAT file is an example of an infinite loop. The file will repeat itself infinitely unless the user stops it by pressing Ctrl−C (or Ctrl−Break).

Infinite loops are a quick-and-dirty programming technique for accomplishing repetitive tasks. Batch files using infinite loops rely upon a certain competence on the part of the user. A rank beginner might respond to the prompt to enter a Ctrl−C by literally typing in the characters C, t, r, l, −, C. (It's been known to happen.)

FOR and conditional loops

To avoid infinite loops, two other looping strategies are used in batch files. They are FOR loops and conditional loops.

FOR loops proceed through a specified sequence of parameters, performing the same processing on each of them in turn. *Conditional loops* involve the use of special error codes. An error code indicates a condition that can be used to control the looping process.

FOR loops   The DOS FOR command allows you to specify a wildcard parameter into which will be substituted one or more items, usually filenames. The parameter then is used with a DOS command until each item has been processed. Don't worry about reading it twice; the FOR command isn't the most straightforward thing DOS does. However, it can save you considerable typing.

The format of the FOR command is:

FOR %variable IN (parameter_list) DO command

The *variable* is a single letter, *A* through *Z*. At the DOS prompt, it's preceded by a single percentage sign. In a batch file, you must put two percentage signs before the variable.

The *parameter_list* is two or more items, filenames, commands, or what-have-you. They must be individual items. DOS considers the space character, comma, and semicolon as separators. In the FOR command, the variable will take on the value of each item in the *parameter_list* when the FOR command runs.

The *command* is a DOS command. It can be an entire command line or anything you normally would type at the DOS prompt, except for another FOR command. The command should act somehow on each item in the *parameter_list*. It does so using the *variable* as a placeholder.

This whole deal can be clarified by the following example. Suppose you wanted to back up dBASE database files in a given subdirectory. In dBASE, the database files have a DBF extension, the memo files have MEM extensions, and index files have NDX extensions.

Ordinarily, to copy all of the files with each of these extensions would require three separate COPY commands. However, by including these three extensions in the *parameter_list*, you can use a single COPY command in a FOR loop as follows:

FOR %F IN (*.DBF *.MEM *.DBF) DO COPY %F A:

This FOR loop uses the variable, %F, as a dummy in the command COPY %F A:. %F itself never gets copied to A:. Instead, %F is used to represent each of the items in the parameter list. In this case, the parameter list contains three parameters, *.DBF, *.MEM, and *.NDX. First, *.DBF is substituted for %F and the command COPY *.DBF A: is executed. Next, *.MEM is substituted for %F and the command COPY *.MEM A: is executed. Finally, the COPY command is executed with the *.NDX command. (Remember, in a batch file, you'd use two percent signs, %%F.)

You also can use the FOR command to execute a single DOS command a number of times. In this case, the DOS command lacks the %F variable; it simply executes once for each item you have in the parameter list. For example:

    FOR %A IN (1 2 3 4 5 6 7 8 9 10) DO ECHO Hello!

echoes the word *Hello!* 10 times at the DOS prompt. That's one time for each item in the parameter list.

Conditional loops   FOR loops execute their commands as many times as there are parameters. Conditional loops, on the other hand, continue until their condition has been met or the user cancels them with Ctrl−C.

A conditional loop usually performs some sort of test to determine whether or not it's to continue executing. This testing is done through the use of the IF command. Although the IF command has other applications in batch file programming, its use is the key to creating conditional loops.

The format of the IF command is:

    IF *condition command*

condition is one of several conditions you'll soon learn about, and *command* is a DOS command. Unlike the FOR command, the *command* in an IF statement can be another IF command.

Statements involving the IF command are called *conditional statements* because they involve testing for a given condition to see whether a specified outcome will result.

You already are familiar with conditional statements—they are a part of your reasoning and vocabulary. For example, you might think to yourself, "If that cinder block hits me in the face, it will doubtless be painful." In this example, the condition to be tested is whether the cinder block will hit you in the face. The outcome in this instance is painful. Note that it will be painful only if the cinder block does hit you in the face, that is, if the condition is true.

The problem with this example is that it is hard to determine exactly what painful is: a direct hit, a scrape, or a close call? Conditions in DOS must be specific, usually as simple as true or false.

The ERRORLEVEL condition   For conditional loops, one condition to be tested is the value of a special variable, ERRORLEVEL. ERRORLEVEL is called an *exit code* in DOS terminology, and can be used to test a variety of conditions.

When a program quits, it returns to DOS with an optional value between 0 and 255. Certain programs and DOS utilities use the ERRORLEVEL value to communicate what functions they performed, or, as the name implies, if any errors occurred. Not every program will return an ERRORLEVEL value, but some do. With those programs, you can use the ERRORLEVEL value to test for various things. The format goes like this:

    IF ERRORLEVEL *x command*

If the program returned an ERRORLEVEL of *x*—or higher—then the command is executed. It's the *or higher* part that causes a lot of batch file programmers to goof.

A good example of using ERRORLEVEL is found in a common utility program, ASK.COM, which has been provided for you on the companion diskette. ASK displays a message on the screen, then checks the user's answer according to which key they pressed. If the user enters a Y, then ERRORLEVEL is set to 0; if the user enters an N, ERRORLEVEL is set to 1.

To use the ASK command in your batch files, it must be in either the current directory or in a subdirectory specified by the PATH command. To see how a conditional loop using the ASK/IF ERRORLEVEL combination works, consider the modified DISTRIB.BAT file shown below:

```
 1: @ECHO OFF
 2: C:
 3: CD \ LOTUS \ DISTRIB
 4: :AGAIN
 5: CLS
 6: ECHO Place the target diskette in drive A.
 7: PAUSE
 8: COPY *.* A:
 9: ECHO Copying completed.
10: ASK Do you wish to copy another diskette (Y/N)?
11: IF ERRORLEVEL 1 GOTO END
12: GOTO AGAIN
13: :END
```

In this version of the batch file, the loop is controlled by the statement IF ERRORLEVEL 1 GOTO END in line 11. If the user types N in response to the ASK command (line 10), an ERRORLEVEL of 1 is returned. In line 11, that value tells the batch file to run to the label END located at line 13. The batch file then ends.

If the user presses Y in response to the ASK command, an ERRORLEVEL of 0 is returned, which is below the 1 mentioned in line 11. Therefore, the IF command fails and execution falls through line 12, GOTO AGAIN. The program then loops back up to line 4, the :AGAIN label.

Conditional loops involving ASK and IF ERRORLEVEL are much more user-friendly than infinite loops, which must be terminated using Ctrl−C. Remember to keep the skill level of the intended user in mind when designing batch files to automate repetitive processes. Also, if you're planning to ask the user to respond to a question, be sure to indicate the appropriate responses by including (Y/N) at the end of the prompt. Your fellow computer users will appreciate these special touches. If nothing else, conditional loops are more professional looking than quick-and-dirty infinite loops.

Conditional branching The IF command can do more than control conditional loops. It also can be used to allow your batch files to make decisions about what action to take based upon a given condition. This ability allows you to truly program your batch files to perform a variety of different tasks depending upon the specific conditions encountered when they are executed.

The three conditional tests that IF is able to perform are:

- EXIST
- = =
- ERRORLEVEL

You already have seen how ERRORLEVEL is tested in the preceding discussion of conditional loops. In this section, you will learn how to use the ERRORLEVEL test in other applications as well.

The EXIST conditional test The EXIST conditional test is used to check for the presence of a given file in the specified directory. It follows the IF command and precedes the name of the file being tested. The format of the IF command when testing for the EXIST condition is:

IF EXIST *filename command*

filename is the name of a file to test for; *command* is executed only if *filename* is found. Note that *filename* also can be a full pathname and can include wildcards.

The following example shows how you would use the EXIST test in a batch file called CP.BAT. CP is a better version of the COPY command. Unlike the DOS version, CP refuses to copy over a file that already exists. Enter CP.BAT using the DOS Editor or your favorite text editor.

```
1: @ECHO OFF
2: IF EXIST %2 GOTO OOPS
3: COPY %1 %2
4: GOTO END
5: :OOPS
6: ECHO The file "%2" already exists!
7: :END
```

Line 2 is what's important. It checks the file you're copying to using IF EXIST. If it's found, the GOTO branches to the OOPS label (line 5) and a message is displayed, telling you the file exists.

If the file isn't found and the IF EXIST test fails in line 2, the file is copied using the standard COPY command. The GOTO in line 4 then branches down to the END label (line 7) and the batch file ends.

The beauty of this batch file is that the COPY command handles any errors. If you don't type in any parameters, COPY returns with an error code; the batch file doesn't have to worry about it. So, most of the error handling is done by the COPY command itself. I say most because this command won't check each file individually when you use wildcards, nor will it work if you specify a drive letter or subdirectory name for the destination. (Solutions do exist, however, they're just beyond the scope of this book.)

The equality conditional test The IF command also can be used to test for the equality of two items. The equality conditional test requires two equals symbols (= =) to represent equality. This test allows you to create batch files that perform a variety of different tasks depending upon the parameters supplied with the batch file call.

Consider the simple batch file, RUN.BAT, which runs either WordPerfect or Lotus 1-2-3 depending upon whether the user specifies WP or 123 after the initial RUN:

```
 1: @ECHO OFF
 2: IF %1 = = WP GOTO WPLAND
 3: IF %1 = = 123 GOTO LOTUSLAND
 4: ECHO I can only run WordPerfect or 1-2-3. Sorry.
 5: GOTO END
 6: :WPLAND
 7: CD \WP51
 8: WP
 9: GOTO QUIT
10: :LOTUSLAND
11: CD \123
12: 123
13: :END
```

If the user specifies RUN WP, then the batch file will match %1 with WP and control will be transferred to the :WPLAND label. If, on the other hand, the user enters RUN 123, control will be transferred to the :LOTUSLAND label instead.

There are several important points to note in the previous batch file. For one thing, you should realize that there are really three possible outcomes. The batch file will either load WordPerfect, load 123, or terminate. In the first case, after the program has been loaded, the subsequent GOTO command (line 9) transfers control of the batch file to the final :QUIT label. Can you see why this is necessary? If the GOTO QUIT command were omitted here, the batch file would proceed to load the 1-2-3 program after the user had exited from WordPerfect.

Another important point to note when using the = = conditional test is the case of the characters being tested. In this batch file, it's assumed that the user will enter WP in capitals. If the user were to enter the command in lowercase, run wp, the test for WP would fail and nothing would be loaded. You could circumvent this by including a separate test for lowercase wp as well:

```
IF %1 = = WP GOTO WPLAND
IF %1 = = wp GOTO WPLAND
```

However, there's even more insidiousness at work here. Run the batch file without typing anything:

```
C:\BATCH> RUN
Syntax error
Syntax error
I can only run WordPerfect or 1-2-3. Sorry.
```

Where did the Syntax error come from?

A *syntax error* is an error produced by a batch file, most commonly when you try to use the IF command equality condition test. In the first instance, you've forgotten to use two equal signs. In the second, one side of the equal sign has evaluated to nothing. If there is no first parameter, %1, in the previous batch file, you get the following statement expanded as the batch file runs:

```
IF = = WP GOTO WPLAND
```

You need something on both sides of the double equal sign. To balance things out, change lines 2 and 3 in the batch file to read as follows:

```
IF %1! = =WP! GOTO WPLAND
IF %1! = =123! GOTO LOTUSLAND
```

Now, if the user types in WP, then WP! will equal WP! and the batch file works. If nothing is entered, then ! = =WP! will be how it's expanded. Although no match is made, you won't get a syntax error.

The ERRORLEVEL conditional test You already have seen one application of the ERRORLEVEL conditional test in controlling the exit from a loop. The initial purpose of the exit code was intended to allow programmers to check the way in which certain applications and utilities quit. For example, if a utility for backing up the hard disk onto floppies successfully backed up everything, the ERRORLEVEL would be set to 0 to indicate a successful backup. A batch file then can test that condition with an IF ERRORLEVEL 0 test.

For simple batch file programming, however, the value of the IF ERRORLEVEL test lies in its use with the ASK utility described previously. This utility has the capability of setting ERRORLEVEL according to a user's response to a question. As you saw in the discussion on conditional loops, a Y response sets ERRORLEVEL to 0, while an N response sets it to 1.

The resulting ERRORLEVEL value then can be tested in an IF ERRORLEVEL conditional test to determine what action should be taken next. The outcome usually will be a GOTO command redirecting the flow of the program to a set of statements elsewhere in the batch file. In conditional loops, this would be back to the beginning of the loop for another pass through the loop procedure.

There are other applications for the ASK command besides exiting from a loop. You can use ASK to determine whether the user wishes to proceed with a course of action or whenever you want to check with the user before proceeding with a sequence of commands. Prompts can take any of the following forms:

```
ASK Do you wish to proceed (Y/N)?
ASK Would you like to continue (Y/N)?
ASK Is this correct (Y/N)?
ASK Would you like to try again (Y/N)?
```

The NOT option Sometimes you'll be more interested in testing the opposite of a condition rather than the condition itself. For instance, the IF EXIST test is used to determine if a file is available. The absence of the file can be tested simply by including the word NOT before the EXIST conditional test:

```
IF NOT EXIST BRAIN.DAT GOTO SCHOOL
```

You also can use NOT with the == and ERRORLEVEL conditional tests. Note that the word NOT always precedes the conditional test. This might seem intuitively obvious for the EXIST and == tests, but many beginners make the mistake of writing:

```
IF ERRORLEVEL NOT 0...
```

which sounds better than:

    IF NOT ERRORLEVEL 0...

Note that the previous command is true only for ERRORLEVEL values of 1 or greater. A good use for NOT with ERRORLEVEL is narrowing down the ERRORLEVEL value. Consider the following:

    IF ERRORLEVEL 63 IF NOT ERRORLEVEL 64 GOTO IT_IS_63

The first ERRORLEVEL test checks for return values from 63 up through 255, for which the ERRORLEVEL test is true. The second IF command (which is okay to do) checks for NOT ERRORLEVEL 64, which is true only for values less than 64. If both tests pass, you definitely have an ERRORLEVEL of 63. (This test will become handy later when you're designing batch file menu systems.)

Chaining

So far, you've seen how batch files can be used to issue a series of DOS commands and load applications. It also is possible to execute one batch file from another. To do so, you simply name the second batch file you want to execute in the first batch file. Using one batch file to run another is known as *chaining*. There is no limit to the number of batch files that can be chained together.

For example, suppose you had an AUTOEXEC.BAT file that set your system configuration at system startup. At the conclusion of this batch file, you want to run PC Tool's PCSHELL program. This could be accomplished by including the PCSHELL.BAT file as the final line of AUTOEXEC.BAT.

While this chaining trick saves the trouble of having to execute the PCSHELL.BAT file separately, it has a number of drawbacks. For one thing, the PCSHELL batch file will be executed automatically whenever the computer is restarted. This situation might not always be desirable. This problem can be overcome by including an ASK...IF ERRORLEVEL test in the AUTOEXEC.BAT file. The following shows how the last few lines in such a file might look:

    ASK Do you want to run PC Shell (Y/N)?
    IF ERRORLEVEL 1 GOTO END
    PCSHELL
    :END

This revised version of the AUTOEXEC.BAT file permits the user to bypass the PCSHELL batch file by typing N at the prompt. However, this version still has several shortcomings.

Remember AUTOEXEC.BAT automatically loads at system startup. There is no opportunity for the user to supply values for any replaceable parameters. Normally, this shouldn't be a problem.

Even so, there's one final limitation to the method of chaining batch files described so far. While application programs return control to the batch file when they terminate, chained batch files do not. Once a new batch file is called from the original batch file, control passes to the new batch file. When that batch file concludes, the user is returned to DOS's command prompt.

At the end of AUTOEXEC.BAT, this isn't a problem; there's no final line to execute. However, you might have batch files that need to reset certain system parameters or move back into the root directory at their conclusion. With the method of chaining described thus far, these steps could be accomplished only by chaining the second batch file to rechain back to the first one, perhaps with some command line parameter that could be intercepted. A better solution is to use a special batch file command, CALL.

The CALL command

The DOS solution to the batch file chaining problem is the CALL command. This command is available only with DOS versions 3.3 and later. If you have an earlier version, upgrade. (Seriously, substitute the COMMAND /C command instead of CALL in all the following examples.)

The CALL command allows you to call a batch file, have that batch file executed, and return control to the original batch file after the second one terminates. Batch files called using the CALL command are sometimes referred to as *subroutines*.

The use of subroutines in batch file programming has several advantages. Obviously, it allows greater control over the execution of the calling batch file. Also, this technique permits a modular approach to batch file programming. A large programming task can be divided into a series of smaller tasks, each of which can be handled easily. Further, the same subroutine batch file can be used, or called, by a number of different batch files. This reduces the amount of programming involved in large projects.

As you work your way into creating batch file menus, you'll see the CALL command in action. Until then, here's the format of the CALL command:

CALL *filename*

The *filename* refers to the batch file subroutine being called. It can include a full pathname as necessary. Here's a trick: it also can be used to call some stubborn programs that halt batch files.

For example, some versions of WordStar wouldn't return control to a batch file when they finished running. To weasel your way around this, just start WordStar from your batch file using the CALL command:

CALL WS

Other stubborn programs might require the same treatment. If you're going to use a batch file as part of a FOR command, it must be called as well.

Another thing to keep in mind is that a called batch file doesn't need to start with an @ECHO OFF command. The ECHO state remains in effect until you turn it off or quit the batch file to return to DOS. (Examples of this are forthcoming.)

Summary

In this chapter, you learned how to extend the power of your batch files. Not only can batch files set up certain conditions for you in DOS and load applications, but they can make decisions and evaluate conditions. This power, provided by such commands as GOTO, FOR, IF, and CALL, allows you to build creative batch files capable of doing interesting things on your system, as well as saving you valuable time.

Incidentally, if you're interested in pursuing the concept of batch file programming further, you should check out TAB Books' batch file programming texts. I wrote two of them: *Advanced MS-DOS Batch File Programming* and *Enhanced MS-DOS Batch File Programming*. I recommend them if you're interested in pursuing the BAT subject further.

The next chapter takes the knowledge you've gained from learning about DOS and batch file programming one notch further. Using batch files, you'll construct a unique and powerful menu system under which you can run your hard disk system.

11

Batch file menu systems

If you have spent any time working with personal computers, you probably have been exposed to some form of menu-driven software. Any program that displays a list of choices or options and allows you to select from among them utilizes menus. When program commands or options are selected from a menu, the program is said to be *menu-driven*.

Menu-driven software is different from software that might use *pull-down menus*. For example, the Editor uses pull-down menus (also called *drop-down menus*, but they really are one and the same). The FDISK utility, which was mentioned in chapter 2, is menu-driven in a more traditional sense. It displays all your options on the screen and you select one from the list.

This chapter is about creating a menu system for running applications on your hard disk. It's all done with batch files and, believe it or not, it's not as hard as it seems. You already know more than enough to get the job done. It's only a matter of becoming familiar with assembling the proper pieces in the right order. You'll know how to do that by the end of this chapter. (Be prepared to amaze yourself!)

Software menus

As with restaurant menus, software menus can take many forms, ranging from one-line menus to elaborate full-screen graphic menu systems. Some programs reserve a portion of the screen for displaying command options. These menus are called *screen menus*. With screen menus, you usually select the option you want by entering the code letters or number corresponding to your choice in response to a prompt on the screen. WordPerfect's Print menu (Fig. 11-1) is an example of a screen menu. (In WordPerfect, you press Shift−F7 to see the menu.)

Other programs place command options in a single line. Such one-line menus often are referred to as *menu bars*. To select a choice from a menu bar, you normally use the left and right cursor control keys (or the Tab key) to move back and forth across the menu bar. Command selection is accomplished by highlighting the desired command or option and pressing the Enter key. Lotus 1-2-3's menu (Fig. 11-2) works this way.

```
Print

        1 - Full Document
        2 - Page
        3 - Document on Disk
        4 - Control Printer
        5 - Multiple Pages
        6 - View Document
        7 - Initialize Printer


Options

        S - Select Printer              Canon LBP-8III
        B - Binding Offset              0"
        N - Number of Copies            1
        U - Multiple Copies Generated by WordPerfect
        G - Graphics Quality            Medium
        T - Text Quality                High


Selection: 0
```

11-1 WordPerfect's Print screen menu.

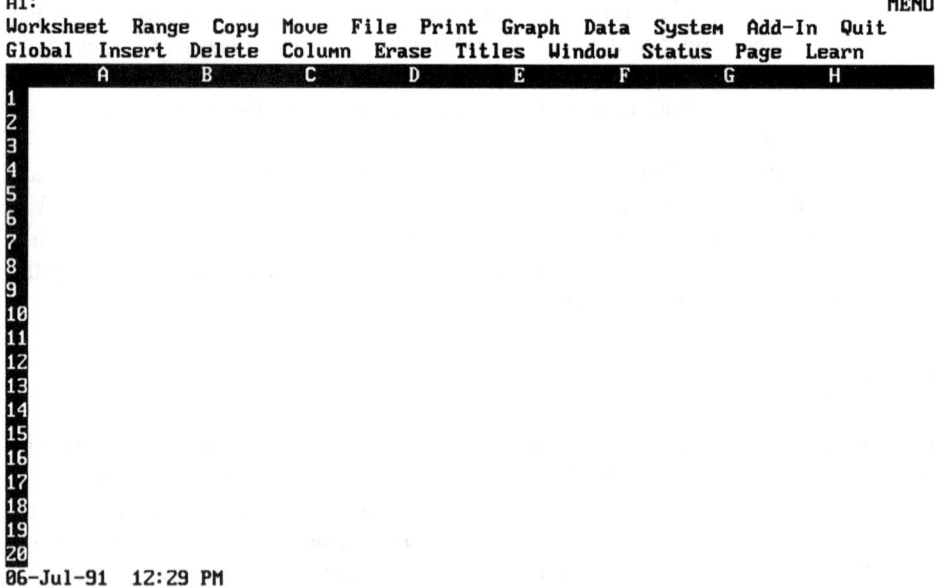

11-2 Lotus 1-2-3's highly-copyrighted menu bar.

Some menu-driven programs provide brief descriptions for each of the choices included in the menu. Still others provide optional on-screen help, selected by pressing a special help key. Sometimes, a single menu is insufficient for displaying all the command choices or program options. In these cases, the programs rely upon additional submenus for displaying additional commands. These commands usually are grouped together in some logical fashion.

The collection of menus, submenus, prompts, and attendant help screens are used to guide a user through a program. The whole deal is called a *menu system*.

You can create customized menu systems for controlling access to files and programs stored on your hard disk. Such menu systems can consist of simple single-screen menus or elaborate systems complete with submenus and optional help screens.

Why use menus?

Menu-driven hard disk management systems have numerous advantages. The most obvious advantage is that a well-organized menu system makes using the hard disk computer easier for both the novice and advanced user.

Menus allow the user to type a little and do a lot; only quick key strokes are required to load programs and locate files. This system saves typing. Also, menus take the memory and guess-work out of working with complex tree-structured subdirectory systems. Along these lines, menus and submenus that correspond to a hard disk's tree structure help multiple users from inadvertently interfering with each other's work areas. If you're networked, all that network gobbledygook can be hidden conveniently behind the friendly facade of a menu screen.

Another reason for using menu systems to control access to the hard disk is security. There are several security considerations that can be addressed through the use of menu-driven hard disk management systems.

As an example, DOS commands can be made part of a special DOS submenu. Within this submenu, one choice could be Format a diskette. This choice would be tied to a batch file that prevents accidental reformatting of the hard disk. By forcing the user to select DOS commands from a menu, you eliminate the possibility of any incorrectly entered commands.

Other security considerations include limiting access to programs and data files. When access to programs and data is achieved through menu choices, password security can be added to ensure that only authorized individuals are allowed access.

Ease of use, convenience, and security are three reasons for developing a menu-driven hard disk management system. With only the techniques described so far in this book and a little help from the MS-DOS Editor, you can develop your own customized menu-driven system for loading programs, accessing data files, and executing DOS commands. No prior programming experience is necessary.

Developing a simple menu system

Developing your own menu system is easy, creative, and fun. Most users get a kick out of designing and implementing their own menus. Also, customized menu systems are modified easily as your system requirements change. Whether your hard disk system is intended for a single user or several different users and no matter what the skill level of the individuals using the computer, a set of customized menus will make your computer more efficient and easier to use and will add a more polished and professional appearance to your hard disk system.

In this section, you'll learn how to create a single-screen menu system. This simple menu system includes the menu screen itself, as well as the batch files to execute the various menu selections. Later in this chapter, you'll see how you can add submenus and help screens to your menu system as well.

For this initial menu system, a simplified hard disk system will be used. The tree structure consists of the following: a subdirectory containing the DOS utilities, \DOS; a word processing subdirectory, \WP; a spreadsheet subdirectory, \123; a database subdirectory, \DB; and a subdirectory for the MENU system and other batch files, \MENU. (See Fig. 11-3.)

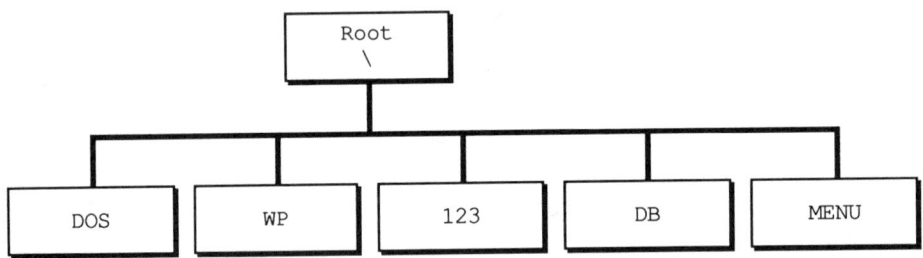

11-3 A simplified tree structure for the sample menu system.

The root directory will be used to hold AUTOEXEC.BAT and CONFIG.SYS. The menu screen text file, the various batch files needed to execute the menu choices and other batch files will be held in the \MENU directory.

Creating menu screens

Menu screens are nothing more than text files designed to display a series of commands or options. To create your menu screens, you can use any word processor capable of generating true ASCII text files. For example, you could use WordStar's non-document mode. Also, you could use WordPerfect and save in the DOS Text mode or use DOS's Edit or EDLIN text processor.

Consider the simple menu screen shown in Fig. 11-4. This screen was created in the Editor (as seen in the figure). The text was eyeball-centered.

A menu such as this could be saved to disk under the name MENU.TXT. In the Editor or whichever program you're using, remember to save the file in the proper subdirectory. In this example, the subdirectory is named MENU.

The menu file can be displayed using the command:

TYPE C:\MENU\MENU.TXT

Even better, this command can be included as the last line in your AUTOEXEC.BAT file. Because a full pathname is specified with the TYPE command, it doesn't matter which drive or subdirectory you're logged to, the proper file will always be displayed.

Once the line has been added to your AUTOEXEC.BAT file, the menu screen will

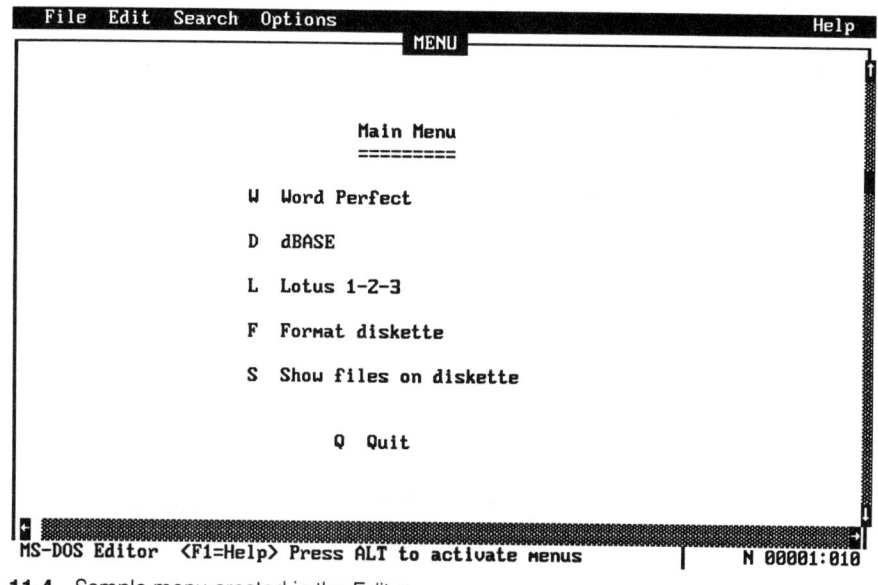

```
 File  Edit  Search  Options                                    Help
┌───────────────────────────┤ MENU ├──────────────────────────────────┐
│                                                                      ↑│
│                                                                      ▓│
│                              Main Menu                               ▓│
│                              =========                               ▓│
│                                                                      ▓│
│                      W   Word Perfect                                ▓│
│                                                                      ▓│
│                      D   dBASE                                       ▓│
│                                                                      ▓│
│                      L   Lotus 1-2-3                                 ▓│
│                                                                      ▓│
│                      F   Format diskette                             ▓│
│                                                                      ▓│
│                      S   Show files on diskette                      ▓│
│                                                                      ▓│
│                                                                      ▓│
│                              Q   Quit                                ▓│
│                                                                      ↓│
│█                                                                    █ │
└──────────────────────────────────────────────────────────────────────┘
 MS-DOS Editor  <F1=Help> Press ALT to activate menus  │    N 00001:010
```

11-4 Sample menu created in the Editor.

11-5 A menu displayed using the TYPE command. Note the DOS prompt that appears below the last line of the menu.

```
                              Main Menu
                              =========

                      W   WordPerfect

                      D   dBASE

                      L   Lotus 1-2-3

                      F   Format diskette

                      S   Show files on diskette


                              Q   Quit

C:\>
```

appear each time the computer starts or is restarted. On the line following this menu, the regular DOS prompt will be displayed, as shown in Fig. 11-5.

Adding user prompts

While this menu might appear obvious to someone familiar to personal computers, the use of the menu can be improved through the addition of a prompt, such as:

Enter the letter corresponding to your choice:

While your first inclination might be to include this prompt as part of the menu screen, the problem would be that the DOS prompt still would appear on the next line. This intrusion of DOS into the menu screen can be distracting, especially to novice users. So, why not change the DOS prompt? This can be accomplished by including a PROMPT command at the end of your AUTOEXEC.BAT file as follows:

```
TYPE C:\MENU\MENU.TXT
PROMPT $_$_Enter the letter corresponding to your choice:
```

The two $_ (new line) meta commands have been added to put a little air between the end of the MENU.TXT file display and the DOS prompt.

Now, when AUTOEXEC.BAT is executed, the DOS prompt, which is the last line that appears on the screen, will read like a prompt to the user to enter one of the letters appearing on the menu. (See Fig. 11-6.) Clever, isn't it?

```
                        Main Menu
                        =========

            W   WordPerfect

            D   dBASE

            L   Lotus 1-2-3

            F   Format diskette

            S   Show files on diskette


                    Q   Quit


        Enter the letter correpsonding to your choice:
```

11-6   Modifying the DOS prompt results in a more meaningful prompt.

Modifying AUTOEXEC.BAT in this manner takes care of all the details needed to display the menu and user prompt on the screen. In practice, however, it's better to place the last two commands into a separate batch file, MENU.BAT, and call this file from the AUTOEXEC.BAT file:

```
@ECHO OFF
CLS
C:
CD \MENU
TYPE MENU.TXT
PROMPT $_$_Enter the letter corresponding to your choice:
```

The reason for placing the TYPE and PROMPT commands in a separate batch file named MENU.BAT is that this batch file now can be called from any batch file that needs it. (This will become apparent in the following section.) The C: and CD \MENU commands are required; they always bring you home to the C:\MENU subdirectory, no matter where you were when you typed MENU.BAT at the command prompt.

You can make the following modifications to AUTOEXEC.BAT:

- Change the PATH to reflect the location of the MENU subdirectory. For example:
  ```
  PATH = C: \ DOS;C: \ MENU
  ```

- Put the command to run the menu file at the end of AUTOEXEC.BAT:
  ```
  CD \ MENU
  MENU
  ```

This chains you right from AUTOEXEC.BAT into the menu system. Now, each time you boot your computer, the menu system will come up automatically. The menu batch file also will be available from any subdirectory or any program that calls it.

Batch files to complete the system

Once the menu text file has been created and the AUTOEXEC.BAT and MENU.BAT files have been established to display the menu on the screen, all that remains is to write the batch files needed to run the system. In this simple case, six batch files are required. These batch files will correspond to the menu item choices and likewise be named: W.BAT, D.BAT, L.BAT, F.BAT, S.BAT, and Q.BAT. Each of these batch files should be located in the \ MENU along with the MENU.BAT and MENU.TXT files.

Three of these files are shown below to illustrate how the menu choices are used to load programs and execute DOS commands. If you do this for your own system, remember to specify the proper drives, directories and commands. W.BAT would look like this:

```
1:  @ECHO OFF
2:  REM This runs WordPerfect from the menu system
3:  CLS
4:  C:
5:  CD \ WP
6:  WP
7:  MENU
```

The batch files for dBASE and Lotus 1-2-3, D.BAT and L.BAT, are similar to W.BAT. Change the REM statement in line 2 to indicate the proper program, then change lines 5 and 6 to correspond to the proper subdirectory and program file name. Everything else remains the same.

Before commenting on the general structure of this batch file, here are the F.BAT and S.BAT files. F.BAT would look like this:

```
1:  @ECHO OFF
2:  REM Formatting a diskette in drive A
3:  CLS
4:  FORMAT A:
5:  MENU
```

S.BAT would look like this:

```
1:  @ECHO OFF
2:  REM See the contents of the diskette in drive A
3:  CLS
4:  DIR A: /P
5:  MENU
```

Each of these batch files does three things:

- Tells the programmer what the batch file does via a REM statement
- Carries out the command (logs to the proper directory, etc.)
- Runs the MENU batch file when it's done

Notice that you don't need to log to the \ DOS subdirectory to run the DOS program FORMAT. Because C: \ DOS is on the search path (as set in AUTOEXEC.BAT), that isn't necessary. Also, because C: \ MENU is on the search path, you don't need to specify a full pathname or log around to get at it either.

The final batch file, Q.BAT, simply resets the system prompt and ends the menu session. The following batch file should suffice for now:

```
1:  @ECHO OFF
2:  CLS
3:  C:
4:  CD \
5:  PROMPT $P$G
6:  ECHO Type MENU to restart the menu system.
```

Submenus and help screens

The preceding example illustrated how you can create a screen and use it in conjunction with the DOS prompt as part of a menu system. The menu system runs one of several batch files to load programs or execute DOS commands. For simple hard disk tree structures, a single-screen menu system such as this one might be sufficient. However, many hard disk tree structures are much more complicated than this simple example. They might contain many different application programs or multiple work areas for each application program.

As an example, consider just the DOS commands in the menu so far. There are two of them, but there could be more. What about system maintenance? Backing up programs could be handled by several menu items. This doesn't even scratch the surface of other disk problems: multiple word processors, multiple users on a single system, different programs for different tasks, and so on.

When you have many menu choices, a single-screen menu would be overly complex. After all, a solid screen of menu items would be more of a hassle than a help. Instead, a better approach would be to create a main menu containing fewer than eight options and use this menu to call for submenus containing specific options for each work area.

Submenu systems

Consider the menu screen illustrated in Fig. 11-7. In this menu, the choices are indicated by multiple letters rather than single characters. This is because the overall system will contain numerous choices and there aren't enough single-letter choices to go around. For instance, both DOS and dBASE begin with the letter *D*.

```
                                    Main Menu
                                    =========

                            WP   Word Processing

11-7  A modified menu for the hard disk.   DB   Database Management

                            123 Lotus 1-2-3

                            DOS DOS Commands


                                 Q   Quit
```

As your menu systems become more involved, you'll find that single-letter options become unworkable. The prompt message will have to be changed slightly to indicate that the user should enter the complete option. A prompt such as the following should suffice:

Enter your choice (WP, DB, etc.):

Notice that the WP, DB, and DOS options are general in nature. They don't refer to a specific application program or command. Instead, they refer to categories. Selecting either one of these options should cause a separate submenu to appear.

For example, Fig. 11-8 shows the word processing menu. This menu contains five choices for working with the various word processing programs available on the disk, plus an option for returning to the main menu.

```
                                Word Processing Menu
                                ====================

                            W    WordPerfect

                            MW   Microsoft Word

                            WS   WordStar

11-8  The word processing submenu.   ED   The DOS Editor

                            GV   GrandView (Outliner)


                                E  Exit to Main Menu
```

As with the main menu, this menu screen could be created using the Editor and saved as a text file, WPMENU.TXT. This menu would be called from the Main Menu by the batch file, WP.BAT:

```
1:  @ECHO OFF
2:  CLS
3:  TYPE WPMENU.TXT
4:  PROMPT $_$_Enter your choice (W, MW, etc.):
```

The various options from within the Word Processing Menu would be executed by batch files named W.BAT, MW.BAT, WS.BAT, ED.BAT, and GV.BAT, respectively. These batch files could be modeled on the W.BAT example, listed previously in this chapter. Note that W.BAT returns to the main menu. This is fine for now, although in the future you could have W.BAT return to the word processing menu: Substitute WPMENU.TXT for MENU.TXT and WP.BAT for MENU.BAT.

The exit option batch file, E.BAT, is shown below:

```
1:  @ECHO OFF
2:  CLS
3:  MENU
```

The other options from the main menu should produce similar submenu screens. For example, Fig. 11-9 shows the database management menu. You could create this menu using the Editor. If so, save it to disk with a logical name, say DBMENU.TXT.

```
Database Management Menu
=========================

1    Order/Entry

2    Invoicing

3    Sort & Report

4    Mailing Labels

5    Customer List/Edit

6    Maintenance


    E   Exit to Main Menu
```

11-9   The database management submenu.

In this menu, a potential problem is solved. The items are chosen by number instead of a single letter or group of letters. You can get away with this only once in your menu system; the single-number batch filenames would otherwise conflict. Also in this menu, see how the *E* menu item is borrowed from the word processing submenu. Because both do the same thing, there's no need to create a new E.BAT file.

The batch file to run this submenu, DB.BAT, would be identical to WP.BAT for the word processing submenu:

```
1: @ECHO OFF
2: CLS
3: TYPE DBMENU.TXT
4: PROMPT $_$_Enter your choice (1, 2, etc.):
```

The differences are in line 3, where DBMENU.TXT is used instead of WPMENU.TXT, and in line 4, where the PROMPT command's text reflects the new menu system.

You probably get the hang of things by now—how the menu screens and batch files all work to create the complete menu system. Providing extended examples here would be counterproductive, because your system has different programs and you might want to create different types of menus than described here. This system gives you the basic foundation upon which you can build a custom menu for your own PC.

Adding help screens to your menu system

Submenus add to the overall user-friendly feel of a menu system. However, the use of a main menu and submenus requires the user to make certain generalizations. While the choices in the main menu might be obvious to the person creating the menu system, a new user might have some trouble figuring out how the menu system works.

One way to overcome this problem is to provide individualized training for each user. Sometimes, however, this isn't practical. In such cases, special help screens might have to be added to the system.

Help screens provide extra information to explain how the menu system works and where specific applications or work areas are located within the menu system. Often, a single help screen, accessed from the main menu, is all that's required. The help feature can be included as an option within the main menu itself.

Figure 11-10 shows a modified version of the main menu, which includes a help option. Another technique is to include instructions for obtaining help within the prompt itself, such as:

```
Enter your choice (WP, DB, etc.) or H for Help:
```

```
                              Main Menu
                              =========

                         WP   Word Processing

                         DB   Database Management

11-10  The modified main menu,    123 Lotus 1-2-3
       including a Help option.
                         DOS DOS Commands

                         H    Help!


                              Q   Quit
```

Help screens are nothing more than text files describing the functions of the menu from which they are accessed.

```
                    Main Menu Help
                    ==============

The following options are available from the main menu:

        Word Processing       - Allows you to run WordPerfect, Word, WordStar,
                                the DOS Editor, or the GrandView outliner

        Database Management - Access the data base functions on this system,
                                including Order/Entry, Sorting, etc.

        Lotus 1-2-3           - Runs the 1-2-3 Spreadsheet

        DOS Commands          - General System Commands, format disks, backup,
                                system maintenance, etc.


   * Type the command letters (WP, DB, 123, or DOS) to access each area.

   * Remember to press the Enter key!

   * Type Q at the main menu prompt to quit.
```

11-11 A sample help screen.

Figure 11-11 gives an example of a help screen to accompany this menu system. This screen was created using the Editor and saved under the filename MAINHELP.TXT. Assume that this help screen is accessed through the batch file, H.BAT:

```
1:  @ECHO OFF
2:  CLS
3:  TYPE MAINHELP.TXT
4:  PAUSE
5:  MENU
```

The H.BAT file displays the text of the file MAINHELP.TXT and then pauses, waiting until the user presses any key. The prompt, Press any key to continue . . . is displayed at the bottom of the help screen thanks to the PAUSE command. After the user has had the opportunity to read the screen, pressing any key causes the MENU batch file to be executed, returning the user to the main menu.

Help screens can be provided for each of the submenus as well, although you'll have to use names other than H.BAT. One other point to keep in mind when creating help screens is to avoid overwhelming the user with too much help. All levels of users feel intimidated by too much information on the screen. Keep your screens simple. If necessary, divide the information into several screens. A good rule of thumb is to limit your help screens to fifteen or so lines. Also, vertical and horizontal centering, indentation, and blank lines help draw the user's attention to the critical information you want to convey.

Summary

You've progressed from simple batch file programs of the previous chapter to complete menu-driven systems in this one. Congratulations! Did you ever think you would be a systems programmer? Actually, you've only just begun. Throughout the remainder of this book, you'll continue to learn more DOS programming tricks and techniques for improving your private little menu-driven system.

While you might feel justifiably proud of the menus you have created in this chapter, the appearance of these menus is rather, well, blah. The next chapter continues work on the menu system, adding snazzy menu screens, complete with special borders and multiple colors.

12
Building up the menu
with ANSI.SYS

Now that you have a functioning menu-driven system for accessing programs and data on your hard disk, you might feel your system is complete. However, there are a number of enhancements you can add. While the system described so far is functional, it admittedly isn't very exciting. The screen displays consist of simple lists of options and a prompt telling the user to select from one of them. Yawn.

You can use your PC's full range of color, special graphics characters, and screen features like inverse video to really jazz up your displays. You also can perform some magic that will allow you to use the ten function keys to call up applications programs instead of entering in a batch filename. This will simplify your menu system significantly, because you'll be able to select options by pressing a single key.

This chapter presents a variety of techniques for enhancing your screen displays and simplifying the use of your menu system. The basic tool here is ANSI.SYS, which gives you extra control of your screen and keyboard under DOS.

Improving your menu screens

To take full advantage of the graphics capabilities of your computer, you should first access what you already have. So far, your menus have consisted of plain old text, plus maybe a few items you already have on your keyboard (such as the equal sign used in the previous menu examples). The PC has many more characters than that, however. To spice up your menus, you will need to have access to the extended ASCII character set.

ASCII files contain only printable characters. Most word processors add additional control characters to denote end of lines, end of paragraphs, special indentations, bold face, underscore, italics, etc. These control characters can produce unexpected results in a batch file or when typed to the screen. (i.e., they look gross).

The standard ASCII-defined character set consists of printable characters, as those available on the standard keyboard: the letters, digits, and characters like the asterisk and pound signs, and other symbols. On all PCs, however, an additional character set also exists. These extended ASCII characters, which really are not defined in the ASCII standard, include a number of special characters such as Greek letters, tiny hearts, smiling faces, arrowheads, and characters for producing single- and double-line border graphics.

Most word processors don't give you access to those special characters. They use them instead to control the format or appearance of the documents they produce. You can't have access to them to create special graphics effects.

Some word processors, including WordPerfect and Microsoft Word, do allow you to work with extended ASCII characters. This means you can use these programs to create fancy screen displays. However, these screen displays can be typed by DOS only as long as you save them as ASCII files. (On the other end of the spectrum, the DOS Editor gives you access to these characters as well, although not as cleanly as WordPerfect or Word.) The screen in Fig. 12-1 was created with WordPerfect using the extended character set to draw the solid menu border and the double line border around the menu heading.

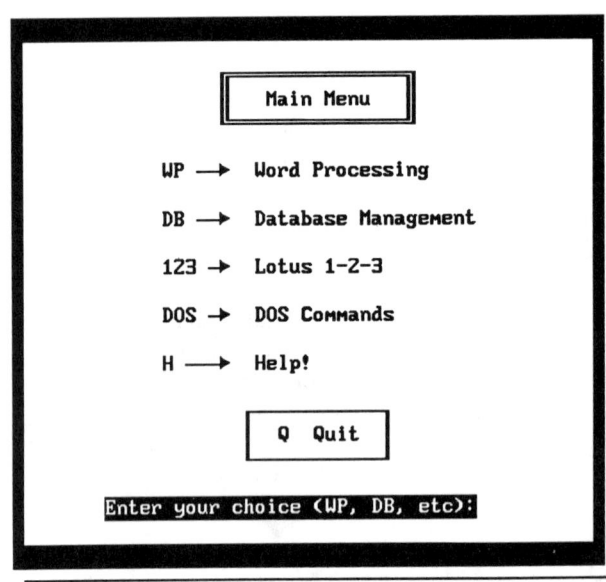

12-1 The improved main menu, including border lines.

The highlighting around the prompt message, Enter your choice, was accomplished through the use of special screen controls. On a color system, controls for changing foreground and background colors could be added as well. These screen controls also are available in the PROMPT command. The techniques for drawing borders and controlling the screen will be described later in the chapter.

Working with the extended ASCII character set

The borders in Fig. 12-1 were created using special characters from the extended character set. These and other drawing characters were shown in Fig. 6-4. Figure 12-2 shows a table displaying the complete extended ASCII character set. Note that these characters

Code	Char.	Code	Char.	Code	Char.	Code	Char.	Code	Code.
0		128	Ç	160	á	192	└	224	α
1	☺	129	ü	161	í	193	┴	225	ß
2	●	130	é	162	ó	194	┬	226	Γ
3	♥	131	â	163	ú	195	├	227	π
4	♦	132	ä	164	ñ	196	─	228	Σ
5	♣	133	à	165	Ñ	197	┼	229	σ
6	♠	134	å	166	ª	198	╞	230	μ
7	•	135	ç	167	º	199	╟	231	τ
8	◘	136	ê	168	¿	200	╚	232	Φ
9	○	137	ë	169	⌐	201	╔	233	Θ
10	◙	138	è	170	¬	202	╩	234	Ω
11	♂	139	ï	171	½	203	╦	235	δ
12	♀	140	î	172	¼	204	╠	236	∞
13	♪	141	ì	173	¡	205	═	237	φ
14	♫	142	Ä	174	«	206	╬	238	ε
15	☼	143	Å	175	»	207	╧	239	∩
16	►	144	É	176	▒	208	╨	240	≡
17	◄	145	æ	177	▓	209	╤	241	±
18	↕	146	Æ	178	█	210	╥	242	≥
19	‼	147	ô	179	│	211	╙	243	≤
20	¶	148	ö	180	┤	212	╘	244	⌠
21	§	149	ò	181	╡	213	╒	245	⌡
22	▬	150	û	182	╢	214	╓	246	÷
23	↨	151	ù	183	╖	215	╫	247	≈
24	↑	152	ÿ	184	╕	216	╪	248	°
25	↓	153	Ö	185	╣	217	┘	249	·
26	→	154	Ü	186	║	218	┌	250	·
27	←	155	¢	187	╗	219	█	251	√
28	∟	156	£	188	╝	220	▄	252	ⁿ
29	↔	157	¥	189	╜	221	▌	253	²
30	▲	158	₧	190	╛	222	▐	254	■
31	▼	159	ƒ	191	┐	223	▀	255	

12-2 The IBM extended ASCII character set.

also can be printed on any printer that supports the IBM extended ASCII character set. That's just about all of them, although you might need to flip a special switch or send the printer a special command to get access to the character set. (Refer to your printer's manual for the details.)

Notice that each character is referenced by a number. These numbers are the extended ASCII code values that represent the characters. Every ASCII character has a corresponding decimal code value. For example, the character *A* has the decimal value 65. Fortunately, you don't have to enter code values for the standard characters; you can just type them from the keyboard. The problem with the characters in the extended ASCII character set is that there are no symbols for them on the keyboard. So, the only way to get these special characters is to enter them as decimal codes.

To enter the decimal code value for any ASCII character, you hold down the Alt key and simultaneously type the decimal code. Note that you must use the numbers on the numeric keypad. The numbers across the top of the keyboard won't work.

For example, if you're in the Editor and want the solid block character, code 219, you would do the following:

1. Press and hold the Alt key (either Alt key)
2. Type 2 on the numeric keypad
3. Type 1 on the numeric keypad
4. Type 9 on the numeric keypad
5. Release the Alt key

When you release the Alt key, the character appears in the Editor.

The special control characters, 1 through 31, also can be produced in the Editor. However, not all of them are Alt-key accessible. Some of the keys, such as 13 and 9, are codes for special keys on the keyboard. (Code 13 is the Enter key; code 9 is a Tab.) To enter them, you must find their corresponding letter key (shown in appendix C) and press Ctrl−P then the Ctrl−letter combination.

For example, to enter the right-pointing wedge, you can type Ctrl−P, Ctrl−P. The letter P corresponds to control code 16, shown as ^P. (See chapter 6, "Inserting special characters," for more information.)

Not all word processors are able to access the extended character set as the Editor is. WordPerfect allows you to work with the drawing symbols and other special characters directly on the screen. Later in this chapter, you'll see how WordPerfect can be used to draw some rather fancy borders and add other enhancements to your menu screens.

If your word processor doesn't allow you to work with the extended character set, you'll need to use the Editor to draw borders around your menu screens.

A sample menu screen

Before actually entering the text and border characters for a given menu screen, it's a good idea to plan out the screen's appearance in advance. For example, notice that the border is centered in the middle of the screen in Fig. 12-1. Also, notice the placement of the text within the borders. Finally, notice the margin between the top of the screen and the top border line. Keep these spacing factors in mind when creating your menu screens.

To create the menu screen in Fig. 12-1, create a file using the Editor. Start off by calling this file MENU1. (Later you can rename it to MENU, MAINMENU, or whatever you like.)

C: \ MENU > EDIT MENU1

Creating the menu border   Inside the Editor, space over to column 10; hit the Spacebar nine times. (Remember, the row column indicator is at the lower right corner of the display.)

The top row is composed of character 219, the solid block. Use the Alt key and your numeric keypad to produce that character.

You need to make 51 of these characters to produce the top line of the display. Rather than do something repeatedly 51 times, produce ten of the block characters, then mark it as a block. Move the cursor to the start of the block, then press and hold the Shift key. Type the End key to select to the end of the line. The block should vanish on the screen, because the inverse of a solid block is an invisible block.

Copy the block by pressing Ctrl−Ins or select Copy from the Edit menu.

Now, paste in the block five times; press Shift−Ins or select Paste from the Copy menu five times. This process will duplicate the block, bringing it out to column 50. To make the last block in the column, enter character 219 a final time.

The final line of the menu consists of a vertical bar, which gives the menu a shadow effect. The bar is character 179. Enter that character using the Alt−keypad trick. Press Enter to start on the next line.

The next 21 lines of the menu boarder basically are the same. Each starts with 9 spaces, character 219, 49 spaces, character 219 again, then character 179. Create one of these lines using the techniques already described in this chapter.

After the initial line is created, select it. Move the cursor to column one and press the Shift key, then press the down arrow key. Now, duplicate the line 20 times. (You'll fill in the center of the menu later.) To duplicate the line, first copy it (Ctrl−Ins), then paste it 20 times (Shift−Ins). The final line should be pasted at line 22 in the editor, according to the row/column indicator.

The second to last line of the display is identical to the top line. So, select the top line, copy it, then paste it on the bottom of the display (line 23).

The final line is composed of the horizontal line drawing character, code 196. There are 50 character 196s, which you can produce the same way you created the top bar. Note that they start at column 11—not column 10.

The final character, the lower right corner, is code 217.

You now have a menu panel. The boarder is done, all that's left is the innards.

The menu contents   To create the text inside the menu and not mess up the boarder, turn the Editor's insert mode off by pressing the Ins key or Ctrl−V. The cursor will change to a large flashing block to tell you the insert mode is off. Now, all text will replace, or over-write, what already is there—and keep our border intact. (If you make a mistake don't press Backspace. If you do, toggle on insert again and try to line up the borders.)

Table 12-1 contains the text tidbits and their row/column values. Insert the text at the proper position inside the Editor. You'll add the final fancy line drawing characters in the last step. (Remember, the text Enter your choice is part of the system prompt; don't include it in the menu.)

Finishing the job   After each of the menu items is a line and a wedge arrow. The wedge arrow is code 16, which you can only enter in the Editor as Ctrl−P, Ctrl−P. There are five such arrows, each of which is at column 28 after each of WP, DB, 123, DOS, and H (see Fig. 12-3).

After each of the main menu items, there is a space, then a line up to the wedge arrow. Position the cursor after each time, then draw the line using the hyphen key or character code 196. Note that overwrite still must be on.

The text Main Menu has a double border box around it. The box starts at row 3, column 28 with character code 201. The top of the box consists of 15 characters code 205. The upper right corner is code 187.

The two sides consists of character code 186. One is at row 4 column 28, the other at column 44.

The bottom line starts at row 5, column 28 with code 200. That's followed by 15 characters code 205, then character 188 at the lower right corner.

Table 12-1 Text items and their row and column values.

Text	Position (row,column)
Main Menu	4, 32
WP	7, 23
Word Processing	7, 31
DB	9, 23
Database Management	9, 31
123	11, 23
Lotus 1-2-3	11, 31
DOS	13, 23
DOS Commands	13, 31
H	15, 23
Help!	15, 31
Q	18, 33
Quit	18, 36

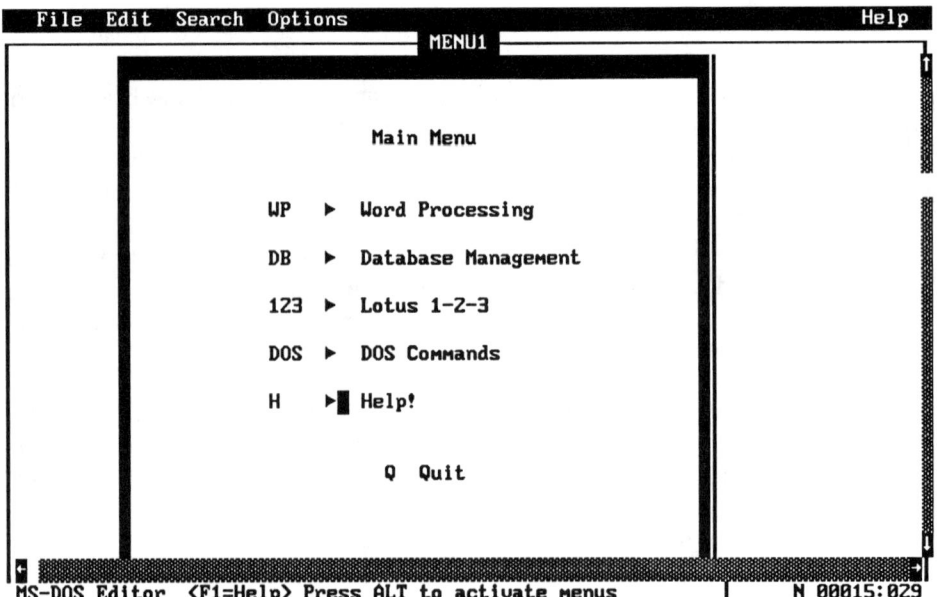

12-3 The menu under construction in the Editor.

The text Quit also has a box around it; however, it is a single border box. The box starts at row 17, column 30 with character code 218. The top of the box is 11 characters, code 196. The upper right corner is code 191.

The two sides of the box are the vertical line drawing character, code 179. One is at row 18 column 30, the other at column 42 in the same row.

The bottom line starts at row 19, column 30 with code 192. That's followed by 11 characters code 196, then character code 217 at the lower right corner.

This screen now is available for use in your MENU batch file. Just make sure you rename it to MENU first.

Fancy menu screens with WordPerfect

The main menu screen created in the last section is a big improvement over the old version. The addition of a border and graphics really enhances the menu, giving it an identity of its own and a professional edge. Unfortunately, using the Editor and the Alt−keypad trick to create such screens is tedious and time-consuming. If you have access to WordPerfect, however, you can create similar screens in a snap. (Other word processors might offer similar features.)

WordPerfect not only allows access to the extended characters and the control characters via the Alt−keypad trick, it also provides you with special commands for drawing on the screen. To draw a border in WordPerfect, all you need to do is select the drawing character you wish to use (for example, say a solid block), then use the cursor keys to draw. Using WordPerfect to draw borders is somewhat like working with the old Etch-a-Sketch boards.

Using the extended character set in WordPerfect

In addition to special commands for drawing borders, WordPerfect allows you to insert any of the extended characters directly into your text. To do so, all you do is hold down the Alt key and type in the decimal code for the character on the numeric keypad. The character appears wherever the cursor is located. This holds true for all characters, even the control characters that must be prefixed with Ctrl−P in the Editor.

To see a list of the Alt characters accessible in WordPerfect, type F3 (Help), then press Ctrl−V. A copy of the chart is shown in Fig. 12-4.

```
      0123456789112345678921234567893123456789 3123456789
  0 -    ☻♥♦♣♠ ·◙○◙♂♀♪☼↕‼¶§▬↨↑↓→←└↔▲▼
100 -                          ÇüéâäàçêëèïîìÄÅÉ∞Æôöò
150 -ûùÿÖÜ¢£¥R ƒáíóúñÑªº¿⌐¬½¼¡«»▓│┤╣║╗╝┐└┴┬├─┼╞╟
200 - ╚╔╩╦╠═╬╧╨╤╥╙╘╒╓╫╪┘┌█▄▌▐▀αβΓπΣσµτΦΘΩδ∞φ∈∩≡±≥≤⌠⌡÷≈°·
250 -  ·√ⁿ²▪
```

12-4 WordPerfect's built-in character reference chart.

Other characters also can be inserted into your text and printed on your printer using Ctrl−V. Note, however, that only the IBM character set (Fig. 12-2) will be displayed on the screen. Any other fancy characters that WordPerfect is capable of cannot be displayed on the screen under DOS. (In the current version of the manual, appendix P lists all Word-Perfect's special characters.)

Line drawing in WordPerfect

WordPerfect provides a useful tool for creating borders, one ideally suited to the subject at hand. The tool is the Line Draw command, which you activate in WordPerfect 5.1 by pressing the Screen Key, Ctrl−F3, then selecting option 2, Line Draw.

When you select the Line Draw command, you're presented with several choices for drawing, erasing, or moving lines:

1 |; 2 ||; 3 *; 4 Change; 5 Erase; 6 Move: 1

The first two choices let you draw lines using either the single or the double line character. The third choice displays an asterisk as the drawing character. However, you can change this to any other character you wish—including the entire range of extended characters.

To draw a border, you first place the cursor at one of the corners of the border rectangle. To use either the single- or double-line character, select the appropriate option (1 or 2). Then, use the cursor keys to move left, right, up, or down as desired. As you press the cursor keys, a line is drawn in the direction you specify. If you change directions by 90 degrees, WordPerfect automatically inserts the correct corner character for you.

For example, to draw a double-line border extending 40 characters across, 10 characters down, and centered on the screen, you would:

1. Turn on Line Draw (Ctrl−F3, 2)
2. Select the drawing character you want, say 2 to draw a double-lined box
3. Use the right arrow key to extend the double line 40 characters to the right (you also can press the repeat key, Esc, type 40, and then press the right arrow key)
4. Press the down arrow key 10 times to draw a vertical line down (or press Esc, type 10, then press the down arrow key)
5. Press and hold the left arrow key to complete the bottom of the box (40 characters)
6. Press the up arrow key to draw the remaining side of the box (10 characters)
7. To exit the Line Draw command, press the Exit Key (F7)

The net effect of doing this is shown in Fig. 12-5. As you're drawing, you might find that your border lines do not meet up as you planned. It's sometimes difficult to determine exactly where to turn the corner (just like the Etch-a-Sketch). If you make a mistake when drawing lines in WordPerfect, just use option 5 to Erase. When this option is selected, any movement using the cursor keys will cause the line to be rubbed out in the direction of the

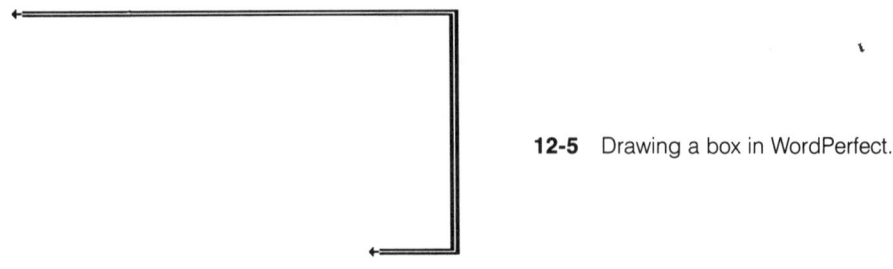

12-5 Drawing a box in WordPerfect.

1 |: 2 ||: 3 ×; 4 Change; 5 Erase; 6 Move: 2   Ln 2.94" Pos 2.73"

arrow key you're using. Note that option 6, Move, can be used to move the cursor without drawing or erasing.

To draw lines using any of the other extended characters, you'll have to substitute that character for the asterisk in option 3. This is done by choosing option 4, Change. This option displays a list of eight drawing options consisting of various sizes and shades of drawing characters (Fig. 12-6).

1 ▒; 2 ▓; 3 ▒; 4 ■; 5 ▄; 6 ▌; 7 ▐; 8 ▀; 9 Other: 0

12-6 WordPerfect's other line drawing characters.

You can either select from one of these or choose option 9, Other. If you select this option, you will see a message displayed at the bottom of your screen:

Solid character:

At this point, you can enter the character code for the character you want. The character you select through this process becomes the new drawing character.

Once you've drawn your border, you can insert the text of your menu. Be careful to use the typeover mode, however, or you'll break up the vertical lines. Once drawn, borders are affected by any editorial changes you make. If you insert additional characters or lines, the borders will be broken up by the insertion, just as any other characters would be. If you do inadvertently break up your borders, you can bring the border lines back into alignment by deleting empty spaces to the left of them or removing extra blank lines.

One way to avoid possible damage to your borders during screen editing is to enter the text of your menu before drawing your borders. Once the text is in place, you can use the Screen key to draw borders around it. Be careful here as well. Make sure you're in the typeover mode or your text will get moved around in strange and mysterious ways.

Saving WordPerfect menu screens as ASCII files

After the menu screen is complete, you'll want to save it in two forms. First, you will want to save the screen as a regular WordPerfect document. Just use the Save key (F10) as usual. You also will want to save the menu screen as an ASCII file.

Like many word processors, WordPerfect places hidden control characters into its files. While you normally don't see these characters when working in WordPerfect, they show up when typed from DOS. Fortunately, WordPerfect provides a conversion command, which can remove these control characters from the file and create a displayable ASCII file.

To save a document as an ASCII file, use the Text In/Out key (Ctrl−F5). This key provides you with several choices. Option 1 will save the document in DOS text format, which is the same as an ASCII file. For WordPerfect 5.0 and later, a third menu comes up. Select option 1, Save, to save the file.

Be careful here, as WordPerfect will suggest the same name that you used to save the file as a WordPerfect document. If you accept this name, WordPerfect will replace the WordPerfect version with the ASCII version. You should use separate names for your WordPerfect and ASCII versions of your menu screens. (Generally, all ASCII files end with a file extension of TXT, although the older ASC extension can be used.)

The reason for maintaining two versions of your menu screens is so you can make editorial changes to the menu easily. These changes are accomplished by bringing up the WordPerfect version of the menu. This version can be edited using any of the WordPerfect commands, including moving or erasing border lines. The border lines in the ASCII versions cannot be edited easily. After making any changes, be sure to resave the file as both a WordPerfect document and as an ASCII file.

Controlling the screen characteristics

Using borders and other graphics characters is only one way to increase the impact of your menu screens. You also can use a number of video tricks to draw attention to your menus and any special messages or prompts to the user.

Your PC provides access to a wide variety of video display features, including bold and inverse video, blinking, underscore, and color—providing you have a color display card and monitor (you can't get blood from a turnip). The remainder of this chapter tells you how you can further spice up your menus and prompts using these secret tricks.

The power of ANSI.SYS

DOS doesn't display fancy text by itself. To do that, you must load a special display device driver, one that lets you access your PC's color and manipulate the keyboard. The most common display device driver is ANSI.SYS, which comes with DOS.

ANSI.SYS is a device driver that gives you access to ANSI commands. These commands are what allow you to control the screen display (also the keyboard) in ways that you can't otherwise do. Through ANSI.SYS and the ANSI commands, you can control the location of the cursor, change video modes, alter the foreground and background colors, and redefine the keys on your keyboard.

Installing ANSI.SYS   You install ANSI.SYS using the DEVICE configuration command in CONFIG.SYS. (Refer to chapter 7 for more information on CONFIG.SYS and the DEVICE configuration command.) For example:

```
DEVICE = C: \ DOS \ ANSI.SYS
```

tells DOS to load the device driver ANSI.SYS, found in the DOS subdirectory of drive C.

Take a moment to examine your system's CONFIG.SYS file to look for ANSI.SYS. Use the following command:

```
TYPE C: \ CONFIG.SYS
```

(If the display scrolls, use the MORE filter and the pipe.)

Look in the output for a DEVICE command line that loads ANSI.SYS. If you can't find one, edit CONFIG.SYS and place into it the proper command. Remember to reset your system after changing CONFIG.SYS. You can work with the ANSI commands only if ANSI.SYS is loaded.

How ANSI.SYS works   ANSI.SYS will control the console device. Because the console consists of the screen and the keyboard, ANSI.SYS will control the way these two components of your system work. The screen and the keyboard will work the way they normally do without ANSI.SYS installed. Without ANSI.SYS, you cannot tap its power.

To make ANSI.SYS do its stuff, you must make calls to it. A call to ANSI.SYS is like saying, "Hey, yo, ANSI.SYS!" and then specifying what screen or keyboard attribute you want to alter.

Calls to ANSI.SYS are made by sending DOS an escape sequence. An *escape sequence* is just an escape character (code 27) followed by a left bracket and one or more special numbers or characters. Unfortunately, these escape sequences cannot be sent directly from the system prompt. Why not? Just try pressing the Esc key to enter the escape character and see what happens.

However, where there's a will, there's a way. In this case, the way is the PROMPT command itself. Also, you can enter the escape character for batch programs and text files using the Editor.

Using PROMPT to call ANSI.SYS

While you can't send escape sequences directly to DOS from the system prompt, the PROMPT command has a way of sending them. If you remember the discussion of the PROMPT command from chapter 4, you'll recall that PROMPT includes a number of meta characters, such as $n, $p, $g, etc. One of those characters is $e, which sends an escape code to DOS. (Ta da!) This escape code can be teamed up with ANSI.SYS to make calls to this device driver.

When you call ANSI.SYS, what you're calling it with is an ANSI command. ANSI stands for American National Standards Institute. What the gang at the Institute has done is to establish standards, one of which describes computer codes for controlling the screen and keyboard. These ANSI commands are all escape sequences. They can be grouped into several categories: cursor functions, erasing, graphics modes, and keyboard reassignment. Each of these functions will be discussed in the following sections. (All of DOS's ANSI commands are listed in appendix D.)

To send an escape sequence to ANSI.SYS via the PROMPT command, you include the PROMPT escape code ($e) followed by a bracket and whatever ANSI.SYS control code you wish to transmit. A few of the more entertaining ANSI codes are listed in Tables 12-2 and 12-3. Note that the left arrow, ←, is used to represent the escape character in

Table 12-2   ANSI cursor commands.

Code	Function
←[r,cH	Move the cursor to row r, column c; The upper left corner of the screen is position 1,1.
←[nA	Move the cursor up n lines, or one line if n isn't specified.
←[nB	Move the cursor down n lines, or one line if n isn't specified.
←[nC	Move the cursor right n lines, or one line if n isn't specified.
←[nD	Move the cursor left n lines, or one line if n isn't specified.
←[2J	Clear the screen.
←[K	Erase the line the cursor is on.
←[s	Save the cursor's position
←[u	Restore the cursor's position (saved with ←[s)

Table 12-3 ANSI screen mode commands.

Code	Screen mode
←[=0h	Monochrome text, 25×40
←[=1	Color text, 25×40
←[=2	Monochrome text, 25×80
←[=3	Color text, 25×80
←[=4	4-color medium-resolution graphics
←[=5	4-color medium-resolution graphics (no color burst)
←[=6	2-color high-resolution graphics
←[=13	Color graphics, 320×200
←[=14	16-color graphics, 640×200
←[=15	Monochrome graphics, 640×350
←[=16	16-color graphics, 640×350
←[=17	2-color graphics, 640×480
←[=18	16-color graphics, 640×480
←[=19	256-color graphics, 320×200

this book. (The left arrow is what you see when you enter Esc into the Editor: Ctrl−P, Esc.)

For example, the escape sequence to clear the screen and home the cursor is ←[2J. In PROMPT command talk that's $e[2J. Note that the *J* must be uppercase. ANSI.SYS is fussy about those things.

To send the escape sequence for clearing the screen and homing the cursor to ANSI .SYS, you could use the following PROMPT command:

PROMPT $e[2J

Don't type that in! You can and nothing will happen—other than your screen will clear after each DOS command to display your new prompt. That doesn't make for very good directory reading. If you did type in that PROMPT string, change it back to your default prompt by just entering PROMPT on the command line.

Escape sequences can be strung together and included with messages to the user. This is the most effective way to incorporate ANSI.SYS into your system prompt. The ANSI command to change the text color is as follows:

←[*n*m

The character attribute and color values for *n* are listed in Table 12-4. You can specify more than one. If so, separate each color value with a semicolon. For example, the command to have blinking yellow text on a red background is:

←[5;33;41m

That's blinking (5), yellow foreground (33), and red background (41). The command to return the text to normal is just:

←[m

Table 12-4
ANSI screen attribute and color codes.

N value	Attribute
0	Normal text
1	High-intensity (bold)
4	Underlined (monochrome monitors only)
5	Blinking
7	Inverse video
8	Invisible text

Color	Foreground N value	Background N value
Black	30	40
Red	31	41
Green	32	42
Yellow	33	43
Blue	34	44
Magenta	35	45
Cyan	36	46
White	37	47

The inverse video escape sequence, ←[7m, and the message Enter your command: could be used as follows:

```
PROMPT $e[7m Enter your command:$e[0m
```

If you wanted to position this prompt to fit the text neatly into a menu screen (hint, hint), you could use the ANSI cursor positioning commands. This technique is covered later in this chapter (although, if you're clever, you probably can look up in Table 12-2 and figure out what the command is already).

The ←[m command is used to change back to normal video. You can omit it if you like the inverse display. Also, feel free to experiment with color options. The following PROMPT command creates that popular bright white characters on blue background screen that so many users strive for:

```
PROMPT $e[1;37;44m$p$g
```

The ECHO$ command

Changing the prompt to demonstrate ANSI commands is a time-honored trick, used by every DOS book writer since day zero. It works, thanks to the $e character that lets you type an escape control code at the DOS prompt. However, it messes up your prompt. I don't know about you, but I can't stand that. So, I wrote the utility ECHO$.

What ECHO$ does is to display text, just like the ECHO command. The difference is that ECHO$ also incorporates all the PROMPT command's meta characters. (Refer to

Table 9-1.) To display inverse text without changing your PROMPT (which is far easier to do, by the way), you could use the following:

```
ECHO$ $e[7m Enter your command:$e[0m
```

The cool part about this command is that I've tossed it on the companion diskette offered with this book. If you'd like to use ECHO$ for each of the following examples, feel free. However, if you want to spruce up your system prompt with ANSI commands, continue to use the PROMPT command.

Cursor and erase functions

ANSI commands allow you to position the cursor anywhere you want. You can move the cursor up a line, down a line, forward or backward across a line, or to a specific position on the screen. The ANSI commands also allow you to save the cursor position in memory, report on the cursor position, and restore the cursor to its former position.

The most useful of the cursor functions is the cursor position function. This function uses the escape sequence:

```
←[r,cH
```

The r and c values are the row and column values. For example, to position the cursor on line 14, column 20, the sequence would be:

```
←[14;20H
```

You have wondered how the prompt in the menu screen displayed in Fig. 12-1 was located within the menu itself. This placement was accomplished through the use of the cursor positioning ANSI command in the PROMPT command:

```
PROMPT $e[21;18H$e[7mEnter your choice (WP, DB, etc.):$e[m
```

See how several ANSI commands have been grouped to make one interesting (and useful) prompt? The batch file required to display this prompt, and the menu, would appear as follows:

```
@ECHO OFF
CLS
TYPE MENU1.TXT
PROMPT $e[21;18H$e[7mEnter your choice (WP, DB, etc.):$e[m
```

The cool part about this prompt is that it always appears in the same spot on the screen. It looks like a real prompt. A day-to-day type of prompt that uses the screen positioning commands could be as follows:

```
PROMPT $e[H$p$g
```

Type in this prompt. The ←[H sequence simply positions the cursor in the upper left corner of the screen—each time the prompt is displayed.

Here is another prompt you might want to try:

```
PROMPT $e[s$e[H$e[7m$e[K$P $D $T$H$H$H$H$H$H$e[m$e[u$g
```

Table 12-5   Function key scan codes.

Key	Normal	Shift	Ctrl	Alt
F1	0;59	0;84	0;94	0;104
F2	0;60	0;85	0;95	0;105
F3	0;61	0;86	0;96	0;106
F4	0;62	0;87	0;97	0;107
F5	0;63	0;88	0;98	0;108
F6	0;64	0;89	0;99	0;109
F7	0;65	0;90	0;100	0;110
F8	0;66	0;91	0;101	0;111
F9	0;67	0;92	0;102	0;112
F10	0;68	0;93	0;103	0;113
F11	0;133	0;135	0;137	0;139
F12	0;134	0;136	0;138	0;140

The top part of the screen is always shown in inverse. Listed will be the current drive and directory, the date, and the time. Yet, the prompt keeps moving down the screen as it always has. Interesting. (Table 12-6 contains the meta and ANSI commands cut up for easier digestion.) This is one of the fanciest prompts around, although it's a bit cumbersome to type. Other prompts can incorporate color commands or fancy text if you like. Don't forget all the meta commands (see Table 9-1).

Keyboard reassignment functions

Another feature of ANSI.SYS is its ability to reassign the function of any key on the keyboard. This includes the function keys, F1 through F12, which can come in very handy for creating menu systems.

Table 12-6   Meta and ANSI commands.

$e[s	Save the cursor's current position
$e[H	Home the cursor
$e[7m	Set the color attribute to inverse text
$e[K	Erase to the end of the line (has the effect of rendering the erased line in the current color attribute)
$P	Show the current drive and directory (plus two spaces)
$D	Show the current date (plus two spaces)
$T	Show the current time
HHHHHH	Backup six times (over the hundredths and seconds display)
$e[m	Normal color attribute restored here
$e[u	Restore the cursor's position, saved with ←[s
$g	Show the standard prompt

Most computer users accept their keyboards at face value. Did you think that, when you entered an *A*, the ASCII code for the letter *A* actually was sent to your computer? This isn't the case. Instead, a special scan code is sent to the computer. In the case of the *A* key, the scan code is 30. There also are scan codes for the shift keys, so the computer can tell whether you are entering a lower or uppercase *A*.

The scan code for the letter you type is translated into the corresponding ASCII code by your computer's BIOS ROM chip. This ASCII value then will be sent on to the screen for display. However, the ANSI.SYS device driver can intercept the ASCII codes before they get to the screen. ANSI.SYS then will generate its own ASCII code, sending it instead to the screen. ANSI.SYS can send an entire sequence of characters. A single key can be reassigned to represent a complete sentence.

The ability to reassign individual keys isn't especially useful. After all, you ordinarily want an *A* when you type the *A* key. (You might want to try some simple key reassignments on your friend's computer, however. This makes a great, if unappreciated, practical joke.) On the other hand, reassigning the values of the function keys can simplify the use of your menus. Consider the menu screen displayed in Fig. 12-7.

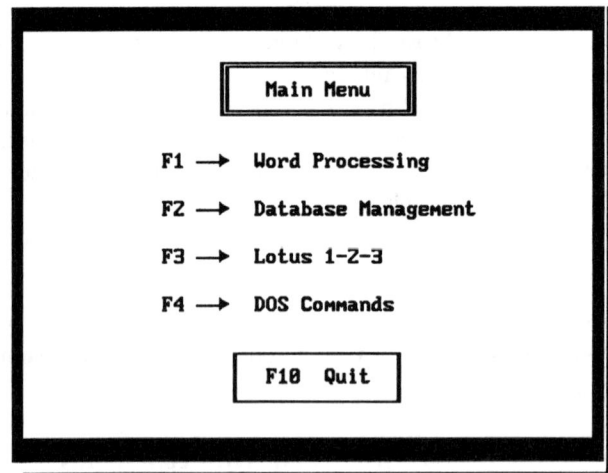

12-7 A menu screen relying on function keys for selecting choices.

This menu refers to the function keys F1 through F4, plus F10, for selecting the options displayed on the screen. The use of function keys to represent menu choices often is preferable to letter choices. There are several reasons for this. For one thing, pressing F1 is faster than typing WS and pressing the Enter key. Also, the function keys are easier for novices to find.

For these reasons, you might want to build your menus around function keys rather than letter choices. To do so, you'll have to use ANSI.SYS to reassign the values of these function keys.

The ANSI command for keyboard reassignment looks like this:

←[*scancode*;"*text*"p

That's the escape sequence followed by a scan code value (the popular ones are listed in Table 12-5), a semicolon, then the text to replace that key in double quotes. A little p ends the command.

These are handy things to have, even outside of a menu system. For example, enter the following batch file, FUNCT.BAT. If you use the Editor, remember that the escape character is entered Ctrl−P, Ctrl−[(or Ctrl−P, Esc).

```
 1: @ECHO OFF
 2: REM Use ANSI to reassign function keys Shift-F1 through Shift-F12
 3: REM ANSI.SYS must be installed for this to work
 4: ECHO ←[0;84;"DIR";13p
 5: ECHO ←[0;85;"CD \";13p
 6: ECHO ←[0;86;"COPY "p
 7: ECHO ←[0;87;"DEL "p
 8: ECHO ←[0;88;"REN "p
 9: ECHO ←[0;89;"CLS";13p
10: ECHO ←[0;90;"PROMPT $p$g";13p
11: ECHO ←[0;91;"PATH C:\DOS;C:\BATCH";13p
12: ECHO ←[0;92;"C:";13;"CD \DOS";13p
13: ECHO ←[0;93;"TYPE "p
14: ECHO ←[0;135;"MENU";13p
15: ECHO ←[0;136;"WP";13p
16: ECHO Done!
```

The previous batch file reassigns keys Shift−F1 through Shift−F12 to various DOS functions. The 13 code at the end of some of the commands simulates pressing the Enter key at the end of a command. Note how it's used in the middle of the command in line 12; that way two commands can be assigned to one function key.

The batch file ends with ECHO Done! in line 16 because it runs silently. The ECHO commands' escape sequences are all gobbled up by the ANSI.SYS driver.

You should note that this batch file uses the ECHO command to send the commands to ANSI.SYS. You also can place ANSI commands into a text file and display it using the TYPE command. In all seriousness, use the PROMPT command as a last resort (or if you only can work at the DOS prompt).

If you're using the ECHO$ command, then note its weakness. Double quotes must be preceded by backslashes:

```
ECHO$ $e[0;59;\"DIR\";13p
```

See how the backslashes are used before the double quotes? Without them, the command won't work.

Once you've reassigned the keys, the effect is permanent. The only way to unassign them is to reboot your machine. Breathe a sigh of relief, however. The changes only take effect at the DOS prompt or in programs that use DOS's standard input (such as the old EDLIN). In standard applications or sophisticated programs like the Editor, the function key reassignments won't work; you'll have access to the application's function key commands.

A menu system based on function keys

To carry this idea of function key reassignment over into your menu system, reassign function keys as you see fit for the menu. Place the new key's definitions into your menu batch files and your submenu batch files. That way, you can reassign the keys depending on which menu level you're at. This technique is one way of eliminating the problem of duplicate names for batch files.

For example, consider the following, new version of the MENU.BAT file:

```
 1: @ECHO OFF
 2: CLS
 3: C:
 4: CD \ MENU
 5: REM Reassign function keys here
 6: REM F1 = Word Processing
 7: ECHO ←[0;59;"WPMENU";13p
 8: REM F2 = Database Management
 9: ECHO ←[0;60;"DBMENU";13p
10: REM F3 = 123
11: ECHO ←[0;61;"123";13p
12: REM F4 = DOS Commands
13: ECHO ←[0;62;"DOS";13p
14: REM F10 = Quit
15: ECHO ←[0;68;"Q";13p
16: TYPE MENU1.TXT
17: PROMPT $e[21;18H$e[7mEnter your choice:$e[m
```

Instead of typing WP and pressing Enter to run the WP.BAT file, pressing the F1 key now runs the WPMENU.BAT file. That file can in turn display its own menu screen and reassign the function keys for its own menu items, as shown below:

```
@ECHO OFF
CLS
REM Re-assign function keys here
REM F1 = WordPerfect
ECHO ←[0;59;"WP";13p
REM F2 = Microsoft Word
ECHO ←[0;60;"WORD";13p
REM F3 = WordStar
ECHO ←[0;61;"WS";13p
REM F4 = The DOS Editor
ECHO ←[0;62;"EDIT";13p
REM F5 = Grandview
ECHO ←[0;63;"GV";13p
REM F10 = Exit
ECHO ←[0;68;"E";13p
TYPE WPMENU.TXT
PROMPT $e[21;18H$e[7mEnter your choice:$e[m
```

Again, the reassignments here give each function key a corresponding batch file to run. The batch file should finish with a command to run the MENU batch file again, which restarts the entire cycle. This process could be repeated for each menu screen and all the menu option.

Don't dwell on the keyboard power of ANSI.SYS. Remember color. Edit your menu text files and spice them up with some color, flash, and pizzazz. However, don't overdo it. It's easy to get carried away with all this stuff. Walk that delicate line between exciting and overdone with the grace of a tightrope artist. (Your users will thank you.)

There's a special feeling that comes from creating your own, customized applications. If you have ever written a simple Lotus macro or dBASE command file, you have experienced this feeling. Just think how proud you'll be to show off your slick, integrated menu system. Won't your computing buddies be impressed?

Summary

Using the menu strategy covered in this chapter, you can create a complete menu system including submenus, help screens, and so forth, all using function keys. When combined with borders, colors, and special video effects, your menus will rival those of professional programs.

Most of the magic here is done via the PC's built-in graphics character set and ANSI .SYS. To use the graphics characters, which are part of the extended ASCII characters, you need a word processor that allows you to enter their values using the Alt−keypad trick—or the Editor will do. To make calls to the powerful functions of ANSI.SYS, you'll need to install that file in your computer's CONFIG.SYS file located in your root directory.

Building your own menu system is fun and a great way to pass the time on a PC. If you're into it, great; however, let me be honest, it's really kind of a waste of time. The next two chapters will introduce you to some powerful menu systems on the professional level, some of which offer features and performance you'd never get from a batch file. Still, don't abandon your efforts from this and the previous chapter—especially if you're having a good time at it.

13
Using DOS Shell

One of the most interesting things to crop up in DOS version 4 was the DOS Shell. Basically, the Shell was an easy-to-use file manager, almost like an apology from IBM for making DOS too cumbersome for some users in the first place. However, the Shell was nice—and came free with DOS. DOS 5 carries on the tradition, offering a similar but more powerful version of DOS Shell.

The newest and most surprising feature of DOS 5's DOS Shell is its ability to task switch. That is, you can switch quickly between several applications without returning to DOS. Each program is swapped out to disk and a new program swapped in its place. You can juggle several applications this way, which makes the DOS Shell useful for overly-productive users as well as the DOS timid neophyte.

This chapter is about the DOS Shell. It covers the Shell in four areas: an introduction to how the Shell works; using the Shell to perform simple and complex DOS tasks; creating menus and setting up your programs to run under the Shell; and task switching. Because all DOS 5 users have the Shell, this entire chapter is devoted to it. Even if you think you're beyond using a shell, take a peek at what the DOS Shell has to offer. You could be surprised.

An introduction to the Shell

The DOS Shell is installed on your PC along with DOS 5. Everybody that has DOS version 4 or higher has the DOS Shell. As long as it's in your DOS subdirectory and that directory is listed on the search path, you'll always have access to it.

To run the DOS Shell, type the DOSSHELL command at the system prompt. A copyright notice will appear, then the Shell's main screen (Fig. 13-1). If you have a mouse installed on your PC, you'll see a mouse pointer, with which you can manipulate the Shell's menus, select options, or work with files.

If you like the Shell, you can make it a permanent part of your system. Simply stick the command to load the Shell, DOSSHELL, at the end of your AUTOEXEC.BAT file. Each time your system starts, the Shell will run.

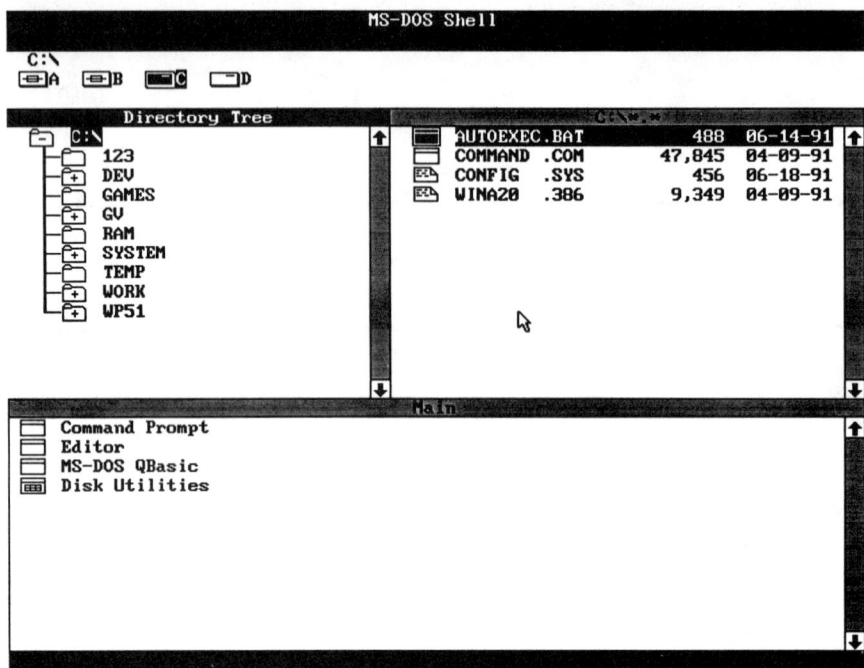

13-1 The DOS Shell.

EGA users note

If you have an EGA display (not VGA), you might need the device driver EGA.SYS in your CONFIG.SYS file. This file helps the EGA display recover when the Shell switches between text and graphics modes. A line in CONFIG.SYS such as the following will do the job:

```
DEVICE = C: \ DOS \ EGA.SYS
```

The C: \ DOS subdirectory is assumed; specify your own DOS directory or whichever directory contains the EGA.SYS file that came with DOS.

A look at the display

If you're running the Shell now, take a look at the screen (or refer to Fig. 13-1). The Shell uses special terms to describe the different parts of the display. The following will help you become familiar with them. (It also helps to break up the display into easily digestible chunks.)

At the top of the display is the *title bar*. It says MS-DOS Shell. Below that, you'll find the *menu bar*, which is similar to the menu bar in the Editor. There are five menus on the menu bar:

- File—file and directory commands
- Options—Shell options and configuration
- View—screen presentations and formats

- Tree—control of the tree structure display
- Help—the help system and tutorial

The Tree menu might come or go, depending on which area of the Shell is active (more on this in a page or two).

Below the menu bar, you'll see the current directory displayed, similar to as it would be in a directory listing. Below that, you'll see the drive icons. There will be one drive icon for each drive in your system: floppy drives, hard drives, RAM drives, network drives, and so on. When the Shell is in the text mode, the drive icons appear as brackets around the drive letter; in the graphics mode, they look like tiny disk drives.

The bulk of the Shell is its midsection, which contains up to four different panels or areas. Each area contains something different, some information about a part of your hard disk. Also, each area has its own area title, at the top of the area panel.

The *Directory-tree area* is below the drive icons in Fig. 13-1. It contains a graphic list of the tree structure on the current drive. The title of the Directory-tree area is Directory Tree.

The *File-list area* contains a list of files for a specific directory on disk (as highlighted in the Directory-tree area). If no files are in the directory, you'll see NO files in selected directory displayed. The title of this area is the pathname of the directory, such as C: \ *.*.

The *Program-list area* contains a list of programs or groups of programs (submenus). This area is the Shell's menu area, where you can install programs you often run or create your own menu system. The title of this area indicates your level in the menu structure or the title of the menu group you're using. In Fig. 13-1, the title is Main for the main menu level.

The *Active Task List area* only appears when you turn on the Shell's task swapping ability. In the Active Task List area you'll see a list of programs the Shell currently has open. You select a program from the list to switch to it.

At the bottom of the Shell's display is the *status bar*. The status bar will give you hints for using the Shell, keystrokes that might come in handy, or just general information, such as the current time.

Changing the display

You can customize the way the Shell presents itself, the number and types of areas it shows, as well as whether the Shell uses text or graphics to show itself.

One handy command worth keeping in mind during this section is the Repaint Screen command, Shift−F5. It will redraw the screen for you, especially if some graphics program or a pop-up utility has messed things up. I use the Shift−F5 key because it's handy. If you like, you also can select the Repaint Screen item from the View menu for the same effect. (Working with the Shell's menus is covered later in this chapter.)

Screen settings   If you have an EGA or VGA display, you can set the number of lines the Shell displays on the screen, as well as whether the display uses the text or graphics screens.

To change the screen settings, select the Display menu item from the Options menu. Press Alt−O, then D for *Display*. The Screen Display Mode dialog box appears, as shown in Fig. 13-2. The screen modes appear in the list window in the center of the dialog

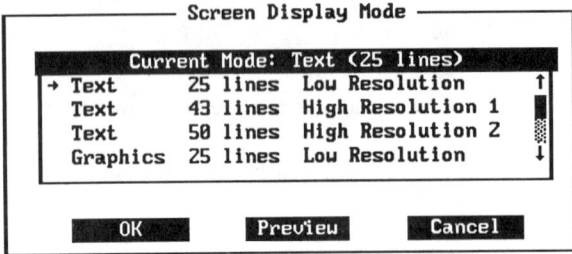

13-2 The Screen Display Mode dialog box.

box. The three columns indicate the screen mode (text or graphics), the number of lines of the display (25, 30, 43, 50, etc.), and the name for the mode (Text, Medium Resolution 1, etc.). Different screen modes appear depending on the abilities of your graphics display adapter hardware.

Select a new mode using the arrow keys, or use the mouse with the scroll bar on the side of the window. The current mode is listed above the window.

To preview a mode, select the Preview button with the mouse, or press the Tab key until the Preview button is highlighted, then press Enter. Press Enter to select the new mode, or Escape to cancel.

Changing colors If you have a color display, you can splash around a few interesting color patterns in the Shell. Select the Colors item under the Options menu. The Color Scheme dialog box appears, as shown in Fig. 13-3. The number and variety of colors shown depends on your display adapter. They're all listed in a window, similar to the options for the Screen Mode Display dialog box.

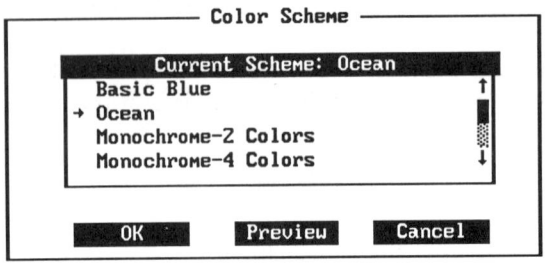

13-3 The Color Scheme dialog box.

Select a color scheme from the Color Scheme dialog box using the arrow keys. Use the Tab key to highlight the Preview button if you want to take a sneak peek at the color setup. Press Enter to accept it or Escape to cancel.

Controlling the area displays When you start the Shell, and without telling it otherwise, it shows you the Directory-tree list, File-list, and Program-list areas. You can customize the Shell to display the areas in up to five options. This is done by selecting the option from the View menu.

To activate the View menu, click on it using the mouse or press Alt−V. You'll see the five display options listed, along with the Repaint Screen and Refresh items. Note that the currently selected view will be dimmed, shown in inverse text, or grayed. That item cannot be selected from the menu.

The following text describes each of the items in the menu and which parts of the display will be visible:

Single File List The Single File List display option shows only the Directory-tree area and the File-list area, side-by-side. The Program-list area isn't visible. The Single File List display is best if you're not using the Shell as a menu system; you can see more files when the Program-list area isn't shown.

Dual File Lists The Dual File Lists display option shows two sets of Directory-tree areas and File-list areas, as shown in Fig. 13-4. This display is best for massive file maintenance workouts: for example, if you're copying files between two drives or subdirectories. This display also is great for comparing directory contents.

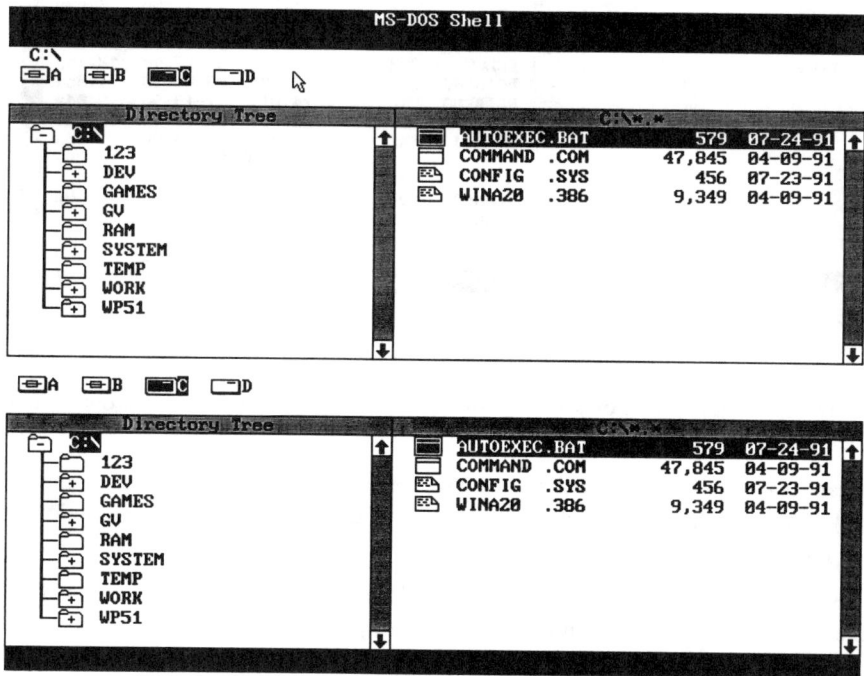

13-4   The dual file list display.

All Files The All File option changes the look of the Shell completely (see Fig. 13-5). The File-list area becomes dominant on the screen. It contains a list of all files on disk. Information about each individual file is listed on the left side of the screen. This type of display is good for file maintenance, especially finding files and weeding out duplicates.

Program/File Lists The Program/File Lists is the standard display, the one the Shell shows when it initially starts (unless you've selected another item). The screen is divided into three list areas, as shown in Fig. 13-1.

Program List The Program List display option is nearly the opposite of the Single File List option; the only area shown is the program list area. If you're using the Shell

```
C:\WORK
[==]A  [==]B  [==]C  [==]D
```

		.		
	AUTOEXEC.DOS	435	03-12-91	2:19p
File	B	19,901	10-24-90	11:32a
Name : AUTOEXEC.DOS	BACK .BAT	57	10-10-90	5:45p
Attr :	BACK2DIR.BAT	20	01-24-91	9:01a
Selected C	BACKTALK.EXE	1,265	06-09-91	7:01p
Number: 1	BACKTEST.BAT	201	03-28-91	12:23p
Size : 435	BACKUP .BAT	714	06-26-91	3:00a
Directory	BACKUP .EXE	36,092	04-09-91	5:00a
Name : WORK	BAG .CPP	2,034	05-04-90	1:00a
Size : 209,783	BAG .H	2,504	05-04-90	1:00a
Files : 8	BANNER .COM	1,684	01-03-85	12:11p
Disk	BATCH .BAT	70	09-25-88	11:37p
Name : DOS 5	BATCH .WP	2,415	11-16-90	11:30a
Size : 42,366,976	BATPROC .EXE	51,790	10-11-90	4:48p
Avail : 16,257,024	BCD .H	7,822	05-04-90	1:00a
Files : 880	BELCH .ASM	888	05-27-90	12:15p
Dirs : 52	BELCH .COM	111	05-27-90	12:15p
	BGIDEMO .C	40,195	05-04-90	1:00a
	BGIDEMO .EXE	74,011	12-19-90	9:04a
	BGIDEMO .OBJ	28,636	12-19-90	9:02a
	BGIOBJ .EXE	11,400	05-04-90	1:00a
	BIOS .H	728	05-04-90	1:00a
	BIP .EXE	6,692	12-01-90	12:43p
	BLANKS .COM	86	07-27-88	9:50p
	BLECH	26,946	07-04-91	12:37p
	BOOT .BAT	94	04-05-91	5:21p
	BOX .C	1,073	07-11-91	1:15p

13-5 The All File display option.

primarily as a menu system or are configuring it for a first- time user, this option is the least intimidating choice.

Any changes you make in the Shell's display are retained when you quit. Running the Shell again will activate the same display options you've chosen previously. (The options are kept in a file named DOSSHELL.INI.)

File display options The File-list area shows files listed by their name, size, and date. All files are shown, except for those files marked by DOS as System or Hidden. (These files have special attributes set, which is the subject of chapter 18.)

You can modify the way files are displayed, how they're sorted, and which files are shown. This is done by selecting the File Display Options item from the Options menu. Doing so shows you the File Display Options dialog box, as illustrated in Fig. 13-6.

The Name field controls which files are displayed. In Fig. 13-6, *.* means all files, although you can enter your own wildcards.

The two items Display hidden/system files and Descending order are check boxes. Click on them using the mouse or press Tab and then the Spacebar to select them. When an X appears between the brackets, that item is on; no X indicates it's off.

The text Sort by is positioned above five radio buttons. Only one radio button can be on at a time (like the old-time car radios). The on item indicates the sorting order that the files will take in the File-list area. The DiskOrder item indicates that the items will be presented in the order they were placed on the disk (the same order the DIR command lists them). Press Enter to accept the settings or Escape to cancel.

```
┌─────────────── File Display Options ───────────────┐
│                                                     │
│  Name:     [*.*·········]                           │
│                                                     │
│                                   Sort by:          │
│                                                     │
│  [ ] Display hidden/system files  (·) Name          │
│                                   ( ) Extension     │
│                                   ( ) Date          │
│  [ ] Descending order             ( ) Size          │
│                                   ( ) DiskOrder     │
│                                                     │
│        ▐  OK  ▌   ┌ Cancel ┐    ▐  Help  ▌          │
└─────────────────────────────────────────────────────┘
```

13-6 The File Display Options dialog box.

Confirmation In the Shell, you can manipulate files much more easily than with DOS. To avoid the pang of accidentally deleting hundreds of files, the Shell has certain confirmation options. The confirmation itself comes in the form of dialog boxes and prompt you with are you sure? type of messages.

To control confirmation in the Shell, pull down the Options menu and select the first item, Confirmation. The Confirmation dialog box appears, as shown in Fig. 13-7. You can control confirmation on three items: when deleting files and directories; when replacing files (such as with a copy or move command), and on mouse operations.

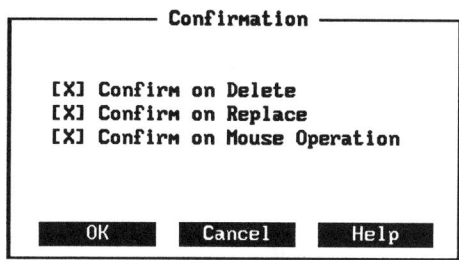

13-7 The Confirmation dialog box.

Set the confirmation according to your tastes. Experienced users probably will want everything toggled off. If you're new to the Shell, keep it all on for now.

Getting help

Anywhere you are in the Shell, at any time, you can press F1 to get help. If you're in the middle of a dialog box or at some prompt, pressing F1 displays helpful information about that item or a list of things you can do at a prompt. This is how the Shell's context-sensitive help works.

More advanced and categorical help is available from the Help menu item, the last item on the menu bar. If you drop down that menu (click on it using the mouse or press Alt-H), you'll see six menu items that deal with help:

- Index
- Keyboard

- Shell Basics
- Commands
- Procedures
- Using Help

Each item covers an individual category of help. The Index item gives you an overview of help; Using Help tells you how the help system works.

You can mess around in the Help system for a while if you like. Use the Tab key to highlight an item or button, then press Enter to view the information. Press Esc to cancel Help and return to the Shell.

Getting out

To exit the Shell and return to DOS you have several options. F3 is the compatibility key, used with the old DOS 4 Shell program. Alt−F4 is the close window keyboard command used in Microsoft Windows. Select the Exit command from the File menu. This is done using the mouse by pulling down the File menu (clicking on it), then clicking on the Exit item. From the keyboard, you can press Alt−F, then X to select Exit.

Using the Shell

The Shell is a handy tool for working with files, especially groups of oddly-related files, files in several subdirectories, and other instances DOS doesn't handle too well from the command line. The following sections describe some basic activities, plus a few hints on working with files and directories in the Shell.

General navigation hints

If you have a mouse, the Shell is a dream to use. Just move the mouse pointer about on the screen, point, and click at what you want. If you've used a mouse with any other application, everything will be a snap.

If you're limited to the keyboard for input (and I never believed I'd write a line like that in a book about DOS), the keys listed in Table 13-1 can be used for general navigation.

Changing areas If you've selected a Shell display configuration with two or more areas, you can move between them by pressing the Tab key. The currently active area will have its area title bar highlighted. Watch for this; the commands you type affect the highlighted area. It's too easy to look at the area you want when another area is highlighted.

The Shift-Tab key combination moves backwards through the areas on the screen.

Note that the Tree menu is accessible only when the drive list at the top of the screen, Directory-tree area, or File-list area is highlighted. If you're in the Program-list area, the Tree menu disappears. The menu contents change from area to area as well.

Looking at the menus The menus in the Shell are activated by pressing the Alt key plus the first letter of the menu you want to drop down. You also can press the F10 key or Alt by itself to wake up the menus, then use the arrow keys and Enter to drop down a specific menu.

Table 13-1   General navigation keys.

Key	Function
Enter	Select the highlighted item
Tab	Move through selections or areas on the screen
Shift – Tab	Move backwards through selections or areas
Arrow keys	Highlight the next/previous item in a list
PgUp/PgDn	Move up or down several items in a list
Home	Move to the start of a list of items
End	Move to the end of a list of items
Letter	Move to the item in a list starting with the letter

Some menu items are dimmed and cannot be selected. Which items are dimmed depends upon whether that item already is active or cannot be accessed from your current location in the program. Try changing areas or selecting another option from the menu to undim an item.

Menu items with a dot, or bullet, by them are currently active. For example, if you turn on the Shell's task swapping abilities, the Enable Task Swapper menu item (in the Options menu) will have a dot by it.

Working the tree

The Directory-tree area contains a graphic description of the directories on a given drive. The drive in question is highlighted in the drive icon list above the Directory-tree area.

To select a new drive, press the Ctrl key plus the letter of the drive in question. You also can click on it using the mouse, or press the Tab key until that area is highlighted, then use the left or right arrow keys to select the drive and press Enter. (The Ctrl key combination works best for me—even though I have a mouse.)

The tree structure shown in the Directory-tree area reflects the root directory and all its subdirectories, shown cascading down the area. You can use the cursor keys to highlight a particular directory: Up arrow, Down arrow, PgUp, PgDn, Home, or End. Each of these keys will move you through the tree. As you move, the files in each highlighted directory will appear in the File-list window.

Some directories have a plus sign in them, which indicates that the directory contains subdirectories. To view the subdirectories, highlight that directory and press the plus key on your keyboard or click on the directory with your mouse. The plus sign in the directory then will change to a minus sign.

To collapse a subdirectory tree, highlight the parent directory and press the minus key on your keyboard or click on the directory with the mouse. (To avoid this happening when you don't want it, click the mouse on the directory's name instead of its icon.)

You also can expand and collapse the tree using the Tree menu at the top of the screen, as shown in Fig. 13-8. The Expand One Level and Collapse Branch menu items correspond to the plus and minus keys on your keyboard. The asterisk key is used to expand an entire branch of subdirectories. Ctrl – * expands your entire tree structure.

```
┌────────┐
│  Tree  │
├─────────────────────────┐
│ Expand One Level  +     │
│ Expand Branch     *     │      13-8   The Tree menu.
│ Expand All        Ctrl+*│
│ Collapse Branch   -     │
└─────────────────────────┘
```

When the Directory-tree area is active, some of the commands in the File menu affect it. The commands are: Delete, which deletes the highlighted directory; Rename, which renames the directory; and Create Directory, which lets you make a new directory. What's missing in the Shell and is present in other shells is the ability to prune and graft. That is, cut, copy, and paste sections of a directory tree. Programs that do this are covered in the next chapter.

Deleting a directory   The Delete command removes a directory, similar to the RD command. Just like RD, you must remove all files and subdirectories from the directory you want to delete. Once that's done, highlight the directory, then choose Delete from the File menu. Zap! The directory is gone.

Renaming a directory   The Rename command is the only way under DOS to rename a directory (other shells also offer this feature). Highlight the directory you want to rename, then select Rename from the File menu. In the Rename Directory dialog box, enter the new name for your subdirectory. Remember that directories use the same naming rules as files (refer to chapter 5, "Subdirectories and paths").

Making a directory   To create a new subdirectory, highlight a directory in the Directory-tree area. Pull down the File menu and select Create Directory. The Create Directory dialog box will appear. Into it, you type the name of the new subdirectory to create in the highlighted directory. Note that you must have the new directory's parent directory highlighted. You cannot create a new directory using a pathname with this option.

If you're working with the Shell and notice some of your changes didn't appear in the Directory-tree area, you can force the Shell to reread the disk and re-create the tree. This is done by pressing the F5 key or by selecting the Refresh item in the View menu.

Working with files

The core of using the Directory-tree and File-list areas is file manipulation. This is the same as is done under DOS (and covered in chapter 4), although it really is more convenient to use a visual shell than a command line.

To work with files, you must make sure the File-list area is active. This is done by clicking in it with the mouse or by pressing the Tab key until that area's title bar is highlighted.

If you need to change directories, use the Directory-tree area. If your work involves working with files between two disks or directories, it's a good idea to change your view. I suggest the Dual File Lists option in the View menu. (If you choose that option, remember to use the Tab key or click in the proper window before you use any commands. Make sure the file you want to work with is highlighted before copying, renaming, or deleting it.)

To work with any file, it first must be highlighted. Once done, you can manipulate it using one of several items in the File menu.

Copying a file   To copy a file, highlight it, then select Copy from the File menu or press F8. A Copy File dialog box appears. Enter the new destination for the file in the To input box, just as you would type a target name for the file with the COPY command.

You also can copy a file by clicking on it with the mouse and dragging it to a new location while pressing the Ctrl key. The mouse pointer changes to a file icon or a dot (in the text mode) when you do so. If it changes to an international no symbol or a double exclamation point in the text mode, then you cannot copy the file to that location.

Deleting a file   To delete a file, highlight it and press the Del key. You also can select the Delete item from the File menu. A confirmation dialog box appears, asking if you're certain you want to delete the file. Press Enter for *yes* and Cancel for *no* or click on the appropriate button in the dialog box.

Renaming a file   To rename a file, highlight it and select the Rename item from the File menu. Type the new name into the Rename File dialog box.

Moving a file   The Shell also allows you to move files, which cannot be done under DOS with one command. (Basically, a move is a copy followed by a delete of the original.) With the file to move selected, pull down the File menu and choose the Move item or press the F7 key. Into the Move File dialog box, type the new location for the file. This works exactly like the Copy command, although the original is deleted.

If you have a mouse, you can drag the file to be moved to its new location. Unlike the Copy command with the mouse, don't press the Ctrl key while you drag; dragging the file alone is enough to move it.

Viewing a file   To peek into a file and see its contents, highlight it, then select View from the File menu or press F9. You'll see the file's contents displayed in either text or hexadecimal (binary) format, as shown in Fig. 13-9. You can toggle between the text or hex display by pressing F9.

Note that you cannot edit a file while you're viewing it. This is possible in other shells, but not the DOS Shell. To return to the File-list area, press Esc (there is no mouse equivalent).

Printing a file   You can print a text file from the Shell by selecting the file, then choosing Print from the File menu. However, you first need to run the DOS print utility, PRINT. You must run PRINT before you enter the DOS Shell program. Personally, I don't recommend running PRINT. If you really want to print files from the Shell, however, you'll have to.

Changing a file's attributes   Every file has associated with it a number of attributes. This book covers the subject in chapter 18. For now, note that the Change Attributes item in the File menu is used to change a file's attributes.

For most file operations, there will be some type of confirmation dialog box to appear. If this annoys you, turn Confirmation off using the Confirmation item under the Options menu.

```
 Display  View  Help
[   To view file's content use PgUp or PgDn or ↑ or ↓.           ]

EGA.INI/VGA.INI
***************** WARNING *********************
This file may contain lines with more than 256
characters. Some editors will truncate or split
these lines. If you are not sure whether your
editor can handle long lines, exit now without
saving the file.

Note: The editor which is invoked by the
      MS-DOS 5.0 EDIT command can be used
      to edit this file.
***************** NOTE ***********************
Everything up to the first left square bracket
character is considered a comment.
************************************************
[savestate]
screenmode = graphics
resolution = medium2
startup = filemanager
filemanagermode = shared
   ↵=PageDown  Esc=Cancel  F9=Hex/ASCII                    12:39p
```

13-9 A file viewed in the Shell.

Selecting files

It's possible to work with groups of files in the Shell. This is better than using DOS's wild-cards, because you can select files individually—even in more than one directory—and then work with them as one large group.

To select an individual file in the File-list window, you move the cursor around using the arrow keys or click on the filename using the mouse. That selects one file.

Selecting a block of files To select a range of files, use the Shift key in addition to the arrow keys. This selects a contiguous block of files (similar to selecting a block of text in the Editor). With the mouse, select a file by clicking on it, then extend that selection by Shift-clicking the mouse.

As an example, to select all files in a directory, press the Home key, then press Shift—End. The Home key moves the highlight to the first file; Shift—End selects all files from that file to the last file in the list. You also can select all the files by choosing the Select All item from the File menu or by pressing Ctrl—/.

Selecting noncontiguous groups Selecting a block of files is fine if the files you want are all listed next to each other. When they aren't, you can select individual files one at a time.

Using the keyboard, you must activate the Add function to select individual files. To do this, press the Shift—F8 key. The word ADD appears by the current time on the status bar. Now, you can use the Spacebar to toggle selections in the File-list area. Use the arrow keys to move, then toggle a selection on or off with the Spacebar.

Using the mouse, press the Ctrl key while you're clicking an entry. This works whether you have ADD toggled on or not.

Note that toggling ADD off with Shift – F8 again deselects your files, as does clicking the mouse in the File-list area without the Ctrl key down. If this happens, you'll need to manually reselect the files.

Selecting across directories If you change directories all your files automatically will deselect themselves. However, you can retain your selections by choosing the Select Across Directories item in the Options menu. When this item is on (it has a dot by it), the Shell remembers your selections as you move from directory to directory.

If you find this too cumbersome or if you have lots of files to select, then consider changing the view in the Shell to the All Files option. It's easier to find and select files with that presentation.

Working with groups of files Once you have a block of files selected, the Copy, Delete, Rename, and Move commands work on the group. This is powerful stuff, so be careful. (Also, you'll notice the mouse icon changes to a stack of files when you drag them around.)

When renaming files, you enter the new name individually for each file. Note that you cannot use wildcards when renaming files in this manner.

Deselecting files After you've manipulated a group of files, they become deselected. You also can deselect files by pressing Ctrl – \ or by choosing the Deselect All item from the File menu.

Working with programs

The Shell gives you access to all your DOS programs and even to DOS itself. For example, the text on the status bar, Shift + F9 = Command Prompt, actually takes you out to DOS, where you can use the command line as you always have.

When you press Shift – F9, you actually are running the program COMMAND .COM, which just starts up another command processor for DOS—like any other program you run. There, you can use DOS commands, run programs, or whatever. Thanks to the Shell's smarts, you'll have almost the full complement of memory in which to do all your command line duties.

To return to the Shell, type EXIT at the DOS prompt.

The Run menu item Within the Shell, you can run individual commands just as you would at the DOS prompt, by selecting the Run item from the File menu. After doing so, you'll see a dialog box where you can enter a DOS command line. Whatever you type will be run just as if you entered that command or program name at a DOS prompt. Unlike Shift – F9, however, you'll be plopped back into the Shell immediately when the command is done.

Opening files The Open item under the File menu is used to run a program highlighted in the File-list area. This item works only for COM, EXE, and BAT files. Once selected, choose Open and the file is run. When the program quits, you'll be asked to press any key to return to the Shell.

You also can open a file by selecting it and pressing Enter or by double clicking on it with the mouse.

Associating files with programs   When you try to open a non-program file, the Shell will beep at you. That is, unless you've associated that file with some application on your PC. The associated application then will be opened and that file will be fed into it, all automatically.

The Shell already comes with some associated files. For example, all files ending in TXT are associated with EDIT.COM, the Editor. If you select any file with a TXT extension and open it, the Shell will load the Editor and place the highlighted file into it for editing.

You can associate files in one of two ways. First, for document files, locate a document in the File-list window, one that has some type of common filename extension. (Associating files works only with files that have extensions.) Then, pull down the File menu and choose Associate. In the dialog box, enter the name of the program with which you want files with a given extension to be associated. If the program isn't on the path, be sure to enter its full pathname.

The second way to associate files is by selecting the COM, EXE or BAT file that runs the program. Then, choose Associate from the File menu. Into the box, you can type a list of extensions with which the Shell will associate the program to filenames. This actually is the smarter way to associate files. The Shell remembers the program's location and will run it directly.

It's best to associate your batch files that run programs rather than the programs themselves. Batch files can change directories and setup applications, which often is required when you run programs from within a Shell.

All the files you associate are remembered by the Shell. It puts special information in the DOSSHELL.INI file, which is retained each time you quit the Shell. By associating files, you bring programs and their files closer together in the Shell. However, there's a way to make this even more convenient by using the Shell as a menu system.

Building menus with the Shell

In addition to being a useful place to organize and maintain files and your tree structure, the Shell also has a mini-menu system. It's not as fancy-looking as the menu system designed in the previous chapter. However, it offers some password security and a few other technomarvels that make it a practical DOS menu system.

The menu system itself appears on the bottom of the screen, the Program-list area in the standard Shell display (see Fig. 13-1). You can make this area fill the entire screen if you like by selecting the Program List item from the View menu.

In the Program-list area, you'll see a list of programs to run, plus submenus or groups. The first level you see is Main, which also is the title of the area. Program items are shown as plain text. Groups appear in brackets.

To select a program item, highlight it and press Enter or select Open from the File menu. Using the mouse, you can double click on an item to open it. For example, to run a copy of the Command Prompt, select that item in the Program-list area and press Enter. (To return to the Shell, type EXIT.)

The Disk Utilities group is a submenu created for you when the Shell was first installed. Highlight it and press Enter or double click on it with the mouse. The title of the

Program-list area changes to reflect the new group. The programs in that group will be visible on the screen (as shown in Fig. 13-10).

You can select any program from the group by highlighting it and opening it. To return to the top group, select the Main item.

The Shell is entirely customizable when it comes to these menus. You can add your own programs and groups and organize them as you see fit. The following sections describe the details.

```
┌─────────────────────────── Disk Utilities ───────────────────────────┐
│ → [Main]                                                            [↑]│
│   Disk Copy                                                            │
│   Backup Fixed Disk                                                    │
│   Restore Fixed Disk                                                   │
│   Quick Format                                                         │
│   Format                                                               │
│   Undelete                                                          [↓]│
├────────────────────────────────────────────────────────────────────────┤
│ F10=Actions   Shift+F9=Command Prompt                          1:15p  │
└──────────────────────────────────────────────────────────────────────┘
```

13-10   The Disk Utilities group in the Shell.

Creating a program group

Suppose you wanted to create a word processing group, into which you'd put your word processing and related programs. This works just like creating a submenu in a batch file menu system, although the Shell is more slick about it.

To create a new group, you first must make sure the Program-list area is selected. Use the Tab key or click in the area with your mouse. Once that area is highlighted, the File menu will have a few new items, one of which is New. Select it. You'll see the New Program Object dialog box displayed, as shown in Fig. 13-11.

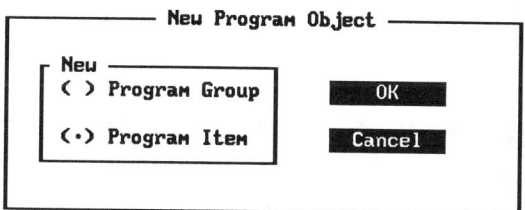

13-11   The New Program Object dialog box.

To add a new program group, select the Program Group radio button and press Enter. The Add Group dialog box then appears, as shown in Fig. 13-12. You need to enter a title for the group (a name), plus optionally some help text and a password.

The Title is the name of the group, as it will appear in the Program-list area. You can enter up to 23 characters, including spaces. Be descriptive. For example, Word Processing.

If you don't want to enter help text and a password, press Enter and the program group is created. It appears in the current group (such as Main) in the Program-list area.

```
┌──────────── Add Group ────────────┐
│                                    │
│  Required                          │
│                                    │
│    Title . . . .   [·················]│
│                                    │
│  Optional                          │
│                                    │
│    Help Text . .   [·················]│
│                                    │
│    Password  . .   [···········]   │
│                                    │
│                                    │
│   ▓▓▓ OK ▓▓▓   ▓▓ Cancel ▓▓   ▓▓ Help ▓▓│
│                                    │
└────────────────────────────────────┘
```

13-12   The Add Group dialog box.

If you do want to enter help text, press Tab to move into that box. You can enter up to 255 characters of help text, describing the program group. For example, for the Word Processing group, you could type The Word Processing group contains: ^m * WordPerfect ^ m * EDIT^m * GrandView. The ^m character is used to force a new line, although the displayed help text will appear wrapped in the dialog box without it.

If you want to enter a password, type it into the Password box. You can enter up to 20 characters including spaces. Note that the password is case sensitive; you must match upper- and lowercase when typing it in. The Shell won't allow access to the group without a password. You can't even change or modify the group without the password!

Once you're done, press Enter. The new group appears in the Program-list area, its title in brackets:

[Word Processing]

To select the group, highlight it. If you want to view help, press the F1 key with the group highlighted. You might see something like the Help dialog box shown in Fig. 13-13. If no help is available, you'll see a dialog box telling you that there is no help available.

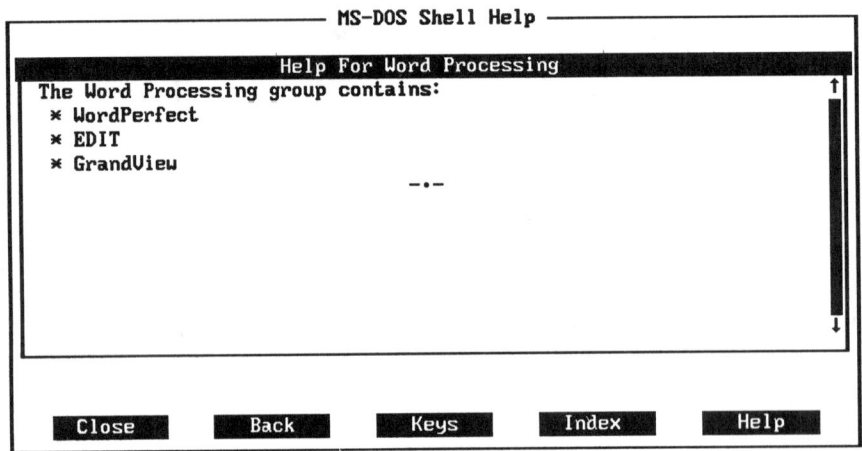

13-13   The help screen for the Word Processing group.

To access a program group, highlight it and press Enter. The group's files and any additional subgroups then will be displayed in the Program-list area.

If the group is password-protected, you'll be prompted for the password when you try to access the group (Fig. 13-14). Enter the password, matching upper- and lowercase letters and typing in any symbols or other characters. Only after entering the proper password will you be allowed access to the program group (or allowed to edit or change the group).

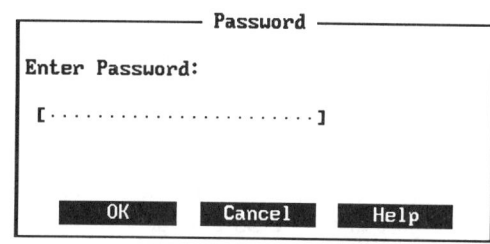

13-14 The Shell asks for an access password.

Changing a program group

To change a program group, highlight it and select the Properties item from the File menu. If the group is password-protected, you'll be prompted to enter the password before you can examine or modify the group.

You modify the group with the an input screen similar to the one used to create it (Fig. 13-12). You can edit or examine entries, fix the help message, or add or remove a password. Press Enter when you're done or Esc to cancel any changes.

If you want to delete a group, highlight it and press the Del key. You'll be asked if that's what you really want to do. Press Enter to delete the group or Esc to cancel.

If you want to change the location of a program group, select that group in Program-list area. Next, choose the Reorder item from the File menu. Now, you can use the arrow keys to position the group where you want it. Press Enter and the group will be moved to where the highlight bar is on your screen.

Creating a menu item

Individual programs are placed into the program groups in the same manner that the groups are created. Make sure you're in the group in which you want to place the program. Highlight that group and press enter. If the group's name is on the area's title bar, then you already are there.

Select the New item from the File menu. The New Program Object dialog box will be displayed (Fig. 13-11). Make sure Program Item is selected and press Enter. The Add Program dialog box will be displayed, as shown in Fig. 13-15. Into this box, you'll enter information about the programs in the group, which is why the box is so detailed.

Remember to press Tab to move from item to item. Pressing Enter ends the setup process.

The Program Title is where you enter the name of the application, as it will appear in the Program-list area: for example, WordPerfect 5.1, GrandView, or Microsoft Word. You can enter up to 23 characters for your description.

```
┌─────────────────── Add Program ───────────────────┐
│                                                     │
│ Program Title . . . . [·····························]│
│                                                     │
│ Commands  . . . . . . [·····························]│
│                                                     │
│ Startup Directory . . [·····························]│
│                                                     │
│ Application Shortcut Key    [······················]│
│                                                     │
│ [X] Pause after exit    Password . .  [············]│
│                                                     │
│    ███ OK ███    ███ Cancel ███   ███ Help ███   ███ Advanced... ███ │
└─────────────────────────────────────────────────────┘
```

13-15 The Add Program dialog box.

The Commands box is where you type the name of the program or the command that carries out the program. If the program is on the search path, then you need only enter its name—just like the DOS prompt. Otherwise, enter a full pathname. For example: C:\ WP51\WP.EXE.

If the program to run has options, you can specify them using replaceable parameters %1 through %9. The Shell will prompt the user to enter the parameters, up to nine of them.

Multiple commands also can be placed in the Commands input box. Each command must be separated by a semicolon. The total length of the line can be no more than 255 characters.

Note that if you specify a batch file you should use the CALL command before it. For example, if you're setting up and running a program like PC Paintbrush in the Shell, use a command such as CALL C:\PBRUSH\PAINT.BAT.

The Startup Directory item is where you specify a directory in which you want the program to look for files. The Shell will log to that directory and attempt to run your program from there.

The Application Shortcut Key box is used for the Shell's task swapping function. It allows you to quickly swap programs in and out by pressing the shortcut key. Note that an application must be active; you cannot start a program by pressing the shortcut key. (This item will be touched upon again later in this chapter.)

The Password input box allows you to assign a password to the program. This works identically to the Password item for a program group (see the previous section); you cannot run the program—or modify its entry in the Program-list area—unless you know the password.

If you want the Shell to display a press any key message after the program runs, toggle on the Pause after exit item.

At this point, the group is created; you can press Enter to finish. The new program item will appear in the current group. To run it (and test it), highlight it and press Enter. (The Advanced options are covered later, in the section on task swapping.)

Changing a program item

Once a program item has been created, you can change its order in the list, copy it to another program group, or delete it. General editing of the program's entry is handled by selecting the Properties item from the File menu.

To change a program's order in the list, highlight the program in question, then select the Reorder item from the File menu. Use the cursor keys to move the highlight bar to the item's new position. Press Enter.

To copy a program item to another group, first select it. Next, drop down the File menu and choose the Copy item. The status bar displays the message: Display the group to copy to, then press F2. Press ESC to cancel.

Use the highlight bar to negotiate the Program-list area's different menus and submenus. When you're at the proper location, press F2. The program item then will be added to the end of that list.

Note that the Copy command retains the original program item's entry. To delete it or delete any program item, highlight it and press the Del key or select Delete from the File menu. A confirmation dialog box will ask you if you want to delete the item. Press Enter to do so.

Note that deleting a program item from the group does not remove that program from your disk. It's removed only as an entry in the Program-list area (and the DOSSHELL.INI file).

Task switching

Here are the spoils of victory. The Shell's task swapping is what every DOS owner can truly use. However, what is task swapping?

Each time you use an application, you must run it either from the DOS prompt or in some type of shell. When you're done, you return to the DOS prompt or shell, then run another program. If you're working on a large project that involves interaction between many applications, this can be a bother.

What task swapping does is to keep the programs you use open and ready for work. When you want to run another program, the current program is saved to disk by the task swapper, in this case DOS Shell. The new program you run then is loaded into memory. To switch back and forth, you press special key commands. That way you can move from one application to another without quitting between them.

Note that task swapping isn't the same as multitasking. In multitasking, all applications continue to run whether or not you currently are using them. In the Shell, task swapping allows you to run only one application at a time, although you can have several on the back burner, ready for your attention at the touch of a key. Because the programs you're not using are inactive, you cannot format disks or use online communications with task swapping. When the program is swapped out, the formatting or communicating would stop (or possibly crash the system).

Configuring the Shell for task swapping

The Shell normally doesn't pop up ready for task swapping; you must activate it. This is done by selecting the Enable Task Swapper item from the Options menu.

When task swapping is on, the Active Task List area becomes visible on the screen, as seen in Fig. 13-16. The Enable Task Swapper menu item also will have a dot by it, indicating that task swapping is on and ready to go.

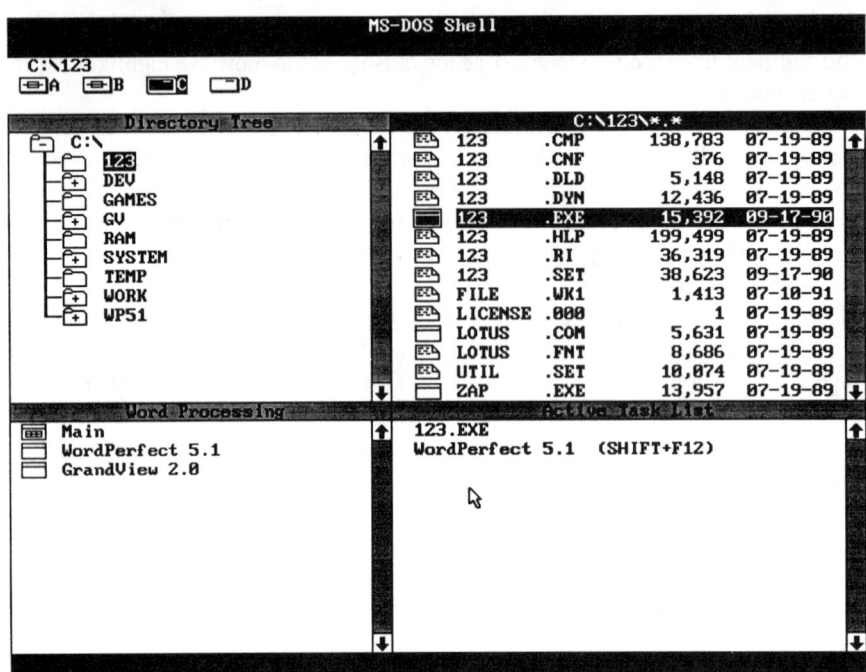

13-16 The Active Task List area.

The Active Task List area shows up only when the Program/File List and Program List screen configuration options are shown. The Program/File List view is shown in Fig. 13-16. The Program List display shows two areas, the Program-list on one side and the Active Task List on the other.

You deactivate task swapping by selecting the Enable Task Swapper item a second time. Note that you should quit all active applications before doing this.

Running applications

You can start applications under the task swapper just as you would at any time in the Shell. You can either select the program from the Program-list area's menu or from the File-list area. However, you cannot swap from a program launched from the Run item in the File menu, nor can you swap between anything you run while you've shelled to DOS with Shift−F9. However, this shouldn't prove limiting.

When you start the program, it runs as it always does. Because task swapping is active, however, you can go back to the Shell without quitting. To return to the Shell, press either of these key combinations:

Ctrl−Esc
Alt−Esc

These key commands return you to the Shell, swapping the application in memory out to disk. In a way, you're quitting the program without quitting. The Shell essentially freezes the program in time. Everything stays as it was until you return to that application, at which time it starts running again.

Once back in the Shell, you'll see your program listed in the Active Task List area (Fig. 13-16). You can select another program to start or work in the Shell for a while. To return to a running application, highlight it in the Active Task List area and press Enter.

If you want to cycle through the programs you already have running, press the Alt-Tab key. This keystroke switches you from one program in the Active Task List to another without stopping back at the Shell between them.

That's about all there is to using the Shell's task swapper. Provided you have enough disk space, everything will work smoothly.

Remember to quit your applications to remove them from the Active Task List. You must quit all active applications before quitting the Shell and returning to DOS. The Shell's task swapper option will stay active until you select it again from the Options menu. So, next time you run the Shell, you'll have access to its powerful swapping abilities.

Setting advanced options

When you create a program item for the Program-list area, there is a button at the bottom of the Add Program dialog box titled Advanced. This button is used to configure applications specifically for use with task swapping.

You can select the Advanced button as you're creating a new program item or when you edit a program item (by highlighting it and selecting Properties from the File menu). The Advanced dialog box appears in Fig. 13-17.

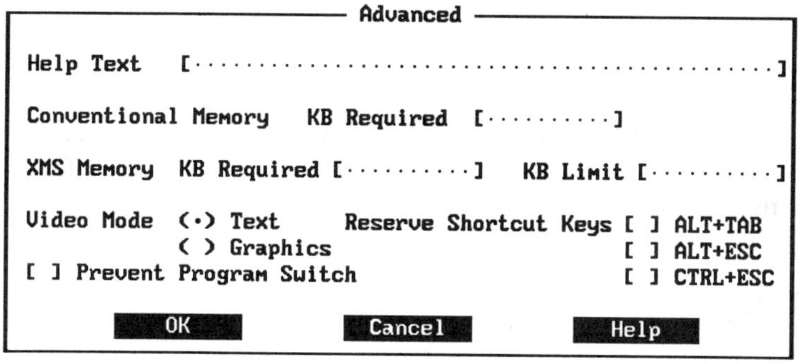
Advanced
Help Text [...]
Conventional Memory KB Required [..........]
XMS Memory KB Required [..........] KB Limit [..........]
Video Mode (•) Text
( ) Graphics
Reserve Shortcut Keys [ ] ALT+TAB
[ ] ALT+ESC
[ ] CTRL+ESC
[ ] Prevent Program Switch
OK
Cancel
Help

13-17 The advanced options for a program item.

The Help Text box allows you to enter up to 255 characters of helpful text, which will be displayed if the user presses F1 when the program item is highlighted. The rules for input here are the same as they are for creating a program group (covered earlier in this chapter).

There are three memory questions in the Advanced dialog box: Conventional Memory KB required; XMS Memory KB Required; and XMS Memory KB Limit.

For conventional memory, enter the amount of memory, in kilobytes, that the program needs to run. Normally, the Shell gives it the full 640K. However, to make task swapping more efficient, you can limit the amount. (Refer to the application's packaging or index for information on minimum memory requirements.)

The XMS, or extended, memory is trickier. Specify an amount only if your application uses extended memory, such as Lotus 1-2-3 version 3. Refer to the application's documentation for exact amounts of memory required, then enter that value in the XMS Required box.

The XMS limit is used to exclude some or all of XMS memory for an application. This is simple memory management; the Shell doesn't want two applications to grab the same XMS memory. Not specifying anything restricts access to no XMS memory; specifying a value of − 1 gives the application all of XMS memory. Any other value is the limit, the maximum amount of XMS memory it can have.

The Video Mode item should be set to Text. Only specify Graphics if you're using the Shell's task swapping and having trouble moving between text and graphics modes.

The Reserve Shortcut Keys item lets your program have control over the task swappers Ctrl−Esc, Alt−Esc, and Alt−Tab key combinations. For example, if your word processor uses Ctrl−Esc to insert the escape character into the text, then you could mark off that item, allowing the program to use that special key combination.

The Prevent Program Switch item is used to block out task swapping for that program. When the program runs, it owns the machine and you cannot swap it out; only by quitting the application can you get back to the Shell. You should always check this option for any telecommunications programs you use.

One item that affects task swapping that's not on the Advanced dialog box is the Application Shortcut Key. This key appears on the initial dialog box you use to create a program item or when editing an existing program item. (Refer to Fig. 13-15.) The shortcut key is created by pressing the Shift, Ctrl, or Alt key plus another key combination, such as Ctrl−F12. That key then becomes the application's hot key and appears next to the application's name in the Active Task List area.

Note that you might not see your key press in the input box right away. After you exit the dialog box and reopen it you'll see the key combination displayed.

You use an application's shortcut key to quickly swap to it when task swapping is active. Only when the task swapper has been engaged does it have any effect; you cannot use the shortcut key to initially load the application.

Summary

Whoa! Not too bad for the makers of DOS, eh?

The DOS Shell adds an interesting new dimension to DOS, giving you file management, menu, and task swapping abilities all, basically, for free. It's not the best shell, but it is interesting and well-featured—certainly more than you could do alone with batch files.

The DOS Shell isn't the last word in DOS shells. Since it's existed (starting with DOS 4.0), third-party developers have made better and more powerful shells to compete with it. That's the subject of the following chapter, "Other DOS Shells." I won't go into each shell as deeply as I did the DOS Shell, primarily because other books will give you more detailed tutorials on these products. However, you'll get a good idea of what's out there and what's possible when you step way beyond the world of batch files and into professional shell programs.

14

Other DOS Shells

Ever since DOS reared its ugly head in 1981, enterprising individuals have sought to improve upon its looks. These improvements vary in approach. Some are menu systems to replace DOS, very similar to what you've worked on in the past few chapters; others use graphics to hide DOS's homely face. However, all of the applications have one goal in mind: making the computer easier to use and the hard disk easier to manage.

This chapter looks at two different, but related, topics. First, you'll learn about menu generators. These are programs to help you create fancy menu systems in a fraction of the time it would take on your own, giving you that professional look without sacrificing your input. Second, you'll discover how DOS shells, those programs that insulate you from the harsh operating system, can revolutionize your use of DOS.

Ordering from the menu

In this part of the book, you've learned how to use the techniques of batch file programming to develop a professional-looking menu system for accessing programs and executing DOS commands. As you can imagine, menu-driven hard disk systems, especially ones using function keys, are quick, efficient, and easy to use. Also, fully menu-driven systems loaded automatically at system startup help keep some users out of DOS.

Menu-driven hard disk management systems can range from the simple to the elaborate. A well-designed menu system includes attractive and eye-catching menu screens, submenus, and help screens to assist the user working with the system. A menu system designed to be used by novice computer users should contain one or more DOS submenus to automate those few DOS commands the user will need.

So far, the advantages of menu-driven systems have been highlighted without consideration for their main disadvantage: they're time-consuming to create—especially in light of the DOS Shell, which can be configured as a formidable menu system, complete with it's own handy help screens.

There are solutions, however. Even beyond the DOS Shell. Among the solutions covered here is a simple menu generator system, provided by the Menu Maker program included on this book's companion diskette. This is followed by a general discussion of menu and shell systems available for DOS. These are all alternatives to both batch file programmed menus as well as the DOS Shell program.

The Menu Maker menu generator

A *menu generator* is a program capable of making, or generating, a menu system for you. You tell it what you want, and it designs the menus or gives you the tools to easily do it yourself. Additionally, these programs come with options and features that make them more powerful than anything you could do with a batch file on a good day.

There are several menu generator programs available. I've written one myself, which I call Menu Maker. Previous editions of this book discussed the program AUTOMENU and offered it on the companion diskette. AUTOMENU now is a full-blown professional program. Other, similar programs exist, each of them offering slightly different ways to create the menu plus an array of features.

In general, menu generators help you draw menu screens, set up batch files for changing directories and loading programs, and have their own keyboard reconfiguration schemes. Many menu generator programs also include password security, which allows you to restrict access to programs or data.

Menu generator programs take much of the drudgery out of setting up menu-driven systems. Menu Maker, for example, is so easy to use, you might wonder why you had to wade through the last three chapters on batch file programming. Actually, any menu generator assumes some understanding of DOS and batch files. While you don't have to write the batch file programs yourself, you actually are programming when you use any menu generator. (Keep in mind that batch files, along with ANSI.SYS, do things the way you want to do them; menu generators usually have some prearranged paradigm for doing things.)

About Menu Maker

Menu Maker is an extremely silly and simple little program. It produces the same basic screens and does the same duties as you've been practicing with your batch files. Its advantage lies in its simplicity, primarily because it's so easy to set up a menu system with it. Its disadvantage is that it's not fool-proof in the same way as batch files aren't (with regard to canceling and peeking at passwords; details later). However, the Menu Maker is a quick system to learn and use (Fig. 14-1).

Menu Maker uses two files: MCREATE, which creates the menu files, and MENU, which displays the menu files created by MCREATE. A third program, VIEW, can be used to display textual information. Everything uses color, which makes the menu interesting for color systems.

The menu file contains a menu title plus up to 15 items for the menu panel. Each menu item has a command key, text to be displayed in the menu, plus the DOS command line that runs that menu item. Optional items include a password plus text to display before the command line is run.

There is no direct submenu ability in the Menu Maker; to run a submenu, you simply create a second menu file and run it from within the first menu. On return, the first menu will run automatically.

```
                    Main Menu

                Press Escape to quit

┌──────────────────────────────────────────────┐
│                                                │
│          1: Word Processing                    │
│                                                │
│          2: Database Management                │
│                                                │
│          3: Lotus 1-2-3                        │
│                                                │
│          4: DOS Commands                       │
│                                                │
│          5: Help!                              │
│                                                │
│                                                │
│                                                │
│              Your choice:                      │
│                                                │
└──────────────────────────────────────────────┘
```

14-1   A sample file created with the Menu Maker.

Each menu file is only about 2.5K in size, which means your entire menu system could easily fit on a floppy diskette (if you wanted it to). Note, however, that you need the MENU program to display and run each menu file. Also, the menu files are basically text, which means anyone can type them out on the screen to see command names and passwords (which is why this is like batch file menus—not very security conscious).

To exit a menu panel, you simply press the Esc key. There's no help system directly available, although you could add a help menu item and have it display useful information. The VIEW utility included with Menu Maker will help out with this. All- in-all, it's really a brainless system.

Building a menu with MCREATE

If you have the companion diskette handy, change to the MENU directory and follow along with the instructions here. (The tutorial creates a generic menu system, so it should work on all DOS computers.) This section assumes you've placed the menu files, MCREATE.EXE, MENU.EXE and VIEW.EXE, into a MENU subdirectory on drive C. If you've placed your program files in a different subdirectory, be sure to specify the proper location for the following examples.

To build a new menu, type MCREATE at the DOS prompt:

C: \ MENU > MCREATE

If you don't enter a menu filename, you'll be prompted for one on the next screen. (If the file specified exists, then it will be loaded for editing, which is covered later in this chapter.) For this sample, use the name MAIN; type MAIN when prompted.

Next you'll be asked to enter three title lines, as seen in Fig. 14-2. Each line can be up

```
Menu Creator
Written by Dan Gookin
Copyright (C) 1990 TAB Books

You use this utility to build or edit menu files as explained
in my book, "Hard Disk Management With DOS 5"

Now using menu filename: MENU

You can now enter up to three title lines for this menu.
Each line can be up to 40 charcters long:

1. Main title [40]   : Main Menu
2. Sub-title [40]    : (DOS command sample only)
3. Third title [40]  : Press Escape to quit
```

14-2 Entering the menu title.

to forty characters long, which is indicated in the brackets. The lines will be centered above the menu panel you'll create next.

For the three title items, enter the following (as shown in Fig. 14-2):

Main Menu
(DOS command sample only)
Press Escape to quit

The main title should always label the menu panel, describing what it does. Examples would be Main menu, Word Processing Menu, etc. You can use the subtitle to narrow down the field. For thc third title, I always put helpful information. In the Menu Maker system, pressing Esc ends the menu, so I always put that note there.

After entering the third title and pressing any key, you'll be prompted to enter the first menu item. All menu files must have one item, with a potential for up to 15 items in each panel. There are five individual elements associated with each menu item:

- The command letter (one character)
- The menu item's name (up to 40 characters)
- The DOS command to be executed (up to 63 characters)
- An optional password (up to 8 characters)
- An optional message (up to 40 characters)

Note that the command letter is one character. Be smart with this option. Although there are 15 possible menu items, if you use numbers you'll only have room for items 1 through 9. You also can specify letters, which is what this example uses.

For the first menu item, enter the following information for the five elements:

1. 1
2. Run the DOS Editor
3. EDIT
4. (leave blank)
5. (leave blank)

This is menu item one, given the command key 1. The menu title is Run the DOS Editor and the DOS command is EDIT. (Note that this only works if the Editor is on your search path; otherwise specify a full pathname.) Elements 4 and 5 are left blank.

After you type in the elements, you'll be asked if you want to enter another. Press Y to enter the second menu item. Type in the following:

1. 2
2. The DIR command
3. DIR /O/L/P
4. DIR
5. (leave blank)

This item simply runs the DIR command with the /O, /L, and /P switches. Note that a password is entered. For the sake of memorization, it's just DIR again. Element 5 is again left blank.

When you're asked if you want to enter another, press Y again. For the third menu item, type in the following:

1. 3
2. DOS command line (shell)
3. (leave blank)
4. (leave blank)
5. Type EXIT to return to the menu

Elements 3 and 4 are blank. When element 3, the command line, is blank, the Menu Maker will simply shell out to DOS, running a copy of COMMAND.COM. The password element is left blank, but element 5, the optional message, is specified. The line you type will be displayed when you select this menu item and it runs the command line or, in this case, shells to DOS.

Type N when you're asked if you want to enter another. The next screen you'll see is the Menu Maker menu, which is shown in Fig. 14-3. There are six options on this menu

```
Menu Creator
Written by Dan Gookin
Copyright (C) 1990 TAB Books

You use this utility to build or edit menu files as explained
in my book, "Hard Disk Management With DOS 5"

Now using menu filename: MAIN

                         Menu Maker Menu
                         ==================

                    (A)dd items
                    (C)hange items
                    (D)elete an item
                    (N)ew title items
                    (S)ave menu file
                    (V)iew menu items
                    (E)xit

                    Choice:
```

14-3 The Menu Maker menu.

that let you examine or change the menu file you've just created; the seventh option quits MCREATE and returns you to DOS. To select an option, type its first letter. For example, type V to view the menu items you've created so far.

If you type V, you'll see the menu items in order. The screen displays Now showing item 1/3, telling you the current item you're looking at as well as the total number of items in the menu file. Press N to look at the next item, P to look at the previous item, or E to return to the menu.

Using option C, you can change the elements in any menu item. For now, everything should be correct, so type E to exit to DOS. (The menu file already has been saved, unless you've changed something, in which case MCREATE will prompt you to save the file.)

Running the menu

To run your menu file, you need the MENU program, following it with the name of the menu file you've created. To see what you've done so far, type the following at the DOS prompt:

C:\MENU> MENU MAIN

MAIN is the name of the menu file you've just created. Figure 14-4 shows you what you should see next—the menu panel you just created using MCREATE. Note how the menu titles are centered at the top of the screen.

```
                      Main Menu
               (DOS command sample only)
                  Press Escape to quit

┌─────────────────────────────────────────────────────┐
│                                                       │
│       1: Run the DOS Editor                           │
│                                                       │
│       2: The DIR command                              │
│                                                       │
│       3: DOS command line (shell)                     │
│                                                       │
│                                                       │
│                                                       │
│                                                       │
│                                                       │
│                                                       │
│       Your choice:                                    │
│                                                       │
└─────────────────────────────────────────────────────┘
```

14-4 The main menu file displayed by the MENU program.

The command keys are displayed followed by a colon and the menu item's name. A prompt appears at the bottom of the screen where you can enter the menu item's command keys.

Press 1 to run the DOS Editor. The menu panel disappears and, providing you entered the proper pathname for EDIT, you'll be in the DOS Editor.

Quit the Editor. A prompt appears at the bottom of the screen:

```
Press any key to return to the menu . . .
```

After pressing the Spacebar (or any key), you're returned to your menu panel.

Now select item 2, the DIR command. This time, you're prompted for a password. The text Password appears at the bottom of the screen, awaiting an entry. The password is DIR; you can type it in upper- or lowercase. Note that whatever you type is displayed as an asterisk on the screen.

Once you've entered the proper password, the DIR command is run. Then, you're returned to the menu.

The final item, 3, runs COMMAND.COM. Select that item. You'll see something like the following:

```
Type EXIT to return to the menu


Microsoft(R) MS-DOS(R) Version 5.00
 (C)Copyright Microsoft Corp. 1981-1991.

C: \ MENU >
```

The message text you entered (as element 5 of this item) is displayed as soon as you run the program. This option isn't practical for running programs, such as the DOS Editor; you won't have time to see it. For running COMMAND.COM or a batch file, however, it can come in handy. (If you do specify a batch file, be sure to use the CALL command before the batch file's name.)

Type EXIT at the system prompt, then press any key to return to the menu.

Once you're back in the menu panel you can press the Escape key to quit, just as it says at the top of the screen.

When you quit the menu, you're returned to DOS. This is rather inconvenient in some cases, especially when you'd like to run shutdown programs, backup files, or do general maintenance after the user quits the menu.

The solution is to run the MENU program from a batch file, such as RUNMENU .BAT. For example:

```
1:   @ECHO OFF
2:   REM RUNMENU batch file
3:   C:
4:   CD \ MENU
5:   MENU MAIN
6:   REM Do other stuff here
7:   REM After the menu quits
```

The previous batch file, RUNMENU.BAT, runs the menu system (line 5). It also has the advantage of letting you include some DOS commands to run after the MENU program quits.

Editing a menu file

Menu files are edited using MCREATE. You specify the menu file after MCREATE at the DOS prompt or type the name of the menu file when prompted after the program starts. For example:

C: \ MENU > MCREATE MAIN

loads the previously created menu into MCREATE for editing. (Because the menu file isn't a plain text file, this is the only way you can modify or change it.) You'll see the Menu Maker menu displayed, as shown in Fig. 14-3. Here, you can add new menu items, delete menu items, or change existing menu items or the menu title. The V option, discussed previously, can be used to view each menu item's elements.

If you wanted to add a new menu item, press A. The item is always added at the end of the list; therefore, with the MAIN menu file, the new item would be item 4. You enter each element for the item just as you did when the menu was first created.

To change a menu item, type C. MCREATE will tell you how many menu items there are and ask you which one you want to edit. Type in the number of that item, say 2 for item 2, and press Enter. The item's elements will be displayed as shown in Fig. 14-5. To replace an item, type its element number, 1 through 5. Pressing 0 returns to the menu.

For example, if you wanted to remove the password (see Fig. 14-5), press 4. You'll be prompted to enter a new password. Just press Enter. Item 4 will be replaced with nothing; therefore, there will be no password.

```
Menu Creator
Written by Dan Gookin
Copyright (C) 1990 TAB Books

You use this utility to build or edit menu files as explained
in my book, "Hard Disk Management With DOS 5"

Now using menu filename: MAIN

There are 4 menu items, which do you want to edit? 2

Settings for menu item 2:

    1. The command letter : 2
    2. The menu item name : The DIR command
    3. DOS  command  line : DIR /o/1/p
    4. Optional  password : dir
    5. Optional  message  :

Change which one, 0 to Exit?
```
14-5 The menu item elements are changed.

A word of warning here: in keeping with the simple-minded nature of this program, you cannot edit the elements. Pressing a number replaces the menu item—even if you press Esc to cancel. The only way to recover from the faux pas is to press 0 to exit, then E to exit from MCREATE. When asked if you want to quit without saving the file, press Y for *yes*. (Maybe someday the programmer will get off his butt and fix this, eh?)

To delete a menu item, press D, then enter the number of the item you want to remove. The item will be displayed before it's deleted. You can press Y or N to delete the item or cancel, respectively.

To change the menu item's titles, press N from the main menu. This method also is the only way you have of viewing the titles. As with the change option, note that you don't edit the titles; the new titles replace the old.

To save all your edits, press S. Then, you can press E to exit back to DOS and run the MENU program again to test your menu panel.

If you try to exit without saving your changes or modifications, you'll be prompted:

You have made changes without saving, quit anyway (Y/N) ?

Press Y to quit without saving, or press N to return to the menu. Then, you can press S to save and exit again.

Submenus

When you're designing a menu system using the Menu Maker, you probably will want some submenus. This is easy to do using the program, although it's not that obvious.

For example, suppose you've created a menu named WORDS for your word processing program. To make that a submenu of the MAIN menu file, you'd need to add a menu item with the following elements in it:

1. W
2. Word Processing
3. MENU WORDS
4. (leave blank)
5. (leave blank)

W is the item's command key and Word Processing is the name of the menu item. The DOS command to run is the MENU program again, which loads the WORDS menu file. When the user selects W from the menu, it will have the same appearance as going to a submenu, when you're just running the MENU program again. You might want to make the title of the WORDS menu file reflect its submenu status:

Word Processing Submenu

Press Esc to return to the Main Menu

When the user presses Esc, the first menu panel will be redisplayed; just as if you'd returned from any other program run from the menu.

Many submenu levels could be created this way. However, there is a limit. Presently, the MENU program takes up 77K of memory. A submenu system would subtract 154K of memory from what you had when you started. So, don't go too many levels deep.

Adding color

Any text displayed in a menu panel can have a dash of color added to it. This text includes the menu titles and all item descriptions. The color is added via a series of special slash-

Table 14-1 Color switches for use in the Menu Maker and Viewer.

Switch	Affect on the text
/U	Blue text/underline on monochrome systems
/B	Bright white text
/R	Red text
/C	Cyan text
/G	Green text
/P	Purple text
/T	Tan text
/Y	Bright yellow text
/W	Flashing pink text (the Warning! switch)
/I	Reversed text
/N	Normal text (white)

commands, which are all listed in Table 14-1. These switches also are used in text files displayed using the file viewer, which is covered in the next section.

These switches change the color or attribute of the text displayed after them. The text remains in that color until you specify another color switch or until the end of the line in MCREATE. (In the viewer, the color stays active until you turn it off.)

For example, if you have a color monitor, modify the MAIN menu file and change the titles to the following:

1. /yMain Menu
2. /g(DOS command sample only)
3. Press /rEscape/n to quit

The main title will be yellow, the subtitle green, and, in the third title, the word Escape will be red. Note how the /n switch turns off the color in line 3. Also, the switches can be entered as upper- or lowercase.

Because the program uses the slash character to identify a color/attribute switch, you must type three slashes to display a single slash on the screen: True///False displays as True/False.

Using the file viewer with a menu

The Menu Maker system comes with a companion utility, the file viewer, VIEW. VIEW is used to display specially-formatted files, primarily those containing the color/attribute switches listed in Table 14-1. Its format is the same as the menu panel display (Fig. 14-6), which makes the VIEW utility ideal for displaying helpful information and blending in well with the menu system.

Here is the format for the file viewer command:

VIEW *filename*

```
                   Formatted File Viewer

                     Press ESC to exit
┌─────────────────────────────────────────────────────────────┐
│  File Viewer                                                  │
│                                                               │
│  The File Viewer is a special text file viewer that incorporates │
│  color text into its screens.  It's used on this diskette to tell you │
│  about the various utilities included.  And you can use it yourself, │
│  along with a text editor, to create interesting documentation files. │
│                                                               │
│  The format for the File Viewer is:                           │
│                                                               │
│  VIEW filename                                                │
│                                                               │
│  Where filename is the name of a specially formatted text file. │
│                                                               │
│  The text file can be no more than 500 lines long (which is a pretty │
│  silly length, when you think about it).  Each line in the text file │
│  must end in a carriage return, and be no more than 70 or so  │
│  characters long.                                             │
│                                                               │
│  Color is added to the text file using special slash-switches.  There │
└─────────────────────────────────────────────────────────────┘
```

14-6 The file viewer is displaying the VIEWME file on the companion diskette.

filename must be specified. It can be any text file, although text files containing the special formatting codes will appear more exciting (see Table 14-1 for a list of the codes).

The viewer ignores all Tabs and any other ASCII characters with a value less than 32 (the space), except for the carriage return and line feed. Extended ASCII characters in the file also will not be displayed. For the best effect, each line in the file shouldn't be more than 76 characters long—preferably less.

As an example of using the file viewer, the file VIEWME on the companion diskette can be examined to see how the various color effects are used. At the DOS prompt you would type:

    VIEW VIEWME

You also should take a look at this file using the TYPE command with the MORE filter. It should show you how the color commands are used to create the interesting effects.

VIEW comes in handy for use in batch files, especially when displaying information. Normally, to exit the viewer, you just press Esc. However, you also can press the function keys, F1 through F10. When you do so, VIEW returns to DOS with a return code (ERRORLEVEL) value from 1 to 10, corresponding to the function key pressed.

As an example, consider the following batch file:

    1: @ECHO OFF
    2: VIEW INSTRUCT
    3: IF ERRORLEVEL 10 GOTO END
    4: IF ERRORLEVEL 2 GOTO SHOWMORE
    5: IF ERRORLEVEL 1 GOTO DEMO
    6: REM Escape pressed, ERRORLEVEL = 0
    7: GOTO END

```
 8:  :DEMO
 9:  REM Demo program run here
10:  DEMO
11:  GOTO END
12:  :SHOWMORE
13:  VIEW SHOWMORE
14:  :END (The batch file is done; return to the menu)
```

The file viewed, INSTRUCT, in line 2, could contain instructions for the user: Press F10 to end, F2 to see more information, F1 for a demo. These ERRORLEVEL values are tested in lines 3 through 5—in reverse order (see chapter 10). The batch file branches to the proper label depending on which key was pressed, which gives you more control over the viewer.

A summary of the ERRORLEVEL return codes produced by the VIEW program is listed in Table 14-2. Note that VIEW requires a file to view, so when you specify it as a command line in MCREATE remember both items.

Table 14-2 The VIEW program's return codes.

Return code/ ERRORLEVEL	Meaning
0	Escape pressed to end the viewer
1	F1 pressed
2	F2 pressed
.	.
.	.
.	.
10	F10 pressed
11	A filename wasn't specified, nothing to view
12	The filename specified couldn't be found or couldn't be opened; VIEW wasn't run

Time logging

One thing some DOS shells are good at is keeping track of the time you spend doing certain activities on your PC. However, you can do that just as easily yourself. All you need is a few DOS tricks and some batch files. Combine that with the Menu Maker and you have an almost professional system.

A batch file program for tracking usage

There are a number of reasons to log computer usage. For example, if you're billing a client by the hour, you need some form of record keeping a bit more convenient than writing the times down (computers are useful for these things, after all). If a number of people from different departments are using the same machine, having the computer keep track of its usage is reliable and efficient—especially because it can be done automatically.

Because PCs have internal clocks, keeping track of computer time is as easy as looking at the computer's clock—assuming that the clock is set properly every day or that the computer has an internal battery-powered clock. To create a usage log, the current time from the computer's clock needs to be written, or redirected, to a disk file.

The best way to keep track of the time you use your computer would be by redirecting the clock's output into a file. For example, a file called LOG could be placed into a special subdirectory. Time-stamping utilities could be used with redirected output to append the time to the log file. The ECHO command could be used to append strings. In the end, you could have a file containing date, time, and project information. This can all be done painlessly using only the tools DOS gives you.

Getting the current date and time

The DOS DATE and TIME commands are used to display the current date and time. However, they also prompt for a new date and time, which means you have to jump through a few hoops to get them to display their date and time strings by themselves. It's possible, but tricky. To pull off this stunt, you need the FIND filter and both input and output redirection.

Creating the ENTER file   For input redirection, you need to create a file on disk that contains only a solitary carriage return—a press of the Enter key. To create that file, use COPY CON: as follows:

1. Make sure you're in your BATCH file subdirectory, the MENU subdirectory, or some other subdirectory in which you put your handy files.
2. Type COPY CON:ENTER and press Enter. ENTER is the name of the file you're creating.
3. Press Enter again to put a single Enter keystroke into the file.
4. Press F6 to end input. This keystroke produces the Ctrl–Z, end-of-file character.
5. Press Enter. This keystroke sends the Ctrl–Z character to DOS.

The file ENTER now has been created. Remember it's location.

Getting the DATE and TIME   Both the DATE and TIME commands display the current date or time, then ask you to enter a new date or time. If you don't want to, just press Enter. Run both DATE and TIME now at your system prompt to get an idea for it.

To make these commands run automatically, use input redirection to supply the Enter keystroke. Try both of the following:

```
DATE < ENTER
TIME < ENTER
```

Specify a full path to the ENTER file if it's not in the current directory.

See how the date and time are both displayed without any input from you? This is the second step to having DOS supply you with the current date and time.

Use the FIND filter The FIND filter displays any lines in a file containing matching text. In both the DATE and TIME commands, the word Current is used on the line with the date or time. Carefully type in the following commands:

```
DATE <ENTER ¦ FIND "Current"
TIME <ENTER ¦ FIND "Current"
```

You're getting closer. Each command now displays only a single line, one which shows you the current date or the current time.

Use output redirection to the LOG file To complete the task, you need to redirect the output of these long and complex commands to your LOG file on disk. That's how you log the current date and time and complete DOS's klutzy but effective attempt at time logging.

Consider the following batch file snippet:

```
 1:  @ECHO OFF
 2:  ECHO Working on the spreadsheet > > C: \ WORK \ LOGFILE
 3:  ECHO Starting the job: > > C: \ WORK \ LOGFILE
 4:  DATE < C: \ BATCH \ ENTER ¦ FIND "Current" > > C: \ WORK \ LOGFILE
 5:  TIME < C: \ BATCH \ ENTER ¦ FIND "Current" > > C: \ WORK \ LOGFILE
 6:  123
 7:  ECHO Finished job: > > C: \ WORK \ LOGFILE
 8:  DATE < C: \ BATCH \ ENTER ¦ FIND "Current" > > C: \ WORK \ LOGFILE
 9:  TIME < C: \ BATCH \ ENTER ¦ FIND "Current" > > C: \ WORK \ LOGFILE
10:  REM Return to menu program here...
```

This batch file could be called using the Menu Maker system. Note the ECHO commands and time and date stamping redirected to the file C: \ WORK \ LOGFILE. That file contains the day's work log. Other batch files on the system probably work the same way, keeping track of activity on this PC (basically, you just change line 6—the program to run).

Also, you should note how the ENTER file is called by its pathname in lines 4, 5, 8, and 9. Always specify a full pathname when you know the exact location of a file.

An easier way

Output redirection...the pipe and FIND filter...input redirection...the ENTER file....ugh. An easier way to do time stamping is with custom utilities that simply spit out the date and time. You still will have to redirect output to a log file, but you won't need to mess with complex DOS syntax.

Three utility programs are included on the companion diskette that will painlessly display the current time. They are STIME.COM, ETIME.COM, and TSTAMP.COM. The first two do roughly the same thing: display the current day, date, and time. The only difference is STIME displays Start Time and ETIME displays End Time before the date and time is displayed. TSTAMP.COM simply displays the time and date without the leading text.

Typing STIME at the command prompt displays something like the following (depending on the date and time):

```
    Start Time = Friday, February 18th, 1994 @ 11:14 am
```
ETIME displays:
```
    End Time = Friday, February 18th, 1994 @ 11:15 pm
```

The program TSTAMP.COM is a little more simplistic. Typing TSTAMP at the command prompt displays the current time and date as follows:

```
    23:16:32 02/18/94
```

All three of these programs read the computer's internal clock and display the current time to the screen. By themselves, these programs are relatively pointless. Yet, by redirecting their output to a LOG file, it's possible to track the time you use on your computer system. Consider the following:

```
    STIME > > C: \ WORK \ LOGFILE
```

Doesn't that read a lot better than the TIME and DATE commands in the previous section—both of which were required to do essentially the same thing.

Consider this batch file tidbit:

```
ECHO Word processing... > > \ WORK \ LOGFILE
STIME > > \ WORK \ LOGFILE
WP
ETIME > > \ WORK \ LOGFILE
```

The ECHO command appends Word processing.. to the \ WORK \ LOGFILE file. After that, the current time is appended to \ WORK \ LOGFILE by the STIME > > command. Finally, the word processing program, WP, is run.

After the word processing is done, control returns to the batch file and the current time is appended to the \ WORK \ LOGFILE file via > > and the ETIME command. The \ WORK \ LOGFILE file now contains something akin to the following:

```
Word processing...
Start Time = Friday, February 18th, 1994 @ 1:14 pm
 End Time = Friday, February 18th, 1994 @ 2:45 pm
```

If a unique batch file were written for each of your programs, at the end of the day, the LOG file might contain something like this:

```
Word processing...
Start Time = Friday, February 18th, 1994 @ 1:14 pm
  End Time = Friday, February 18th, 1994 @ 2:45 pm
Updating Customer File...
Start Time = Friday, February 18th, 1994 @ 2:51 pm
  End Time = Friday, February 18th, 1994 @ 3:02 pm
Telecom to Seattle Branch...
Start Time = Friday, February 18th, 1994 @ 3:05 pm
  End Time = Friday, February 18th, 1994 @ 4:16 pm
Backing up files for today:
Start Time = Friday, February 18th, 1994 @ 4:30 pm
```

End Time = Friday, February 18th, 1994 @ 4:52 pm
System Shutdown:
17:02:26 02/18/94

The TSTAMP program was used at the end of the day to log when the system was shut down. The last program run each day might be a SHUTDOWN batch file (see chapter 16), in which case it's a good idea to save the shutdown time in the batch file.

The only disadvantage to indicating only the start and end time for each job is that it still takes a bit of brain work to figure out how much time was spent on each project. The \ WORK \ LOGFILE file helps to show when you started and when you stopped work on each project, but does not show totals. This might not be that big of a problem seeing that most time cards show only a start and stop time. However, keep in mind this machine is a computer and it's capable of next to anything.

Norton's TM utility

One commercially available program capable of keeping track of computer usage is included with the Norton Utilities series of programs. Besides displaying the current time, Norton's TM program also keeps track of elapsed time—just like a stopwatch. By specifying certain parameters, TM can give you the exact number of minutes and seconds elapsed since you've started a particular job. Up to four of these stopwatches can be used to keep track of up to four different elapsed times.

TM is not a memory-resident program. However, it uses a secret portion of low memory at address 4F0 hexadecimal called the *Intra-application Communications Area*, or *ICA*. There, TM stuffs the starting times for each of its four stopwatch functions. When you access TM to display the elapsed time, it looks at memory location 4F0 for the start time, then displays the elapsed time.

The format of the TM command is:

TM [START|STOP|COMMENT] [/C*n*][/L][/LOG][/N]

All parameters are optional with TM. When no parameters are specified, the current time is displayed, right justified on the screen:

11:08 am, Tuesday, February 26, 1991

The optional /L switch is specified to left justify the output:

11:10 am, Tuesday, February 26, 1991

When START is specified, a special stopwatch starts ticking away seconds. The /C*n* switch is used to select one of four stopwatches:

TM START /C2

This command starts stopwatch number two. If no /C*n* number is specified, stopwatch number one is used. To see the elapsed time, type TM STOP. The current date and time are displayed, followed by the elapsed time since TM START was entered:

C: \ > TM STOP

11:08 am, Tuesday, February 26, 1991
15 seconds

If the TM START command is used again, the stopwatch starts all over. Specifying /Cn with STOP displays the elapsed time for that particular stopwatch.

The COMMENT option displays a one word comment before the time string. COMMENT can be only one word. Any extra words on the same line after COMMENT are ignored:

```
TM /L STARTING
```

displays:

```
STARTING 11:10 am, Friday, February 26, 1988
```

The /N switch suppresses the listing of the current date and time. TM STOP /N displays only the elapsed time since the last TM START command was issued:

```
C \ > TM STOP /N
                    33 minutes, 15 seconds
```

The /LOG switch is used to add a carriage return/line feed combination to the end of TM's output. As with the utilities STIME, ETIME, and TSTAMP, TM's output can be redirected to a log file. If this is the case, the /LOG switch should be specified to prevent TM's output to the log file from appearing all on one line:

```
TM STOP /L/LOG >  \ WORK \ LOGFILE
```

The previous command appends something similar to the following to the LOG file:

```
11:59 am, Wednesday, February 27, 1991
38 minutes, 9 seconds
```

By using combinations of TM's switches, it would be possible to add elapsed time comments to your /USER/LOG file. Because multiple stopwatches can be used, one timer for each user of the computer can be maintained. Consider the following additions to an earlier batch file tidbit:

```
ECHO Word processing... > >  \ WORK \ LOGFILE
STIME > >  \ WORK \ LOGFILE
TM START /C1
WP
ETIME > >  \ WORK \ LOGFILE
TM STOP /C1/N/L/LOG > >  \ WORK \ LOGFILE
ECHO "--" > >  \ WORK \ LOGFILE
```

TM START /C1 starts stopwatch one. When the job is done, the TM STOP /C1/N/L/LOG produces a left-justified string displaying only the elapsed time for stopwatch one. This string is then appended to the \ WORK \ LOGFILE file. (ECHO "--" has been added to clean up the \ WORK \ LOGFILE file a bit.) At the end of the day, the \ WORK \ LOGFILE file probably will look like this:

```
Word processing...
Start Time = Friday, September 2nd, 1994 @ 1:14 pm
  End Time = Friday, September 2nd, 1994 @ 2:45 pm
1 hour, 31 minutes, 5 seconds
```

```
--
Updating Customer File...
Start Time = Friday, September 2nd, 1994 @ 2:51 pm
   End Time = Friday, September 2nd, 1994 @ 3:02 pm
1 hour, 11 minutes, 52 seconds
--
Telecom to Seattle Branch...
Start Time = Friday, September 2nd, 1994 @ 3:05 pm
   End Time = Friday, September 2nd, 1994 @ 4:16 pm
1 hour, 11 minutes, 6 seconds
--
Backing up files for today:
Start Time = Friday, September 2nd, 1994 @ 4:30 pm
   End Time = Friday, September 2nd, 1994 @ 4:52 pm
22 minutes, 16 seconds
--
System Shutdown:
17:02:26 09/03/94
```

A special time could be set at the start of each day to keep track of the total time the system was on. For example, suppose stopwatch three were used for this purpose. The elapsed time then could be appended to the \WORK\LOGFILE file as part of the SHUT-DOWN batch file program:

```
BACKUP C:\ADMIN\WP A: /S/M
ECHO "Backup completed" >> \WORK\LOGFILE
ECHO "System Shutdown:" >> \WORK\LOGFILE
TSTAMP >> \WORK\LOGFILE
ECHO "Total up-time today:" >> \WORK\LOGFILE
TM STOP /C3/N/L/LOG >> \WORK\LOGFILE
```

This bit of code works, assuming the following TM command exists in the AUTOEXEC .BAT file:

```
TM START /C3
```

Now, the total time the system was on (up-time) can be tracked. This ability might come in extremely handy for maintenance records or repair work where the average amount of time you use your computer daily is important.

DOS shells and front ends

For many years, personal computer users had to deal with their computers' operating systems much the way users on large systems did. Personal computer operating systems mimicked the command structure of minicomputers and mainframes. DOS is a descendant of an earlier microcomputer operating system, CP/M, which itself has antecedents in the larger computer world.

Operating systems that rely on single-character prompts, terse commands, and cryptic error messages couched in computerese might be fine for die-hard computing types (who read assembly language programs with their Cap'n Crunch at breakfast), but what about the rest of us?

Apple Computer recognized that not everyone is as adventurous as those bold computer pioneers who strode forward to conquer the uncharted realms of DOS with nothing but their ten digits and a box of Ding Dongs to sustain them. The Apple Macintosh revolutionized the way personal computer users looked at computing. The user interface took on an entirely different meaning. No longer did users have to struggle with DEL *.*, COPY PROG.BAS B:/V, and Invalid command or file not found. Instead, users could look at cute little pictures on the screen, play with friendly mice, and point at what they wanted.

Actually, in fairness, it should be noted that the icon-based interface popularized by the Macintosh was developed as a large computer interface by a research team at XEROX. However, the prevailing reaction to such a cutesy interface was: "Real hackers don't use icons!" So, the project languished until it was revived by the Apple Lisa in 1983. DOS users were quick to jump on the user-friendly bandwagon and a host of products designed to simplify DOS were released. Most of these fell into one of two categories: shells and front ends.

DOS shells actually sit on top of DOS. They display their own easy-to-use interface to the user. When the user indicates the command to be executed, the shell program performs the steps necessary to accomplish the command. Usually, this task involves passing parameters down to DOS and having DOS do the actual work.

Windows is an example of a DOS shell. It uses graphics and windows on the screen and employs cute icons and friendly dialog boxes to represent operating system activities such as deleting files. With the addition of an optional mouse, this user- friendly program converts your PC into something suspiciously resembling an Apple Macintosh.

DOS front ends, on the other hand, are little more than window dressing for the DOS operating system itself—menu systems like Menu Maker and anything you could create with a batch file. User commands are handled directly by DOS; only the interface has been changed to protect the naive. Such programs make DOS easier to use without disguising the basic nature of the operating system itself. Files still are represented by their filenames—extensions and all—and commands retain their DOS nomenclature (COPY still is COPY, etc.)

While the subject of windows, icons, and mice is an interesting one and something you might consider looking into, it's not really a practical way to go. For one, computers must be equipped with top notch graphics displays to make everything look good. The standard graphics adapters make those fancy windows and icons look like mush. Also, without the mouse, using those programs is even more clumsy than using DOS. Sure, it's a cute picture on the screen, but cute doesn't help getting the job done if you still have to explain details to the person using the computer.

Better than those windowing applications are commercial DOS shells. These are professional packages that lie somewhere between Menu Maker, DOS Shell, and a cumbersome shell like Windows.

New commercial shell programs come out just about every week. I once did a review for *COMPUTE!* magazine of about 15 of them. There probably are hundreds more, yet only a few stand out as being different.

Basically, the bottom line is trying to make the computer easier to use. This usually is done in a DOS shell by displaying a menu of applications or categories. Submenus usually contain the programs to run. The better DOS shells also have their own utilities, including some fancy file rescue utilities that might come in handy. Also included are methods for tracking computer usage, password protection, and the facilities for redesigning or creating your own custom menus.

For this book, I've chosen three such DOS shells that you might be interested in:

- Direct Access
- The Norton Commander
- XTree Pro Gold
- PC Shell

These shells were chosen from the crowd because of their interesting methods of accomplishing tasks, their features, their presentation, their ability for a DOS guru such as yourself to use them, their ability for a non-DOS guru to use them, and their longevity. There also is a space consideration here. So as not to be totally rude, I've listed some other shells you might want to consider at the end of this section.

Direct Access

Direct Access is one of the oldest DOS shell/menu programs around. Not only is it one of the oldest (a program named 1DIR is older), it's consistently been a best seller for years. There's a reason for this: Direct Access does the job and does it will.

Direct Access is low on the frills department. There are no graphics (although it will display your corporate logo on startup), no poppity-zippity sounds or exploding windows. You just see a menu with options, as in Fig. 14-7.

It's up to you to build your own main menu and connecting submenus, but this isn't a problem. The menu creation screens are laid out logically and are easy to follow. What you see when you're done is a clean screen, perhaps with some hint of colors (very tastefully done), and your menu options. Novices pick up on it very quickly. Direct Access is the preferred choice of many educational institution's computer labs, as well as software stores for running demos.

Direct Access also offers password protection for certain menu items, as well as time usage tracking. Password protection comes in handy on computers used by several people or on demonstration or lab computers. The usage tracking can be used on single computers used by several people to determine how much time is being used by whom and for what. On computers used by one person, usage tracking can be used for billing purposes and, for curiosity's sake, just to see what it is you do on your computer.

The only major ticket item lacking from Direct Access is any file manipulation utilities. However, this isn't a drawback. You can add any utility on your hard drive to a Direct Access submenu. Overall, it's a very competent and clean DOS shell.

Direct Access
Fifth Generation Systems
10049 N. Reiger Rd.
Baton Rouge, LA 70809
(504) 291-7221
(800) 873-4384

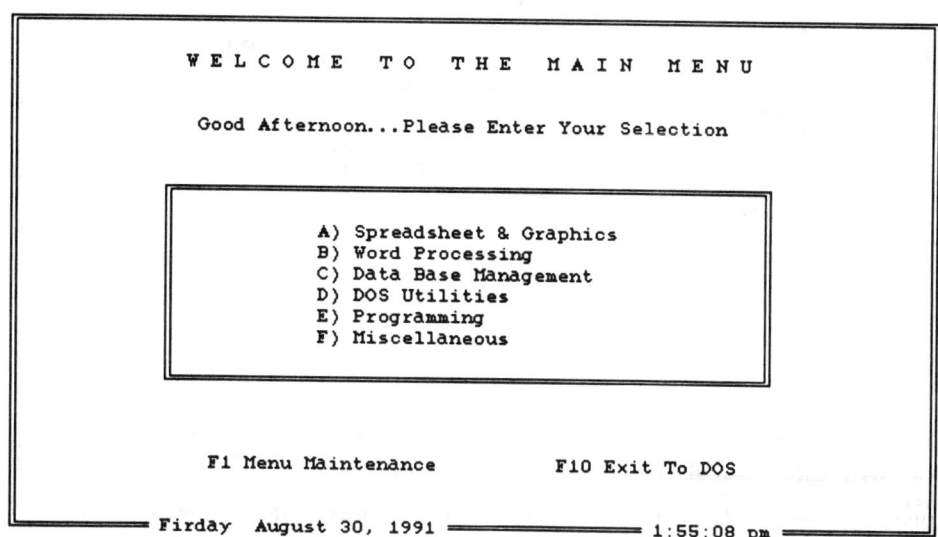

```
                  W E L C O M E   T O   T H E   M A I N   M E N U


              Good Afternoon...Please Enter Your Selection


         ┌──────────────────────────────────────────────────────┐
         │                                                        │
         │          A) Spreadsheet & Graphics                     │
         │          B) Word Processing                            │
         │          C) Data Base Management                       │
         │          D) DOS Utilities                              │
         │          E) Programming                                │
         │          F) Miscellaneous                              │
         │                                                        │
         └──────────────────────────────────────────────────────┘



              F1 Menu Maintenance            F10 Exit To DOS


     ═══════ Firday  August 30, 1991 ══════════════ 1:55:08 pm ═══
```

14-7 Direct Access's main menu uses a simple easy-to-follow design.

The Norton Commander

Where Direct Access is simple, elegant, and uncomplicated, the Norton Commander's strength lies in it's kitchen-sinkness. The program is definitely for utility lovers, as well as hard disk manipulator types. True, it's a DOS shell, but the shell part is hard to see through the fancy displays, the many commands, options, and various utilities tossed into the program. No, it's not really messy, but it's not for the DOS fainters either.

The strength of the Norton Commander lies in its jumbo jet cockpit approach to working with your hard disk. You have at your disposal the DOS prompt for entering commands, a pull-down menu system at the top of the display, a left or right (or both) panel system for displaying files or information about files, and a row of function key options at the bottom of the screen. (The screen is depicted in Fig. 14-8.) If you have a mouse, the Norton Commander will sense its presence and even let you use it to manipulate the commands.

Due to its complexities, beginning users probably will shy away from the Norton Commander. This is too bad. Yes, you really do need to read the manual to find out what's going on; however, contrary to what's popular in the field of computer manuals, this one is pretty good—even funny in spots. So, you can get out of the program whatever you like. Also, it's customizable, allowing you to install your own programs and options.

The bottom line on the Norton Commander is that it's a utility lover's DOS shell. If you're into having a handful of interesting programs, features, and options always available as you run your computer, then the Norton Commander is worth looking into—especially if you feel a simple menu program such as Direct Access doesn't do enough for you. (They actually are at opposite ends of the DOS shell spectrum.)

The Norton Commander
Symantec Corporation
10201 Torre Ave.
Cupertino, CA 95014
(408) 253-9600

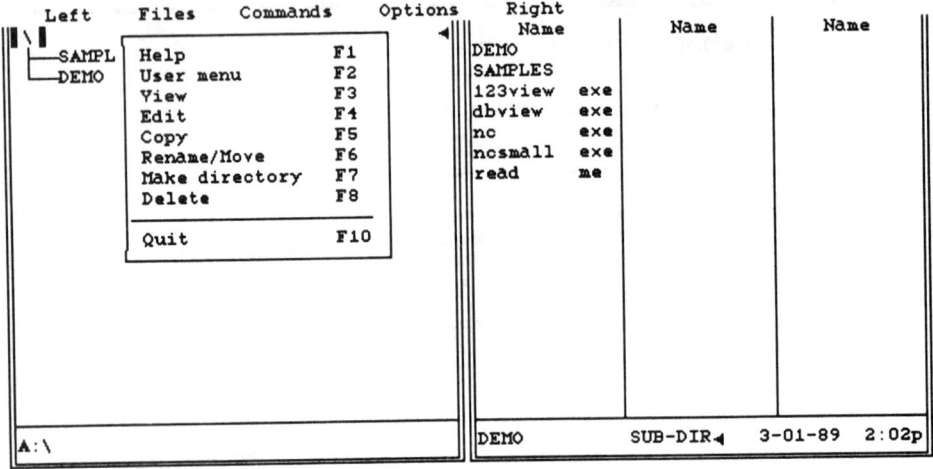

```
   Left      Files    Commands    Options     Right
                                            ◄     Name          Name            Name
  ║ \ ║
  ┌─SAMPL  ┌─────────────────────────┐ DEMO
  └─DEMO   │ Help              F1    │ SAMPLES
          │ User menu         F2    │ 123view    exe
          │ View              F3    │ dbview     exe
          │ Edit              F4    │ nc         exe
          │ Copy              F5    │ ncsmall    exe
          │ Rename/Move       F6    │ read       me
          │ Make directory    F7    │
          │ Delete            F8    │
          ├─────────────────────────┤
          │ Quit              F10   │
          └─────────────────────────┘




 A:\                                      DEMO      SUB-DIR◄   3-01-89   2:02p
```

A:\>
1Help 2User 3View 4Edit 5Copy 6RenMov 7Mkdir 8Delete 9Menu   10Quit

14-8 The Norton Commander's main screen is divided into two parts, with function keys on the bottom and a menu bar on the top.

XTree Pro Gold

It started as XTree. Then, came XTree Pro. Now, XTree Pro Gold pushes the adjective-spectacular into the outer limits of descriptiveness. XTree Pro Gold is the latest incarnation of an old shareware program, XTree, that started as a simple directory tree manipulator. Today, it still is basically a directory tree editor and file manager.

At XTree's core is the concept of pruning and grafting. As any arborealist will tell you, that's the art of cutting a tree branch and stitching it back at a different location—something DOS can't do with subdirectories. XTree did it first and everyone else copied. However, while everyone else added feature upon feature (*featuritis*), XTree stayed sleek and simple—a Swiss Army knife with one or two very good blades (Fig. 14-9).

XTree Pro Gold also has its own menu system, similar to the simple menu system found in DOS Shell. It's not the end-all to DOS shells; however, for good directory maintenance, XTree is the one to beat.

XTree Pro Gold
Executive Systems, Inc.
4330 Santa Fe Rd.
San Luis Obispo, CA 93104
(805) 541-0604

PC Tool's PC Shell

PC Tools is a big, big package. I know an author who worked on one of those 40 pound books on PC Tools. He calls it the kitchen sink of software programs. Every year, with every new version, PC Tools grows more kitchen sinkier.

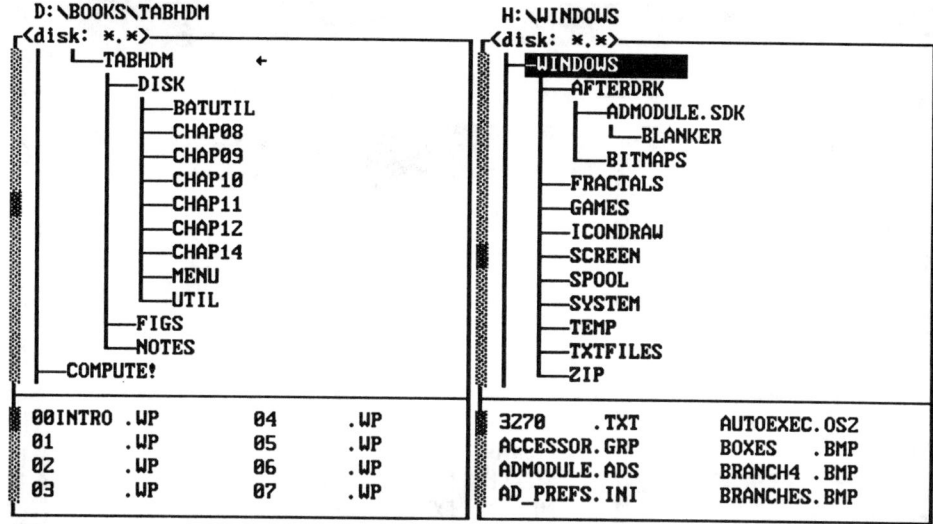

```
D:\BOOKS\TABHDM                          H:\WINDOWS
┌<disk: *.*>─────────────               ┌<disk: *.*>─────────────
      └─TABHDM         ←                     ■WINDOWS
              ┌─DISK                         ├─AFTERDRK
              ├─BATUTIL                      │    ├─ADMODULE.SDK
              ├─CHAP08                       │    └─BLANKER
              ├─CHAP09                       │    └─BITMAPS
              ├─CHAP10                       ├─FRACTALS
              ├─CHAP11                       ├─GAMES
              ├─CHAP12                       ├─ICONDRAW
              ├─CHAP14                       ├─SCREEN
              ├─MENU                         ├─SPOOL
              └─UTIL                         ├─SYSTEM
        ┌─FIGS                               ├─TEMP
        └─NOTES                              ├─TXTFILES
  ├─COMPUTE!                                 └─ZIP
─────────────────────────────          ─────────────────────────────
  00INTRO .WP      04      .WP            3270    .TXT    AUTOEXEC.OS2
  01      .WP      05      .WP            ACCESSOR.GRP    BOXES   .BMP
  02      .WP      06      .WP            ADMODULE.ADS    BRANCH4 .BMP
  03      .WP      07      .WP            AD_PREFS.INI    BRANCHES.BMP
─────────────────────────────          ─────────────────────────────
ALT DIR    Edit  File display  Graft  Hide/unhide  Log disk  Prune
COMMANDS   Release disk  Sort criteria  Tag  Untag  Wash disk  eXecute  Quit
           F2 format  F3 relog directory  F10 config
```

14-9   XTree Pro Gold's simple and intuitive display.

While it comes with a large collection of utilities, the soul of PC Tools—its command center—is a modest though fully-equipped DOS Shell called PC Shell. It's very similar to DOS Shell, although with a more interesting appearance on EGA and VGA displays (see Fig. 14-10). The tools are complete and can be overwhelming.

For basic file work, the Shell is a wonderful place to go. The menus in the advanced mode are long and complex, with many commands, but nothing's out of the way—save for directory maintenance. A submenu item, the directory maintenance actually is performed by an external program, DM.EXE (short for directory maintenance). The screen is shown in Fig. 14-11.

The left side of the screen shows interesting graphics displays, illustrating the number of files in each directory. You can prune and graft easily using this module. However, the entire program is terribly cumbersome and does eat up a lot of disk space. Personally, if you only need a front end, a shell, a menu system, or simple tree maintenance, I think some of the other options here are lighter and swifter. If the diversity attracts you, however, PC Tools is worth it at the price. (Later chapters will discuss additional features the program offers—an impressive array of stuff.)

PC Tools
Central Point Software, Inc.
15220 NW Greenbrier Pkwy., #200
Beaverton, OR 97006
(503) 690-8090

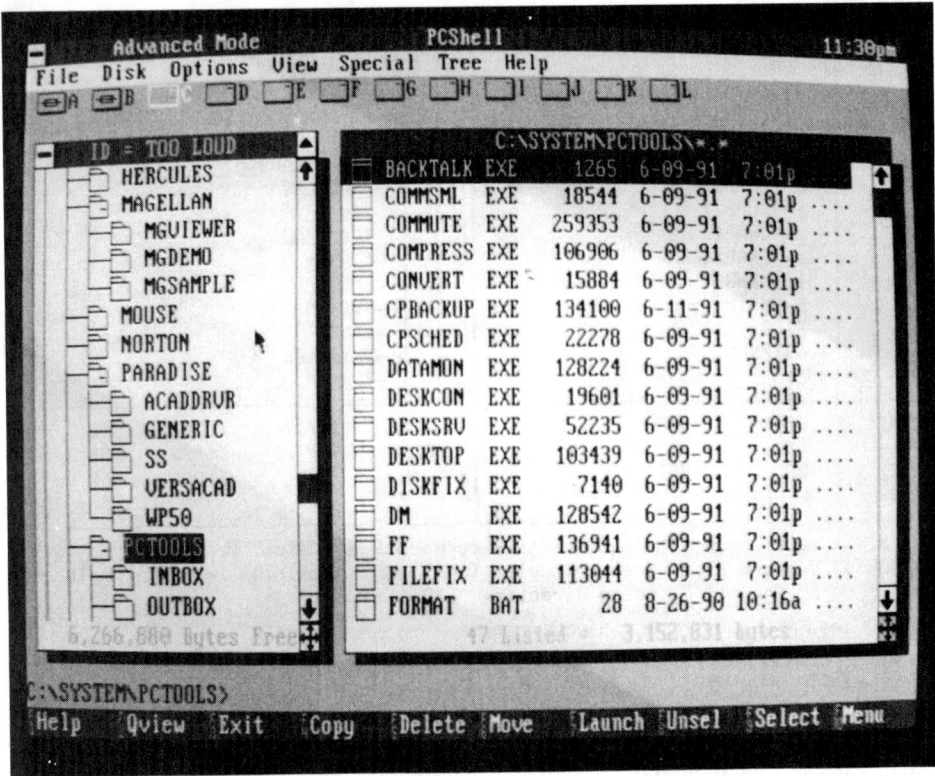

14-10   PC Tools' PS Shell program—everything you need, more than you want.

Other shells

There are more shells for DOS laying around than Neptune ever tossed up on a beach. For example, anyone who buys a Tandy computer usually walks out of the store with a copy of DeskMate. DeskMate is a fun graphic shell complete with an array of mini- programs. It's good for beginners and will help ease you into using a computer and software, but it's not enough. DeskMate only wets your appetite and, eventually, you'll need something more. Also, DeskMate is lame on disk utilities. (Note that any PC can run DeskMate, not just the Tandy line.)

In the first and second edition of this book, the AUTOMENU program was discussed at length. When the first edition came out, AUTOMENU actually was a shareware program—a try-then-buy piece of software. Today, it's a professional-level program and quite useful. If you can't find it in a store, check out the previous diskette that came with this book; it still is available as diskette #786 from the PC-SIG Library. Call them at (800) 245-6717 or (800) 222-2996 in California.

There also is a fun menu system called Menu Works from Power Systems. It comes with a manual that's the same size as a diskette, so you often will find Menu Works sitting by the cash register in your computer dealer. Frankly, I don't care for the pop-up windows and flash of the program. Some users might find it fun. If you do, buy two of them.

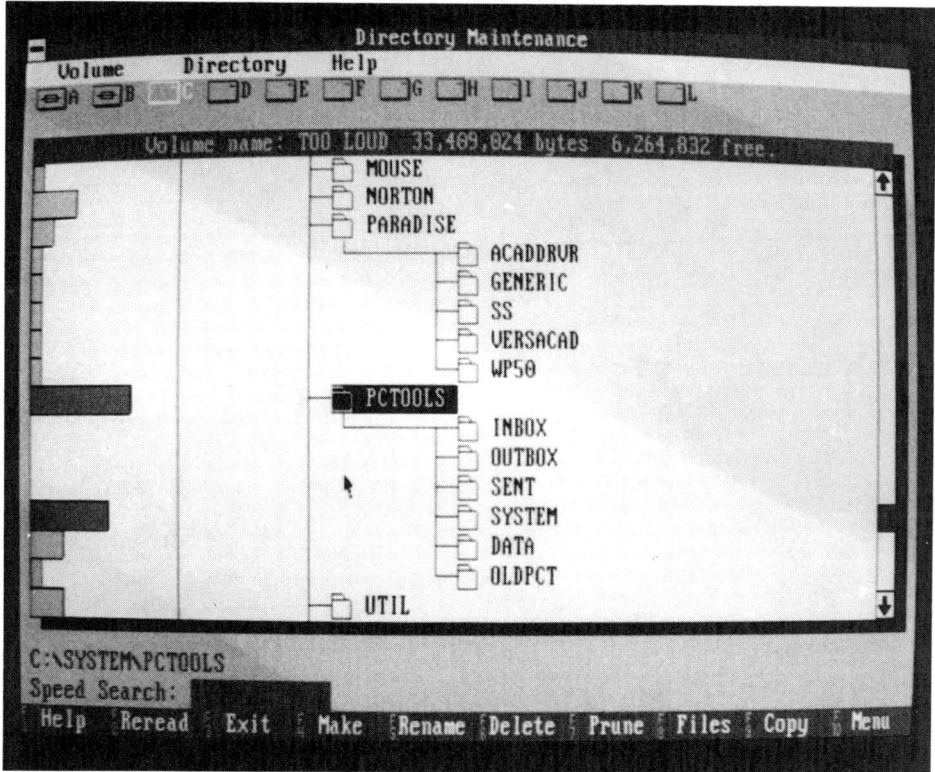

14-11 PC Tool's directory maintenance module.

Summary

This concludes this chapter, as well as part II of this book. During this chapter and the last few chapters, you've been shown several methods for creating customized professional-looking menu screens for guiding yourself and others through the intricacies of your hard disk tree structure.

Yet, there is more to hard disk management than the tasks of organizing and accessing programs and data. There are two other important issues of concern to hard disk owners. Hard disk security includes data backup security; file access security; virus detection and prevention; password protection; data encryption; and other topics related to the security of your data. Hard disk optimization is the methods and practices that will extend the performance, reliability, and life of your computer system.

Part III
Hard disk security

Hard disk security isn't all passwords, secret codes, locking out prying eyes, and tossing a bundle of backup diskettes into a fire safe every night at five o'clock. It's a software—as well as hardware—solution to maintaining the integrity of your data. After all, you've worked hard and put a lot of effort into the information stored on your system. This part of the book will show you how to sleep sounder at night knowing that information is safely kept.

Hard disk security is the subject of this part of the book. Chapter 15 covers the subject of data recovery, prevention, and cures—new material for DOS 5. Chapter 16 deals with backup and restore, basic elements of hard disk management, and file security. Chapter 17 covers password security, illegal computer access, and the trendy topic of computer viruses. Chapter 18 is about the interesting topic of hiding files and file attributes.

15

Prevention and cure

Remember that nightmarish scene from *The Marathon Man* when Sir Lawrence Olivier is torturing Dustin Hoffman with a dentist's drill? He keeps asking, "Is it safe?" Well, thanks to DOS 5, you can breathe a big sigh of relief and say, "Yes, everything is safe now." Starting with version 5.0, DOS comes with a battery of safety nets—prevention and cures—for which DOS users used to go elsewhere. Everything you need to resurrect a deleted file or unformat an accidentally formatted disk now comes with DOS. It's about time.

The best way to protect your data is to frequently back it up. Sadly, that's not always the case. Restoring data from backup diskettes can be time consuming. An easier alternative, thanks to DOS 5, is the quick-fix—two utility programs that undelete files and recover accidentally-formatted disks. The prevention is provided via a utility that remembers a lot of things DOS forgets, making data recovery quick and easy.

This chapter is about DOS's cures for missing or accidentally lost data. These cures are provided via three programs: MIRROR, UNDELETE, and UNFORMAT. Incidentally, this chapter concentrates on DOS's cures only. Other programs exist to fix the ills of DOS (the three covered here have powerful siblings in PC Tools). Some of the third-party utilities are mentioned later in this book. When they are, their data recovery prowess will be mentioned there as well.

The deep, dark truth

It finally is safe to spread the word about some little-known DOS trivia. When DOS deletes a file or reformats a disk—even a hard disk—it actually doesn't erase anything. I know, this is scandalous; however, what DOS actually does is opt for speed instead of thoroughness (if you can swallow that).

Consider the deleted file. When you use DEL or ERASE to zap a file from disk, DOS does only two things. First, it looks in the directory for the file's entry. Once found, DOS takes the first letter of the file and replaces it with character E5 hex (229 decimal). Second, DOS looks at the file's first entry in the FAT and zeros it out, to show that part of the disk as unused. The file has been deleted in DOS's eyes.

The truth is that the file only has been banished. What DOS doesn't do is go out to disk and physically rub out the file's bytes, replacing them with zeros. The file still exists—even its directory entry still is there, except for the E5 byte replacing the filename's first letter. From that directory entry stub, you can even locate the file's first entry in the FAT. Once that first entry is replaced, the rest of the FAT entries (if any) can be found and, ta-da, the file is recovered.

This is a somewhat simplistic explanation. Some verification is involved as well. For example, if a new file is created and uses space formerly occupied by the deleted file, then the first file cannot be recovered. Because of this, deleted files can be fully recovered only if the recovery is done immediately.

The story is the same for reformatted diskettes. Recall from chapter 2 that, when a previously formatted diskette is reformatted, DOS simply verifies it. The root directory, FAT, and boot sector are rewritten. The rest of the diskette, complete with all its data, subdirectories, and programs, isn't zapped. Providing that you don't write any new files to the diskette, a full recovery is possible.

By itself, DOS can quickly and effectively recover any deleted file or reformatted diskette. The commands that do this are UNDELETE and UNFORMAT. They're easy to use and are covered toward the end of this chapter.

While UNDELETE and UNFORMAT are the cures, an ounce of prevention is provided via the MIRROR command. MIRROR is a memory-resident utility that monitors deleted files and assists UNDELETE in a speedy full recovery. Additionally, MIRROR can be used to take a snapshot of a disk's boot sector, root directory, and FAT. That snapshot can be hidden elsewhere on the diskette, which then makes the UNFORMAT command work in an ultra-speedy manner for a full disk recovery.

An ounce of prevention

DOS's MIRROR command has three distinct uses:

- MIRROR can copy and record a hard disk's partition table information. That information, saved on a floppy diskette, can be used to recover the hard drive's partitions in case of a boot sector failure.

- MIRROR can take a snapshot of any disk's boot sector, FAT, and root directory. That information is stored in a file, safely tucked away elsewhere on disk. In case the disk is accidentally formatted, the information in the file MIRROR creates can be used with the UNFORMAT to fully recover the disk.

- MIRROR can go memory resident to secretly monitor all deleted files. MIRROR saves information about the files, which then can be used with the UNDELETE command to quickly and safely recover the files.

The MIRROR command is powerful stuff and is not hard to understand or use. The following sections will describe each version of the command in detail.

MIRROR, the partition saver

A hard disk actually has two boot sectors. The first is the physical disk's boot sector, which contains a partition table (created by FDISK). The partition table shows the computer which partition is the boot partition and points the boot program off in that direction. The second boot sector is a logical disk's boot sector, similar to the boot sector of a floppy diskette. That's the boot sector that actually loads DOS.

If something dreadful happens to your hard drive and the partition boot sector is zapped, then the whole hard drive is gone. You cannot reconstruct the boot sector and expect any data left on the disk to survive. For some reason it just doesn't work. However, by using the MIRROR command, you can safely record a copy of the boot sector and partition information and save it on a floppy diskette.

The format of the MIRROR command to save a hard disk's boot sector and partition information is:

MIRROR /PARTN

That single command will read the partition table (boot sector) information for all physical hard drives installed in your system. The information must be saved on a floppy disk. The file will be called PARTNSAV.FIL. (As a suggestion, put the file on a bootable floppy or any disaster recovery diskettes you might have created; see the next section.)

After entering the MIRROR /PARTN command, follow the directions on the screen. This command needs to be used only once. Only if you add a new hard drive or repartition an existing drive will you need to run MIRROR /PARTN again.

If anything ever happens to your hard drive and the partition table becomes damaged (such as you get one of those *Hard drive? What hard drive?* type of error messages), you can use the UNFORMAT command to restore the partition information. The format of the UNFORMAT command in that instance is:

UNFORMAT /PARTN

After entering this command, follow the instructions on the screen. When the partition information is restored, you might need to further use the UNFORMAT command to recover information on the diskette; refer to the UNFORMAT command covered later in this chapter. Only restore the partition if any damage has occurred.

Building a recovery diskette

If the information on your hard drive is important, you should consider building a disaster recovery diskette, as mentioned previously. This diskette would contain emergency files, utilities, and other tools to help you restore a hard drive run amok.

To create this diskette, use the FORMAT command to make it bootable:

FORMAT A: /S

The diskette should be created in drive A, seeing that it's your only other bootable drive. After the diskette is formatted, keep it handy. Label it *Disaster Recovery* or *Emergency*. You'll want to put your PARTNSAV.FIL file there (or copy it there), plus any other emergency files or recovery programs and tools. This chapter, as well as the next few, will give you some ideas for further creating the diskette and what to put on it.

MIRROR, the disk saver

MIRROR can be used to record information about a disk's logical boot sector, FAT, and root directory to aid the UNFORMAT command with unformatting. Without this information, UNFORMAT still will recover a disk; however, it takes longer and files in the root directory are given generic names. (Everything else on the disk is okay.) However, if you use MIRROR to help UNFORMAT recover a disk, recovery is quick and complete, *sans* hassle.

To help MIRROR recover accidentally formatted disks, use it in the following format:

MIRROR [*drive:* [*drive:.* . .]] [/1]

drive indicates one or more disk drives from which MIRROR will record boot sector, FAT, and root directory information. If *drive* isn't specified, the current drive is assumed. MIRROR records information about the drives in a file named MIRROR.FIL. The file is saved in the root directory, but exists toward the back of the disk, away from the area the FORMAT command destroys when it reformats the disk.

The optional /1 switch tells MIRROR to retain only one copy of the MIRROR.FIL file. Otherwise, MIRROR will make a backup of that file, MIRROR.BAK, each time it's run, saving the older disk information. The older file can be used during recovery for comparison purposes. Normally, however, most people specify the /1 switch to keep only one file on disk—to keep the root clean, as it were.

The following command is a sample of the MIRROR command. This command is something you should consider putting in your AUTOEXEC.BAT file, to be run each time your computer starts:

MIRROR C: D: E: /1

When this command is run, MIRROR will save important disk information for all hard drives, C through E. Only one copy of the MIRROR.FIL will be maintained. These drives now are fully protected against accidental reformatting. If you do need to use the UNFORMAT command on them, recovery is almost guaranteed.

You also can use the MIRROR command on a floppy diskette. However, be wary of MIRROR.FIL files that are too old. If you use an old MIRROR.FIL file with the UNFORMAT command, the results could be disastrous and unrecoverable. So, if you need to MIRROR a floppy, do it often.

MIRROR and deletion tracking

MIRROR's last incarnation is its memory-resident deletion-tracking function. This function monitors all files DOS deletes from the drives you specify. When used in conjunction with the UNDELETE command, MIRROR in this mode makes for a smooth and total file recovery.

To activate MIRROR's deletion tracking, use it in the following format:

MIRROR /T*drive*[-*files*]

drive is a disk drive in your system. That specific drive will be monitored by the MIRROR command with deletion tracking. If you want to monitor more than one drive, you must specify an individual /T switch followed by that drive's letter. On each drive you're monitoring, MIRROR creates a secret file named PCTRACKR.DEL. In that file, MIRROR will place a list of recently deceased files, aiding in their recovery with the UNDELETE command.

− files indicates the number of files you want MIRROR to track. This overrides the number of files MIRROR normally monitors. It can make the PCTRACKR.DEL file smaller on disk if that's a concern. The number of files MIRROR normally keeps track of is shown in Table 15-1.

**Table 15-1
MIRROR's deletion-tracking
default -files value and the relative
size of the PCTRACKR.DEL file.**

Disk size	Standard -files value	PCTRACKR.DEL file size
360 K	25	5 K
720 K	50	9 K
1.2 Mb	75	14 K
1.4 Mb	75	14 K
32 Mb	202	36 K
(higher)	303	55 K

In some cases, you can anticipate not wanting to keep track of over 300 deleted files. With the average directory containing less than 100 files, specifying a *− files* value of 100 will save you some disk space on most hard drives. (That should handle most DEL *.* cases.)

Note that the PCTRACKR.DEL file isn't created until after you've deleted files on a volume. Yes, I know, this all makes for more files in the root directory, but the trade-off is worth it.

The following is an example of using MIRROR's deletion-tracking function on the hard drive C:

    MIRROR /TC − 100

The /T switch tells MIRROR to monitor deleted files on drive C, up to 100 files. This command is ideal to put into AUTOEXEC.BAT, to help assist the UNDELETE command if you later need to delete files. (Although UNDELETE can work without deletion tracking, it just works better with it.)

You also can combine both MIRROR's disk saving and deletion-tracking abilities. For example:

    MIRROR C: D: E: /1

MIRROR both creates the MIRROR.FIL file and monitors deleted files on drives C, D, and E.

Note that MIRROR is only memory resident when deletion tracking is turned on. Also, MIRROR is loaded automatically into an upper memory block if you have created them; there's no need to specify the LOADHIGH command. (For more information on DOS's memory management and the LOADHIGH command, refer to chapter 20.)

Undeleting files

There is a special pang of dread you feel when you've deleted an important file. I did it while cleaning up my utility directory just the other day. Instead of deleting an old data file, I razed the program file that created it—not what I wanted. A few happy moments later, however, I typed the UNDELETE command, followed by the file's name. The file was back and happy and beloved even more than ever before.

Undeleting files used to be the realm of Peter Norton, the once and always PC Utility God (although his praises aren't sung as often now as they were in The Old Days). Norton was the first to develop the Unerase utility—a classic. Unerase did the miraculous job of breathing new life into the vapor of vanished DOS files—an amazing feat. Now, DOS can do the same thing (and young users are as bewildered about Norton's legend as they are about the Beatles).

Before starting with the descriptive part, here's another Hard Disk Management rule: *never use a recovery tool as an excuse for negligence*. Sure, DOS can breathe life into the nostrils of dead files; however, that shouldn't encourage you to be lazy with the DEL, ERASE, or even FORMAT commands. Even with MIRROR installed, using your brain now is better than relying on software tools later. Consider this: the COPY command is instant death here. If you copy one file over another, you cannot get it back using UNERASE. You have been warned.

The format for the UNDELETE command—in its fully panic-driven mode—is as follows:

UNDELETE filename [/LIST | /ALL] [/DOS | /DT]

filename is the name of the file you want to recover. It also can be a wildcard, which allows for quick recovery of all files just deleted using a wildcard.

The [/LIST | /ALL] and [/DOS | /DT] items are optional either/or's. You can either specify /LIST or /ALL and /DOS or /DT. I'll talk about what they do in a few lines. First, here is how you would undelete the file DOODLE.TXT using the UNDELETE command:

UNDELETE DOODLE.TXT

If deletion tracking isn't installed, you'll see something like the following:

Directory: C: \
File Specifications: DOODLE.TXT

Deletion-tracking file not found.

MS-DOS directory contains 1 deleted files.
Of those, 1 files may be recovered.
Using the MS-DOS directory.

?OODLE TXT 166 6-28-94 12:06p . . .A Undelete (Y/N)?

Press Y to recover the file. DOS will ask you for the file's first letter (because it was removed when the file was deleted). In the previous example, you'd press D, then DOS would tell you File successfully undeleted. It's back! It's back!

If deletion tracking has been installed, the entire operation becomes easier. You still use the UNDELETE command in the same format; UNDELETE knows whether or not deletion tracking is on or off. You would see the following after typing UNDELETE DOODLE.TXT:

Directory: C:\
File Specifications: DOODLE.TXT

Deletion-tracking file contains 1 deleted files.
Of those, 1 files have all clusters available,
          0 files have some clusters available,
          0 files have no clusters available.

MS-DOS directory contains 1 deleted files.
Of those, 1 files may be recovered.

Using the deletion-tracking file.

DOODLE TXT 166 6-28-94 12:06p . . .A Deleted: 7-15-94 5:25p
All of the clusters for this file are available. Undelete (Y/N)?

Press Y to recover the file.

With deletion tracking on, file recovery is a snap; DOS now knows if the file can be fully recovered and what its first letter was. Notice that the display gives you both statistics for DOS's way of undeleting a file—which is primitive—and the deletion-tracking method. Deletion tracking is much more thorough and actually can tell you the possibilities of recovery based on how clusters are used on a disk. Definitely, it's the preferred way to go.

You can force UNDELETE to ignore deletion tracking by specifying the /DOS switch. Likewise, you can force it to use deletion tracking by specifying the /DT switch. However, if the file was deleted before you installed MIRROR with deletion tracking, UNDELETE with the /DT switch won't be able to locate it.

The /LIST switch can be used for a preview of deleted files that can be recovered. UNDELETE scans the current directory or the path specified and reports how many files can be recovered using deletion tracking and how many are deleted according to DOS. This is a good way to test-run the UNDELETE command before attempting a recovery.

The /ALL switch is the no-questions-asked switch. For example, to recover DOODLE.TXT and not have UNDELETE stop to ask if it's okay, specify the following:

UNDELETE DOODLE.TXT /ALL

This switch is handy if you have deletion tracking on and have just zapped a group of files with a wildcard. To recover them, use the same wildcard with UNDELETE and the /ALL switch. For example:

UNDELETE *.* /ALL

If you use /ALL and deletion tracking hasn't been installed, DOS will assign # as the first character of each recovered file. When deletion tracking is on, the first character will be restored just as it was before.

Note that time is of the essence here. You should use the UNDELETE command immediately after using the DEL or ERASE commands. Time-wise, the files can sit on disk all night—for months. If you run any other DOS commands or copy any files before you use UNDELETE, however, recovery might not be possible.

Finally, UNDELETE cannot restore subdirectories removed with the RD command. In that instance and under other circumstances where UNDELETE doesn't work, you can try to get the file restored from a recent backup archive. The next chapter contains all the details.

Formatting disks

Before discussing how diskettes are unformatted, here's a meticulous look at the FOR-MAT command, which is, after all, responsible for reformatting diskettes that you might one day need to unformat.

The FORMAT command prepares disks for use under DOS. All disks must be formatted before the operating system can use them as a storage device.

For all disks, whether they've been formatted previously or not, the FORMAT command creates the boot sector, FAT, and root directory. For previously unformatted floppy diskettes, FORMAT also creates all the tracks and sectors, taking the disk size information from your PC's BIOS (although you can direct FORMAT to create a diskette of a different size—more in a moment). For previously formatted floppy disks and all hard disks, FORMAT simply verifies the tracks and sectors already there. This is all basic disk information, most of which is detailed in chapter 2 if you want to take a look back.

The general format of the FORMAT command is as follows:

FORMAT *drive*

drive is required, indicating the disk drive containing the disk to be formatted. Every drive in your system qualifies, even hard drives.

Beyond the drive requirement, FORMAT has a parade of optional switches—11 in all. Of those, only five are worth worrying about. The rest of the switches are to keep FORMAT compatible with previous versions of DOS.

The five switches you should concern yourself with are /S, /Q, /U, /F, and /V. The six older switches are /B, /T, /N, /1, /4, and /8. Crack open the DOS manual if you really want to find out what they're all about.

The /S switch is the system switch, used with FORMAT to make a system, or bootable, disk. Specifying the /S switch is similar to using the SYS command after FORMAT. Basically, /S directs FORMAT to copy DOS's system files (IO.SYS, MSDOS.SYS, and COMMAND.COM) to the newly formatted diskette. This was discussed previously in chapter 2.

/Q is a handy switch. It's the QuickFormat switch. By using it, you can reformat a diskette in a matter of seconds. Incidentally, the speed improvement comes from the fact that /Q directs DOS to skip the disk verification stage. So, only use /Q when you're certain a diskette is okay.

Personally, any time I need to reformat a diskette, I use the /Q switch. This is for two reasons: it's faster and it's easier for DOS to recover a diskette that has been QuickFormatted. (It's even easier if you use the MIRROR command, covered earlier in this chapter.)

The /U switch is the near opposite of the /Q switch. FORMAT /U specifies an unconditional format; the entire diskette will be formatted and all old data will be destroyed. Essentially, /U forces FORMAT to think of the diskette as a fresh one, right out of the box. Note that there's no chance for recovery when a diskette has been reformatted with the /U switch.

The /F switch now is the standard switch you use to format a diskette of a lower capacity in a high-capacity drive. Simply specify the size of the diskette after the /F switch. Table 15-2 lists valid values you can specify after /F and a colon.

Table 15-2   Values for use with FORMAT's /F switch when formatting different sizes of diskettes.

Diskette size	/F: values
160 K	160, 160 K, 160 K
180 K	180, 180 K, 180 K
320 K	320, 320 K, 320 K
360 K	360, 360 K, 360 K
720 K	720, 720 K, 720 K
1.2 Mb	1200, 1200 K, 1200 K, 1.2, 1.2 Mb 1.2 Mb
1.4 Mb	1440, 1440 K, 1400 K, 1.44, 1.44 Mb, 1.44 Mb
2.8 Mb	2880, 2880 K, 2880 K, 2.88, 2.88 Mb, 2.88 Mb

This subject is confusing to most PC users. Here are some rules to remember:

- Use the proper diskettes for each of your drives. Use high-capacity diskettes in high-capacity drives and low-capacity diskettes in low-capacity drives.

- Do not try to fool the computer by punching holes in a $3^1/_2$-inch diskette to make it high capacity. It might hold the initial format, but any addition access to the disk will render it useless.

- When formatting a low-capacity diskette in a high-capacity drive, make sure you're using a double-sided/double-density (DS/DD) diskette. Use the proper FORMAT command (see Table 15-3).

- Do not format a high-capacity diskette to a lower capacity. For example, you can format a high-capacity diskette to only 360 K. However, that diskette cannot be read by any 360 K disk drive; you've just wasted a diskette.

If you do want to format a low-capacity diskette in a high capacity drive, Table 15-3 will show you which commands to use. The diskette sizes are listed on the top of the table; drive sizes (capacities) are on the left side. If you've ever used DOS 3.3, you'll notice how much saner the /F switch values are than the old method.

Also, whenever you reformat a low-capacity diskette in a high-capacity drive, you must specify the /U switch. Even on new formats, /U guarantees that the FORMAT command will properly format the diskette.

**Table 15-3   The /F switches for formatting
low-capacity diskettes in high-capacity drives.**

	160 K	180 K	320 K	360 K	720 K	1.4 Mb
360 K	/F:160	/F:180	/F:320			
1.2 Mb	/F:160	/F:180	/F:320	/F:360		
1.4 Mb					/F:720	
2.8 Mb					/F:720	/F:1.44

Finally, the /V switch is used to prespecify a volume label. This switch eliminates the annoying label question after the disk has been formatting. Specify the label following /V and a colon. If the label contains spaces, you'll need to put it all in double quotes. For example:

FORMAT A: /V:"DATA DISK"

The previous command applies the label DATA DISK to the diskette formatted in drive A. As a drawback, note that all succeeding diskettes you format (when asked Format another?) also will have the same label. Go figure.

Unformatting disks

Starting with DOS 5.0, you can unformat an accidentally formatted diskette using DOS's UNFORMAT command. As with UNDELETE, the UNFORMAT command works scads better when you've used MIRROR on the drive. Still, UNFORMAT is capable of unformatting any recently formatted diskette using only DOS's information. However, the results are a little muddled, such as misnamed files in the root directory and waiting up to half an hour for DOS to locate files, but it works.

As with UNDELETE, the sooner you use UNFORMAT after a diskette has been formatted the better. Also—and please remember this—don't yank a partially-formatted diskette out of the drive. Wait for the diskette to be fully reformatted first. Then, use UNFORMAT.

The basic format of the UNFORMAT command is:

UNFORMAT *drive*

drive is the letter of the disk drive containing the diskette to be unformatted.

Before proceeding with an actual unformat (it really is a bomb-defusing-tense situation), you might want to try a test run. For example:

UNFORMAT A: /J

The /J switch tests the MIRROR.FIL file on the diskette. It verifies that MIRROR.FIL actually matches the disk information. You want to make sure the MIRROR.FIL file is up to date. If not, then you need to tell UNFORMAT to ignore it; using an old MIRROR.FIL file could be worse than no recovery at all.

Another test switch you can try is /TEST, which does a dry-run through of the unformatting process, but without the MIRROR.FIL file's assistance.

When you're ready to go, use the following command:

UNFORMAT A:

Specify the proper drive to unformat in place of A: in the previous command. If you want to ignore the MIRROR.FIL file, then use the /U switch:

UNFORMAT A: /U

If you're working on a hard drive and want to rebuild the partition table previously saved with the MIRROR /PARTN command, use the following command:

UNFORMAT /PARTN

You'll need the diskette with the PARTNSAV.FIL file on it, as created by the MIRROR command (refer to the first section in this chapter). If you use the /L switch with /PARTN, you'll see a comparison of the existing partition with that saved in the PARTNSAV.FIL file. That's a method of testing the partition, to see if it's worthy of restoration.

At any time, you can use the optional /P switch to direct the MIRROR command to send its output to the printer as well as the display.

If you're building a disaster recovery diskette, consider copying the files UNFORMAT .EXE and UNDELETE.EXE to that diskette. Other files you might want to copy, especially those to assist in recovering a hard drive, include the following:

FORMAT.COM
SYS.COM
FDISK.EXE
DEBUG.EXE

These files can be located in your DOS directory. Each of them might help in some form of hard disk recovery, should the need arise.

Summary

DOS comes with some interesting cures for some common and forgivable offenses: UNDELETE to recover deleted files and UNFORMAT to rescue accidentally reformatted disks. The sin of negligence is unforgivable, so don't take the presence of these commands lightly. Use MIRROR to assist in undeleting and unformatting and with general hard disk management, as you see fit. Keep a disaster recovery diskette handy and continue to build upon it as you learn more about hard disk security.

The next chapter covers the cure-all for every DOS problem, no matter what. It's the subject of archiving information on your hard drive, which is handled by the BACKUP command. Equally potent, although often forgotten, is the RESTORE command. Together, these two commands can help you undo just about any malevolent deed done to the hard drive. However, everything works only if you practice the art of backup like a religion. (Don't worry, you'll be a convert soon.)

16

Backing up data and programs

Hard disks perform so flawlessly that most of the time you can forget about these reliable beasts. Still, problems might occasionally happen. When they do, it's important to be prepared. This preparation involves some preventive maintenance on the software side—some data security provided by DOS in the form of a backup program.

This chapter is about preventive maintenance. Primarily, the subject is archiving information from the hard drive onto floppy diskettes. Essentially, what you want are two copies of your data, just in case. DOS provides two programs for this, BACKUP and RESTORE. Additionally, third-party programs can do the job faster and more effectively.

Beyond the software solution, this chapter also touches upon the subject of tape backup. These are all solutions to the same problem: keeping an extra copy of vital information handy in case something happens to the hard drive.

Preventive maintenance

In my opinion, only an idiot would jump out of a plane. Many idiots do. I did once, along with several of my computer buddies back in 1984: the First (and last) Annual Idiot Programmer's Jump. We even invited celebrities and the media (although only Steve Wozniak, creator of the Apple computer, expressed a true desire to join us).

Jumping out of a plane was a dumb thing to do. It would have been even dumber had each of us not had a handy safety device—the parachute—securely strapped to our bodies. To make things even safer, several of us embraced the reserve chute option. For some reason, hurtling yourself into space at 3000 feet seems somehow mentally better when you have two parachutes instead of one.

Now, think of your hard drive. Don't you love your hard drive and all its data more than life itself? Think of the time that went into creating that data. Think of how important all that data is to you, your business, everything you do, etc. There's money there; your time invested into your hard drive.

Now, try to imagine all that data as your life. Where is your parachute? Seriously, things can happen to a hard drive that figuratively are the same as tossing your PC out the open door of a DC-3, 3,000 feet over the southern California desert. Where is your data parachute?

Creating a data parachute is done by archiving information from your hard drive to a secondary storage medium. That archival copy is a duplicate of the original information on your hard drive. Should anything happen to your hard drive or any of the information on it, you can reconstruct it using the archival copy.

Obviously, keeping an archival copy up to date is important. Information changes on your hard drive daily. Making an archive of your hard drive's changing data on a daily basis is critical—like keeping that parachute tightly strapped to your body.

Under DOS, there are several ways to archive the information on your hard drive. DOS itself provides a utility program, BACKUP, that does the job. BACKUP's counterpart, RESTORE, is used to put the files back on the hard drive should the Big Scary ever happen. Better than that, third-party backup programs exist that do the job smoother and faster than DOS's backup. Even better still, you can get devices such as tape drives to make backups even less painful.

It's surprising that the topic of pain needs to be mentioned. It's almost like some fool not wanting to wear his parachute because it's too binding. Yet, that clown will jump out of a plane and expect to land okay. The same silliness can be applied to backing up.

When you back up a hard drive, you're shuffling lots of diskettes back and forth. All backup programs typically back up to floppy diskettes. If you have the 2.8 Mb diskettes, it might take only a few of them to fully back up a hard drive. With 360 K diskettes, however, that's a huge stack of diskettes, plus a lot of time spent swapping them back and forth as the backup progresses. Even with the benefits of the backup parachute, people neglect to back up for this very reason.

Backing up doesn't have to be painful. For example, you need to do a full hard disk backup only once a week, maximum. Daily backups are a must, yet they might take only two or three diskettes, plus perhaps 10 minutes of your time. With all the benefits of having a backup handy, you would think every hard disk owner would do this. Still, they don't.

Often, it takes something like a total disk crash to convince users to back up their computers. I lost three months of data once due to a hard drive crash. The power dropped in my office for only a split second. Yet that outage was enough to fry the circuitry on my hard drive. I had a daily backup of my book but no other recent backup of the hard drive. I lost three months worth of batch files, new programs, downloads, and other projects I had been working on.

Don't let the same mistake happen to you. Follow the instructions here and back up! It's the second half of basic hard disk management (along with organization) and is the most important.

You don't have to back up the whole hard drive every day. For me, that would take almost an hour, even with a fast backup program. For a file server with 300 Mb of storage, that process would take several hours. Truly, if you had to back up that way, no one would do it.

Instead, the following sections provide some general rules to follow when archiving your data.

Back up your work files daily Backing up your work files means making a duplicate copy of your files on a floppy diskette. You can get by simply by using the COPY or XCOPY command—provided that everything fits on a diskette. Otherwise, you can use the BACKUP command, which can copy files across several diskettes (or copy one large file to two or more diskettes).

A daily work file backup is what I do at the end of the day; I copy this book's directory and all its subdirectories, which contain the figures and tables, to a set of floppy diskettes. It takes maybe seven minutes. That way, if anything happens to the hard drive, I'll be only one day behind in my work.

Perform an incremental backup daily An incremental backup is a backup of only those files on your hard drive that have been changed or modified. Each file has assigned to it certain attributes, one of which changes when you modify the file. Most archiving programs can scan for those files and copy only them to a backup diskette. Once the file is backed up, DOS changes the archive attribute back to zero.

This approach is good if you're working with files all over a diskette. Each day, you'll be certain to archive all the files you've modified. For each day, you keep a different set of diskettes: one for Monday, one for Tuesday, and so on.

Back up the entire hard disk weekly Here is the time-consumer. A full hard disk backup takes a few minutes, but it's security. Once the hard drive is backed up, you can start over again with your incremental backups on Monday—even using the same set of diskettes (if they're reliable diskettes). The cycle repeats weekly and a recent safety copy of everything is maintained.

Now, consider a disaster. On Wednesday, somebody from marketing removes the \ WORK branch from your hard drive. It's gone. Here's the steps that you can do:

1. Yell at the person. (This step is optional.)
2. Whip out last week's full hard drive backup.
3. Restore the \ WORK branch from that backup diskette set. This brings your hard drive back to the way it was last Friday.
4. Restore Monday's incremental backup.
5. Restore Tuesday's incremental backup.

Once the backups are restored, your computer should be the way it was when you came in Wednesday morning. The backups saved you from having to reconstruct your hard drive and saved the poor marketing person's job.

It's perfectly okay to be flexible here. For example, here is my personal strategy for backup:

- Back up working subdirectories every day
- Do an incremental backup every Friday
- Back up the full hard drive on the first of each month

If something happens in the middle of the week, I have only Friday's incremental backup to work back to. Yet, what's important to me here is my daily work backup. Outside of that subdirectory, few items are changed or modified on my hard drive. So, this flexible scheme works for me.

With any backup scenario you create, remember to keep one or more backup disk sets. Yes, this involves a heavy investment in floppy diskettes, but it's nicer to have several useful backup diskette sets than to rely on one flaky one. For example, I recently had to trash a backup diskette set on one computer because two diskettes turned out to be rotten. Because that was my only backup disk set, the whole backup was rendered useless.

DOS's BACKUP command

The BACKUP command is DOS's file archiving command. You can use it to back up the whole hard drive or only a subdirectory branch or to perform an incremental backup or a backup based on a specific date and time. Also, the BACKUP command is the only DOS command that will copy a large file across several floppy diskettes.

Keep in mind that BACKUP is not the same as COPY. The files on a BACKUP diskette are all neatly packed into a special file format. That format is readable only by DOS's RESTORE program. The RESTORE program can put a file only back onto the original drive and subdirectory from which it was backed up. This makes BACKUP and the files that it creates unique.

The format of the BACKUP command is:

BACKUP *pathname drive*: [/S][/M][/A][/D:][/T:][/F:][L:*filename*]

pathname is the disk drive from which you're backing up. It must be a pathname, such as C:\ *.* for drive C. This drive is referred to as the *source drive*, although you can back up anything from a single file to the entire drive.

drive is the floppy drive to which you're backing up, or the *target drive*. The target will always be a single drive, which is normally your A drive, although, if you have a drive B, you can also back up to it.

It's important that the source drive not be write protected, otherwise the backup will fail. Also, if your computer is part of a networked system, BACKUP will not archive programs you don't have access to. Refer to your network guide for more information.

The optional switches are discussed throughout the rest of this chapter.

An example

The following is an example of backing up all files from the hard drive to floppy diskettes that you'll be placing in drive A.

You can start by approximating the number of diskettes you'll need for the backup. This estimate is done by taking the total number bytes used by the files you're backing up and dividing it by the size of the diskettes you're using. For example, if you have 14 Mb of files to back up, you'll need 10 or 11 1.4 Mb diskettes.

To find out how many diskettes you'll need, you can use the CHKDSK command. As one of its many duties, CHKDSK reports the amount of space used by files on a diskette. For example:

```
C:\ > CHKDSK

Volume DOS 5 created 09-21-1990 1:26p
Volume Serial Number is 16CE-9B67

    42366976  bytes total disk space
```

```
   77824  bytes in 4 hidden files
  104448  bytes in 49 directories
25638912  bytes in 915 user files
16545792  bytes available on disk

    2048  bytes in each allocation unit
   20687  total allocation units on disk
    8079  available allocation units on disk

  655360  total bytes memory
  637616  bytes free
```

In this example, there are 25,638,912 bytes on the disk used in 915 files. If you divide that amount by 1024, you get a hair over 25 Mb (25,038 K actually). If you're backing up to 1.2 Mb diskettes, you perform simple division:

25 Mb ÷ 1.2 Mb = 20.8 diskettes

Figure that you'll need 20 diskettes, but prepare 22 of them just in case.

For the backup diskettes, it's a good idea to format them first. The BACKUP command is able to format the diskettes for you, providing the FORMAT command is on the PATH and the diskettes are of the same size and capacity of the drive used (which they always should be).

If you don't format the diskettes before the backup, then definitely label them. Apply a sticky label to each diskette and number them, one through however many you have. You also might want to label the first one according to which type of backup it is: *Full Disk C:*, *Incremental Monday*, *Working Group*, etc.

When the diskettes are ready, you'll use the following command to back up all files on your hard drive C:

BACKUP C: \ *.* A: /S

The source drive is C, specifically all the files in the root directory of drive C. The target drive is A. The /S switch directs the BACKUP command to archive all files in all sub-directories on the source.

After pressing Enter, you'll see something like the following:

Insert backup diskette 01 in drive A:

Warning! Files in the target drive
A: \ root directory will be erased
Press any key to continue . . .

Note that any information already on the target diskette will be erased. This is okay for a backup diskette set.

The directions on the screen tell you to insert the first backup diskette into drive A, close the drive door, and press the Enter key. DOS then begins archiving all the files from drive C to the floppy diskette in drive A, starting with the root directory.

BACKUP will let you know what it's doing, displaying the pathname of each file as it's archived to the floppy diskette. As subsequent diskettes are required, BACKUP prompts you to insert them:

Insert backup diskette 02 in drive A:

Warning! Files in the target drive
A: \ root directory will be erased
Strike any key when ready

Be careful here. BACKUP is too dumb to check for the same diskette left in the drive. If you've mistakenly left the same diskette in the drive, you won't be warned and your backup set will be ruined.

You'll continue to shuffle diskettes until the entire hard drive, or whatever was specified by the BACKUP command, has been completely archived to floppies. Then, you should rubber band them and put them away in a safe place. For example, at the office where I used to work, we locked up all our backups in a fire safe each night.

Note that BACKUP can archive only from one hard drive at a time. If you have more than one hard drive, you'll need to run the BACKUP command once for each of them.

What happens behind the scenes

The BACKUP program is not COPY. If you take a look at a target diskette after the backup operation was completed you'll see a directory listing like the following:

Volume in drive A is BACKUP 001
Volume Serial Number is 16CE-9A38
Directory of A: \

BACKUP   001   1456640 08-31-94 11:41p
CONTROL   001   617 08-31-94 11:41p
        2 file(s)   1457257 bytes
                        0 bytes free

This diskette actually might contain dozens of files. All of them are stored carefully in those two solitary files you see in the above directory listing. That's the maximum number of files you'll always have on any DOS backup diskette—no matter how many files were backed up to it. Basically, BACKUP stores all the source files in one large file. In the previous example, it's named BACKUP.001, the 001 indicating that it's the first backup diskette. The file CONTROL.001 contains information about each file stored in BACKUP.001: its full pathname, date and time, and its internal location in the larger file. Only the RESTORE program can extract out your files. (So, you see I wasn't kidding when I said BACKUP isn't the same thing as COPY.)

This version of the BACKUP command has been the same since DOS version 3.3. So, you can back up and restore between DOS 3.3, 4.0, 4.01, and 5—no sweat. However, this version of BACKUP is 100% incompatible with previous versions of BACKUP, which stored files in a dissimilar manner. With that in mind, here is the last rule of using DOS's BACKUP: *it's best to back up and restore using the same version of DOS.*

If you have a version of DOS older than 3.3, back up and restore your hard drive with the latest version. If you upgrade, back up using the new version of DOS.

Doing an incremental backup

The previous example backs up the entire hard drive, which could take weeks on some of the larger systems. You should do an incremental backup daily (or weekly, if you're lazy like I am). That backup will contain only those files modified since the previous backup, which should be no later than the day before.

To tell DOS to incrementally back up, you specify the /M switch. The *M* stands for modify. What you're telling the BACKUP command to do is to archive only those files with their archive, or modify, attribute. That includes everything created, copied, or updated since the last backup.

```
BACKUP C: \ *.* A: /S /M
```

will scan the entire hard drive C for all files that have been modified. Only they will be copied to your backup diskettes. Be sure to keep each day's diskette set separate. Label each accordingly: *Monday*, *Tuesday*, etc. Keep each in a separate place. Unlike a full hard drive backup, the incremental backup will take only a few diskettes to accomplish, typically two to five, depending on the diskette's capacity.

Backing up a work area

Each day, at the end of the work day, I run the following batch file, named BACK.BAT:

```
@ECHO OFF
BACKUP D: \ BOOKS \ TABHDM \ *.* A: /S
```

The directory D: \ BOOKS contains all my book projects. TABHDM is the directory containing this book's chapters. There are subdirectories which contain figures, files for the companion diskette, and other stuff. The previous backup command backs up this entire part of the tree structure onto 1.2 Mb diskettes in drive A (currently two of them).

You could use a similar command and a similar batch file to back up your work. Note that my batch file is called BACK.BAT and not BACKUP.BAT. The reason is that BACKUP is the name of a DOS command and I don't want to confuse the two (also, BACK is faster for my lazy fingers to type).

For example, suppose you put all your work into a PROJECT subdirectory. Then, back it up daily with the following command:

```
BACKUP C: \ PROJECT \ *.* A: /S
```

This is a complete backup of a subdirectory branch—not an incremental backup. If you wanted to be extra safe, you could include two batch files in your BACK.BAT program. The first is a complete backup of your work area; the second could be a full incremental backup of the entire hard drive.

Technically speaking, what you really might want to do is a differential backup of your work area. A differential backup is a backup that doesn't change the modify attribute of the files that are backed up. That allows for modified files to be included in the second incremental backup. However, DOS's BACKUP program lacks the ability to do a differential backup, so you can peruse the third-party backup programs for information to see if they have that ability.

Backup's switches

You already have been introduced to BACKUP's /S and /M switches. The following sections describe BACKUP's other switches. They're not used as often as /S and /M, primarily because, if you really are into this, you'll buy a third-party backup program and skip DOS's BACKUP.

/A   The /A, or *append*, switch adds files to the backup disk. Normally, BACKUP erases all files on the root directory of the target disk. When the /A switch is used, those files that are backed up are added to the files already on the target disk.

```
BACKUP C:\MYBOOK\CHAPT1?.* A: /A
```

backs up all files named CHAPT1?.* to the disk in drive A, adding those files to any already found there. The disk in drive A must be the last (highest numbered) disk from any previous backup.

To start the backup, DOS prompts:

```
Insert last backup diskette in drive A:
Strike any key when ready
```

DOS adds the files specified on the source to those already on the target. Even if the files are of the same name, they're still appended to the BACKUP.XXX file on the target. (However, you can pull out individual versions of the files using RESTORE.)

/D and /T   The /D and /T switches are used together to back up files on or after a certain date. This is not the same as the /M switch. Even if a file might have been backed up since the date listed it still will be backed up when the /D switch is specified. For example:

```
BACKUP C:\DBASE\CUST*.DAT A: /D:10-19-91 /T:5:45p
```

Only the customer files (CUST*.DAT) created or modified after 5:54 p.m. on October 19th, 1991 are backed up to drive A.

The format for the date and time strings depends on the country settings for DOS. Refer to chapter 7 and the COUNTRY configuration directive.

Note that you can use the /D switch without the /T switch, but not vice-versa.

/F   The /F switch causes BACKUP to format an unformatted diskette at the size specified. Normally, BACKUP will always format an unformatted diskette, provided that the FORMAT command is on the search path (refer to chapter 9). What the /F switch does is to force the FORMAT command to format a diskette of a different size.

For example, if you really wanted to make BACKUP take longer and be even more excruciating, you could use 360 K diskettes in your 1.2 Mb drive. If so, you would specify /F:360 as an option for the FORMAT command. (All the /F options are the same as for the FORMAT command's /F switch; refer to Table 15-2.)

/L   The /L switch is used to create a backup log file. /L is followed by a colon and the pathname for a file to contain information about the backup. If a filename isn't included, the file BACKUP.LOG is created in the root directory of the source drive.

A typical BACKUP.LOG file contains something like the following information:

```
9-1-1994 5:59:35
001 \ BOOKS \ CHAPT1.DOC
001 \ BOOKS \ CHAPT2.DOC
001 \ BOOKS \ CHAPT3.DOC
001 \ BOOKS \ CHAPT4.DOC
001 \ BOOKS \ CHAPT5.DOC
```

The first entry shows the date and time of the backup. The remaining entries list the diskette number and the pathname of the files on that diskette. Each time you back up, new information is appended to the BACKUP.LOG file. You can use the log file created to keep track of the file's locations or simply for verification purposes.

The RESTORE command

After you've done your backup, store your diskettes away in a safe place. Normally, there's no need to use these diskettes—they're just there for insurance (your parachute). Hard disks are fairly robust and perform flawlessly. However, if something does go wrong or if you've accidentally deleted a file or want to restore a file or subdirectory to a previous condition, you need to get access to your archived file diskettes. This is done with the RESTORE command.

The format of the RESTORE command is:

RESTORE *d: pathname* [/P][/M][/S][/B][/A][/E][/L][/N][/D]

d: is the disk drive containing your backup diskettes.

pathname is the name of the file you want to restore or a pathname to restore. Using the RESTORE command's /S switch you can restore additional files located in subdirectories under the specified pathname (examples forthcoming).

Note that, if your computer is part of a networked system, the RESTORE program will not restore programs you currently do not have access to. Refer to your network guide for more information.

Restoring the full hard drive

Restoring all files from all backup diskettes to the hard drive isn't something you'll be doing every day. In the old days, this often was done after you'd updated your version of DOS. Today, it might be done after you repartition a drive, add a new drive to your system, or after the much-dreaded hard drive crash.

The RESTORE command to put all your files back on the hard drive is:

RESTORE A: C: \ *.* /S

This is the reverse syntax of the full hard drive BACKUP command. First comes the source drive, A:, which will contain the backup diskette set. Second is the destination,

C: \ *.*, the root directory of drive C, all files. Finally comes the /S, the subdirectory switch. That tells the RESTORE command to put all the files back on the hard drive, starting with the root directory. RESTORE will create the subdirectories for the files as the restoration process continues.

After you start RESTORE, it asks:

Insert backup diskette 01 in drive A:
Press any key to continue . . .

This is a good argument for labeling and numbering your diskettes. Locate the first backup diskette, put it in drive A, then press Enter. You'll see something like the following displayed:

*** Files were backed up 09-01-1994 ***

*** Restoring files from drive A: ***
Diskette: 01

The RESTORE command will start listing the names of the files it restores. As it finishes each diskette, you'll be prompted to insert the next one in sequence. The length of the entire operation depends on how many backup diskettes you have and the wildcard you're using to restore the files.

Restoring an individual file

Occasionally, you might want to restore only a single file or group of files using a wildcard. In the old days, this was how you undeleted a file—provided that the backup was recent enough.

The format to restore an individual file is the same; simply specify the filename with the RESTORE command:

RESTORE A: C: \ STUFF \ DOODLE.TXT

will scan the backup diskettes in drive A, looking for the single file DOODLE.TXT. Note that a full pathname must be specified. Also, RESTORE will put the file back only in its original directory. (If the directory doesn't exist, RESTORE will create it.)

Now, here's the rub. RESTORE scans each backup diskette for the files to be restored—every one, until the file is found. RESTORE asks you to insert each diskette sequentially until the indicated files are all found and restored. If DOODLE.TXT (or the file you specify) is on the last diskette, then you'll insert the diskettes from the first through the last before the file is found. Unlike other backup and restore programs, RESTORE doesn't know off the bat where a file is located. Ipso facto, this can be a real pain.

Note that the filename doesn't always have to be *.*. For example:

RESTORE A: C: \ *.DOC /S

will replace only all the *.DOC files from the backup diskette set. Because it's starting at the root directory and the /S switch is specified, all *.DOC files from the entire disk will be restored.

Restoring a partial subdirectory branch

Restoring a subdirectory branch is done in a similar manner to restoring a single file:

```
RESTORE A: C: \ WP \ BOOKS \ *.* /S
```

With this command, only the files in the \ WP \ BOOKS directory on drive C—plus all the files in all subdirectories beneath it—will be restored.

Restore's optional switches

In addition to /S, RESTORE has eight other optional switches. They're described in the following sections.

/P When the /P switch is specified, RESTORE checks each file on the backup diskette to see if it's read-only. (Read-only files are discussed in chapter 18, "File security.") If the file is read-only and the file already exists on the hard disk, RESTORE will ask:

```
Warning! File filename
is a read only file
Replace the file (Y/N)?
```

To replace the version already on disk with the one on the backup disk, press Y. Pressing N leaves the file as it is—the previously backed up file is not restored.

/N The /N switch is used to search out and restore files on the backup diskettes that no longer exist on the target. In other words, if you accidentally have erased a file on your hard disk and want it back, you can use the RESTORE command with the /N switch. For example:

```
RESTORE A: C: \ WORK \ IMPORTNT \ *.DOC /N
```

After entering the previous command, RESTORE directs you to insert your backup diskettes sequentially starting with the first one. It will scan each diskette for any files matching the target file specified in the example—all DOC files in your \ WORK \ IMPORTNT subdirectory on drive C. If any DOC files are found in the backup set that don't exist on the hard drive, they'll be copied over. (This option probably should be /W, for *Whew!*)

As long as you keep a recent backup around, you can rescue any accidentally deleted file or subdirectory using RESTORE and its /N switch.

/D The /D switch is a test switch, used to preview the restore. When it is specified, no files will be restored, yet RESTORE will show you a list of possible files that would be restored. For example:

```
RESTORE A: C: \ WP \ BOOKS \ *.* /S /D
```

Everything will work just the same as if the /D switch wasn't specified. RESTORE will prompt you to insert various backup diskettes. You'll see the names of files displayed, but nothing will be restored.

The /D switch is good to use for test restoring a file that you think might not be on a backup diskette set. (There really is no other way to look at the diskette and see if the file you need is on there.)

Date and time switches RESTORE has four interesting switches that allow you to restore files from a backup diskette set based on their date and time. For example, a file entry in a directory might look like this:

    ADIR   TXT   362 9-01-94 5:45a

ADIR.TXT was created at 5:45 a.m. on Thursday, September 1, 1994 (probably by someone who stayed up all night working). The dates and times used by RESTORE's special date and time switches refer to that date—not the date of the backup nor the current date.

There are two sets of date and time commands for RESTORE. There are switches to restore files created or modified on or before a specific date or time: /B and /E. Also, there are switches to restore files modified on or after a specific date or time: /A and /L. Table 16-1 shows how each of the these switches affects the RESTORE command.

Table 16-1
How the switches affect
the RESTORE command.

	Date	Time
On or after:	/A	/L
On or before:	/B	/E

The /A switch RESTORES only files modified on or after the indicated date. For example:

    RESTORE A: C: \ *.* /S /A:08-01-94

restores to the hard drive only those backup files that were modified or created on or after August 1, 1994. The following command would back up only those files modified on or before July 31, 1994:

    RESTORE A: C: \ *.* /S /B:07-31-94

The time switches, /L and /E, work only by the time of day, like BACKUP's /T switch. To get specific with the time, you need to specify both a time and date switch with RESTORE.

Note that RESTORE doesn't like it if you use the /B, /A, and /N switches in any combination.

Some final notes on BACKUP and RESTORE

Backing up your hard disk is a must. Yet, RESTORE is a program that is rarely (and hopefully never) run. There's no real need to back up and restore the hard disk unless something goes wrong with the hard drive. As a precautionary measure, it's suggested you do a complete backup, with the remote possibility of a necessary restore, before the following operations:

- When your computer is modified, either by yourself or a professional. This includes adding a memory card or other expansion option, a second hard disk, or some other hardware modification.

- When you use a new hard disk controller card with the same hard disk you presently are using. Each controller card formats the drive differently; therefore, when you use a new card, you'll need to back up, format, and restore your files to the hard disk now using the new controller.

- Before a major move involving the computer. This includes a move between offices, across town, or some long distance when the hard drive could be damaged.

- Always back up your hard disk before you take the computer into the shop (if possible). Even if they're fixing something unrelated, it's still a good idea.

A daily backup batch file

A special batch file can be written to ensure that a daily backup of important data files is done. This batch file should be run at the end of each working day.

Just like the AUTOEXEC.BAT file is run when the computer is first booted, the SHUTDOWN.BAT file can be run just before the computer is turned off. However, unlike AUTOEXEC.BAT, which is automatic, you'll have to get into the habit of typing SHUTDOWN at the end of each working day. One way to ensure that the SHUTDOWN batch file is run at the conclusion of each session is to include it as part of the Q.BAT file in your menu system (refer to chapter 11).

A typical SHUTDOWN batch file would be as follows:

```
 1: @ECHO OFF
 2: CLS
 3: REM Change to working subdirectory
 4: C:
 5: CD \WORK
 6: ECHO Insert today's work file backup disk into drive A:
 7: REM Full work group backup:
 8: BACKUP C:\WORK\*.* /S
 9: CLS
10: REM Do full hard drive incremental backup
11: ECHO Insert the incremental backup diskette set "C" for today
12: DATE < C:\BATCH\ENTER
13: BACKUP C:\*.* A: /S /M
14: CLS
15: REM And backup hard drive D, too:
16: ECHO Insert the incremental backup diskette set "D" for today
17: DATE < C:\BATCH\ENTER
```

18: BACKUP D: \ *.* A: /S /M
19: ECHO Backup completed. Bye!

This program does both a full backup of a work subdirectory (line 8), as well as an incremental backup of two hard drives (lines 13 and 18).

See how the DATE command is used with input redirection in lines 12 and 17? Refer to chapter 14 for more information.

You might want to add other commands to your SHUTDOWN.BAT or Q.BAT file. For example, deleting temporary files can be done, you can copy data files to a hard drive from your RAM drive (if any), or include output redirection/append to send shutdown information to a log file.

Commercially available backup programs

Many private software developers have realized the limitations of DOS's BACKUP and RESTORE programs—mainly that they're slow. Because computers are supposed to be time savers, any program that can do a job better and faster is worth looking into.

Points to consider

Some points to consider when looking for a third-party backup package are listed in the following sections. A later section has some examples of popular backup applications.

Speed Commercial backup programs are notably faster than DOS. They do this by packing more files on a diskette or by using a special high-density (and non-DOS compatible) diskette format. It might take time initially to format your backup diskettes under the special format; however, in the long run, the backup will be quicker.

The handiest speed feature of all third-party backup programs is that they know when you've removed one disk and inserted another. This conveniently avoids the annoying press any key message DOS's BACKUP displays.

The ability to restore DOS's RESTORE program works. Commercial backup software relies upon its speed as a selling point. They only rarely will mention the speed of a restore—let alone the restore's efficiency. Can you restore single files, groups of files, files by date and time, just as DOS's RESTORE can? Can you mark unrelated files and restore them? Can you restore files to a drive and directory other than their originals?

File groups Some backup software can back up files by subdirectory or by file group. A file group is a set of files or wildcard specs that you provide, even files across several drives. The backup program will read through that list and back up only those files that match. If the application also has such a feature with its restore half, then it's all the better.

Macros and automation Does the software allow you to back up at preset times? This scheduling feature usually is part of some automation scheme, one that usually involves mini-programs, similar to batch files, called *macros*. Basically, a macro is a series of keystrokes that can fire off various options in the backup program. It's a plus if you can automate the backup process, including bells and whistles to alert various users when they need to back up.

Compatibility A good reason for not going with a commercial backup program is compatibility. BACKUP and RESTORE come with each version of DOS. They're a staple. Know them once and you don't have to learn them again on a new machine. Because they come with DOS, they'll be on every DOS system you ever work with. Commercial backup programs usually are compatible with themselves, but they usually can't read other backup programs (nor DOS's) formats.

Flexibility in backup devices Nearly all backup programs can archive files to floppy diskettes. However, can they back up to tape drive systems or removable hard disks?

Backup applications

There are lots of popular backup programs on the market. The grandaddy of them all is Fifth Generation Systems' FastBack. Two others mentioned in this section are PC Tools' CP Backup and one from Peter Norton, the Norton Backup.

All these packages are fast; refer to their own advertisements and documentation for the various speed tests, etc. They can restore and back up with ease and all have controls for setting just about any backup option you can think of. The following information isn't meant to be a product comparison; buy whichever package you feel works best with the way you do.

FastBack FastBack (Fig. 16-1) is the original fast backup program and the first backup utility outside of DOS. It offers fast reliable backup; can format diskettes to super-large capacities; has file selection criteria or *gating* technology, history databases, password protection and file encryption; it offers scheduling facilities and programmable backup sessions; and is easy to use and pretty to look at.

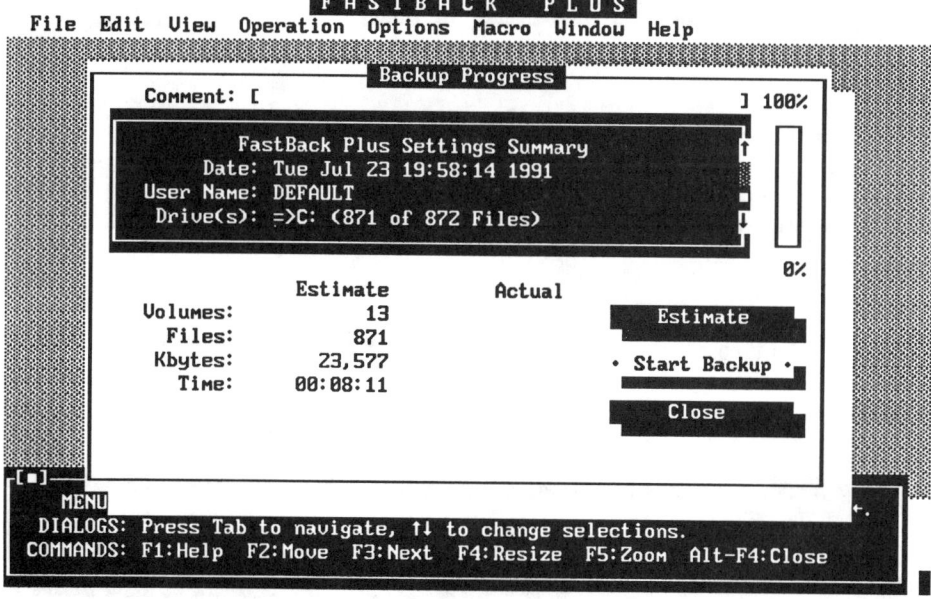

16-1 FastBack's evaluation of the hard disk backup.

A well-thought feature of FastBack is its express menu system. Several common backup scenarios are preprogrammed for you. The full hard disk backup even comes up automatically when you first start the program. There also is a description of creating an emergency restore disk in the manual. This is the kind of forethought I admire in computer programs. It makes FastBack a regular part of my laptop's hard disk routine.

FastBack
Fifth Generation Systems
10049 N. Reiger Rd.
Baton Rouge, LA 70809
(504) 291-7221
(800) 873-4384

PC Tools and CP Backup One of the many programs that come with PC Tools is CP Backup (Fig. 16-2). However, if you don't want the entire kitchen sink, you can buy CP Backup separately. Either way, it's a decent backup program, fast and reliable—and getting better all the time. (My advice is to buy PC Tools entire kitchen sink application.)

I must confess that I personally use this package on my desktop system. The main reason is that PC Tools gives you more for your dollar than buying any other backup package separately. With version 7, the backup program also has gotten smarter and is more customizable than before.

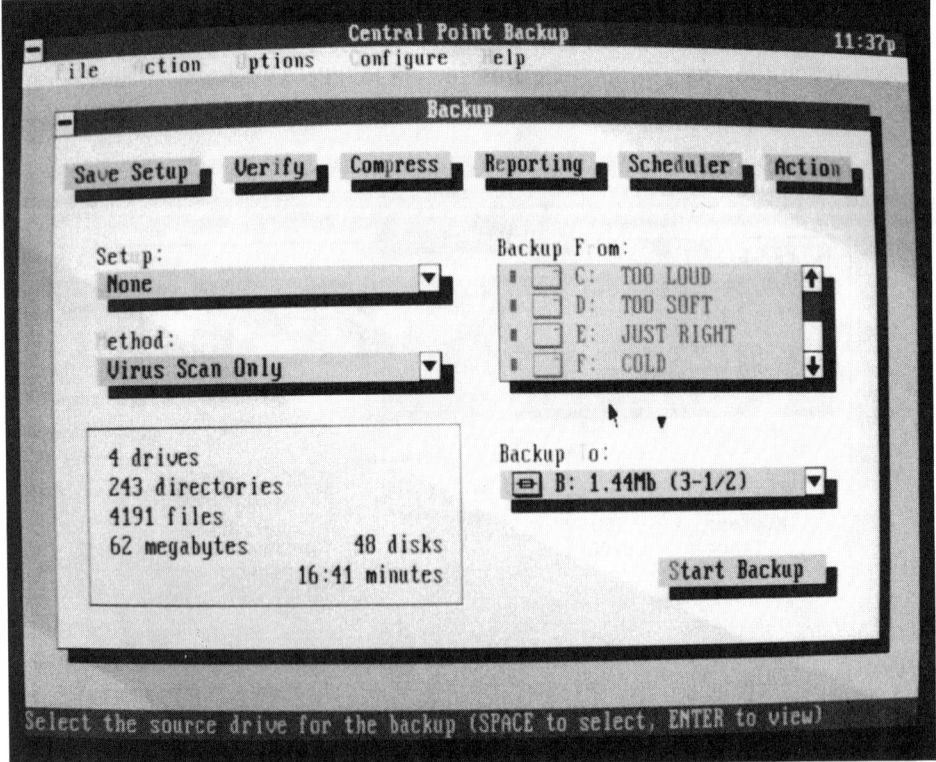

16-2 CP Backup's flashy and informative screen.

PC Tools
CP Backup
Central Point Software, Inc.
15220 NW Greenbrier Pkwy., #200
Beaverton, OR 97006
(503) 690-8090

The Norton Backup   The Norton Backup (Fig. 16-3) is a capable and slick program, complete with all the bells and whistles you'd expect from the god of PC Utilities. It has macros and scheduling and is very flexible. Its only sour spot is that it's pricey.

The Norton Backup
Symantec Corporation
10201 Torre Ave.
Cupertino, CA 95014
(408) 253-9600

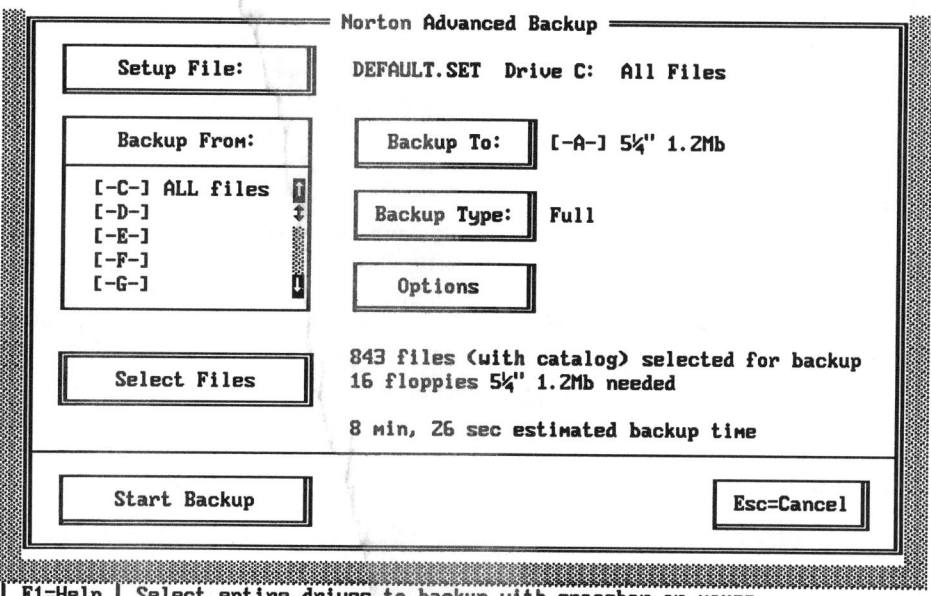

16-3   The Norton Backup's advanced screen.

PARK: extra hard disk precaution

Most PCs with hard disks, or the hard disk itself, will come with a special software disk. What's on this disk depends on the brand and model of your computer, the type of hard disk, and where you bought your hard disk. One program on this disk you should pay special attention to is PARK. (It also might be called HEADPARK, HARDPARK, DISK-PARK, SHIPDISK, SIT, or might incorporate the name of the computer. Sometimes PARK is an option from a diagnostic menu program.)

What PARK does and how you use it are crucial to the longevity of your hard disk. Yet, the PARK program really is quite simple. Its sole job is to instruct the hard disk drive to park the read/write heads on the far outside of the hard disk.

If you recall from the earlier discussion of hard disks, the read/write heads are responsible for storing and retrieving information from the hard disk. This device sits only microns above the hard disk itself. If the read/write head were to come into contact with the hard disk, irreparable damage could occur. With the hard disk spinning at 3,600 RPM, this contact is equivalent to a head-on collision at 60 MPH. Such hard disk collisions are known as *head crashes*.

The PARK program prevents a possible head crash. Because PARK moves the read/write head to the far outside of the disk (where no data is stored), any head crash would not interfere with your data.

For older hard disks, I recommend you PARK your hard disk just before turning the computer off. Newer hard drives—all ESDI, IDE, and SCSI drives—are self-parking. However, when you move the computer, you should always use the PARK program to lock down the heads. Even if the computer's just going to be off a few days, I advise running PARK. (You never know when an earthquake will hit.)

Due to the variety of PARK and PARK-like programs, it's impossible to discuss how each is used here. However, it's important to note that, for each brand of hard disk, there is a unique PARK program. Your friend's PARK program might not work on your hard disk. (It might make your hard drive go nuts, but it won't mess up your data.) You should use only the PARK program that came with your hard disk or one you know will work properly.

Also, all PARK programs behave differently. Some merely move the read/write heads to the outside of the disk, then return you to DOS. Others park the read/write head, then lock up in a loop, instructing you to turn off your computer. Still others might sit and continually beep at you until you turn the computer off. Unfortunately, this is something you have little choice over when you use your PARK program. However, the most important thing to remember is that PARK can prevent a possible head crash.

Tape backup

Seeing the inefficiency of floppy diskette backup, several companies offer the convenience of backup onto tape. These devices, the tape drives, now are so inexpensive that they commonly appear in a third disk drive bay, along with drives A and B. If you don't have one already and you're weary of the floppy disk shuffle backup, then a tape system is worth consideration.

Streaming tape systems

The most popular alternative to backing up data on floppy disks is a *streaming tape backup*. The streaming tape drive is like a high-quality cassette recorder. It copies all data from the hard disk in one, fell swoop, putting that information onto a special cassette tape. Because the primary purpose of the tape drive is to back up a hard disk, it's very fast.

Streaming tape drives can be installed either internally or externally. Internal models occupy the same size as a half-height disk drive and might require an expansion board or plug into the floppy or hard disk controller. External models mount outside the computer. In most cases, the external tape drives use the computer's own power supply. However, some do require an external power supply or have one available as an option. The external models generally operate off the 37-pin external drive connector on the back of the floppy disk controller, in which case, they won't take up valuable slot space. They also might come with their own controller card.

An advantage to external drives is that they can be shared by a number of computers. For example, an external tape backup system could be carted around to various computers in the office. Each user could connect their computer to the tape drive, perform the backup onto their own tape, and roll the cart to the next user. As long as the external drive is one of the plug-in types, this would save the expense of buying a tape drive for each computer system.

The entire backup operation from hard disk to cassette takes about 40 minutes for a full 40 Mb drive. The multiplication factor is about one minute per megabyte used on the hard disk. Sure, it might not compare that well with the time required to back up a hard disk to floppies. With a tape drive, however, you need to insert it only once. Then, when the backup is done, the cassette cartridge can be put back into its box and stowed away in a safe place. According to the software, you can set the thing up and leave for the night. That way, who cares how long it takes (at least you don't have to sit and swap diskettes).

Incidentally, tape drives were the original form of mass storage for computers—not hard disks. Information was recorded and retrieved from reel to reel tapes. However, because the tape is one long continuous surface, this meant all data on the tape had to be accessed serially, one file after another. The advantage disks had over tape was that disks could use random access; any point on the disk could be read simply by moving the disk's read/write head to that spot. This saved time over searching through a serial reel to reel tape.

Information storage on tape

Information is stored on tape using two methods: start-stop and streaming. *Start-stop* refers to the way tapes were used in the old days for accessing data. *Streaming* is a continuous flow of tape, used primarily for backup. Some streaming drives are capable of start-stop data storage, but at a much slower speed than dedicated start-stop tape drives.

Streaming tapes are always moving. The information is written to the tape by a write head. A few fractions of an inch away, a read head reads back the data that was just written. This is how streaming tape drives detect a write error. When an error happens, the write head rewrites the bad information, all while the tape still is moving.

For example, suppose an error exists in a block numbered N. The read head catches the error while the write head is writing block $N+1$. The write head then attempts to rewrite block N, then $N+1$ again. If all is okay, the remaining blocks are written ($N+2$, $N+3$, etc.) as the tape continues to move. So, on the tape, the block order would be:

N $N+1$ N $N+1$ $N+2$ $N+3$ $N+4$ . . .

The first N contained the error. Block $N+1$ was written before the error was detected, so the following block is a rewrite of block N again. Using this error detection scheme, data can be written to the tape in one continuous motion.

If an error occurs during a restore (when the tape is being read), the drive will back up and reread the bad block. Read errors aren't corrected the same as write errors. Instead, special information is stored on the tape along with the data. This information tells about the data, such as the block number, and includes a CRC (Cyclic Redundancy Check) error check. When the information is read from tape, another CRC error check is performed and the two CRCs are compared. If they aren't equal, the tape rewinds and the data is read again. If after a given number of attempts the data cannot be read, an error message is displayed or, depending on the type of tape software, the block is ignored.

Tape drive buying tips

Cost is about the most important item when looking for a tape drive. These devices are expensive (sometimes as much as buying a second hard drive). They also are an extremely specific item for the computer. As with anything you buy for the computer, the cost should be weighed against the alternatives—in this case, backing up using floppies. For large volume disks where backups are crucial, such as file servers and network drives, tape drives are worth the price. For other systems, tape drives are more convenient than diskette backups; however, cost-wise, you should ask yourself if they really are worth it.

Other than cost, the next most important items to look for in a tape backup system are the formatted capacity of the tape, the data transfer rate, and the speed of the drive.

The formatted capacity of the tape is important in relation to the size of your hard disk. Unlike floppies, tape systems will not pause when the tape gets full and ask you to insert the next tape. The tape backup must be smooth and contiguous. For a 20 Mb hard drive, you'll need a 20 Mb capacity tape drive and 20 Mb tapes. (For specific tape systems, check to see that the capacity of the drive and tape cartridge match that of your hard disk.)

Tapes also can be used to back up one small portion of a hard disk, such as a group of files or subdirectory. Although the formatted capacity of the tape can be as large as your hard disk, you can put several backup sessions on a single tape. For example, if your company's order entry information takes only 1 Mb of storage, you could back up each day's information using a single tape. (The tape keeps a directory of its information, just like a disk does.)

The data transfer rate, the speed at which information is read from or written to the tape, is measured in kilobytes per second, Kbytes/sec. The higher the number of Kbytes/sec, the faster information is transferred to and from the drive. Between 90 and 100 Kbytes/sec is a good transfer rate for a tape drive.

The speed of the tape drive is measured in inches per second (IPS). The larger the formatted capacity of the tape and the faster the tape speed (IPS), the less time a tape backup will take. For example, a tape capable of holding 40 Mb and recording at 30 IPS will take approximately 24 minutes to do a full 40 Mb backup. If the tape speed is tripled to 90 IPS, the backup takes only 8 minutes.

Final buying considerations might be the physical size of the drive and its interface. Some tape drives are fairly large and would tend to be external-only. Others can occupy the space of the typical half-height disk drive.

The interface on the drive should be PC bus or use the same size connector on the back of the floppy diskette controller. SCSI, Small Computer Serial Interface or Scuzzy, tape drives can be used only if your computer is equipped with a SCSI controller card. These tape drives are high-performance devices, often more efficient than PC bus tape drives. SCSI will doubtless be the wave of the future; however, unless your computer sports a SCSI port, you shouldn't mess with a SCSI tape drive.

One final note: some tape drives are not considered to be a logical device. You don't treat a tape drive as drive D: (or T:). You cannot load or execute programs from the tape drive, nor can you save directly to the tape drive using DOS. The tape drive is simply a device for storing backups. Only special software controls the action of the tape. As far as DOS is concerned, the tape drive does not exist.

Summary

BACKUP provides an insurance policy by archiving files from the hard disk to diskette. RESTORE, if needed, brings the archived files back. Whether you use the DOS backup or not, you should always keep a safety copy of your data handy. The more recent the copy, the less sweat will dot your brow if anything ever goes wrong. (No more finger wagging— I think you've got the message.)

The subject of this part of the book really is hard disk security. BACKUP gives you security because your data is secured in two locations. When most users think of security, however, they think of access and prevention. The next chapter takes a very serious look at this subject, including the daunting issue of computer viruses.

17

Preventing illegal computer access

Hard disk security involves more than just backup. It's about your sensitive data and information you might not want the world to see. This doesn't imply that you should be overly paranoid. Yet, the concept of the computer virus is deadly enough to make even the one-computer office a security target. Even if you don't have national defense files on your system, your data is important to you.

This chapter deals with several parts of hard disk security. Up front is virus security or keeping your data safe from hard drive-altering programs. This topic is followed by a discussion of access security on the user-level. Large computer systems use passwords to grant access—even passwords to prevent access to specific subdirectories and files. DOS by itself lacks this ability. However, there are tools you can add to make password security possible.

Illegal access

If the information stored on your computer is trivial, then there's no need to worry about illegal access. That computer in your den isn't a target for international espionage and no disgruntled family member is going to erase the December budget—especially with Christmas so close. However, not every PC is like that.

Consider the office PC. It might be used only by one reliable person, but what's to prevent someone else from sauntering by and taking a snoop in the payroll files? Oh, you can run a shell with a password. However, anyone smart enough to want to know how much you make a month can boot the PC from a floppy disk and have access to all your hard drive files from drive A.

There are lots of interesting batch file and BASIC password schemes and various DOS tricks you can pull to protect your data. However, anybody can boot a PC from a floppy drive and have access to your files. Batch file passwords? Forget it! The same person can type out a batch file and see how it runs. The passwords generally are listed in the file somewhere. Only a third-party password program, one that really can lock up your hard drive, will keep the snoopers out.

A good way to stop a meddler in their tracks is to use data encryption. A file scrambled with a special utility requires a secret password for access. Without that password, the file just looks like so much random text. The password is encrypted in the file, which adds extra protection from prying eyes. (The subject of data encryption—a good general form of anti-personnel security—is covered in the next chapter.)

Okay, relax. Take a second to calm your nerves. Stop being suspicious. Assume that all your employees love you or that any sensitive information is safely tucked away on your computer and you lock it up in Fort Knox at the end of the day.

One day, the computer starts acting funny. That file you just saved doesn't appear in the directory. You save again and the system locks. Frustrated, you reset. However, when the computer boots you see a chilling message:

Ha! Ha! Have a nice day!

By no means is this cute. It means you definitely have a computer virus. A nasty program has found its way onto your computer, laid dormant for a while, then reared its beastly head. If you're lucky, you'll see only the message and no data is lost. Other viruses might zap your hard drive or randomly scramble data.

How did the virus get there? Usually through an infected program. It could be something you bought in a store; however, more likely, a computer virus is spread from a program you've acquired on a floppy diskette from an unwitting friend or downloaded from an online service or local bulletin board system (BBS). The infected program passed the virus on to you. From there, you could have passed it along to other systems.

Fortunately, viruses aren't that devious on the PC. On the Macintosh, viruses proliferate. On a PC, you must run a COM, EXE, or SYS (device driver) program to spread a virus around; data files are rarely infected. A recent backup probably will get you all your data files back intact if the virus destroyed them.

Nasty relatives to the virus exist as well, one of which is the Trojan horse. The *Trojan horse* works like its namesake. You run a program that you think does one thing and it winds up doing something else. These programs aren't viruses in that they don't multiply and infect other programs (although the media confuses the two for panic's sake).

An example of a Trojan horse was an old program file named EGADEMO. It purportedly ran through a series of graphics demonstrations for your EGA card. After the display was over, you saw the message Arf! Arf! Gotcha! It turned out that, while you were watching the pretty displays, EGADEMO was busily erasing your hard drive. This is nothing a recent backup—or some precaution—couldn't cure.

True, this virus stuff is enough to make normal users suspicious about experimenting with new software—or even upgrading. At a large defense contractor in my home town, their computer manager removed all the floppy drives from hundreds of PCs to keep them from running any of the millions of virus-infected programs out there. This hysteria is unnecessary.

As long as I've got you alarmed (and I'm sitting here all hyped to write about The Virus), the following sections discuss some things you can do to prevent and deal with computer viruses. Password protection is covered in the second half of this chapter.

Avoiding the plague

To fight the battle, you can spend hundreds of dollars on virus-protection software. When the virus idea was new, lots of fly-by-night companies appeared that offered nifty $400 solutions. I got a laugh from several computer consultants who charged users $150 an hour to remove a virus they didn't have. (The consultant confessed to me it was a flaky disk drive. She ran CHKDSK twice, then sent the client a bill.)

Most of the time, any virus you suspect probably will be a random disk error. Face it, programs screw up, DOS screws up. Things happen all the time. PC software is an electronic house of cards ready to tumble at the slightest sneeze. For example, yesterday my computer was acting all weird. Was it a virus? Hmmm. I reset and, lo, everything worked normally. No virus. However, to be sure, I ran a special virus-checking program that came with PC Tool's CP Backup. That program is covered later, along with the Certus hard disk protection program and the Mace Utilities. The following section gives you some immediate DOS hints for assisting with viral protection.

DOS-by-itself solutions

Here are a few handy things you can do to avoid The Virus. These are all DOS solutions and are by no means guaranteed to stop a virus from infecting your computer. However, they might slow it down a tad.

Create an incorruptible boot diskette   The best example of an incorruptible boot diskette would be your disaster recovery diskette, as discussed in chapter 15. Any older bootable floppy generally can be considered uncorrupted. Unfortunately, DOS 5 doesn't come with any virgin bootable diskettes (it's an upgrade kit, not a new version), so you can't boot with it.

The incorruptible boot diskette should be used to start your system if you think you have a virus. Oftentimes, the virus will infect COMMAND.COM or one of the boot files on your hard drive. Booting from an incorruptible boot diskette prevents the virus from running.

Make your program files read-only   A read-only file is one that only can be read from. You cannot write to the file, change it, modify it, overwrite it, or delete it. This makes it harder for the virus to infect the program.

To make all your program files read-only, you'll use the ATTRIB command as follows:

```
ATTRIB +R C:\*.COM /S
ATTRIB +R C:\*.EXE /S
```

You should do this for each of your hard drives. (A full description of the ATTRIB command and read-only files is offered in the following chapter.)

Write protect floppies   Write protecting especially applies to distribution diskettes, public domain software diskettes, and any diskette you'll use to install software on your hard drive. Obviously, if you need to write to the diskette, such as with a backup or file transfer, then you shouldn't write protect it. However, for an important diskette, such as a boot disk or the disaster recovery diskette, write protect it.

Incidentally, you write protect a 5¼-inch diskette by placing a tab over the write protect notch on the diskette's side. For 3½-inch diskettes, the disk is write protected when you can see through the little hole in the diskette's corner (the tile is off the hole).

Never boot from a floppy If that new game a pal gave you requires you to boot from the floppy diskette or the game won't run, don't bother. Any diskette that self-starts or grabs control of the computer is suspect. The exception to this rule is the incorruptible boot disk or your disaster recovery diskette.

Beware of unknown programs If you don't know where a program came from, don't run it. However, don't make yourself overly suspicious. PRINTER.EXE might look unusual in your WordPerfect directory, but it's a legitimate program with a purpose.

Keep others away from your PC You should prevent other people from using your system, especially to test software. Consider designating an older PC as a test system if you need to evaluate software or run demonstration programs.

Don't pirate software There isn't a recorded case of any computer software developer shipping a virus with their product. However, if you borrow the software from a buddy, you're asking for trouble.

Remove files you don't use A hard drive can be a big place. With all that space, you might find yourself storing files that you rarely access and programs that you don't use. If so, remove them. Personally, I have a \TRASH subdirectory into which I place files I'm not using but don't quite want to delete. After a month in the TRASH directory, I zap the files.

Backup Nothing is more secure than having a backup copy of the data on your hard drive. If the virus has stopped your computer, then you can start from a bootable floppy, restore your hard drive, then run some virus-removal software. On the PC, viruses cannot infect data programs, although they can scramble the data. A recent backup will get all your data files back. If you own all your software, then you can reinstall the original programs if need be.

If you do think a virus has invaded your system, these following sections show a few things you can do to:

Check for consistency The Virus is a common scapegoat for everyday computer flubs. Before The Virus, people either assumed they were doing something wrong or that the software was buggy. Today, everyone is too quick to suspect a virus.

If you have a problem, try to repeat it. If the file won't save, try saving it under a different name. If the computer won't boot, turn it off and try again in a few seconds. Try booting from a floppy diskette. Also, check the operating conditions. Is it too hot out? A feverish computer tends to reset itself spontaneously.

Take a moment to review your situation. Did you add any new device drivers to CONFIG.SYS recently? Did you change any existing drivers? If so, undo the changes and reset the system. (This happened to me once. For the life of me I couldn't figure how my RAM disk device driver had disengaged both floppy drives, but it did. No virus.)

Only if the problem repeats consistently or if you see a nasty message or something obviously peculiar should you assume you have a virus.

Check COMMAND.COM's size and date   The most obvious item for a virus to infect is your system files, typically COMMAND.COM. Each version of DOS is different, so each COMMAND.COM will have a different size. To be safe, get a hard copy of COMMAND.COM's directory listing—and toss in the two other hidden-system files as well (IO.SYS and MSDOS.SYS or IBMBIO.COM and IBMDOS.COM). With your printer on, use this DIR command:

```
DIR C:\ /A > PRN
```

Keep that hard copy around and verify the size of COMMAND.COM or the other two files if you suspect a virus.

Maintain a disaster recovery diskette   You might want to create several of disaster recovery diskettes. The Certus program, covered later in this chapter, makes you create a critical diskette during its installation. You can use that safe diskette to boot your computer and run virus detection and recovery utilities whenever anything nasty happens. You might want to create other diskettes for your other favorite utilities as well—including any third-party backup programs.

Re-SYS the system   If your system files are infected, you can replace them with the originals using the SYS command. To do this, you must boot from an uncorrupted floppy diskette, one that preferably has the SYS.COM file on it. Then, do the following:

```
SYS C:
```

That command transfers the system files from the uncorrupted floppy up to the hard drive. If any of the hard drive's system files were infected, they're gone now.

Other disaster recovery measures also might be necessary. If the virus has erased your hard drive, then you'll need to start all over with low-level formatting, partitioning, and high-level formatting. Then, restore your most recent backup and be careful in the future. You also should run the MIRROR program before any of this happens (refer to chapter 15).

DOS's solutions are rather limited. Most of them hinge upon incorruptible floppies and fancy footwork beforehand. If that doesn't make you feel safe enough, you can grab some professional-level virus scanning and prevention utilities.

PC Tools' anti-viral solutions

PC Tools comes with three utilities that can assist you in virus detection and prevention. If you really are serious about it, you'll need Central Point's Anti-Virus program, which constantly checks for viruses, prompts for routine virus scans, and can remove viruses once they've attacked. Otherwise, you can use the following utilities that come with PC Tools:

CP Backup PC Tools' backup program has a built-in utility for virus scanning. What it does is to look for telltale virus signatures in all the files on your system. It does this without backing up any software, so you can use this feature as a quick test of any potential viruses on your hard drive.

To run the virus scan, start the CPBACKUP.EXE program, either from PC Shell or at the DOS prompt. Select the Backup item from the initial menu. On the main backup screen, select Backup Method from the Options menu. In the next box, toggle on the Virus Scan Only item (it's off by default).

Next, select all the files on all hard drives in your system. Highlighting all the drives listed in the Backup From list will do the job (see Fig. 17-1).

When you're ready, select the Start Backup button. No actual backup will take place, although every file on your system will be scanned for known viruses. The next screen will show each filename displayed as it's peeked at for signs of infection. When the operation is completed, you'll see a summary of files scanned, viruses found, and file's you've renamed.

Note that CP Backup doesn't remove the virus; only the Central Point Anti-Virus program will do that. If a virus is found, you're presented with a dialog box showing the type of virus and the name of the infected file. Rename the file with a V*xx* extension, with *xx* being a number 00 through 99 in sequence of the infected files found. Additionally, exclude that file from the backup; no one wants a virus on the backup diskettes.

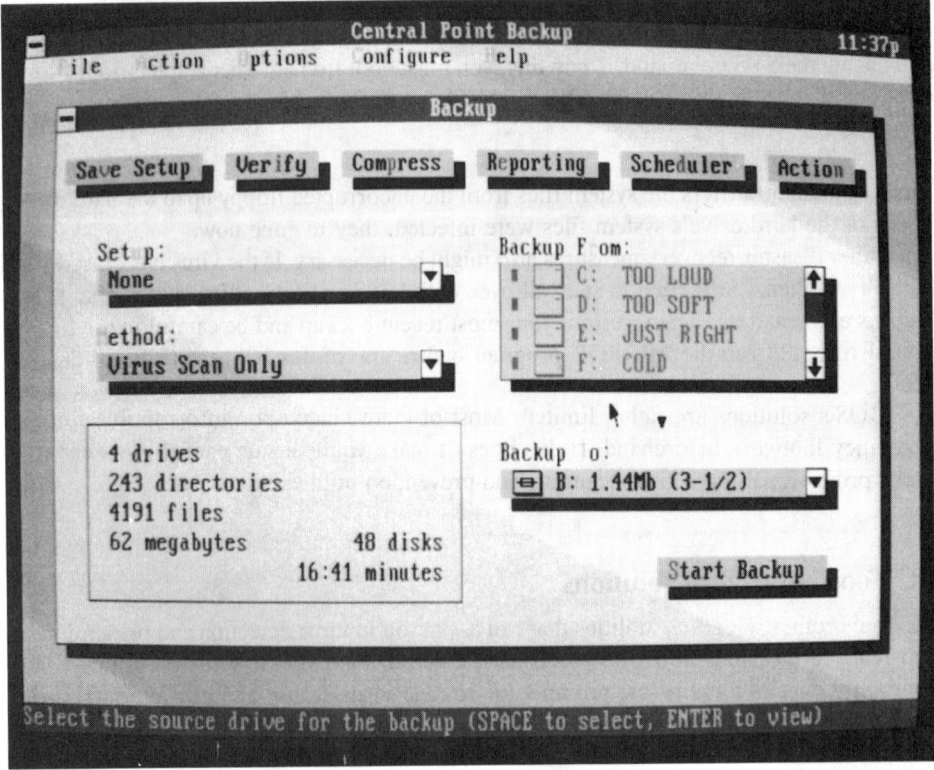

17-1 CP Backup is configured to scan viruses on the hard drive.

You optionally could use the WIPE utility to completely zap out the file; refer to the PC Tools' manual. Also, you could just go ahead and order the Anti-Virus program for further fixing.

VDefend   The VDefend utility is a memory-resident scanner, which you can install either in CONFIG.SYS or AUTOEXEC.BAT (it comes in both SYS and COM file flavors). With VDefend installed, each time you run a COM or EXE program, it will check it out, comparing it with the signatures of 400 some-odd viruses. (You can get updates to the list at periodic intervals from Central Point.) This sounds like it would slow down your system, but the effect is barely noticeable.

VDefend also prompts you if any program attempts to low-level format a hard drive. It doesn't forbid low-level formatting, but it will tell you one is about to happen. If that isn't what you want, it's time to track down the program or virus that's responsible for the low-level format attempt. If you want to low-level format, the program will let you proceed.

PC Tools
Central Point Anti-Virus
Central Point Software, Inc.
15220 NW Greenbrier Pkwy., #200
Beaverton, OR 97006
(503) 690-8090

Certus

Certus is Latin for *certainty*. You might not recognize the name, but how about *vaccine*? Vaccine was the original name for the program, the first and best solution to the PC virus. The company changed the product's name a few years back. With the name change, they added lots of features that you'll be reading about all over this chapter. The basic one remains vaccine-like: Certus is excellent virus protection for your PC.

Before moving on, I have to make an observation. In my opinion, the Certus manual, at least the one I have, is perhaps the worst computer manual I've ever read. It's long on hot air and short on descriptions of how to use the programs. There, I've said it. The information in the following sections is more lucid than anything you'll find in the manual (although this is by no means a complete treatise on Certus).

Installation and the critical diskette   Before starting installation, you should create a bootable floppy diskette. That diskette will become Certus' critical diskette, which could someday assist you in hard disk recovery. However, the diskette must be a system diskette and you must create it before installation. Do so by grabbing a diskette for the highest capacity of your A drive and using the following FORMAT command:

    FORMAT A: /S

Once that's done, you can begin installation.

Certus installation is very thorough; however, if you want to stick it in a directory other than C: \ Certus, you'll have to specify the proper directory. For example:

    INSTALL /IP *pathname*

pathname is the directory in which you want to put Certus. Also, if you don't want Certus to modify your AUTOEXEC.BAT file, specify the /NE switch. Instead, Certus will create the batch file RUNCTS.BAT, which will contain the same commands it would otherwise stick in AUTOEXEC.BAT.

On my system, I skipped installing Certus into AUTOEXEC.BAT. Instead, I run the RUNCTS.BAT program with the following line at the end of my AUTOEXEC.BAT file:

CALL C:\SYSTEM\CERTUS\RUNCTS.BAT

One of the things installation does is to create a critical diskette, which you can use to help repair your hard drive in case of a mishap. If the INSTALL program didn't create it (or you skipped that option), you can create a critical diskette with the following command:

SHELTER INSTALL

Make sure the bootable system diskette is in drive A before you press Enter.

The critical diskette serves many purposes under Certus. Primarily, it's a disaster recovery diskette, which you can use to start your system or repair the hard drive after a disaster. You can skip this step in installation, although I recommend that you don't. Once the critical diskette is created, write protect it.

One important step in installation is to create a user password and a supervisor password. These passwords are used when you run Certus or perform specific sensitive operations. (You can even use them to totally lock up the hard drive, which is covered later in this chapter.)

I recommend that you use a password; don't skip that option. Be sure to remember your passwords. Make them something simple, yet not obvious. If security is your goal, then the more difficult you make your passwords, the harder it will be for someone to crack into your system.

You can change your password after installing the program by using the PCHANGE program.

CERTUSVS, the virus scanner   When you first install Certus, it performs a scan of all program files on your hard drive. The purpose is to hunt down any infected files—even before the program installs itself. The program that does this is CERTUSVS, the virus scanner.

CERTUSVS works with a database file, VIRUSDB.DAT, which contains information about hundreds of known viruses. From a menu or command line interface, you can direct CERTUSVS to scan for viruses in memory, in your hard disk's boot sector, and in all files on your system. CERTUSVS reports its results and optionally kills any viruses as it's found.

A memory-resident version of CERTUSVS is available. VSRES provides additional run-time virus checking as programs are loaded and saved in memory. This is in addition to the memory-resident protection offered by the Certus program itself (covered later).

Killing a virus   If CERTUSVS finds a virus, it can kill it. This is done by starting the program with the /KILL ON switch or by selecting that option from the menu. (Nearly all Certus' programs are command line and menu driven. If you don't specify any command line parameters, the menu version is run.)

If a virus is found, CERTUSVS prompts you with *Kill it?* You press Y to remove the file or N to skip it. Note that, when CERTUSVS removes a file, it rubs it completely off the disk, erasing all bytes used by the file, its directory entry, and its FAT. No recovery is possible.

Once the infected file is gone, you'll want to replace it with an untainted original. Before doing so, write protect the floppy diskette. Then, perform CERTUSVS on that disk as well:

CERTUSVS A: /KILL ON

To use the menu system, type CERTUSVS by itself. Once you're sure the original is free from infection, copy it back to the hard drive, then reboot.

The manual offers additional advice on fixing and reinstalling software (page 52, if you have the same manual I do). The critical diskette will help with boot, FAT, and root directory infections. Do not reinstall your infected software from a backup diskette. After realizing you have a clean system, it's a good idea to do a full hard disk backup.

Running Certus   When Certus installs itself, either in AUTOEXEC.BAT or by creating its own RUNCTS.BAT file, it runs several programs.

CERTUS, the program, checks all program files on your system against an internal database of programs on your system (CERTUS.DAT). It compares the files to see if any have changed or have been modified. If so, you're altered to that fact.

Additionally, CERTUS sits in memory and keeps a sharp eye on important parts of the disk. If any attempt is made to alter the disk's boot sector or partition table, you'll be alerted. Also, as each program is loaded, it's checked by CERTUS against the database of programs on your system. This provides additional protection against programs that might modify after they run.

A daily log of files that CERTUS checks (in other words, all programs you run) is maintained for security purposes. For the long term, a log is maintained as well. These two files, DAILY.LOG and HISTORY.LOG, are hidden in the Certus subdirectory. (To find them, use DIR /A:H. You can list them with the TYPE command only by specifying their full name.)

CHKBOOT, another program run at boot time, will verify the integrity of the disk's partition tables, boot sector, system files, and FAT table. If an error is found, you'll be alerted to the error's presence and given an opportunity to correct it. (This usually involves the critical diskette.)

Other utilities run at startup will update the DAILY.LOG and HISTORY.LOG file, as well as make safety copies of system files in case of a hard drive crash. The system can be recovered using the critical diskette.

The QUICK utility   Certus comes with many utilities. One of them mentioned a lot in the manual is QUICK. QUICK scans programs on your disk, comparing them with the information Certus already has set in the CERTUS.DAT database. If necessary, you can use QUICK to add new programs to the database. Also, QUICK can be used globally to change the attributes of files on your hard drive. While it's true that the DOS ATTRIB command can do this as well, QUICK combines with Certus in memory to make these changes permanent. When you lock down a file with QUICK, it stays locked down and nothing can change it.

QUICK can be menu- or command-line driven. The command line version is

```
┌────────────────────────QUICKMNU────────────────────────────┐
│ ▐Complete▌ File Add Verify Protect Unprotect Subdir External │
│ Execute the command line                                     │
└─────────────────────────────────────────────────────────────┘

┌─────────────────Description of current settings────────────┐
│                                                             │
│ Verify using CERTUS's database all files matching CERTUS's  │
│ file extensions include all subdirectories of \.            │
│                                                             │
│                                                             │
└─────────────────────────────────────────────────────────────┘

┌───────────────────────Quick Command Line───────────────────┐
│ C:\SYSTEM\CERTUS\QUICK /V /S \*.@                            │
└─────────────────────────────────────────────────────────────┘
```

17-2 QUICK's menu.

QUICK; the menu version, shown in Fig. 17-2, is QUICKMNU. QUICKMNU basically creates a command line and passes it off to QUICK.

When combined with CERTUS, QUICK really can lock down a program tight—tighter than DOS ever could. For example, consider the following QUICK command:

QUICK /L+ /S C:*.@

This command sets all file attributes (system, hidden, and write-protect) for all command files on your hard drive. The files can be run, but they cannot be deleted, modified, or copied to a floppy. (You can use QUICK to remove this protection as well.) The DOS ATTRIB command cannot do this by itself.

Increasing security The SETCTS utility is used to change the security level of Certus and includes a number of interesting options for the security-conscious. Before running SETCTS, you'll need to enter your password. Then, you can modify Certus either for today's session or permanently (see Fig. 17-3).

Once you choose something to modify, you'll see the main menu screen, as shown in Fig. 17-4. The options displayed tell Certus how to work. For example, Windows tells Certus to display a pop-up window for each COM or EXE program verified as it's run. Surveillance on hard disk checks direct disk writes to hard disks, floppy disks, or both. Write to floppies allows you to lock out the floppy drives, preventing information from being written to them. FAT backup tells Certus to make a safety copy of your FAT when the system starts. Attribute lock is used with QUICK to prevent other programs from changing or modifying file's attributes. (Only QUICK can change the attributes; it requires a password.)

Uninstalling Certus Finally, if Certus is too much for your single-user system, you can remove it using the UNCTS utility. UNCTS is located on the Utilities distribution diskette. This is the only way to fully remove the program— especially when CERTUS is running (it doesn't like it when someone, or something, tries to delete it). You also might want to use the QUICK utility to remove protection from all Certus's files on disk:

QUICK /L– C:\CERTUS*.*

Reset after you're done.

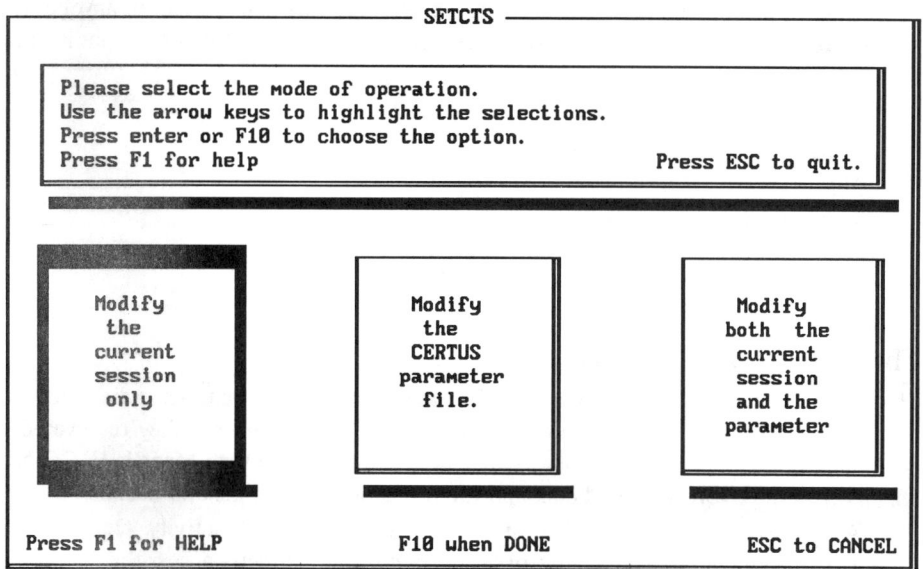

17-3 SETCTS's menu.

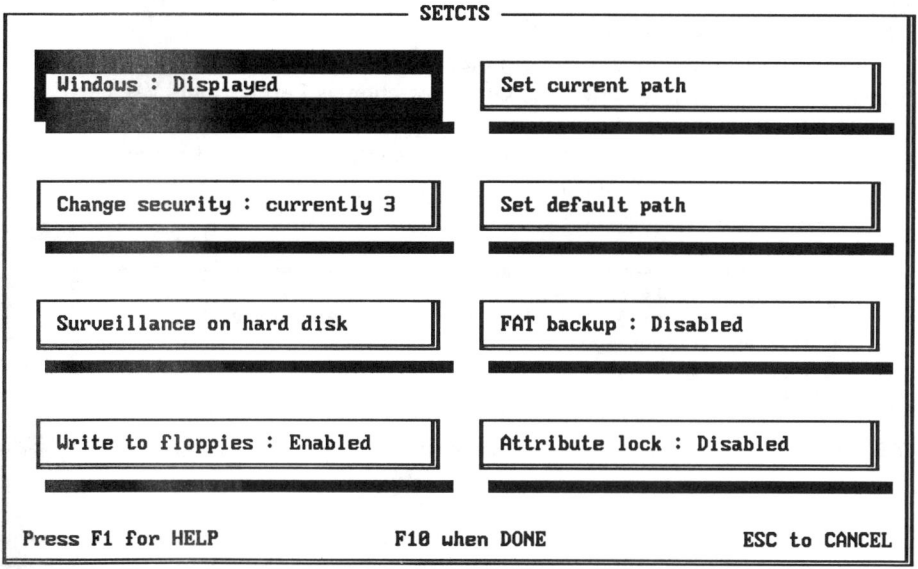

17-4 SETCTS's modification screen.

I've been a little hard on Certus, primarily because the manual needs a heavy dose of organization and some sympathy for those not familiar with the program. Fortunately, Certus does have phone support. The developers listed that number anywhere in the manual where it suggests you call them.

The program is competent and serious. The serious part is important to anyone who uses a hard drive and values the data on it. Certus might be confusing at first, but it's reliable and well supported.

Certus
Certus International Corporation
13110 Shaker Square
Cleveland, OH 44120
(216) 752-8181
(800) 722-8737

The Mace Utilities' Vaccine

The Mace Utilities are known primarily for the defragmentation and hard disk recovery tools—one of the first such DOS utilities available. (In that capacity, they're covered in detail in chapter 19.) One of the many bonus programs included with Mace is VACCINE, which offers three levels of hard disk and file protection against general nastiness.

VACCINE is a memory-resident program that monitors disk activity. Once started, it's at Level 1, which offers tight control over programs that directly access the disk's boot area, DOS's system files, the root directory, and the FAT. If any access is made to these areas, VACCINE pops up with a message alerting you to the potential damage. Note that this not only stops viruses, but also programs that have run amok, as well as dangerous activities with programs like DEBUG.

To bring VACCINE up to Level 2 protection, you type VACCINE 2 after it initially is loaded. Level 2 (Fig. 17-5) offers the same protection as Level 1, plus VACCINE monitors all direct disk access. This includes access made by programs like CHKDSK and all sector editors (such as Mace's MUSE). Again, you'll be warned of the action by VACCINE and given the chance to cancel it or to go ahead.

```
===============[Mace VACCINE]===============
 A program wants to perform an absolute write to the system
 area of your hard disk. Partition, Boot, FAT, or Directory
 data may be destroyed.
 Type Y to allow this operation, N to disallow it, or X to
 disable all protection.
===============[Protection Level = 2]===============
```

17-5 VACCINE at Level 2 is preventing the author from doing something stupid to his hard disk's boot sector.

At Level 3 protection, VACCINE is used with a second program, SURVEY, to check each program file on your system as it's loaded. SURVEY initially is used to scan your hard drive and make a record of all program files. When VACCINE is boosted to Level 3, it compares the programs you run with the HELP.CRC database of files. If any file size, date, or time has changed, you'll be alerted. (You can add files to the database when you update your system by running SURVEY /P.)

If VACCINE ever does report any oddities with any programs you've run and you suspect that the program is infected, you can use Mace's DESTROY utility to blast it off your hard drive—removing it a total of six times.

These three programs, VACCINE, SURVEY, and DESTROY, make for an interesting combination of anti-virus utilities. What's lacking, however, is any scanning software that confirms infection. So, be extra careful before you utterly destroy a file six times.

Mace Utilities
Fifth Generation Systems
10049 N. Reiger Rd.
Baton Rouge, LA 70809
(504) 291-7221
(800) 873-4384

The Norton Anti-Virus

Norton makes an Anti-Virus program as well. I don't have one, so I can't write intelligently about it. If you're curious, contact Symantec. They'll send you information or a demo diskette.

Norton Anti-Virus
Symantec Corporation
10201 Torre Ave.
Cupertino, CA 95014
(408) 253-9600

Password security

Passwords are used on mainframe computers and public bulletin board systems (BBSs). Each of the system's users is assigned his or her own unique password that only he or she knows. The password positively identifies the user, because only he or she knows what it is. Once the password is entered, it acts like a key, unlocking only certain doors. The system can direct users to the specific areas of the system they have access to. Not only will the password prevent the user from wandering around, but it prevents other users from getting into that user's area.

Two password security systems are covered here: the BOOTLOCK program that comes with Certus and the DiskLock program from Fifth Generation Systems.

Certus' BOOTLOCK program

When the Certus virus protection program runs, it asks you for your password. This program can be stuck in AUTOEXEC.BAT, but it can be defeated. For example, anyone still can access the hard drive by booting from a floppy disk or by pressing Ctrl−C to cancel AUTOEXEC.BAT, just as they would any batch file. Two simple tricks and the power of Certus's password is lost.

However, Certus comes with two utilities that can password protect your hard drive fully. The first is BOOTLOCK and the second is KEYBD.SYS.

BOOTLOCK is used to lock up your hard drive when DOS is loaded from a floppy diskette. Anytime you boot from a floppy and attempt to access the hard drive, you'll get an Invalid drive type of error. The hard drive is effectively locked.

To lock up your hard drive, run BOOTLOCK and step through the questions it asks you. You'll need your critical diskette, which will be the only way to access the locked up hard drive should you forget your password. Note that you cannot run BOOTLOCK unless you know the password you've created when you installed Certus.

Step through each of the menu choices and follow the instructions on the screen (see Fig. 17-6). After running BOOTLOCK, you really won't notice much of a change. However, boot from a bootable floppy diskette (not the critical diskette) and try to access your hard drive. You can't.

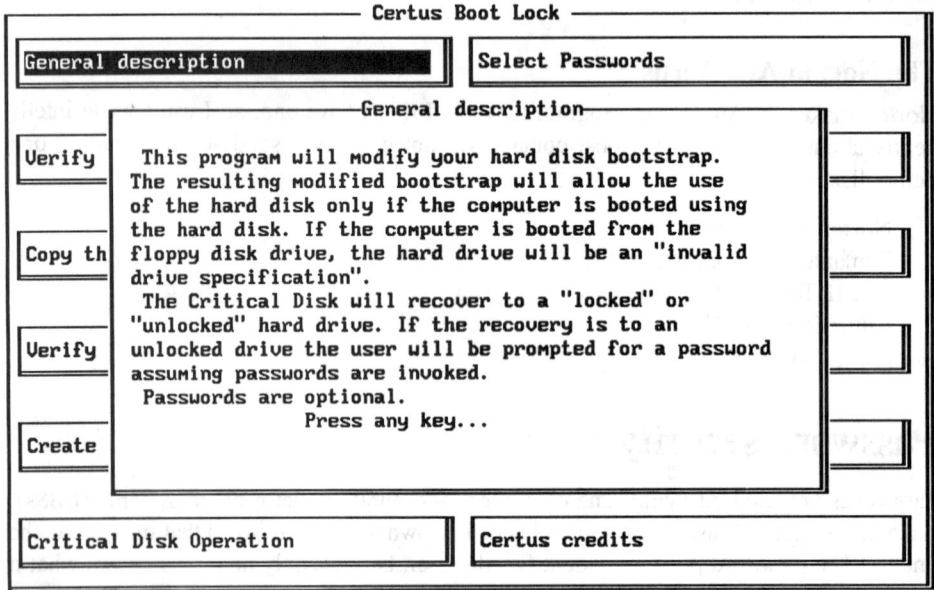

```
───────────────── Certus Boot Lock ─────────────────

│General description          ║ │ Select Passwords       ║
                    ─────────General description─────────
│Verify  │   This program will modify your hard disk bootstrap.
         │ The resulting modified bootstrap will allow the use
         │ of the hard disk only if the computer is booted using
         │ the hard disk. If the computer is booted from the
│Copy th │ floppy disk drive, the hard drive will be an "invalid
         │ drive specification".
         │   The Critical Disk will recover to a "locked" or
         │ "unlocked" hard drive. If the recovery is to an
│Verify  │ unlocked drive the user will be prompted for a password
         │ assuming passwords are invoked.
         │   Passwords are optional.
         │              Press any key...
│Create  │

│Critical Disk Operation      ║ │ Certus credits         ║
```

17-6 BOOTLOCK.

The hard drive now is protected from illegal floppy disk access. The next step in password protection process is to lock out the Ctrl−C or Ctrl−Break key presses that can cancel AUTOEXEC.BAT. That's done by using the KEYBD.SYS device driver in CONFIG.SYS.

Edit your CONFIG.SYS file and place a line similar to the following in it:

DEVICE = C: \ CERTUS \ KEYBD.SYS

Remember to specify the proper path for your Certus subdirectory; in the previous command, C: \ CERTUS is assumed.

The KEYBD.SYS command disables the Ctrl−C and Ctrl−Break keystrokes. Now, no one can cancel AUTOEXEC.BAT as it runs.

In AUTOEXEC.BAT, you should run the Certus program, which requires a password for access. Your system now is password protected. Running CERTUS also will reactivate the Ctrl−C and Ctrl−Break keystrokes, so other programs can use them or so the user can Ctrl−C out of AUTOEXEC.BAT. However, security has been achieved; the hard drive is protected.

If you don't run CERTUS, then the Certus utility program RKEYBD.COM can be run to restore Ctrl−C and Ctrl−Break.

The only limitation to this system is that you have only one password for your entire system. For a single-user system, that's no problem. If several users have access to the system, however, they all will be using the same password. Further security can be achieved by using file encryption, which is covered in the next chapter.

Fifth Generation Systems' DiskLock

DiskLock, from Fifth Generation Systems, is an excellent password protection program. I found it much easier to use than BOOTLOCK. In addition to password-protecting the hard drive and locking out access from a booted floppy, DiskLock offers individual file and directory locking as well as file encryption and decryption.

DiskLock is installed from a DISKCOPY of the original diskette. You must make a DISKCOPY—and keep that copy around. It's your only method of uninstalling the program, should you decide to do so.

DiskLock installs everything and protects the entire hard drive during installation. Unlike BOOTLOCK, there are no hidden hurdles to jump over. Everything is done for you.

The key to the protection is how DiskLock originally scans the hard drive, ensuring that no floppy disk can access it. The DISKLOCK.SYS device driver is responsible for initially asking for your password—so there's no chance of someone breaking into AUTOEXEC.BAT.

Once DiskLock is in memory, it offers several hard drive lockup options. You can set a timer to go off after a certain period of inactivity. DiskLock then will blank your screen and wait. Only if you know DiskLock's special hotkey can you see your screen again; however, what you see will be encrypted. When DiskLock accepts your password for access, it then unscrambles the display. You also can lock up your system immediately and blank the screen by pressing DiskLock's hotkey combination.

To change your password, hotkey combination, or the inactivity timeout, you run the DiskLock program, DL (see Fig. 17-7). You also can use this program to individually protect files and directories, as well as for data encryption and decryption.

DiskLock's ability to lock files and directories might seem rather lame to you. However, that's only if you're logged into the system as the primary user. A secondary password can be assigned (which is set under the Password menu). It then must be activated under the Configuration menu (Set Access Level). When that's done, any user logging into the system using the secondary password won't have access to the locked files and directories. Those areas of disk will be inaccessible—like they didn't exist.

The primary password should be given only to the office computer master and be used only by that person. This feature can further be used to protect system files from deletion by unwitting users. DiskLock also keeps a log of illegal access attempts, although it doesn't log usage time for valid password accounts.

I like DiskLock. It's simple and effective. DiskLock didn't hurt my brain like BOOTLOCK did. So, if you want simple and effective password protection and encryption, go for DiskLock. While it doesn't offer Certus' virus protection, if security is your only concern, nothing beats it.

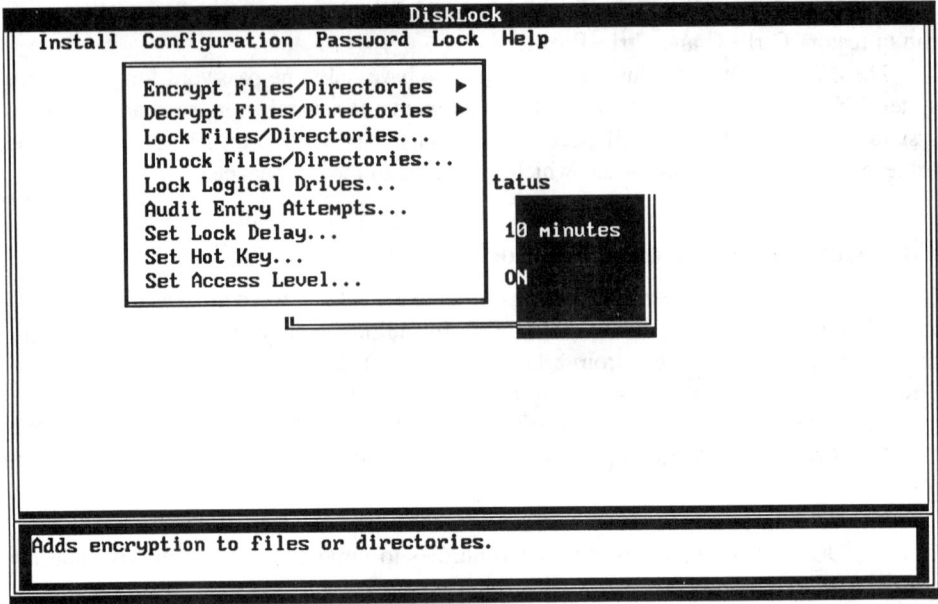

```
┌──────────────────────────────────────────────────────────────────┐
│                            DiskLock                                │
├──────────────────────────────────────────────────────────────────┤
│  Install   Configuration  Password  Lock   Help                    │
│         ┌────────────────────────────────┐                         │
│         │ Encrypt Files/Directories   ▶  │                         │
│         │ Decrypt Files/Directories   ▶  │                         │
│         │ Lock Files/Directories...      │                         │
│         │ Unlock Files/Directories...    │ tatus                   │
│         │ Lock Logical Drives...         │                         │
│         │ Audit Entry Attempts...        │ ████████████            │
│         │ Set Lock Delay...              │ 1█ minutes  █           │
│         │ Set Hot Key...                 │             █           │
│         │ Set Access Level...            │ ON          █           │
│         └────────────────────────────────┘             █           │
│              ██████████████████████████████████████████            │
│                                                                    │
│                                                                    │
│                                                                    │
│                                                                    │
│                                                                    │
│                                                                    │
├──────────────────────────────────────────────────────────────────┤
│ Adds encryption to files or directories.                           │
│                                                                    │
└──────────────────────────────────────────────────────────────────┘
```

17-7   DiskLock's menu-driven program.

DiskLock
Fifth Generation Systems
10049 N. Reiger Rd.
Baton Rouge, LA 70809
(504) 291-7221
(800) 873-4384

A real SCREAMER

In my efforts to find public domain password protection programs, I came up mostly empty handed. Nothing is going to beat Certus' BOOTLOCK or FGS's DiskLock. Any other program that sticks a password in AUTOEXEC.BAT or CONFIG.SYS can be circumvented by booting from a floppy diskette. However, I did find one amusing password-like program, SCREAMER.

SCREAMER is a memory-resident password program and screen blanker. It's rather limited, to be sure. However, it has one hilarious side-effect. If an illegal access attempt is made, the program will scream through your PC's speaker the following message:

Help! Don't touch me! Unauthorized use of this computer. Help!

It's a little fuzzy, but it's charming.

The format for SCREAMER is as follows:

SCREAMER [*codekey*] [/M] [/U]

Without any options, SCREAMER comes with an information box and asks if you want to blank the screen. The program is a good screen blanker and works for just about any display, except Hercules. It asks for a code key, a single key you press to regain access to your computer. Once that's done, SCREAMER asks if you want to blank the screen. If so, the screen goes black. Only by pressing the code key will you regain access. Otherwise, your computer screams at you (again and again).

You can predefine a code key by specifying a single key as *codekey* after SCREAMER. This would work in an AUTOEXEC.BAT or any batch file to add password protection (and annoying screeching).

The /M switch makes SCREAMER memory resident. You activate the program by pressing Ctrl−Spacebar. SCREAMER then will pop up and prompt for your code key password and ask if you want the screen blanked. No other access is permitted at this point, unless you press the proper key.

The memory-resident feature provides great *I'm-at-lunch* security. I can activate SCREAMER while in WordPerfect by pressing Ctrl−Spacebar. By not blanking the screen, what you see is WordPerfect. Yet, only by pressing the proper key can anyone gain access. (Otherwise, the PC screams away.) Don't forget your code key.

To uninstall SCREAMER from memory, use the /U switch.

SCREAMER is a shareware program and the author would like $5 for it. The program definitely is worth five bucks. To get SCREAMER and to register the program, write to the following address:

Leithauser Research
4649 Van Kleeck Drive
New Smyrna Beach, FL 32169

SCREAMER has been included on the companion diskette, but it's only being distributed on the diskette. You have not paid for it. So, if you use SCREAMER and enjoy it, fork over the dough.

Other ways of protecting the hard disk

Besides using a password, there are other ways of keeping unauthorized people from using your computer. In addition to a software password, some computers, such as most AT-class and 386 machines, come with a lock and key. Once the key is turned, the computer is locked and it sits tight until it's unlocked.

Depending on the make of the computer, the key can do a number of things. With most computers, turning off the key disables the keyboard and prevents the computer from being reset or booted. If you step out of the office for a moment, locking the computer ensures that no one else uses it while you're out. Because the keyboard is turned off, there's nothing they can do. If the computer is off and locked, turning the computer on won't make it boot. Your system is secure.

Some computers with locked keys might boot up and run AUTOEXEC—all with a disabled keyboard. Others simply will sit there until the key is turned. Still other AT compatibles use the key as a mere decoration. Internally, the key isn't connected to anything.

With some networked systems, the key might be used to lock your system out of the network. This measure would prevent other users on the network from accessing your system's hard disk. Again, this depends on the type of computer and networking software available.

The LOCK.COM utility

A software form of the lock and key is included on the companion diskette. The LOCK .COM program has the effect of putting a giant write-protect tab on the hard disk. Once LOCK.COM is run, no file on the hard disk can be changed, renamed, modified, or deleted. It just won't work.

LOCK.COM is a memory-resident program. What it does is to intercept all access to the hard disk. When the LOCK is on, it tests to see if the hard disk is being accessed to change information. If so, it immediately tells the operating system that the hard disk is write protected. LOCK does allow the hard disk to be accessed to simply read information without any complications.

The best aspect of LOCK is that it won't allow the hard disk to be reformatted. With the LOCK on, a hard disk FORMAT only verifies information on the hard disk; nothing is erased.

To install LOCK, type LOCK at the DOS prompt:

```
C:\ > LOCK
Your hard disk is not Write- & Format-protected
Run LOCK again to turn it OFF.
```

Any attempt to change anything on the hard disk will produce a write-protect error. For example, an attempt to rename the file LETTER to LTTR results in:

```
C:\STUFF> REN LETTER LTTR
Write protect error writing drive C
Abort, Retry, Ignore?
```

Once LOCK is installed, it can be turned on or off again by typing LOCK at the DOS prompt. For example:

```
C:\ > LOCK
LOCK is now OFF (no hard disk protection).
Run it again to turn it ON.
```

Now, the disk is back to normal. Any attempt to change or modify a file on the hard disk will not be stopped. To turn lock on again, type LOCK once more.

Summary

Hard disk security covers many aspects, with backup being central. Beyond backup comes data security and preventing illegal access. The big Virus Scare has led to many anti-viral programs, among them Central Point's Anti-Virus and other tools, as well as the Certus suite of anti-virus and hard disk protection programs.

Password protection offers further security for the hard drive, preventing access to your important data and programs from snoopy users as well as virus-infecting programs. Unfortunately, under DOS, password security is rather limited. DiskLock only gives you two passwords, Certus' BOOTLOCK, only one. That's too few for an entire hard drive. However, this is the most secure form of protection available at present.

Beyond password protection comes individual protection of files and their contents, as well as directories. This is accomplished under DOS by means of data encryption, which is covered in the next chapter on file security.

18

File security

If more than one person uses the computer and a password security system seems limited or if you're the only one using your computer and you find a password system overwhelming, you might look into individually protecting files. This can be done with DOS by changing the attributes by which DOS describes each file. It also can be done by data encryption.

This chapter discusses file security measures, some of which are built into DOS. DOS allows certain files to be made invisible; only DOS can see them. DOS also can mark files as read-only, which has the effect of putting a write-protect tab on a single file. As a secondary line of defense, data files can be encrypted, or scrambled, according to a specific key. Anyone who doesn't know the key would not be able to interpret information in the file.

Protecting files under DOS

Besides the information displayed by the DIR command, each file has special information associated with it. Part of this information controls whether a file or subdirectory is visible or invisible (hidden from a DIR listing). Anyone who's interested in data security certainly will see how hiding files can be very practical. Keep in mind, however, that this level of protection isn't foolproof; anything DOS can do is easily undone by someone with the right knowledge.

There are two ways to protect a file using the special information DOS associates with it. First, you can make a file invisible. Second, you can make a file read-only, or write-protected. Granted, these measure aren't smart enough to guard your files against a devious computer virus, but they are smart enough to protect them from sloppy users and carelessness. (More information on fighting The Virus is provided in chapter 17.)

File attributes

Every file in the directory has an attribute byte associated with it. Inside this byte are eight attribute bits that tell DOS a few things about the file. For example, one attribute bit, the modify bit, lets the BACKUP program know if a file has been changed or modified since the last backup. Each time the file is changed or modified, DOS switches this bit's value from 0 to 1, or from off to on.

The eight attribute bits DOS associates with each file are listed in Table 18-1. With regards to bits 4 and 3, every subdirectory and the volume label (name of the disk) take up space in the directory. They are considered files by DOS even though they aren't used as such. Bit 5 is reset when a file is created or modified after the BACKUP and XCOPY commands. That one bit is referred to as the *modify*, or *archive*, *bit*.

Table 18-1   Attribute bits associated with each file.

Bit	If ON (set to 1) means . . .
0	File is read-only
1	File is hidden
2	File is a system file
3	File is a volume label entry
4	File is a subdirectory
5	File has been backed up
6	Nothing
7	Nothing

Bits 2, 1, and 0 commonly are used with system files. Bit 2 informs DOS that the file is a system file, either IO.SYS or MSDOS.SYS. Bit 1 hides a file, making it invisible. Bit 0 puts a protective lock on the file, preventing it from any modification or deletion.

There normally is no reason to change any of these attribute bytes. DOS assigns them as needed or to protect its own system files. However, you can manipulate them to add your own level of file security. This can be done with DOS's ATTRIB command.

The ATTRIB command

The ATTRIB, or attribute, command allows you to modify the attributes of any file on disk—including subdirectories, starting with DOS 5.0.

The format of the ATTRIB command is:

ATTRIB [±R][±A][±H][±S] *filename* [/S]

The R, A, H, and S items are used to set or reset a file's read-only, archive, hidden, and system attributes. A plus in front of the character turns that attribute on; a minus turns it off. You can specify more than one attribute at a time, but separate each by a space. Note that there is no slash before the plus or minus sign.

filename is required. It can be a single file or a group as specified by wildcards. When one or more of the R, A, H, or S items is specified, it changes that attribute for the filename or group of files. If the items aren't specified, then the ATTRIB command will display the current attributes of the files.

The optional /S switch is used to change or check the attributes of any files in any subdirectories under the current directory.

By itself, ATTRIB followed by a filename displays the attributes of the file or files listed:

```
C:\ > ATTRIB *.*
  SH    C:\IO.SYS
  SH    C:\MSDOS.SYS
  A     C:\CONFIG.SYS
  A     C:\COMMAND.COM
      R C:\WINA20.386
  A     C:\AUTOEXEC.BAT
```

IO.SYS and MSDOS.SYS are both system and hidden files. CONFIG.SYS, COM-MAND.COM, and AUTOEXEC.BAT have their archive bit set, meaning they've been copied or modified since the last backup. WINA20.386 has its read-only attribute set.

Changing a file's attributes

To change the attribute of any file or group of files, specify an attribute item with a plus or minus sign before the filename. The A, or archive, attribute is a harmless one to experiment with. Try the following in your root directory of drive C:

```
ATTRIB − A *.*
```

This command removes the archive attribute from all files in the root directory. You might get the following feedback:

```
Not resetting hidden file C:\IO.SYS
Not resetting hidden file C:\MSDOS.SYS
```

Hidden files have special protection.

To verify your work, use ATTRIB *.* to see that no files have their archive attribute set.

The A attribute is turned on only when a file has been modified. Once that file is backed up or XCOPYed, its A status is switched off.

Technically speaking, the bit in the file's attribute byte is set to 1 by BACKUP or XCOPY. When the A attribute is turned on, either by changing the file or by using the ATTRIB command, the bit in the attribute byte is reset to 0. If this sounds backwards, that's because it is.

The only real advantage of changing the A attribute is when backing up or XCOPYing files. When the /M switch is used with BACKUP or XCOPY, those programs only look for files with the A attribute. Using ATTRIB, you can selectively turn on or off the A attribute and choose which files will be backed up or XCOPYed. For example:

```
ATTRIB + A *.*
```

sets the A attribute on each file in the current directory. Now, every file will appear to DOS as if it were modified since the last backup. This includes all those files in an incremental backup no matter what. Using the ATTRIB command you can selectively include or exclude files from being backed up. For example:

```
ATTRIB − A \*.* /S
```

In the previous command, the S switch is used with the pathname, \ *.*, to match all files in the root directory and all files in all subdirectories, e.g., all files on the drive. With the − A item specified, the archive attribute will be removed from all files.

Making files read-only

Files with their R attribute set have a read-only status. Any attempt to delete, rename, or modify these files results in an error. This gives you a minor form of file security; although viruses still can weasel their way into a file, you cannot accidentally delete it with DEL *.*.

For example, to protect program files on a hard drive, you'd enter the following two ATTRIB commands:

```
ATTRIB +R \*.COM /S
ATTRIB +R \*.EXE /S
```

These commands add + R, the read-only attribute, of all COM and EXE files on the hard drive. Those files can no longer be deleted, renamed, modified, or changed. However, they can be run, because they're read only. This can be done with any sensitive files you don't want to delete. Simply use that file's name with the ATTRIB command and the + R option.

If you later discover you need to change or delete a file, switch its read-only status off. For example:

```
ATTRIB − R NOVEMBER.WKS
```

normalizes the file NOVEMBER.WKS, removing its read-only protection. To remove the read-only protection for all files in the current subdirectory, use:

```
ATTRIB − R *.*
```

Hiding files

The ATTRIB command also can be used to hide files, rendering them invisible. The file won't appear in the standard DIR command listing and won't be included in any command using the *.* or any other matching wildcard.

To hide a file from view, use the ATTRIB command with the + H item. For example:

```
ATTRIB +H CLAUDE
```

will hide the file, CLAUDE, from view. You still can access it using any DOS command or program by specifying its full name, otherwise it's ensconced.

You also can hide subdirectories with the ATTRIB command. Just specify the sub-directory's name and it's invisible:

```
ATTRIB +H UTILITY
```

makes the UTILITY directory, a subdirectory of the current directory invisible.

To make a file or subdirectory visible again, you need to know its full name, then use it with the ATTRIB command and the −H option.

Now, I need to tell you about the drawbacks. While DOS 5.0 started the trend of the ATTRIB command making a file invisible, it also introduced the /A switch with the DIR command. From chapter 3, you recall that the /A switch displays all files in the directory regardless of their attribute. /A:H displays only hidden files. This wrecks any file security hiding files brings.

You also can use the ATTRIB *.* command to display hidden files. Because ATTRIB *.* lists the attributes of all files in the current directory, it will display anything you have there—anything, that is, except for hidden subdirectories. However, you still can locate hidden subdirectories using the DIR /A:H command.

Sneaky file names

DOS allows certain special characters to be used when naming files. Although the DOS manual doesn't specifically state these characters can be used, they're accepted by DOS and serve as an interesting method of file security. It should be noted that, because these characters are not specifically mentioned, this procedure might not work with future releases of DOS.

Normally, a file name can contain any ASCII character (letters, numbers, or punctuation symbols) except the following:

. " / \ [ ] : * | < > + = ; , ?

Also, a file cannot contain any control character (^C, ^A, etc.), or a space. This leaves a wide variety of characters available on the keyboard for naming files. Additionally, it allows certain characters not available on the keyboard to be used for naming files. These are the extended ASCII characters. (See appendix C.)

The extended ASCII characters can be typed at any time using the Alt key and your keyboard's numeric keypad. (Some utility programs (i.e., Borland's SuperKey) disable this feature.)

For example, the extended ASCII character number 219 is a solid block. To type this character, press and hold the Alt key and type 219 on the numeric keypad. When you release the Alt key, the solid block appears.

This can be done with regular ASCII characters as well. Try typing the following numbers. For each, press and hold the Alt key and type the number. Release the Alt key after the number is entered:

72, 101, 108, 108, 111, 33, 32, 1

The extended ASCII set contains a variety of characters. However, character 255 is a blank. If a file were renamed using this blank character, it would appear as a mysterious blank in the directory listing.

For example, suppose the file TEST1 is on disk. To rename this file as the extended ASCII character 255 type:

REN TEST1 [Alt−255]

Hold Alt and type 255 on the numeric pad.

TEST1, which now is named [255], appears as follows in a DIR listing:

```
Volume in drive A has no label
Volume Serial Number is 0521-16DE
Directory of A:\

              84 2-11-94   2:16p
TEST2         85 2-11-94   2:25p
TEST3         85 2-11-94   2:25p
       3 file(s)       254 bytes
              1455600 bytes free
```

Unlike hiding a file, [255] is listed. Its name is blank, but the size and date show up. The other files in this directory also could be changed to blanks. Remember, no two files can share the same name, so TEST2 could be renamed [255][255], TEST3 could be renamed [255][255][255]. Up to 11 files can be named in a single directory using the [255] blank character.

As long as no one else using your computer knows about the extended ASCII names for files, other bizarre names can be created. Try renaming a file as [224][225][226]. The new filename appears in the directory as alpha, beta, and gamma, the first three letters of the Greek alphabet.

Along the same lines, it might be a good idea not to give certain files on disk obvious filenames. For example, PAYROLL.WKS is one file any curious office employee might want to take a peek at. Renaming the file SAMPLE.WKS, or even MEMO.DOC, might be enough to keep potentially prying eyes away.

PC Tools' Data Monitor

PC Tools' Data Monitor program is a memory-resident utility that provides extra protection for sensitive files and directories on your system. It's not particular to computer viruses, but I think it's rather neat. Data Monitor definitely fits into the same vein of data protection as the other utilities covered here (but it's important enough to warrant its own section).

Data Monitor is a single program, DATAMON.EXE, that contains five individual modules (see Fig. 18-1). Three of these, Delete Protection, Directory Lock, and Write Protection, should be of special interest to security-conscious hard disk users. All five of the options are discussed in the following sections.

When you first run Data Monitor, you'll want to configure several of its options, tuning them to the way you prefer. This configuration is done only the first time you run DATAMON.EXE. From that point on, you can load the program and have it run in memory without having to set options manually. Individual items can be switched off using DATAMON at the DOS prompt after it's loaded.

Delete Protection

Delete Protection works similar to DOS's MIRROR command. One of the Delete Protection's options is the Delete Tracker, which essentially is the MIRROR command. A better option, in my opinion, is the Delete Sentry.

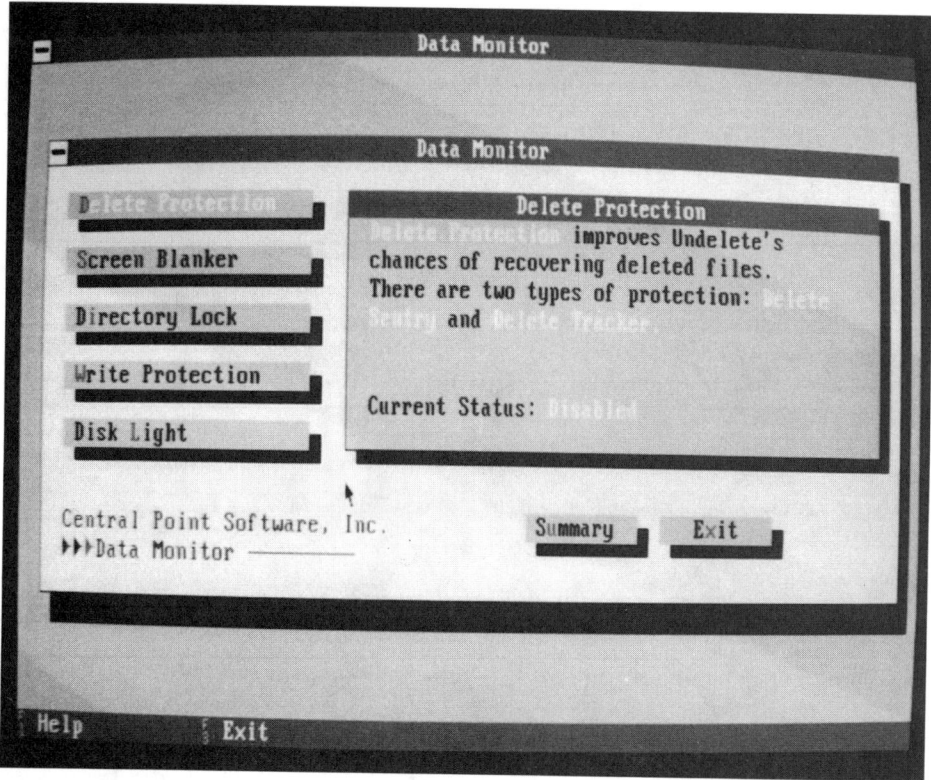

18-1 PC Tools' Data Monitor.

Unlike Delete Tracking, the Delete Sentry doesn't record just the filename and other tidbits of information about a deleted file. Instead, Delete Sentry takes all deleted files and carts them off—in their entirety—to a hidden subdirectory on your disk. The files sit there until you rescue them or the Delete Sentry optionally will purge, or delete, them after a given time interval.

Figure 18-2 shows the Delete Sentry configuration screen. The options displayed are the standard setup options.

I really like Delete Sentry. It's not a particularly security-conscious command, but it's along the lines of the KILL batch file I wrote for another book. Basically, KILL is used instead of DEL or ERASE and copies files off to a \TRASH subdirectory. No file actually is deleted. Delete Sentry is more efficient and totally automatic, but still works on the same principle.

Screen Blanker

The Screen Blanker is a screen saving program that blanks your display after a given interval. It has an optional password, which must be typed to regain access to the system after you've been away. This module of the Data Monitor works similarly to the SCREAMER program mentioned in chapter 17—although it doesn't screech out a warning if an illegal access is attempted.

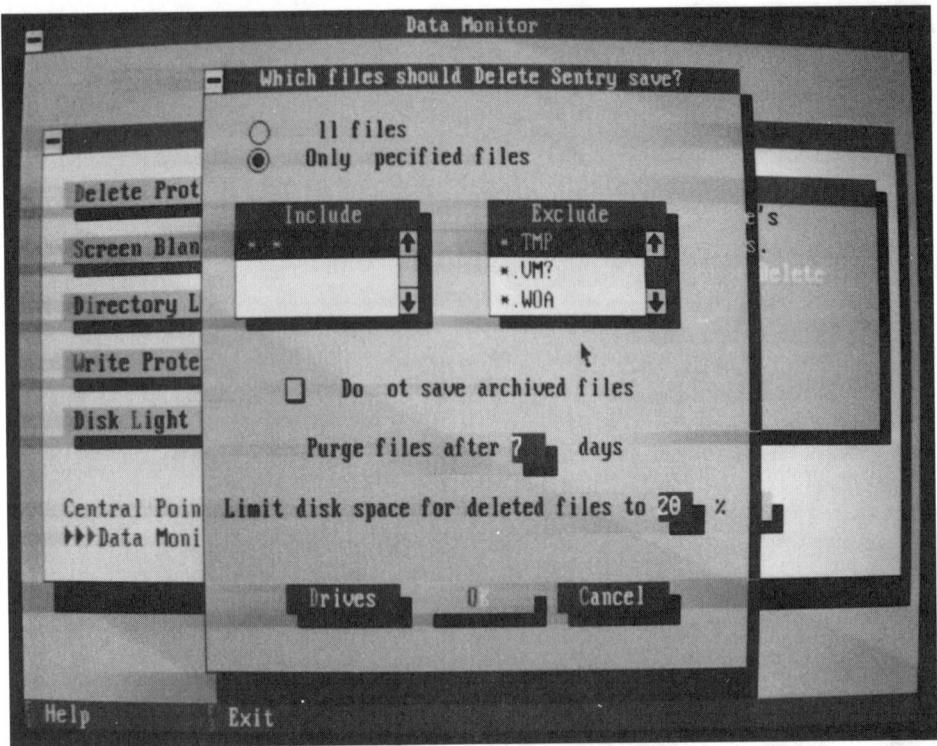

18-2 Delete Sentry's configuration screen.

Directory Lock

Directory Lock (Fig. 18-3) is a module designed for file security. Using Directory Lock, you assign one or more subdirectories on your system as special password-protected directories. Whenever any attempt is made to access that directory, you'll be greeted with a password prompt. Additionally, all files copied to that directory will be stored in an encrypted format, decryptable only if you know the password.

The Directory Lock program only locks one directory name. For example, if you have several WORK directories on your drive, you can specify that name and Directory Lock will protect all of them. When you use the CD command to change to that directory, you'll be prompted with a password dialog box. Only by entering the password can you access the directory.

To re-lock a directory once you've accessed it, you type the following:

```
DATAMON /DATALOCK+
```

The /DATALOCK+ switch turns the lock back on. Once again, you have a locked directory.

The inherent drawback here is that only one password is assigned for all the locked directories. This is okay for a single user; however, for multiple users on one PC, it provides little protection.

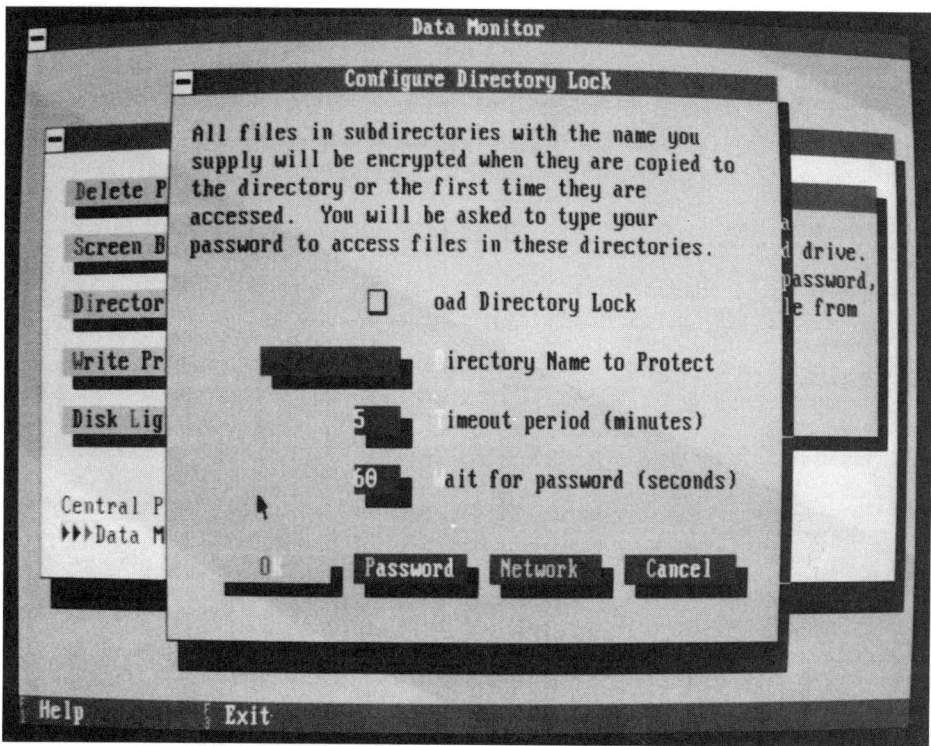

18-3 The Configure Directory Lock dialog box.

Write Protection

The Write Protection feature (Fig. 18-4) of Data Monitor is used to intercept attempts to access specific areas of disk or certain files. Write Protection is a higher order of protection than that offered by the ATTRIB command and DOS's file attributes. What the Write Protection module does is to actively examine all DOS access to the files you specify and prompt you when an access attempt is made.

Write Protection monitors four items: the entire disk, the system areas (boot track, partition tables, etc.), floppy drives, and files specified by wildcards or individually. If any attempt is made to access the disk or files you've specified, a warning dialog box appears. In the warning box, you can select to allow or disallow the access or to disable Write Protection's monitoring.

Disk Light

The Disk Light module is rather trivial. What it does is to graphically show disk access by flashing the drive letter in the upper right corner of your screen. The letter is followed by an r for read operations and a w for writes.

If you already can see a drive light on your computer, this is dumb. However, if you're attached to a network drive or if your computer sits under a desk, it's an interesting item to have.

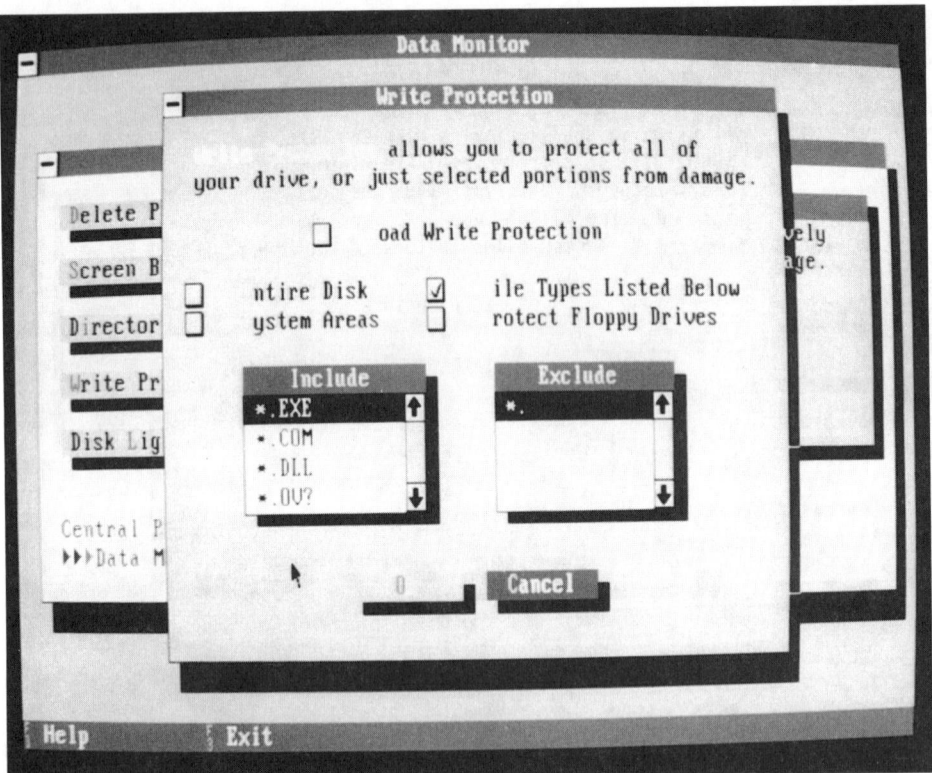

18-4 The Write Protection configuration dialog box.

All of these modules are set and loaded using the DATAMON program, which you can install in your AUTOEXEC.BAT file. While DATAMON is configured using a menu-driven system, it's possible to control the program using the command line. Indeed, using the command line is how you access the program once it's been loaded into memory.

PC Tools
Central Point Software, Inc.
15220 NW Greenbrier Pkwy., #200
Beaverton, OR 97006
(503) 690-8090

All about data encryption

Data encryption is the systematic scrambling of information in a file, making that information unreadable. Because the information is scrambled systematically, or according to a pattern, it can be unscrambled and returned back to its original form. Scrambling information in this manner is referred to as *encryption*. Unscrambling is referred to as *decryption*.

Encrypting a file typically involves the use of a key, or password. This key works like the secret decoder rings of old. These decoder rings had two movable circles on them, one inside the other. On both circles were the alphabet. If the decoding pattern were $A-P$, the inner circle was turned so that its A matched the P on the outer circle. The relationship between the characters on both circles looked something like the following:

```
ABCDEFGHIJKLMNOPQRSTUVWXYZ
PQRSTUVWXYZABCDEFGHIJKLMNO
```

Kids then could use this relationship to translate strings such as:

```
TPI BPAID BTPA!
```

Into:

```
EAT MALTO MEAL!
```

Encrypting a computer file on disk works surprisingly similar to this. (Who'd have ever thought?) Every character of the file is translated using a special key. The key also is used to decrypt the file back to its original state.

Very simple data encryption routines operate like a secret decoder ring. Every character in the file is added or subtracted from a certain key value. However, these schemes usually prove too simple for most practical encryption. (After all, knowing any kid with a secret decoder ring was capable of reading your encrypted files would prove distressing.) Because of this limitation, more advanced methods of encrypting computer data are used.

The following sections elaborate on this concept, using the BASIC programming language that comes with DOS. Note that this program is used purely for demonstration purpose; I wouldn't expect anyone to seriously encrypt anything with it.

Data encryption using BASIC

Imagine an encryption method that works like a decoder ring, except the decoding key is not a single character but a string of up to 255 characters. This method is used in the file CRYPT.BAS (a BASIC language file) included on the companion diskette. Encrypting files works by adding the key string of characters in sequence to each character in the file.

For example, suppose the key string is TESTING. The file to encrypt contains the following:

now is the time for all good men.

The CRYPT.BAS program works by adding the key string TESTING to each character in the file as follows:

```
TESTINGTESTINGTESTINGTESTINGTESTI
now is the time for all good men.
```

The result is a bunch of strange characters, which are not easy to read nor understand. Unless you know the exact string of characters and their length, decrypting the file would take quite a while. (Keep in mind, this program still is an elementary form of data encryption and is not foolproof.)

To decrypt the file, the same key string of characters is subtracted from each character in the file. Only the exact key string of characters can properly decrypt the file. So, by adding the key string to the string of strange characters, the result is:

```
now is the time for all good men.
```

This method of encryption works on data and program files, as well as straight text, or ASCII, files. Just don't forget the key string.

The following program demonstrates the encryption routines discussed earlier. It's written in the BASIC programming language, which is supplied with some versions of DOS as GWBASIC and with DOS 5 as QBASIC. (It also could be BASICA.) You can type in this program yourself to see how data encryption and decryption can work.

To enter BASIC, type the name of your BASIC programming language. For example:

```
C: \ > QBASIC
```

QBASIC works a lot like the DOS Editor, which was covered in chapter 6. The Editor is a subset of the QBASIC program.

After starting QBASIC, press Esc to skip using the survival guide and you'll be placed into the QuickBASIC program interpreter, where other programs for your PC can be written.

Carefully type in the program shown in Fig. 18-5, including the line numbers. Double check your work to make certain you don't mistype anything.

If you have the companion diskette, you can quickly load the program from there. It's named CRYPT.BAS. You would load it using the following command:

```
QBASIC CRYPT.BAS
```

You also can select the Open command from QuickBASIC's File menu.

After you've loaded or typed in the program, save it as CRYPT.BAS; pull down the File menu and select the Save option. Name the file CRYPT (the BAS extension is added automatically to all BASIC language files).

Exit QuickBASIC by selecting the Exit item from the File menu.

To run this BASIC program from DOS type:

```
QBASIC /RUN CRYPT
```

The Crypt program displays the following:

```
A Sample File Encryption Program in BASIC
Written by Dan Gookin, Copyright (C) TAB Books
```

```
Will you be <D>ecrypting or <E>ncrypting? (D or E):
```

Press D or E to decrypt or encrypt a file, respectively. Next, the program asks:

```
Enter the INPUT file:
```

If you're encrypting, enter the name of the file you'll be encrypting. If decrypting, enter the name of the already encrypted file you'll be decrypting. Then, you will be prompted to:

```
Enter the OUTPUT file:
```

If you're encrypting a file, type the name of a new file on disk, one that will contain the encrypted data. If decrypting, enter the name of the file that will contain the decrypted output. In both cases, the output file should be a new file on disk.

Next, you're asked to enter the key string:

```
Enter the keyword pattern:
```

```
100 KEY OFF
110 COLOR 7,0
120 WIDTH 80
130 SCREEN 0,0,0
140 CLS
150 PRINT "A Simple File Encryption Program in BASIC"
160 PRINT "Written by Dan Gookin, Copyright (C) TAB Books"
170 PRINT
180 PRINT "Will you be <D>ecrypting or <E>ncrypting? (D or E): ";
190 B$ = INPUT$(1)
200 B$ = CHR$(ASC(B$) AND 95)
210 IF B$><"E" AND B$><"D" GOTO 190
230 PRINT B$
240 PRINT
250 LINE INPUT "Enter the INPUT file: ";FILEIN$
260 LINE INPUT "Enter the OUTPUT file: ";FILEOUT$
270 PRINT
280 LINE INPUT "Enter the keyword pattern: ";KEYWORD$
290 KEY.LEN = LEN(KEYWORD$)
300 IF KEY.LEN = O THEN 280
320 REM *****************************
330 REM Encryption/Decryption routines
340 REM *****************************
350 OPEN FILEIN$ FOR INPUT AS 1
360 OPEN FILEOUT$ FOR OUTPUT AS 2
370 FOR X=1 TO KEY.LEN
380    IF EOF(1) THEN 460
390    D$ = MID$(KEYWORD$,X,1)
400    A$=INPUT$(1,1)
410 ON INSTR("DE",B$) GOSUB 480,510
420    PRINT#2,C$;
430    PRINT C$;
440 NEXT X
450 GOTO 370
460 CLOSE
470 END
475 REM *****************************
480 REM Decrypt it:
490 C$ = CHR$((ASC(A$)-ASC(D$)) MOD 255)
500 RETURN
510 REM Encrypt it:
520 C$ = CHR$((ASC(A$)+ASC(D$)) MOD 255)
530 RETURN
```

18-5 The CRYPT.BAS BASIC program for file encryption.

Type up to 255 letters, characters, or symbols. Press Enter when you're done. Remember this string; it's the key by which information will be encrypted. Once you have entered the key, the Crypt program reads information from the INPUT file and, depending on whether you selected D or E, it decrypts or encrypts that file's information and saves it to the output file.

This is a simple—and limited—method for encrypting files. Note that BASIC has trouble reading in binary (non-text) files. Even then, anyone good at the game Crypt-o could decipher the file, given time.

Description of CRYPT.BAS

The following explanation of the CRYPT.BAS program is provided for those interested in BASIC programming. It is not required reading, so feel free to skip up to the section titled

"Using PC Tools' PC Secure." If you're interested in the BASIC programming language, refer to your library or book store for a complete selection of good, introductory BASIC programming texts.

Lines 100 through 170 set up the computer screen and display the title of the program. Lines 100 through 140 establish that the screen's function key display is off, the colors used are black and white, the computer is in the 80 column mode, the screen pages are all set to 0, and that the display is clear.

Lines 180 through 240 determine whether the program is decrypting or encrypting. Line 180 displays the prompting message. Line 190 reads one character from the keyboard. Line 200 makes that character uppercase using a logical AND instruction. In line 210, the character entered is compared against E and D. If the input does not match E or D, execution branches back to the input statement in line 190. If the input does match, that letter is displayed.

Lines 250 and 260 get the input and output file names and assign them to variables FILEIN$ and FILEOUT$.

Line 280 gets the encryption keyword pattern and assigns it to the variable KEY WORD$. Line 290 assigns the variable KEY.LEN to the length of the encryption keyword string.

The actual decryption/encryption is done in the FOR-NEXT loop between lines 370 and 450. First, each file is opened in lines 350 and 360. Then, the program incrementally reads a character from the key word (line 390) and from the file (line 400). Line 410 branches to the appropriate encrypting or decrypting routine depending on whether D or E was entered. Line 420 prints the resulting encrypted or decrypted character to the output file and line 430 prints the character to the screen.

Line 440 completes the loop. Line 450 continues the program until the end of the input file is detected by line 380. Once the last character is read from the input file, the IF-THEN test in line 380 branches program execution to line 460 where the files are closed and the program ends.

The actual encrypting routines are in lines 480 through 530. The equation is the same for both, except that addition is used for decryption and subtraction is used for encryption. The MOD 255 function keeps the resulting character within the values of a character to prevent BASIC from producing an error.

Using PC Tools' PC Secure

Yet another utility that comes with the PC Tools package is PC Secure. PC Secure lets you encrypt and decrypt files on disk. This program gives instant password protection to your files and, in some cases, the encrypted file actually is smaller on disk than the original.

Once a file is encrypted, it's very safe. Only with the password can the file be decrypted. Unlike the simple letter-for-letter encryption of a decoder ring or the CRYPT .BAS program, PC Secure uses complex algorithms for coding a file. Only the password keyholder has any chance of decrypting the file. Because of this, you should always remember your password.

The best thing about PC Secure, and file encryption in general, is that each file can be given its own unique password. Every other security measure covered so far in the book involved one master password for the whole system. This is the first time that individual passwords can be assigned to files or directories, which makes this security system viable for a single PC used by several people.

Setting up PC Secure When you first run PC Secure (PCSECURE.EXE), you'll be asked to specify a *master key password*. This password is the universal password that gives you access to all encrypted files. If you ever forget a file's individual password, the master key will help you recover it. Don't forget your master key password and don't share it with other users of the system.

Figure 18-6 shows PC Secure's main operations window, where files are encrypted and decrypted and various options are set.

18-6 PC Secure's main window.

The File menu is used to encrypt or decrypt single files or groups of files. All files encrypted during a single session will use the same password (one you specify, not the master key password). You can switch this option off if you like.

The Options menu lets you select the type of encryption, file attributes for the encrypted file, whether you want the encrypted file to overwrite the original file, whether you want the original file to be deleted after encryption, and other various and sundry options.

The Help menu contains helpful information and hints on how to use the program.

Encrypting a file To encrypt a file using PC Secure, pull down the File menu and select Encrypt. The File Selection panel appears, as seen in Fig. 18-7. Select the file you want to

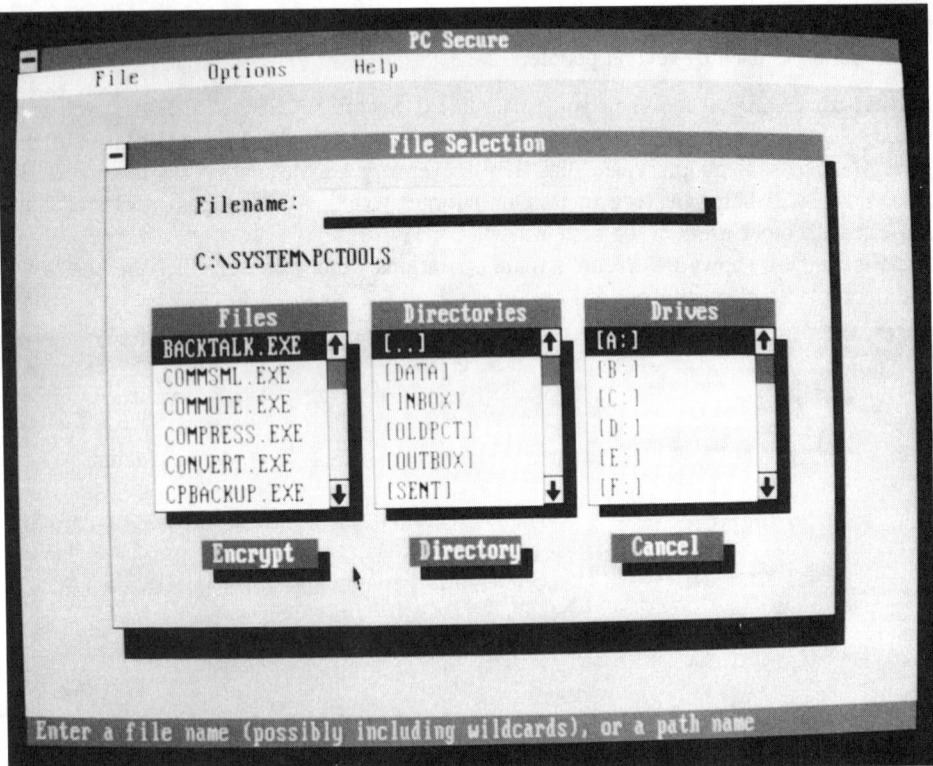

18-7 The File Selection panel allows you to select one or more files for encryption.

encrypt. Next, you'll be asked to enter a password initially and then again to verify it. Remember that password.

The next window you'll see shows you the program's progress as it encrypts the file. If you've selected the Delete Original option (from the Options menu), the encrypted file takes the same name as the original, overwriting it. If not, the encrypted version of the file will have the same filename but with an SEC extension.

To make sure the file is totally scrambled, return to DOS and type the file to the screen or try to load it into the application that created it. The results will be predictably Greek. The file is secure.

Decrypting a file Decrypting a file is similar to encrypting it. Select Decrypt from the File menu, then enter the name of the file you want to decrypt. You'll be prompted for the password. The decryption process will take place, then the file will be restored to its original condition.

Using the U.S. Government DOD standards The most popular and foolproof encryption scheme is referred to as the Data Encryption Standard, or DES, which is defined by the National Bureau of Standards. (It's the same encryption standard used on our tax forms.) This encryption scheme is so powerful that the United States government prohibits the export of programs which use it—even to friendly countries!

To use the government's high standards of encryption with PC Secure, start the program with the /G switch (*G* standing for *Government* or *G-men*). PC Secure's Options menu will be preset to the Government's standards when /G is specified. Full DES encryption will be used and the original file will be overwritten seven times. This encryption setup is harder to crack than the standard encryption.

If you're really, really security conscious, a file can be encrypted with two passwords. This is done by starting PC Secure with the /M switch. Two different users can enter one password each to encrypt each file. Only with both passwords can the file be decrypted. You can specify both the /G and /M switches.

DiskLock's data encryption

Aside from slapping one or two passwords to your entire hard disk, subdirectories, or individual files, Fifth Generation Systems' DiskLock can be used to encrypt and decrypt files. The Encryption and Decryption options are under the Configuration menu.

After selecting Encryption, you select the type of encryption you want: FastCrypt, Proprietary, or the DES Encryption standard. Following that, you select the drive containing the files. Then, you're presented with a directory tree and file listing (Fig. 18-8). Select the files or directories you want encrypted. DiskLock asks for a password, verifies it, then encrypts the selected files.

Depending on the type of encryption, the files might be invisible and inaccessible to the secondary user (Fast Encryption), scrambled for the primary user (Proprietary Encryption), or compacted into a single file (DES encryption). You can restore the encrypted file's contents only by using the DL utility. To run DL, you need the master password as well as the file's encryption password.

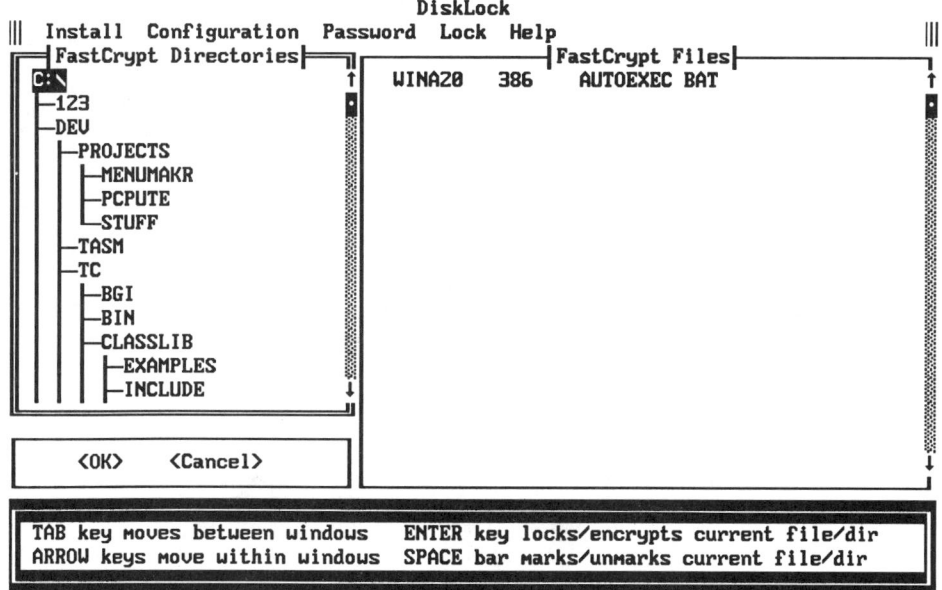

18-8 Files and directories are selected for encryption.

To decrypt the files, select the Decryption item from the Configuration menu, choose a drive, then select the encrypted files from a screen similar to Fig. 18-8. Files will show up only if they're encrypted. If so, DiskLock will prompt you for the password, then restore the files to their previous state.

This encryption feature, along with DiskLock's password protection, which was covered in the previous chapter, make DiskLock a program worth looking into. If you don't want the bulk of PC Tools and feel that Certus' anti-virus protection isn't needed, then DiskLock is an elegant solution.

Summary

This chapter covered several types of file security measures. Using DOS, you can give files a modest form of protection by setting their hidden or read-only attributes using the ATTRIB command. Unusual or secret filenames also can be used to thwart some users. Additional file security can be offered through file protection programs, such as PC Tools' Data Monitor. The best form of individual file protection, however, is via file encryption and programs such as PC Secure and DiskLock. This is the most reliable way to keep information in a file safe (although the file still can be deleted).

This wraps up the third part of this book, on hard disk security. The next and final part of this book deals with hard disk optimization and tuning your system to peak levels of performance.

Part IV
Hard disk optimization

Everything covered thus far in this book, the organizational information provided in part I, menus and shells in part II, and security in part III gives you a firm grip on controlling your hard disk. You should be fairly proficient in operating, maintaining, and organizing the hard disk by now. Yet, there still are many interesting things going on behind the scenes that are crucial to hard disk performance.

Hard disk optimization and performance is the subject of this part of the book. Chapter 19 is about tuning your hard disk's performance and increasing its storage capacity. Chapter 20 is about improving system and disk performance using DOS 5's memory tools, RAM drives, and disk caches. Chapter 21 wraps up the book with a discussion of specialized forms of hard drives and how to upgrade your hardware.

19
Storage optimization

There are dozens of special tricks for speeding operations on a hard disk, as well as methods for increasing hard disk capacity. Many of these techniques are deceptively simple, yet achieve astounding results. By using all or a combination of these optimization strategies, you could improve your hard disk's performance by as much as 300%.

This chapter is about improving hard disk performance and capacity. The performance part is handled by special formatting techniques, special methods of data storage, and general disk cleanup. Storage optimization is accomplished by special programs that compact data as it's stored to disk or by programs that fool the hard drive into storing twice as much data than it was designed to hold—and it all works.

Note that none of these tricks are things you can do with a screwdriver in your own spare time. Because most of them mess with the actual structure of the hard disk, it's a good idea to have a current backup made just in case. However, once their job is done, you immediately will notice the increased power, speed, and performance of your hard disk.

Housekeeping

Nothing beats routine hard disk management, a portion of which is housekeeping. This involves deleting files you no longer need, copying files that are just sitting around to floppy disks for long-term storage, renaming files, creating new subdirectories, moving files here or there, and general disk maintenance. All of that is what I call housekeeping.

Routinely, you should scan your system and perform housekeeping. Anytime you have an extra 20 minutes to kill, break out a disk utility and scan for redundant files or those named KILL, TEMP, or JUNK. Delete them if you no longer need them.

A handy tool to use for this is Lotus' Magellan (Fig. 19-1). It's more than a DOS shell, although it can function as one. Primarily, Magellan is a hard disk information tool, with which you can see a file's contents just as you would if you were running the program that created that file—even graphics files. You can tag files, copy, delete or move them to a new location, search files for certain information, perform a fuzzy search, and generally manage information on disk in a smooth and efficient manner. (I wrote a book on the subject, *Working With Magellan*, which is available from Windcrest if you're interested.)

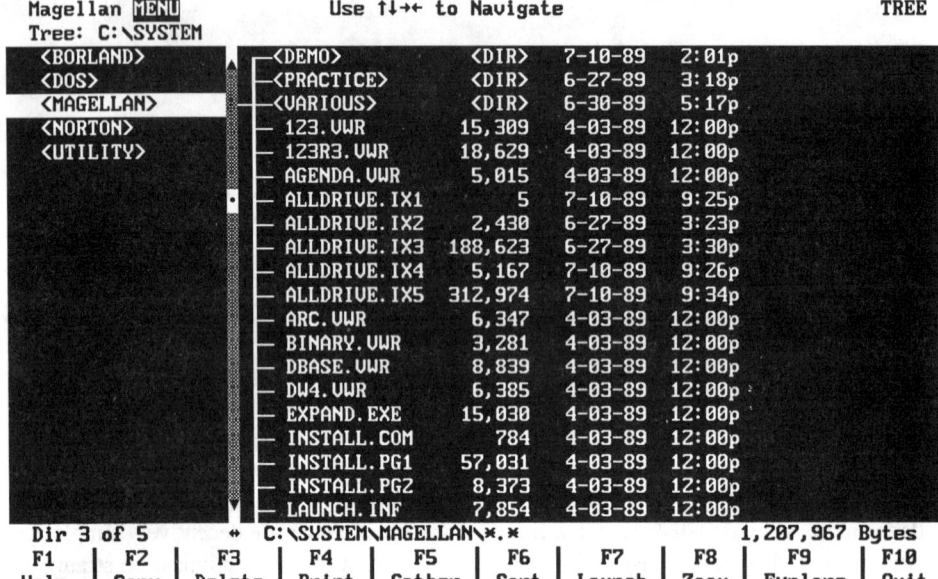

<BORLAND>	─<DEMO>	<DIR>	7-10-89	2:01p
<DOS>	─<PRACTICE>	<DIR>	6-27-89	3:18p
<MAGELLAN>	─<VARIOUS>	<DIR>	6-30-89	5:17p
<NORTON>	─ 123.VWR	15,309	4-03-89	12:00p
<UTILITY>	─ 123R3.VWR	18,629	4-03-89	12:00p
	─ AGENDA.VWR	5,015	4-03-89	12:00p
	─ ALLDRIVE.IX1	5	7-10-89	9:25p
	─ ALLDRIVE.IX2	2,430	6-27-89	3:23p
	─ ALLDRIVE.IX3	188,623	6-27-89	3:30p
	─ ALLDRIVE.IX4	5,167	7-10-89	9:26p
	─ ALLDRIVE.IX5	312,974	7-10-89	9:34p
	─ ARC.VWR	6,347	4-03-89	12:00p
	─ BINARY.VWR	3,281	4-03-89	12:00p
	─ DBASE.VWR	8,839	4-03-89	12:00p
	─ DW4.VWR	6,385	4-03-89	12:00p
	─ EXPAND.EXE	15,030	4-03-89	12:00p
	─ INSTALL.COM	784	4-03-89	12:00p
	─ INSTALL.PG1	57,031	4-03-89	12:00p
	─ INSTALL.PG2	8,373	4-03-89	12:00p
	─ LAUNCH.INF	7,854	4-03-89	12:00p

Dir 3 of 5   ↔ C:\SYSTEM\MAGELLAN*.*   1,207,967 Bytes

F1	F2	F3	F4	F5	F6	F7	F8	F9	F10
Help	Copy	Delete	Print	Gather	Sort	Launch	Zoom	Explore	Quit

19-1 Magellan at work.

Magellan grows on you. It's not a full-featured shell like PC Tools and doesn't have nearly that many utilities. However, it does have its own UNDELETE command, as well as commands for backing up and archiving files—including the ZIP utility, which is covered later in this chapter. The support from Lotus is outstanding as well. I just received an upgrade diskette from them that offered mouse support and additional file viewers—all free of charge (and that wasn't because I wrote a book on it, either).

Magellan
Lotus Development Corporation
161 First Street
Cambridge, MA 02142
(617) 577-8500

There's a program available on the companion diskette that also can help you with your hard disk housekeeping. FD, for Find Duplicates, will locate and display all files on all hard drives on your system that have similar names. It's a memory pig, so make sure you have at least 512 K of RAM on your system to run it. (If not, you can use it on only one drive at a time.)

For example, Fig. 19-2 shows a test run of FD on my C drive. I edited down the list because it was very long; there was a lot of duplicate filenames on the drive. Only a few, however, were true duplicates, as seen by the file's date and time (TALK.CFG in Fig. 19-2). Others could be duplicates, with the same size but different dates and times.

See all the README.* files? If you read them and followed whatever instructions they offered, kill them. The same goes for any INSTALL programs or similar files you no

```
FD - Find Duplicates
Written by Dan Gookin
Copyright (C) 1991 TAB Books

Now scanning current drive C:
1555 files found in 56 directories.
Now sorting the list ................................. done.


File: DS800.EXE
      30400  01/17/89 10:39:24 am    C:\SYSTEM\PARADISE\ACADDRVR
      30400  06/10/88 03:15:08 pm    C:\SYSTEM\PARADISE

File: FF.EXE
       8682  05/27/90 10:34:11 am    C:\SYSTEM\UTIL
     136941  06/09/91 07:01:00 pm    C:\SYSTEM\PCTOOLS
       9042  01/03/89 04:51:00 pm    C:\SYSTEM\NORTON

File: INSTALL.EXE
     134259  06/09/91 07:01:00 pm    C:\SYSTEM\PCTOOLS
      34312  01/03/89 04:51:00 pm    C:\SYSTEM\NORTON
      57817  09/01/90 05:05:01 am    C:\SYSTEM\V

File: README.DOC
        485  03/20/91 01:05:00 am    C:\SYSTEM\UTIL\PKLITE
       7211  11/09/90 12:00:00 am    C:\SYSTEM\MAGELLAN
        873  10/01/89 01:02:00 am    C:\SYSTEM\UTIL\ZIP
       5619  03/06/88 09:46:02 am    C:\SYSTEM\MOUSE

File: README.TXT
      10882  10/03/88 07:32:23 am    C:\COMM\LAPLINK
       5184  06/09/91 07:01:00 pm    C:\SYSTEM\PCTOOLS
      10188  05/02/90 06:03:00 pm    C:\SYSTEM\PCTOOLS\DATA
      10188  05/02/90 06:03:00 pm    C:\SYSTEM\PCTOOLS\OLDPCT

File: TALK.CFG
       4641  08/26/90 02:10:16 pm    C:\SYSTEM\PCTOOLS\OLDPCT
       4641  08/26/90 02:10:16 pm    C:\SYSTEM\PCTOOLS\DATA

  52 groups of duplicate files found.
```

19-2 A small chunk of FD's output.

longer need. However, note that FF.EXE in Fig. 19-2 probably is three different programs, as seen by their sizes and different locations on the disk; you wouldn't want to
delete them.

FD isn't a utility for removing your duplicate files. However, it is a tool to help you
perform file housekeeping. While running it for this demonstration, I discovered many
files that were duplicated between two directories. The total disk savings after I deleted the
extraneous copies was some 500 K. That's not a bad trick to save half a megabyte of disk
space—and you're not even at the part in this chapter where hard disk compression is discussed.

If you can, use a tool like Magellan or FD regularly. Most hard drives fill up to capacity unnecessarily. One solution is to buy a second drive or replace your current drive with
one of a larger capacity (see chapter 21). However, most users should be able to clean off a
few megabytes with good housekeeping.

Cleaning up the directory

The order of files in a directory listing can be very important to the speed at which the programs are loaded. This is true because, when DOS searches the current directory for the name of a program file, it starts with the first directory entry and reads through the entire directory looking for a match. If your file is at the end of the directory, it will take longer for DOS to find and run it. This situation is okay if you have five files in the directory, but a BIN or UTIL subdirectory with 100 files takes a while to churn through.

Files are listed in a directory in the order they were added. Therefore, a simple trick to speed up the time DOS takes to load a program is to put all the COM, EXE, and BAT files at the start of the directory. Even more efficient would be to place the most often used programs first in the directory. Unfortunately, this isn't easy to do after the programs already are on your disk. However, it can be done with some interesting utility programs.

Before I discuss the utilities, you also should familiarize yourself with another slow-poke in a directory: the tombstone. Like driving your car over a speed bump, tombstones can slow DOS down as DOS reads through a directory looking for a file.

Tombstones are created when files are deleted. When that happens, DOS places a special available tag in that file's directory entry. This tag over the old file entry is the tombstone. (The file actually isn't erased from disk, which is why the UNDELETE command can recover it; see chapter 15.)

When DOS happens upon a tombstone directory entry, it skips over it, which adds to the time it takes for DOS to search for and load a program. Not much time is added, granted, but consider if fifty files were deleted from one directory. That's fifty extra stops DOS has to make.

When DOS adds new files to a directory, it puts them in one of two places: at the end of the current list of files or in one of the tombstones left by deleted programs. For example, the following directory has three files:

(1)	CFS		4520	1-23-93	5:44p
(2)	JOBLOG	88	7516	2-17-94	4:44p
(3)	SCHED	WCF	8404	11-11-93	8:08p

(The numbers are added for reference.) If a new file were added, the directory appears as follows:

(1)	CFS		4520	1-23-93	5:44p
(2)	JOBLOG	88	7516	2-17-94	4:44p
(3)	SCHED	WCF	8404	11-11-93	8:08p
(4)	LOAN	WKS	3680	11-17-94	11:34p

However, if the file JOBLOG.88 was deleted before the file LOAN.WKS was added, the directory would appear as:

(1)	CFS		4520	1-23-91	5:44p
(4)	LOAN	WKS	3680	11-17-91	11:34p
(3)	SCHED	WCF	8404	11-11-91	8:08p

DOS makes an attempt to fill in the tombstones left by deleted files only as new files are added to the directory. By getting rid of the empty directory entries as well as sorting the files in the directory, DOS could search through the entries much faster.

This task is something that cannot be done at all using DOS. You need a special piece of software designed to physically sort a directory on disk. This isn't the same as piping the output of the DIR command through the SORT filter or using DIR's /O switch.

The utility programs that sort directory entries carefully pick up all directory entries, then sort them in whichever order you specify: alphabetically or by extension, size, or date. Additionally, any tombstones left by dead programs are overwritten by the sorting processes.

Before sorting the directory, you might want to ensure that the COM, EXE and BAT files will come first by renaming them. Renaming the file doesn't change their contents; however, they will need to be renamed again after the sort. For example, the following commands could be performed before the sort:

```
REN *.COM *.000
REN *.EXE *.001
REN *.BAT *.002
REN *.*.003
```

In computer sorts, numbers take on a lower value than letters. The numbers 0 through 9 have a higher sort priority than the letter *A*. Just make certain there are no other files with the same extensions in the directory.

The last REN command renames files without extensions. If this wasn't done, then they would be sorted first—which defeats the purpose.

Once the files are renamed, you would sort them using the special utility.

After the sort is performed, files in the directory will be listed 000 (COM) first, 001 (EXE) second, and 003 (BAT) third. Other files will follow based on their extensions. Any tombstones in the directory will be removed. To rename the COM, EXE, and BAT files back to their original names, use the following commands:

```
REN *.000 *.COM
REN *.001 *.EXE
REN *.002 *.BAT
REN *.003 *.
```

There's one warning to keep in mind when you do this: removing a file's tombstone means you cannot recover the file using UNDELETE. Nothing can recover a deleted file once you've physically sorted a directory.

The Norton Utilities

The quickest and easiest directory sorting/squeezing program is called DS.EXE or DIR-SORT.EXE, available as part of the Norton Utilities. DS physically sorts directory entries by either filename, filename extension, date, time, file size, or a combination of each. Additionally, DS will sort out all of a directory's tombstones.

Norton's DIRSORT uses optional letters to sort the directory based on filename (N), extension (E), date (D), time (T), or size (S). If the optional /S switch is specified, Norton's DS will sort all directories starting with the current directory on down. For example, to use DIRSORT to sort the COM, EXE, and BAT files renamed in the previous section, you would use the following:

```
C: \ > DS E /S
```

After a few moments, all files in all directories on drive C will be sorted and the tombstones removed.

If you only want to sort by filename, then you can use the following:

```
DS N
```

I use this command periodically on my data file subdirectories. It sorts the files by name, as well as removes any tombstones.

The Mace Utilities

Paul Mace is a hard disk utility legend, even though he considers himself an aviator. Paul's even written a few books on hard disks and file recovery, which go into lots of detail on the subject.

The Mace Utilities started out as the first hard disk defragmentation utility (covered in a later section), but they also offered directory squeezing and sorting. Presently, the Mace Utilities is distributed by Fifth Generation Systems. The directory squeezing and sorting utilities have been offered as external utilities in addition to being part of the defragmentation program.

The directory squeezing is handled by SQZD. It basically plods through one or all directories and removes all the tombstones. The directory sorting program is done by SORTD. It sorts files in one or more directories by their name, extension, date and time, or size. Finally, the beach bunny program is handled by SANDYD.

One interesting aspect about SQZD and SORTD is that SORTD doesn't remove references to deleted files. Norton's DS does, but Mace has kind of split DIRSORT into both sorting and tombstone-stomping programs. My advice is to squeeze, then sort all directories on a drive. That's done by the following two commands with the Mace Utilities:

```
SQZD C:
SORTD C: EN
```

In the previous example, SORTD will sort files based on first their extension (E), then the name (N). The drive letter forces both programs to work on the entire hard drive.

Using PC Tools Compress

PC Tools has a utility, Compress, that can arrange the order of files in a directory. Files can be arranged individually or by specific extensions using the Files to Place First option in the Options menu.

Of the directory sorting programs covered here (Norton's DIRSORT and Mace's SQZD and SORTD), Compress is the only one that gives you total control over file order. However, the directory sorting and tombstone kicking aren't offered individually, as with Norton's and Mace's utilities. Compress really is a specific disk optimization tool and is covered in more detail later in this chapter.

The curse of fragmentation

DOS allocates space for programs in chunks called *clusters*. The size of the cluster depends on the size of the disk. For 360 K diskettes, the cluster size is one sector, 512 bytes. DOS allocates one sector each time you add a file to disk. Even if the file is less than 512 bytes in size, DOS allocates the full 512. This number is not reflected by the DIR command; DIR reports the actual physical size of the program. However, the total bytes free at the end of the DIR command shows the total space left on the disk has decreased by the size of one cluster.

A 512 byte cluster isn't that bad. However, on a hard drive, the cluster size is four sectors, or 2048 bytes. That's a lot of space for DOS to allocate, especially for a directory full of 120 byte batch files. Yet, it would be even harder for DOS to keep track of 512 byte clusters on a large hard drive. The present FAT system for file allocation would easily become overworked, errors would occur, and the storage system would be unreliable. So, users live with 2 K clusters on a hard drive (and the typical file is between 5 K and 8 K in size, so it's okay). When a program is erased, the clusters that it used become available. They actually don't get erased, but DOS alters the file's directory entry and marks the clusters as available in the FAT. When a new file overwrites the erased file's clusters on disk, it does so under a best-fit circumstance. Especially if a file is too large, it must be split up to fill in several of the holes left by previous programming. This is known as *fragmentation*.

Fragmentation isn't bad. DOS still keeps track of the file's pieces in the FAT. When it loads the file, it will reassemble the pieces. However, this process slows down the disk. A larger file in several pieces takes time to load and save to disk. As you do your housekeeping, more and more holes are created by deleted files. New files you create fill in those holes. The result is a fragmented drive. Performance decreases as the percentage of fragmented files grows.

Using CHKDSK to check for fragmentation

To see which files are fragmented in a given directory, you can use DOS's CHKDSK, check disk, command. As one of its many features, CHKDSK displays fragmented files matching the filename specified. The fragmented filenames are displayed as well as the number of noncontiguous blocks of the file. (A *block* is a sequence of clusters the file occupies on disk.)

For example, on your hard drive, log to one of your working subdirectories and type the following command:

```
CHKDSK *.*
```

If there are no fragmented files, CHKDSK will inform you All files are contiguous. Otherwise, you might list files as follows:

```
C:\COMMAND.COM Contains 2 non-contiguous blocks
C:\WINA20.386 Contains 3 non-contiguous blocks
```

The files listed are fragmented. Some are split up into two blocks, some more than that.

Although CHKDSK does point out which files are noncontiguous, it does little to remedy the situation. For a defragmentation cure, you must go to a third-party disk utility or program.

The DOS manual has offered some bizarre recommendations for dealing with disk fragmentation. One recommendation was to COPY the files to another disk, then copy them back. However, this does not guarantee they will become contiguous and generally will result in poorer performance from the hard disk. Another suggestion was to back up the hard drive, reformat it, then fully restore. Yeah, right.

Mace's FragCheck

Included with the Mace Utilities is a program FRAGCHK.EXE, FragCheck. It's used to find fragmented files on a single hard drive and list them in a fancy display. Unfortunately, you cannot redirect the output to a printer or a file, but the summary the program produces (Fig. 19-3) is worth it.

```
 v1990        M A C E   F R A G M E N T A T I O N    C H E C K        12-15-89

    FILE                                                         FRAGMENTS
    C:\SYSTEM\MACE\SQZD.EXE                                          2

    Press a key...
    C:\SYSTEM\MACE\SURVEY.EXE                                        2
    C:\SYSTEM\UTIL\MUB.EXE                                           9
    C:\SYSTEM\UTIL\MFT.EXE                                           4
    C:\SYSTEM\UTIL\MFT.HLP                                           2
    C:\SYSTEM\UTIL\TRAN.EXE                                          4
    C:\SYSTEM\UTIL\NU.EXE                                           14
    C:\SYSTEM\UTIL\DATAMON.EXE                                       9
    C:\TEMP\CASTLE.SEC                                               3
    C:\TEMP\ESI.EXE                                                  5
    C:\WORK\05                                                       4

    Total number of fragmented files: 90
    Total number of fragments: 320

    Done; press a key...
```

19-3 Mace's FragCheck.

FragCheck actually is the first part of the defragmentation process done by Mace's UNFRAG program, which is covered later in this chapter. It gives you a good grip on your hard drive's fragmentation situation, plus you can run the program after using a defragmentation utility to see how good of a job it's done.

The blessing of defragmentation

When total hard disk fragmentation hits about 5%, you should consider defragmenting the drive. When it hits 10%, you're seriously compromising your hard drive's performance;

defragment at once. How do you find out these percentages? How can you defragment the drive? The answer lies in third-party programs.

Defragmentation utilities are interesting and complex programs. Basically, they reorder files on your hard drive by moving them off the disk, either to memory or to an unused part of the disk, then copy them all back in a contiguous manner.

This is tricky stuff. If you reset during defragmentation, the result might be a totally scrambled hard drive. Further, you need to unload all memory-resident programs before defragmenting. Also, get out of Windows or DESQview or any other multitasking or task swapping program (like DOS Shell). It's a good idea to fully back up your hard drive before defragmenting as well.

The Mace Utilities come with two batch files, ON.BAT and OFF.BAT. These are ideal for use when setting up your computer for defragmentation.

OFF.BAT renames AUTOEXEC.BAT and CONFIG.SYS, then prompts you to reset before defragmenting the drive. The result of doing this is that you start off with a clean system—nothing is in memory to botch up defragmentation. After you've defragmented, you run ON.BAT, which renames AUTOEXEC.BAT and CONFIG.SYS back to their original names. Reset and your system is back to normal.

Batch files similar to Mace's ON.BAT and OFF.BAT are included on the companion diskette for you to use with whichever defragmentation utility you prefer. The following sections go over three of the defragmentation utilities: Mace's, Norton's, and PC Tools'.

The Mace Utilities

Paul Mace is one of the canonized saints of the Hard Disk Crusades. The Mace Utility's original claim to fame is that it actually could unformat a reformatted hard drive—way before anyone else thought that was possible. (Before the FORMAT command included a warning prompt, just about everyone and his uncle was reformatting the hard drive.)

The Mace Utilities package contains dozens of programs, such as SQZD, SORTD, and FRAGCHK (which were discussed earlier). All of the programs and performance enhancement utilities can be run from a handy interface, the MACE program (Fig. 19-4).

Before running Mace, especially if you want to defragment your drive, remember to run the OFF.BAT batch file. This program ensures that no memory-resident program will interfere with the defragmentation process.

If all you want to do is defragment your disk, select the Optimize Disk item from the Performance menu. The manual suggests that you run the REMEDY program (under the Solutions menu) at least three times before your first attempt at defragmentation. This is done by starting REMEDY with the /3 switch. Then, proceed with the Optimize Disk item.

Personally, I recommend doing the following. These are all the command line names and options for the programs run through the Mace shell. Note that you should have a formatted data diskette in drive A. All these files come with the Mace Utilities.

Type OFF to run OFF.BAT. The OFF.BAT file renames AUTOEXEC.BAT and CONFIG.SYS to *.TMP. This is highly impractical for running your system but is ideal for running Mace. Reset to reboot your computer without your device drivers and memory-resident programs.

Change directories to your MACE subdirectory. Type the following:

```
FRAGCHK C:
```

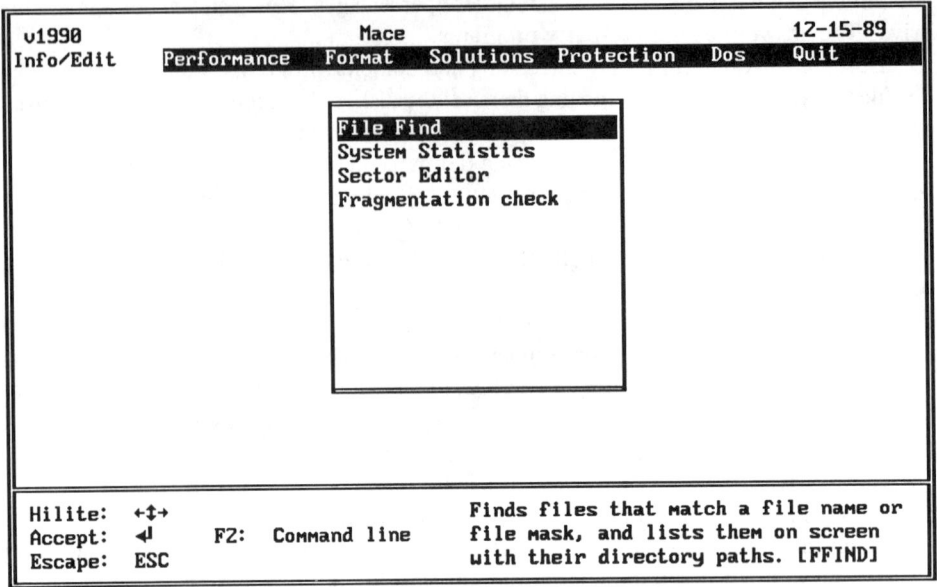

```
v1990                        Mace                       12-15-89
Info/Edit  Performance   Format   Solutions  Protection   Dos    Quit

                        ┌─────────────────────────────┐
                        │ File Find                   │
                        │ System Statistics           │
                        │ Sector Editor               │
                        │ Fragmentation check         │
                        │                             │
                        │                             │
                        │                             │
                        │                             │
                        │                             │
                        │                             │
                        └─────────────────────────────┘



  Hilite:  ←↕→                     Finds files that match a file name or
  Accept:  ↵      F2:  Command line file mask, and lists them on screen
  Escape:  ESC                     with their directory paths. [FFIND]
```

19-4 The MACE program and the interface to all of the Mace Utilities.

The previous command checks for fragmented files on drive C. This will give you a good idea of what kind of a job the UNFRAG program will do—a preview, if you will. (The defragmentation program, UNFRAG, does this automatically, so you can skip this command if you like.)

Type the following command to run REMEDY:

REMEDY C: A: /3 /T

REMEDY is a disk utility that scans the specified drive for bad or questionable sectors. The A: tells REMEDY to send its report to drive A. (Because the hard drive is being scanned, you'll need to specify a different drive.) This item is optional. The /3 switch directs REMEDY to perform its scan three times. The /T switch tells REMEDY to only test the drive; files won't be moved away from the bad sectors.

After REMEDY is done, you might want to examine its report to see if any nasties were found on your hard drive. Use the following command:

TYPE A:REPORT.M__U

Use the Ctrl−S key to pause the display. (If you want to use the MORE filter, remember to specify a full pathname; AUTOEXEC.BAT didn't run and your system probably lacks a search path.) If you see any bad clusters listed, you might want to run REMEDY again. This time, don't specify the /T switch. If REMEDY reports any problems reading or writing to the drive, then don't defragment at this point. (Refer to the Mace Utilities manual for instructions on repairing the disk.)

SORTD C: E

is run to sort your directory entries by filename. If you want to put the COM, EXE, and BAT files first, then rename them as described earlier in this chapter.

```
SQZD C:
```

should be run after SORTD to remove the file tombstones. (Remember, SORTD doesn't do that.)

Finally, the defragmentation utility, UNFRAG, is run. Type the following command to run the defragmentation utility:

```
UNFRAG C: A: /R /P
```

With the previous command, UNFRAG will defragment files on drive C and send its report to drive A. (Note that the report is named REPORT.M__U—the same as for the REMEDY program.)

The /R switch directs UNFRAG to reorganize the disk and arrange files according to their order in the directory. If you've sorted your directories with COM, EXE, and BAT files first, then this will make loading them even faster (although only slightly faster).

The /P switch directs UNFRAG to pack the disk, moving the files in tight together, not just defragmenting them. Together, both /R and /P add time to the defragmentation process. If you're in a hurry, you don't need to specify them. (Without them, UNFRAG still will stick together all the fragmented files.)

The entire defragmentation process could take up to two hours for a severely fragmented drive. Your computer will reset after it's done.

Once you're done, run the FRAGCHK program again. It will report that zero files are fragmented (although your system files still might appear in the list; UNFRAG doesn't mess with them).

Finally, use the ON.BAT program to rename AUTOEXEC.BAT and CONFIG.SYS back to their original names. You're all done.

Norton's Speed Disk

If time isn't on your side, you can defragment your drive using the Speed Disk program that comes with the Norton Utilities. Speed Disk is a fast defragmenting program. It doesn't rearrange files on disk, nor pack them tight like Mace's UNFRAG. It only pieces together severely fragmented files. However, Speed Disk does it fast and safe—so quick you could almost include it as a line in your AUTOEXEC.BAT (or SHUTDOWN.BAT) files.

To run Speed Disk, type SD followed by the drive to optimize:

```
SD C:
```

If you want it to be faster, specify the /Q (quick) switch. If you want a more complete optimization, specify the /C switch.

For a preview of the process, you can specify the /R switch:

```
SD C: /R
```

Speed Disk will come back with a quick summary. For example:

```
Total of the entire disk: 95% unfragmented
```

Five percent fragmentation indicates that you might want to optimize the disk. As with Mace's FRAGCHK, you might want to use the /R switch again after optimizing the disk to verify that Speed Disk did its job.

PC Tools' Compress

Compress, yet another tool in PC Tools' suite of hard disk utilities, is perhaps the smoothest and most complete disk defragmentation tool. Upon running Compress, it will perform an instant analysis of your hard drive and decide which type of compression will work best. If no compression is needed, you'll be alerted to that fact.

What makes Compress so unique is that it has dozens of options covering a wide range of things you can do to manipulate data stored on your hard drive. The Compression Technique menu (Fig. 19-5) is an example of this versatility. It even offers you suggestions for when you use each technique. Note the File Sort option, which can be used to physically sort directories (covered earlier in this chapter).

Set any options you might want (such as file order in the directory) before you compress. Then, choose the Begin Compress item from the Compress menu, or press F4. The display probably is the most visually interesting of the three programs mentioned here.

After compression is complete, you'll be given the option of running MIRROR on the drive. This is Central Point's own version of DOS's MIRROR command. What it will do

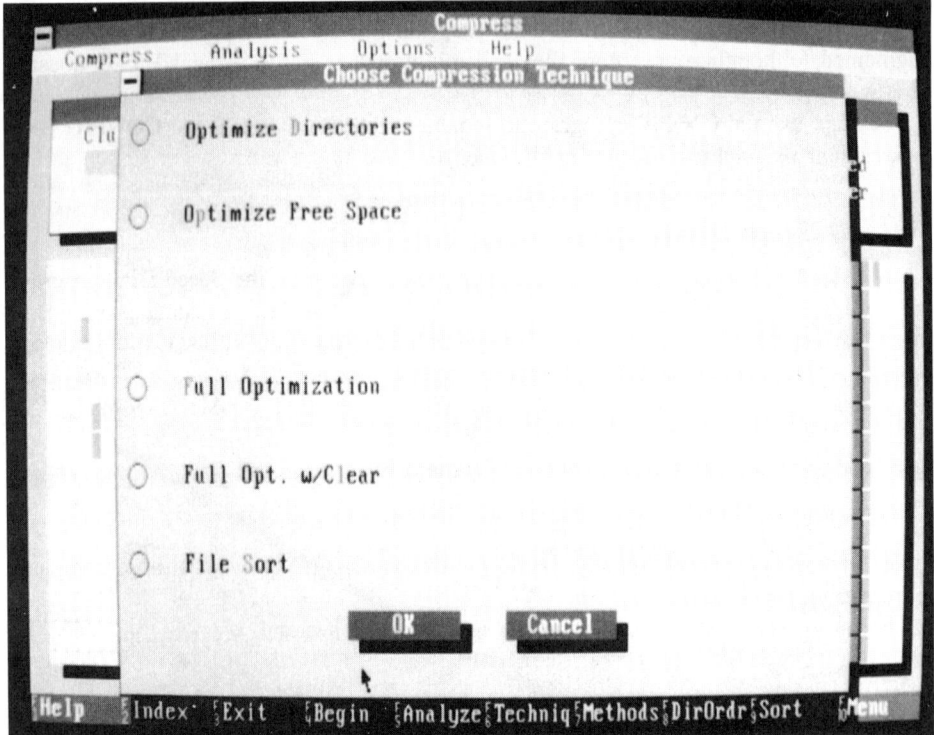

19-5 The Choose Compression Technique dialog box.

is create the UNFORMAT information for your drive. I highly recommend selecting this option.

When the whole operation is over, you should reset your computer. Any drastic improvement in speed won't be noticed right away. If your disk fragmentation was 10% or greater, however, after a time, you'll notice a more peppy hard drive.

Improving the low-level format

Aside from packing and defragmenting files on disk, there are certain formatting techniques that optimize disk performance on a very low level. As technology races ahead, more and more of these techniques become available. They take standard middle-of-the-road hard disks and turn them into real storage monsters.

When DOS formats a disk, it lays down a series of tracks and sectors, as discussed in chapter 2. Because tracks can be placed on both sides of a disk or on the many sides, or platters, of a hard disk, they are considered *cylinders*.

Cylinders are numbered starting at the outside of the disk with cylinder 0. They move in sequentially to the highest numbered cylinder, which usually is somewhere in the 600s for most hard drives. The sectors, however, are not numbered sequentially. Unlike numbers on the face of a clock, sectors are placed around the disk in a specific pattern according to the interleave factor.

For example, sectors on a 360 K floppy diskette are numbered from one through nine. Yet, if you were to shrink yourself down, sit on a floppy drive's read/write head and watch the sector numbers fly by, you would see the following:

1 3 5 7 9 2 4 6 8

This is referred to as a 1:6 interleave. The next sequentially numbered disk sector actually is six physical sectors away. Figure 19-6 shows how this numbering scheme might look on the disk.

The reason for having an interleave is because the disk is spinning as information is read. The disk controller performs an error-checking calculation on it called a Cyclic Redundancy Check, or CRC, on each sector after it's read. This check assures that the information read from the disk is identical to the information originally written to the disk. If there is a difference, a CRC error occurs and the controller makes another attempt to read the sector. If after a given number of attempts the sector cannot be read, the disk controller informs DOS and an error message is displayed.

While the disk controller is calculating the CRC, the disk continues to spin. By the time the CRC is calculated on sector 1, the next sector (sector 3 in Fig. 19-6) has passed under the read/write head. The interleave is created so that when the drive is done reading sector 1, it's poised and ready to read sector 2, which on the disk actually is six sectors away, as seen in Fig. 19-6.

The original hard disk in the PC/XT used a 1:6 interleave. The IBM PC/AT's disk drive and most common 20 Mb and 40 Mb drives, use a 1:3 interleave, as seen in Fig. 19-7. Superfast hard drives on 386 computers use a 1:1 interleave, which is simply each sector on the disk numbered sequentially. Because the system is so fast, there's no need to interleave.

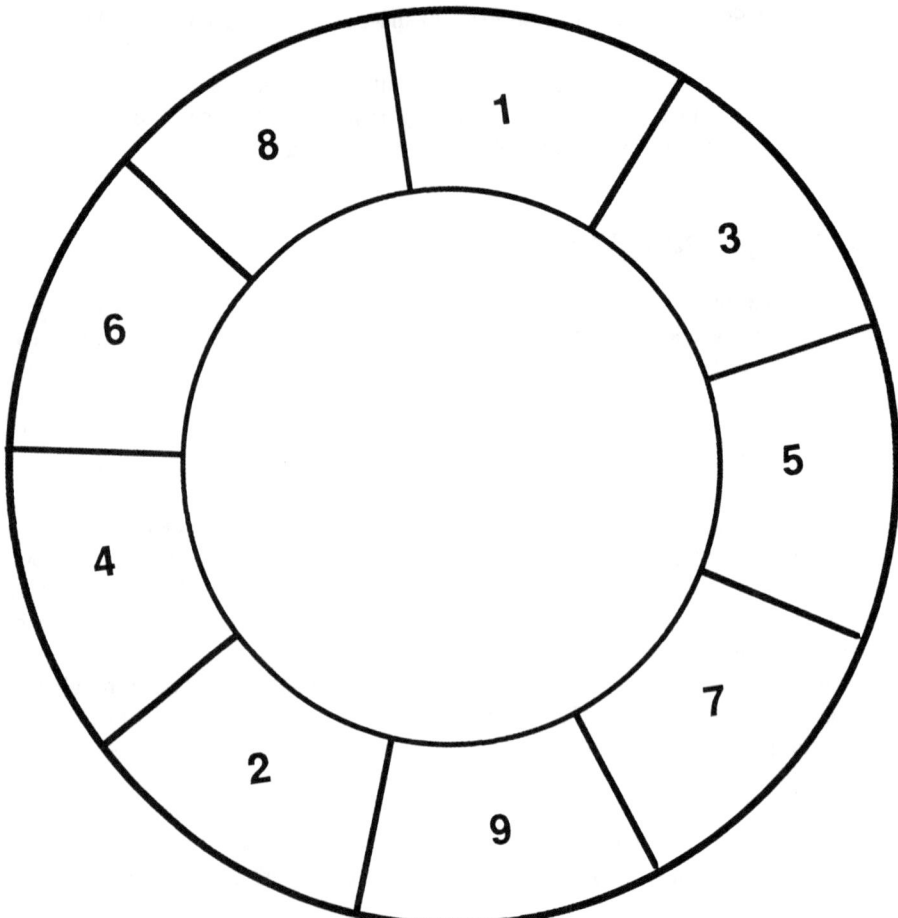

19-6 The 1:6 interleave found on a 360 K floppy diskette.

The interleave is invisible to DOS and to your programs. It's maintained by the disk's controller. So, when DOS or your program reads information from disk, it's read sequentially, even though the sectors really don't sit that way on disk. As a matter of fact, many technical books leave out the subject of disk interleave because it's done automatically by the disk's controller.

A potential problem with a hard disk's interleave factor is that it might be inefficient. The interleave might be too conservative for the disk controller or might be too liberal, causing the controller to skip over sectors and wait a complete disk revolution for the next sector. Either way, an improper interleave slows the performance of a hard disk.

This can be fixed by resetting a disk's interleave factor. Alas, that's only done when you initially low-level format a diskette. Because that's destructive, doing so means you have to go through the labors of a full hard disk backup (including all logical disk partitions). Then, you need to start over again with the low-level format, FDISK, the high-level format, and finally a restore operation. Yuck!

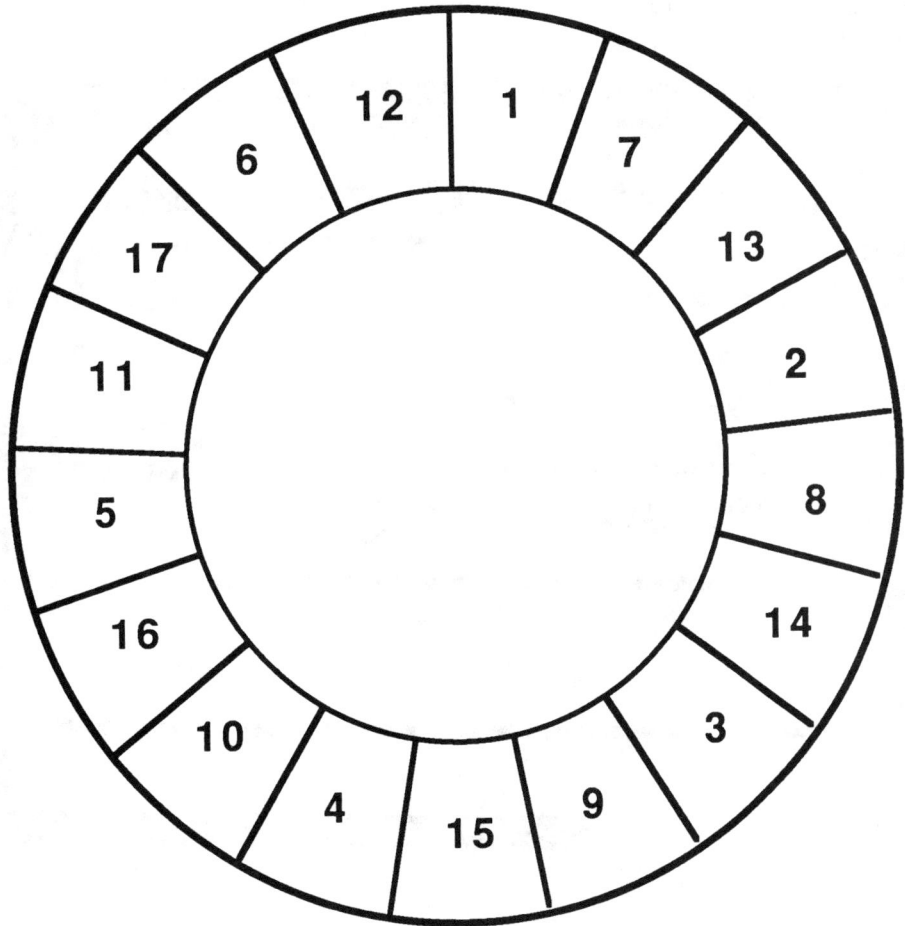

19-7 The 1:3 interleave found on most common hard drives.

Rather than bother with that pain, you can use some special non-destructive low-level reformatting programs. These will help you evaluate your hard disk's interleave, as well as reformat the drive with a more efficient interleave if the disk calls for it. All of this is done without destroying a sector of data.

Even if you have a superfast hard drive with a 1:1 interleave, performing a low-level format has been known to revitalize a borderline hard drive. It has something to do with lazy magnetic particles that tend to flake out if they aren't accessed after a while. So, a non-destructive low-level reformat might be in store as a part of yearly computer maintenance.

PC Tools' DiskFix

DiskFix is PC Tools quick and handy disk repair shop. It helps remedy many hard disk ills, can recover and rebuild lost files and directories, scans the disk for potential defiled sectors, and can perform a non-destructive low-level format as well as analyze and mend the interleave factor. The program's main screen is shown in Fig. 19-8.

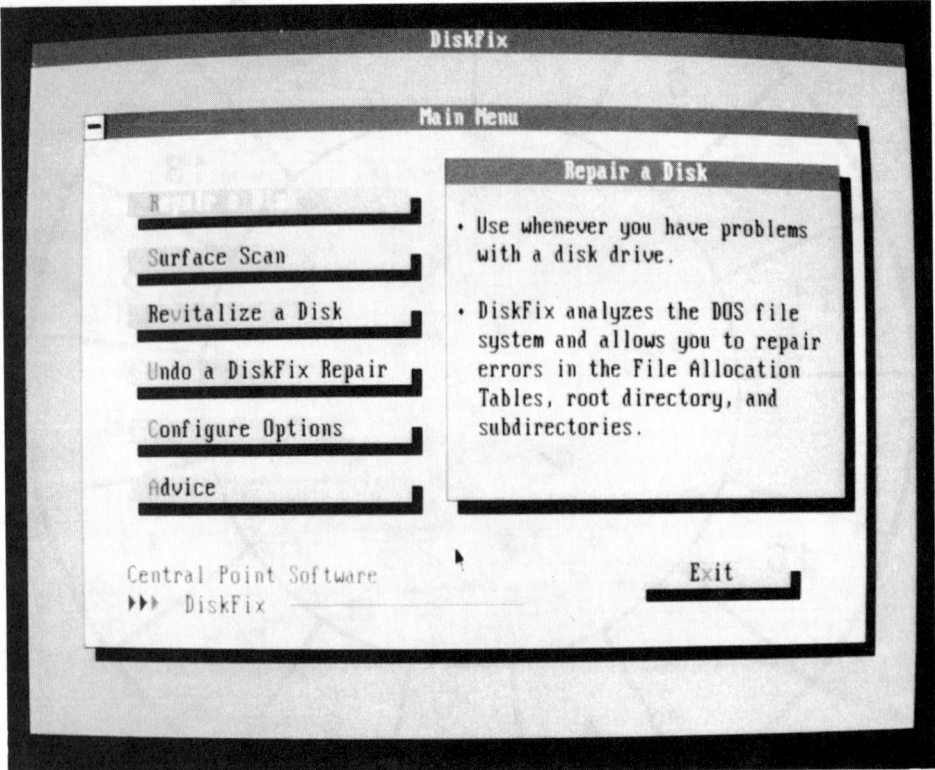

19-8 DiskFix's main menu.

The low-level format and interleave option is the third in the list, Revitalize a Disk. After selecting that option, DiskFix immediately analyzes the disk to see what needs to be done. This analysis is to ensure that no disk errors exist that could compromise the reformatting.

DiskFix continues its battery of tests with a disk timing test (which has a great-looking display), followed by a physical parameter test. It's in the physical parameter test where you'll see your hard drive's current interleave ratio. If the interleave can be improved upon, the program will show several interleave ratios plus the best desired ratio for the drive. If the interleave is okay or if the drive cannot be low-level formatted (and that's the case with some of the SCSI, ESDI, and IDE drives), then you optionally can perform a surface scan to revitalize the disk.

If you do proceed with a low-level reformat, I suggest you go through the maximum pattern testing before continuing. You want to make sure you select the correct interleave for your drive; this is nothing to mess with.

One thing that annoys me about this program is that, after a program is run, the hard drive light blinks on and off. I don't know if that means an error or what, but it bugs me.

Other low-level formatting tools

Other commercial applications might exist to give you a better interleave factor, without you having to resort to reformatting the entire drive. One commonly mentioned is Steve Gibson's SpinWrite, as well as Prime Solution's Disk Technician. I don't have either of these packages, though both do carry a well-earned reputation. Refer to your software dealer or magazine reviews for additional information before buying one or the other or when comparing them with PC Tools' DiskFix.

Making more disk space

If you need more disk space, you can do one of three things. First, you can buy new hardware that gives you extra storage. This approach involves buying a second hard drive or just replacing one you have. If you've made a good initial hard disk buying decision, this isn't something you should be doing a few weeks after buying your computer. However, you might do it sometime down the road. (This topic is covered in chapter 21 just in case.)

Second, you can always archive or copy programs to floppy diskettes. This should be done as a part of general housekeeping, especially for files that are gathering dust on the hard drive. They're just taking up space, so why not copy them away? However, if you're copying off full applications or files you need and end up copying them back on, you need more disk storage.

Third, you can squeeze more disk storage by compacting programs on disk as they're saved to disk or by using special software that creates more space on your hard drive by some form of techno-magic. These techniques really aren't magic, but they're covered in the next few sections. Take a look if you're one of the many PC users who find yourself growing short on disk space.

Archiving utilities

Archiving utilities are some of the most popular utility programs for the PC. They originated from the electronic Bulletin Board Systems (BBS) that dot the nation. It's more convenient and takes less time for a BBS user to download software (copy it from the BBS to their own system) as one file rather than to get 10 or 20 larger files. For your hard disk, the archiving utilities allow you to store groups of files in a tight, compact form, saving disk space.

Note that archiving on your hard drive is best for files you want to keep handy, yet files you don't access often. For example, after each of my books returns from the publisher, I archive all the files, documents, and figures into one handy ZIP file. That ZIP archive file is one file on disk that contains all the other files—and it uses less space than the other files altogether.

If I need one or more files after they've been archived, I can UNZIP one or all of them. Using an archive file viewer, such as Lotus' Magellan, I can peek into an archived file, extract text or other information, then be on my way without using up any disk space.

These ZIP files are archive files created by Phil Katz's popular PKZIP program. Its counterpart, PKUNZIP, is used to scan ZIP archives and optionally extract files from them. Both of these programs, as well as other convenient utilities, come in the ZIP package, which is available from major online systems, computer clubs, or software ware-houses, such as PC-SIG.

Creating a ZIP file   To create a ZIP archive, you use the following format:

    PKZIP – A *zipfile filenames*

The – A is the add switch. The *zipfile* is the archive filename, which will be created if it doesn't already exist. *filenames* can be a single file, a group of files specified using wild-cards, or a list of files in a file on disk. All of those files will be added to the zipfile. Once that's done, you can delete the originals; the ZIP file will contain them all in a compressed format. The disk savings can be up to 50%.

If you want to archive an entire subdirectory branch, you can specify the – R switch. For example, here is the command I'll use to create a ZIP file of this book, its disk, fig-ures, and all the other files associated with it (some 3 Mb of stuff):

    PKZIP – AR TABHDM *.*

Both A and R are specified together. PKZIP will create TABHDM.ZIP and place all the files in all subdirectories associated with this book into TABHDM.ZIP. (This assumes I use the command in the book's main directory.)

UNZIPping files   If you want to extract one or more files from a ZIP file, you use the PKUNZIP program. The format is:

    PKUNZIP *zipfile* [*filenames*]

Again, *zipfile* is the archive filename. The ZIP extension is optional. The *filenames* are optional. If they are not specified, PKUNZIP will extract all the files. Otherwise, you individually can specify one or more files to extract. The file remains in the ZIP file, still in a compressed form—you're only extracting a copy of it.

Viewing ZIP files   You can check the contents of a ZIP file using the PKZIP program in the following format:

    PKUNZIP – V *zipfile*

PKUNZIP will display a formatted listing of the files in the zipfile, with their original sizes, dates, and special codes used to verify the integrity of each file.

If you want to order PKZIP, you can order it directly from the following address:

PKZIP, PKUNZIP, PKSFX
PKWARE, Inc.
7545 N. Port Washington Rd.
Glendale, WI 53217

PKZIP also is available from the PC-SIG Library. Ask for diskette #1364.

Increasing disk storage

Creating archive files solves the problem of some software you want to keep handy, but it doesn't cure everything. Program files and data files you need and use still take up valuable space on disk. You cannot archive and then unarchive them as you need them; that occupies too much of your time. Instead, you need to turn to a solution that takes the amount of space used by all files on disk and reduces it drastically.

Several methods of increasing disk storage always have been available. The memory-resident Cubit program used to compress files as they were saved to disk and decompress them as they were loaded into memory. However, that process added time to all disk activities and proved unreliable. Alternatives always have come up, but two I'm presently fond of are Stac Technology's STACKER and Sundog Software's Squish Plus.

Stac Technology's Stacker   Stacker is a combination software hardware solution that started catching fire in the PC industry in early 1991. It offers hard disk space savings that literally double the amount of storage space your PC has.

Stacker works in the background, monitoring all DOS's disk writes. As files are saved to disk, they're compressed. As files are loaded from disk, they're decompressed. This is nothing novel, yet Stacker does it at what seems like the speed of light; you'll never know the compression is taking place. Because it monitors all disk writes, none of your hard disk snooping utilities will ever know the difference—and that's only the software version. The hardware version of Stacker is a coprocessor card that makes the Stacker software compression work even faster.

The Stacker solution works for all hard drives. Alas, it doesn't work for floppy drives or RAM drives (which limits its laptop appeal), but it is a reliable and popular solution if you're tight on disk space and can't afford another drive.

> Stacker
> Stac Electronics
> 5993 Avenida Encinas
> Carlsbad, CA, 92008
> (619) 431-7474

Squish Plus   I first learned about Squish Plus for a book I wrote on laptop computers (*The Concise PC Notebook and Laptop User's Guide*, Windcrest book #3921). Squish Plus is a device driver that creates a disk within a disk. The Squish drive actually is a special file on your hard disk that acts as if it were another disk drive. You can use all DOS commands on the drive, run programs there, even copy and store new files. Because it really is a file on disk controlled by the Squish device driver, however, it saves disk space every time you copy a file to it.

The only downside to Squish Plus is that you must have a good-sized chunk of hard disk space free to initially create the Squish drive. Yet, once it is created, you can start moving files there and save on disk space.

Incidentally, the Squish drive can be password-protected and all files copied to it are stored in an encrypted fashion. This should please security-conscious users.

> Squish Plus
> Sundog Software Corporation
> 264 Court Street
> Brooklyn, NY, 11231
> (718) 855-9141

Summary

This chapter was packed with information about getting the most from your hard disk. A wide variety of topics, including hardware and software techniques, were covered. These tricks included general housekeeping; sorting and squeezing your directories; defragmenting files; adjusting the hard disk's interleave factor; archiving or ZIPping files to keep them handy, yet save on disk space; and using special disk compression software to save disk space as files are written and read.

All of these tricks are more-or-less physical solutions to optimizing hard disk performance. In the next chapter, you'll see how your computer's memory, or RAM, can be used to maximize disk access and overall computer performance.

20

Memory optimization

PCs store information in one of two places: in internal memory or on disk. The computer's RAM, or Random Access Memory, is used for the temporary storage of information; disks are used for permanent storage. To hold information in RAM, electrical current must refresh the RAM circuitry constantly. Once the power is turned off, any information in RAM is gone. Because of this, information needs to be saved to a more permanent site on disk. Disks retain information even when the power is off.

The subject of this book is hard disks, yet that doesn't mean your PC's memory doesn't play a role in optimizing your hard disk. This chapter continues the discussion of disk optimization, but with the concentration on interaction between your computer's RAM and disk storage. Some amazing things are possible.

Memory in a PC

In the old CP/M days of computing, memory was a scarce commodity. The computer's operating system, programs, and data all had to fit inside a tiny 64 K bank of memory. It appears tiny today because computers typically come equipped with ten times that much memory—and more. Still, that much memory isn't considered enough, which makes it even more amazing that people got all their work done using CP/M computers with only 64 K of RAM.

The original IBM PC introduced in 1981 had only 64 K of RAM out of a potential 640 K. This made sense, because all other computers at the time also had only 64 K of RAM. Software houses developed for the PC were used to working in a 64 K environment. To make the best use of that space, they divided the 64 K RAM up into sections for their own program and for data. For example, the ancient VisiCalc spreadsheet (the predecessor of 1-2-3) occupied about 30 K of RAM and left the rest of memory for spreadsheet data.

The PC's true potential for memory was 640 K. Actually, the 8088 microprocessor inside the PC could access, or address, 1 Mb (1024 K) of memory. However, part of that memory was set aside for future expansion. The upper 384 K of all PCs, and all machines compatible with it, is reserved memory or upper memory. The lower 640 K, called *conventional memory* or *DOS memory*, is where DOS and your programs run (see Fig. 20-1).

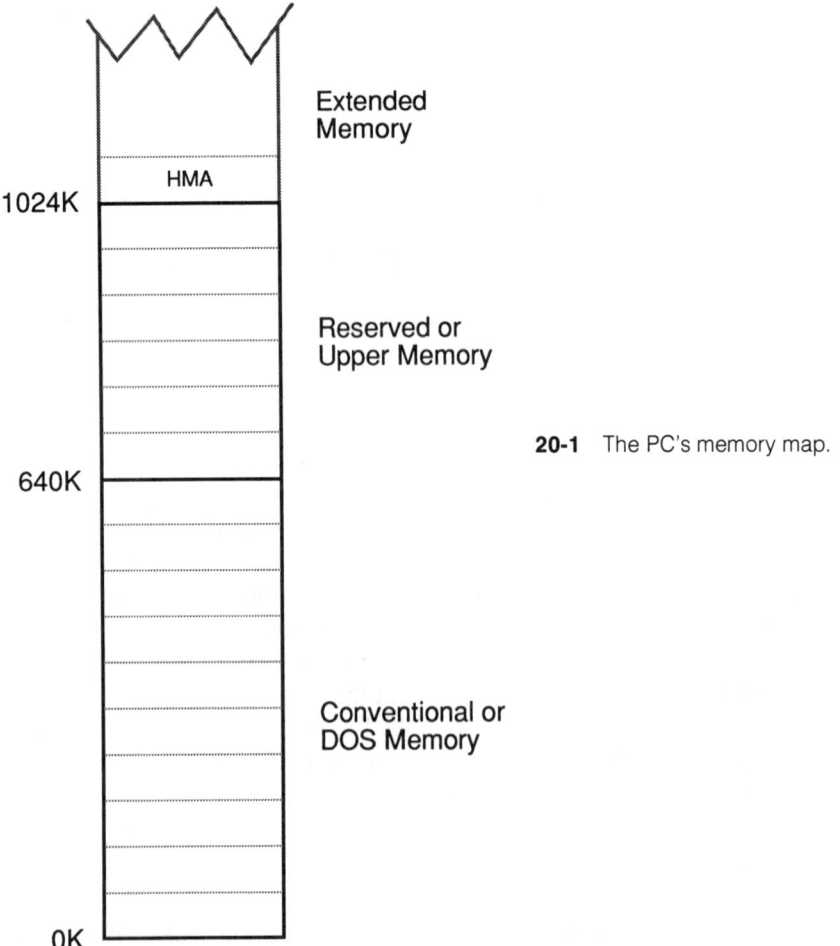

Extended
Memory

HMA

1024K

Reserved or
Upper Memory

20-1 The PC's memory map.

640K

Conventional or
DOS Memory

0K

This still is true today, because all PCs—no matter which microprocessor they use—are compatible with the original model.

Unfortunately, even 640 K of RAM proved to be too puny for RAM-hungry PC applications. Most programs maxed out on RAM in 1985. To solve this problem, several schemes were developed to put more memory in the PC. But no matter what, one adage remains the same: to keep compatible with DOS, all PCs can only have a maximum of 640 K in which to run programs.

Any extra memory you add in a PC is just that—extra memory. It's used to store information; programs can only run in conventional memory, the basic 640 K.

EMS memory

As the size of programs increased, the software houses began to see a real limitation with 640 K of RAM. Most programs could get along fine in 640 K. However, graphics programs and spreadsheets needed more memory. Users that created large spreadsheets discovered that memory disappeared quickly. Software designers were pushing the PC to the limit of its performance. They wanted more RAM.

The solution for all PCs and all DOS programs was EMS, the Expanded Memory Specification. Expanded memory is simply extra memory in a PC. It's not memory beyond the 1 Mb mark. Instead, think of expanded memory as a pool of memory sitting in a PC, memory that any DOS program can access and use.

Any PC can have up to 32 Mb of EMS memory, although most users typically will have anywhere from 512 K to 2 Mb—which is enough. That memory is accessed through a page frame, which is a 64 K chunk of reserved memory (see Fig. 20-2). That page frame lets any EMS-aware DOS program swap memory back and forth from the EMS memory pool into conventional memory.

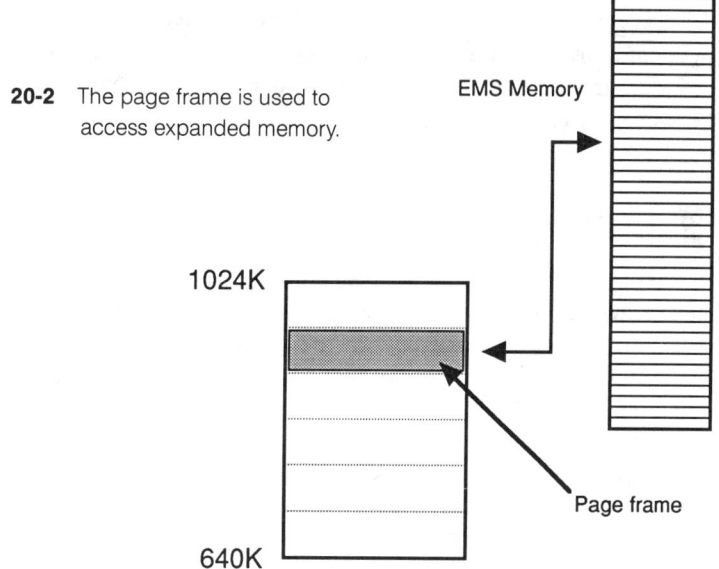

20-2 The page frame is used to access expanded memory.

Many programs will take advantage of EMS memory: WordPerfect, Lotus 1-2-3, PC Tools, Windows, and on and on. If you don't think you own any programs that take advantage of EMS memory, reread your manual; you might be surprised. However, if you really don't own any EMS-aware programs, you can always put that memory to use as a RAM disk or as cache memory. Each of these tools will help speed up disk operations. Because they aren't in standard memory, they don't subtract space from running your programs. (RAM disks and cache memory are elaborated upon later in this chapter.)

The issue of extended memory

Expanded. Extended. Where else but the computer industry would you have such similar sounding yet different terms to describe memory?

Extended memory is memory above the 1 Mb limit on 80286, 386, and later microprocessors (see Fig. 20-1). These microprocessors have the ability to directly address 16

Mb to 4096 Mb of memory—many times greater than the original 8088. If you have any extra memory installed in your 80268 or 386 machine, that memory is all extended memory. There's nothing wrong with extended memory, except that DOS cannot use it. Therein lies the rub.

For DOS to run on an 80286 or 386 PC, the microprocessor needs to be in its real mode. In the real mode, those microprocessors cannot access extended memory. Only in the processor's protected mode can extended memory be accessed. DOS is a real-mode-only operating system. Only OS/2 and some variations of UNIX can run in the protected mode—but not DOS. (Yes, Windows claims it wants extended memory; however, internally, it converts it all to expanded memory.)

All is not lost, however. You still can use extended memory as a RAM disk or as cache memory. Some programs will access extended memory through various dark and techno-magic secrets. However, the majority of the programs want expanded memory.

Incidentally, to get expanded memory on an 80286 AT class PC, you must add an expanded memory card, just as you would for the standard 8088 model PC. To get expanded memory on a 386 system, you can convert some of your extended memory into expanded. This subject is explained in the next few sections.

DOS 5's memory magic

One of the best things DOS 5 has to offer is memory management. While DOS programs still are limited to operate below the 640 K barrier, DOS 5 does provide memory management abilities for 80286 and 386 systems. The end result of these mnemonics isn't more than 640 K, but rather a greater portion of that 640 K in which you can run programs. Other benefits are available as well, making DOS 5's memory magic something worth having.

Alas, these memory tricks won't work on an 8088/8086 vintage PC. For those systems, my best advice is to add and use as much EMS memory as you can. Otherwise, prepare to open up new vistas for your 80286 and 386 systems.

Controlling extended memory

The first step in taking control of your memory is to set up extended memory for use under DOS. Yeah, I know, I said you cannot use extended memory under DOS. Yet, some programs can use it for storage (you'll see examples of them in the latter parts of this chapter). To access extended memory, you need some form of memory driver. The driver contains all the functions for using and allocating extended memory and adheres to a certain standard. Under DOS, the standard is the *Extended Memory Specification*, or XMS.

The DOS 5 XMS device driver is HIMEM.SYS. It's installed in your CONFIG.SYS drive as the main control program for all access to extended memory in your system. Note that you must have at least 350 K of extended memory to use HIMEM.SYS.

For example, the following command installs HIMEM.SYS into your CONFIG.SYS file:

```
DEVICE = C:\ DOS \ HIMEM.SYS
```

Note that the C: \ DOS subdirectory is assumed in the example; be sure to specify the full pathname to the HIMEM.SYS driver on your system. (For more information on CONFIG.SYS and the DEVICE configuration command, refer to chapter 7.)

This command should always come before all other device drivers in CONFIG.SYS, especially those that deal with memory. For example, if you're using an EMM.SYS device driver for an EMS memory expansion card on your 80286 system, put that device driver command after HIMEM.SYS.

With HIMEM.SYS installed on your system, you've done two things. First, you've established XMS control over extended memory. Second, you've created what's called the *High Memory Area*, or HMA.

The HMA is a bonus. It's an extra 64 K bank of memory DOS can use. That bank starts at memory address 1024 K and goes up into the first 64 K of extended memory (Fig. 20-1). This works because of a fluke in the microprocessor that allows DOS to see the extra 64 K bank of memory beyond the 1024 K limit.

Loading DOS high

With the HIMEM.SYS driver installed and the XMS established, you now can put the HMA to work. This is done under DOS 5 by loading DOS high.

The HMA's 64 K bonus bank has been put to use in many programs. For example, both Windows and DESQview use it—Windows even comes with its own HIMEM.SYS driver. Under DOS 5, you can use the HMA for DOS's kernel and the disk buffers. The end result is extra memory savings without cramping down on your basic 640 K.

To load DOS high, you use the DOS configuration command in CONFIG.SYS. The format is:

DOS = HIGH

That's it. Elsewhere in CONFIG.SYS, you'll need the HIMEM.SYS device driver installed. Without it, there is no HMA and DOS can't load itself high. With all the gears meshing together, however, DOS = HIGH will load DOS into the HMA and free up about 50 K of conventional memory. Both DOS and its internal buffers (created using the BUFFERS command) now will sit in the HMA.

Sadly, this is as far as you can go with DOS 5 on an 80286 system. The rest of the solutions offered are only for 386 systems. However, you should look into some interesting third-party memory management programs, as well as consider buying an expanded memory card for your 80286 system.

Creating expanded memory

Further memory magic is provided on 386 systems by using a second memory management device driver, EMM386.EXE. This program is dual-purpose. It can be used both as a command line program as well as a device driver—even though it has an EXE filename extension.

EMM386.EXE does two things for your 386 system. It creates what are called *upper memory blocks*, or UMBs. Also, it can convert extended memory over into the more useful expanded memory for use under DOS. Creating the UMBs is covered in the next section.

Under DOS, you often will find programs that want expanded memory—expanded memory, not extended. All the extra memory in your 386 system is extended memory. A few programs, notably Windows, want extended. For most software, however, expanded memory is desired.

To take advantage of the EMM386.EXE device driver to create expanded memory, your 386 system must have at least 2 Mb of total memory. Then, to create the expanded memory, use EMM386.EXE in CONFIG.SYS as follows:

```
DEVICE = C: \ DOS \ EMM386.EXE [memory]
```

memory is optional and indicates the amount of extended memory you want to convert into expanded memory, in kilobytes. If you don't specify a value for memory, EMM386.EXE converts 512 K.

There are two important things to note with the above command. First, be sure to specify the proper location for EMM386.EXE on your hard drive. Second, remember that the device driver has an EXE extension, not SYS. If you reset to test this command and see a Device driver not found type of error message, that's probably the reason.

```
DEVICE = C: \ DOS \ EMM386.EXE 1024
```

converts 1 Mb of extended memory into expanded memory. If any additional extended memory exists in the machine, it will be extended memory, available for whatever program wants it.

Note that EMM386.EXE requires the HIMEM.SYS driver to be installed in memory. Because of this, only specify the DEVICE command that loads EMM386.EXE after the command that loads HIMEM.SYS. Also, do not use this command with Windows; Windows wants extended memory, not expanded.

Creating upper memory blocks

To free up more of your basic 640 K of RAM, you can move your device drivers and memory-resident programs, loading them high, similar to the way DOS is loaded high. However, while DOS sits in the HMA, device drivers and memory-resident programs must be loaded into UMBs, upper memory blocks.

Upper memory blocks are unused locations of reserved or upper memory. When IBM designed the PC, they set aside 384 K for future expansion. Because the PC's design has more or less stabilized, only a few items have found their way into the expansion area: video memory and the video BIOS; the hard disk controller's BIOS; network cards; the EMS page frame; the main BIOS; and the BASIC programming language ROMs on some systems (see Fig. 20-3).

The interesting thing about upper memory is that it's not full. There is space between the various ROMs and BIOSs. The EMM386.EXE device driver can take advantage of the spaces and fill them with usable RAM. That's what creates the upper memory blocks. (A further step is required to load your device drivers and memory-resident programs into those blocks.)

Before you use EMM386.EXE to create the blocks, you need to tell DOS about it. This is done by specifying the UMB switch with the DOS configuration command:

```
DOS = UMB
```

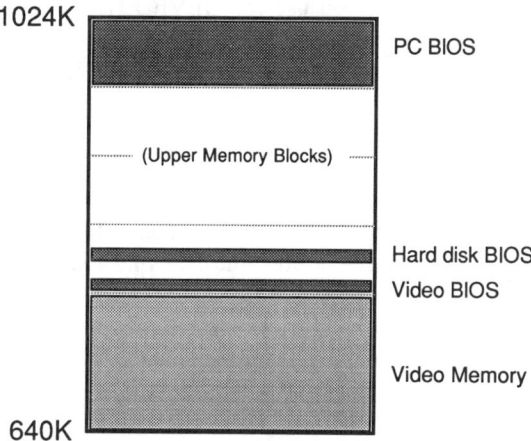

1024K

PC BIOS

(Upper Memory Blocks)

Hard disk BIOS

Video BIOS

Video Memory

640K

20-3 Upper memory blocks are unused areas of reserved memory.

If DOS already is equal to HIGH, you can specify both items on the same line:

DOS = HIGH,UMB

To direct the EMM386.EXE device driver to create upper memory blocks, you have two options. First, if you're using EMM386.EXE to convert extended memory into expanded, use this format:

DEVICE = C: \ DOS \ EMM386.EXE *memory* RAM

The RAM option is used to create the upper memory blocks, in addition to converting memory kilobytes of extended memory into expanded.

The second option is used if you don't need any expanded memory converted, yet you want upper memory blocks. Here is the format:

DEVICE = C: \ DOS \ EMM386.EXE NOEMS

The NOEMS switch tells EMM386.EXE to create the UMBs only; no extended memory will be converted. NOEMS primarily is used when you want to save conventional memory and create UMBs. When your applications need 100% extended memory, however, there's only one application that presently lends itself to the task: Microsoft's Windows. Because of that, I call NOEMS the *Windows switch*.

Once the UMBs are created, you can use two DOS commands to load your device drivers and memory-resident programs into them: DEVICEHIGH and LOADHIGH.

Loading device drivers high

Normally, DOS loads device drivers into conventional memory. This makes sense, seeing that your basic 640 K is all you have to run programs and that a device driver is basically a program. Through the magic of DOS 5, however, you now can load a device driver high, into an upper memory block (provided you create them first).

To load a device driver high, you use the DEVICEHIGH configuration command instead of DEVICE. It really is that simple. Some DOS 5-aware device drivers will load themselves high automatically whether you use the DEVICE or DEVICEHIGH commands.

```
DEVICEHIGH = C: \ MOUSE \ MOUSE.SYS
```

loads the MOUSE.SYS device driver into an upper memory block. Depending on the driver, you can save anywhere from 14 K to 28 K of conventional memory by doing this. Everything works as it did before, it's just that the driver now is loaded high and out of the way.

Occasionally, a few sleight of hand tricks are required to load a device driver high. This situation is when the MEM command comes in handy. MEM, short for *memory*, will display which programs are in memory and which are loaded high. This is done by typing the following at the DOS prompt:

```
MEM /C ¦ MORE
```

The /C switch stands for *classify* and directs the MEM command to output the names of all files currently in memory, as well as a summary of memory usage. If you've created upper memory blocks, you'll see any files loaded high as well.

If you notice a device driver doesn't load high, it might help to check its size in the output of the MEM /C command. If the device driver is rather large, it might help to load it first, changing its order in your CONFIG.SYS file.

Another problem arises from expanding device drivers, which can crash the system. To avoid this problem, you need to determine the driver's size in memory using MEM /C, then specify the hexadecimal size value for the driver in the DEVICEHIGH command as follows:

```
DEVICEHIGH SIZE = hex driver.SYS
```

hex is the size of the device driver in hexadecimal; *driver*.SYS is the device driver name. Presently, I know of no device drivers that expand such as this, but that doesn't mean there aren't any out there.

Most of your common device drivers can be loaded high: MOUSE.SYS, ANSI.SYS, and a few other DOS chestnuts. The following shows a CONFIG.SYS file listing with all the memory management tricks discussed so far:

```
DEVICE = C: \ DOS \ HIMEM.SYS
DOS = HIGH,UMB
DEVICE = C: \ DOS \ EMM386.EXE 512 RAM
DEVICEHIGH = C: \ DOS \ ANSI.SYS
DEVICEHIGH = C: \ DOS \ MOUSE.SYS
```

Loading memory-resident programs high

Memory-resident programs typically are loaded in AUTOEXEC.BAT. Programs, such as DOSKEY, pop-up calculators, memory-resident print modification routines, and so forth, all stay in memory and either modify something or provide an extra utility at the touch of a hotkey. Yet, all this stuff takes up memory; therefore, if you've created UMBs, why not load your memory-resident programs high just like device drivers?

The command to load a memory-resident program high is LOADHIGH, which can be abbreviated LH. To load a memory-resident program high, just stick LH in front of it; nothing else is required:

    LH DOSKEY

Unlike DEVICEHIGH, there's no size option or anything else to worry about.

If there aren't any more UMBs for the program, then it's just loaded low, as it was before.

You can use LOADHIGH with just about any memory-resident program. Don't use the command with regular programs or batch files; the results will be unpredictable and predictably bad.

This is the last memory management trick DOS 5 has to offer. Third-party memory managers will do more for you and, generally, free up more memory. If you wish to pursue this subject further, I suggest picking up a good, thorough book on the subject.

RAM disks and how they work

One of the best things you can do with extra memory in your PC is to put it to work as a RAM disk. RAM disks go by a number of names: RAMDRIVE, VDISK, MEMBRAIN, and so on. Basically, a RAM disk is a superfast disk drive created in memory. Because it's in memory, it's going to behave a lot faster than any physical disk drive. Disk access will be quicker and reads and writes will appear nearly instantaneous. The RAM disk will operate as fast as your computer's memory.

Most RAM disks are created with a device driver in your CONFIG.SYS file. The RAM disk has a specific size and location, either in conventional, extended, or expanded memory. DOS assigns a letter to the RAM disk, usually the next highest letter in your system. You can create as large a RAM disk as you have memory for or create several smaller RAM disks—whatever you want.

DOS treats the RAM disk just like any other disk in the system. You can copy files to it, run CHKDSK, use the DIR command—anything. The only drawback is that all information on a RAM disk disappears when you turn off the PC; like the rest of memory, RAM disks are not permanent. Because of this, any new information you place on a RAM disk should be copied back to a real disk before turning off the power. (That's an excellent application for a SHUTDOWN.BAT file.)

DOS's RAMDrive

A RAM disk driver is included with DOS. With MS-DOS it's called RAMDrive. Other versions of DOS might call it VDisk for Virtual Disk. Both commands are similar, although this book standardizes on RAMDrive.

Using RAMDrive you can create any number of RAM disks in either conventional, extended, or expanded memory. I recommend using whichever you have the most of, preferably extended or expanded memory.

To create a RAM disk on your system with RAMDrive, you need to use the RAM-DRIVE.SYS device driver. (VDisk's device driver is named VDISK.SYS.) The format is as follows:

```
DEVICE = C: \ DOS \ RAMDRIVE.SYS [size] [sector] [dir] [/E | /A]
```

Remember to specify the proper full pathname to RAMDRIVE.SYS. In the previous example, C: \ DOS is assumed.

size is optional and indicates the size of the RAM disk. It can be anywhere from 16, for a 16 K RAM disk, up through 4096 for a 4 Mb disk. If *size* isn't specified, RAMDrive creates a 64 K disk.

sector refers to the size of the sectors used in the RAM disk. DOS usually allocates 512 bytes to a sector; however, you can specify values of 128, 256, or 512 bytes. If a sector size isn't specified, 512 bytes are assumed. The only time I recommend using a size other than 512 is when you're working with small files. On my batch file RAM drive, I use a sector size of 128 bytes (because most batch files are only 100 bytes in length). Note that you must specify a *size* value if you use the sector option.

dir refers to the number of directory entries allowed in the RAM disk's root directory. This can be any number from 2 through 1024, with 64 being the default. I always specify this value when I'm copying a known number of files to the RAM disk— especially when I know the number of directory entries won't be changing. Note that you must specify both a *size* and *sector* value if *dir* is specified.

You can use either the /E or /A switch to create the RAM disk in extended or expanded memory, respectively. If neither switch is specified, the RAM disk is created in conventional memory, which probably isn't what you want.

Note that you can use the DEVICEHIGH command to load the RAMDRIVE.SYS driver into an upper memory block (see the previous section). Only the actual driver, some 1.4 K, is loaded high; the RAM disk itself is put into conventional, extended, or expanded memory as specified.

The following command in CONFIG.SYS is used to create a 720 K RAM disk in expanded memory:

```
DEVICE = C: \ DOS \ RAMDRIVE.SYS 720 /A
```

If you have drive C as your highest-lettered drive, then the RAM drive will be drive D. When your system starts, you'll see the following startup message:

```
Microsoft RAMDrive version 3.06 virtual disk D:
Disk size: 720k
Sector size: 512 bytes
Allocation unit: 1 sectors
Directory entries: 64
```

The following two lines in a CONFIG.SYS file install two RAM disks into extended memory. The first disk is 64 K in size, the second, 1024 K:

```
DEVICE = C: \ DOS \ RAMDRIVE.SYS /E
DEVICE = C: \ DOS \ RAMDRIVE.SYS 1024 /E
```

There now are two virtual disks in memory. The first was assigned to drive D, the second to drive E. The first is 64 K in size, the second 1024 K.

DOS normally gives you up to drive E without any fuss. So, if you only have a hard drive C, you can create two RAM drives, D and E. If you add any more, however, you'll need to use the LASTDRIVE command in CONFIG.SYS. That will set the highest drive letter DOS allows. For more information, refer to chapter 7 and the LASTDRIVE configuration command.

RAM disk techniques

There are many interesting things that can be done with a RAM disk. Keeping in mind the RAM disk's speed, it can do nothing but improve the time that disk-intensive operations take. This is where RAM disks really shine. Because batch files are fairly disk intensive, you can copy them to a RAM drive for superfast operation. Then, you can put that drive letter on your path and you have access to all your batch files.

The following four RAM drives are created on my personal system:

```
Drive I    C:\DOS\RAMDRIVE.SYS 32 128 128 /E
Drive J    C:\DOS\RAMDRIVE.SYS 1024 512 128 /E
Drive K    C:\DOS\RAMDRIVE.SYS 512 512 128 /E
Drive L    C:\DOS\RAMDRIVE.SYS 720 512 128 /E
```

The first, drive I, holds all my batch files. This is why it's only 32 K in size and has a sector size of 128 bytes. However, note that the directory entries have been bumped up to 128—the same with all the RAM disks.

Drive J is where I transfer all my utility files, which normally are held in a UTIL subdirectory. Currently, I have close to a megabyte of files there.

Drive K holds DOS. I've pared down DOS to fit into a 512 K RAM drive. This was done primarily by removing the DOS Shell and QBASIC files to another directory.

Drive L is my temporary files directory. It's a 720 K drive created to match the size of the 720 K floppy diskette. (Note that you cannot DISKCOPY between the two drives.)

To make four RAM drives work, the following is a section of my AUTOEXEC.BAT file:

```
ECHO Moving Batch Files...
XCOPY C:\SYSTEM\BATCH\*.* I:\  > NUL
ECHO Moving Utilities...
XCOPY C:\SYSTEM\UTIL\*.* J:\  > NUL
ECHO Moving DOS...
XCOPY C:\SYSTEM\DOS\*.* K:\  > NUL
REM Reset path to RAM drive files:
PATH = I:\;J:\;K:\
SET TEMP=L:
```

See how the batch files, utilities, and DOS are copied to the RAM disk? Then, the RAM disk letters are used on the path: I, J, and K. Everything runs blisteringly fast from the RAM drive. The TEMP variable is set to drive L, which further speeds DOS.

If the ideal of separate drives bugs you, you can use the JOIN command to attach a RAM drive as a subdirectory on part of your main hard drive. Although it still is a real RAM drive, DOS will treat it as if it's just another subdirectory.

For example, the following JOIN command attaches the RAM drive D to a subdirectory RAM on drive C:

```
JOIN D: C:\RAM
```

If \RAM doesn't exist, DOS creates it. If it does exist, it must be empty of files for the JOIN command to work.

After a RAM drive is joined to your hard drive structure, you can use it like any other subdirectory, put it on the path, etc. However, all files run from that directory will run faster because it secretly is a RAM drive.

To unJOIN a RAM drive the following command is used:

```
JOIN D: /D
```

In the previous command, the RAM drive D is unJOINed from whichever subdirectory it was attached.

The great RAM disk warning

Because the RAM disk is memory, when the power goes off or even if the computer is reset, any information stored on the RAM disk is gone forever.

You should always check a RAM disk before shutting down your computer. This could be another function of a SHUTDOWN batch file. A good way to test for files in a RAM disk would be to include the following statements in your SHUTDOWN.BAT file:

```
REM RAM disk assumed to be drive D:
IF NOT EXIST D:\*.* GOTO EMPTY
DIR D: /W
ASK Backup the files in the RAM disk (Y/N)?
IF ERRORLEVEL = =1 GOTO EMPTY
XCOPY D:\*.* C:\RAMDISK /S/E
:EMPTY
```

This batch file assumes the RAM disk is drive D. The IF NOT EXIST test determines whether the RAM disk is empty. If no files exist (*.*), batch file execution jumps to the EMPTY label and SHUTDOWN.BAT continues.

If files do exist, a directory is displayed. The ASK statement waits for keyboard input. Either Y or N must be typed before the batch file continues. If Y is typed, an errorlevel of 0 is returned; N sets the errorlevel at 1.

If N is pressed, execution branches to the EMPTY label and files in the RAM disk are not saved. If Y is pressed, the XCOPY program is used to copy all files and all subdirectories from the RAM disk to the subdirectory \RAMDISK on Drive C. (This could be replaced with whichever directory you find most appropriate for the files in your own RAM disk.) Once the files have been saved, the batch file continues.

Disk caching

A *cache* (pronounced *cash*) is a secret storage place. Pirates often had a cache of jewels buried on some desert island. Modern day terrorists have caches of weapons hidden somewhere. On a less-evil side, squirrels have caches of acorns stowed away for winter. Computers, not necessarily associated with pirates, terrorists, or squirrels, also can use caches. In this respect, a cache is a secret storage place in memory that speeds up disk operations.

A disk cache is not a RAM disk, although they are similar and easily confused. A disk cache monitors disk activity. It logs all reads and writes from disk, then keeps a copy of what was read or written in its own cache memory. If the computer makes a second request to read information from disk and that information is already in the cache, rather than reload the information from disk, it's read from cache memory. In computer jargon, the read request was satisfied from cache memory. Because the cache is memory, it's much faster than reading the data from disk.

The disk cache always makes sure whatever it holds in memory is safely saved on disk. When you save a file to disk, a copy is sent to disk and physically stored there. A second copy also is saved in cache memory. This is what makes it different from a RAM disk, where the information is only saved in RAM. If you wanted to access the same information again, the cache would intercept the call to disk and, instead of reloading the duplicate information, would simply copy it out of its own RAM. The disk access light won't glow and the information will be loaded much faster than without the cache.

The best way to test a disk cache is with a database or accounting program that uses many modules. Databases are perhaps the most disk-intensive programs. Each record is read from disk as it's individually called up. In the last section, you read how putting a database on a RAM disk speeds up certain operations (such as sorting). Using a cache, those operations still would be accelerated. However, unlike the volatile RAM disk, the cache is only a copy of what is already on disk. If a power failure occurred, nothing would be lost in the disk cache.

Disk caches are an excellent disk speed-up tool. They function simply based on the observation that most disk operations are repetitive. Like defragmenting your hard disk, you might not notice the full effect of a disk cache until after you've used one a while. The only drawback to a disk cache is that it uses memory. However, as long as memory isn't a problem, a disk cache is a quick and excellent RAM-based speed-up tool.

DOS's SMARTDrive

DOS's own cache program is SMARTDrive. Like RAMDrive, SMARTDrive is a device driver you install in your CONFIG.SYS file. Unlike RAMDrive, you only need to install one SMARTDrive for all hard drives in your system.

The format for the SMARTDrive cache program is:

```
DEVICE = C: \ DOS \ SMARTDRV.SYS [max] [min] [/A]
```

As usual, specify the proper path for SMARTDRV.SYS on your system; in the previous command, C: \ DOS is assumed.

Without any options, SMARTDrive creates a 256 K disk cache. Up to 256 K worth of information will be saved as it's read from disk. New information replaces old in the cache. Essentially, however, your disk's performance will improve the longer the cache stays in place.

max is used to indicate the maximum size of the cache in kilobytes. Values for *max* range from 128 through 8192, with the default being a 256 K cache.

min is a tricky value. It indicates the minimum size of the cache and can be any value from *max* on down to zero, with zero as the default. Theoretically, a program can adjust the size of the cache memory, reducing it if need be. In practice, the only program that does this is Windows. If you don't run Windows, you don't need to specify a *min* value.

The /A switch is used to place the cache into expanded memory. By not specifying /A, SMARTDrive will use extended memory for the cache. You cannot set up the cache in conventional memory.

As with RAMDrive, you can use the DEVICEHIGH command with SMARTDRV .SYS. Only the drive will be loaded high; the cache memory will remain in expanded or extended memory.

```
DEVICE = C: \ DOS \ SMARTDRV.SYS 512
```

creates a 512 K disk cache in extended memory.

Commercially available disk caches

There are a lot of disk caches available on the market. Some give you write-ahead caches. Some are read-only caches. Some have features that will block out certain drives, while others will cache everything.

Personally, I've found that most cache programs tend to interfere with DESQview and QEMM and everything else running amok in my PC. However, some of the third-party packages offer a bit tighter rein on disk caching. Two worth mentioning are Golden Bow's Vcache and Mace's MCache.

Vcache   One of the most interesting cache programs available comes from Golden Bow Systems of San Diego, California. There really are three versions of Golden Bow's Vcache program: CACHE is for conventional memory; CACHE-EM is for EMS memory; and CACHE-AT is for Extended memory. Only one program should be used at a time, depending on where you wish to place it in memory.

Vcache can be installed at any time simply by typing the appropriate program name at the command prompt. It also can be included as part of the AUTOEXEC.BAT file. Unlike many similar programs, CACHE can be removed to free the memory it uses.

Vcache offers both read and write caches and even comes with a handy summary feature. It can be used as a device driver or a memory-resident program, although, if you load it as a device driver, you cannot unload it.

Golden Bow has even thrown in a whole suite of utilities with the Vcache programs, including screen speed-up programs, keyboard tuners, and even caching software for your floppy drives. It's impressive. It's the only cache I'll use on my demanding system.

Vcache
Golden Bow Systems
2665 Ariane Dr., Suite 207
San Diego, CA 92117
(619) 483-0901

Mace's MCache Fifth Generation Systems' Mace Utilities comes with three disk caching programs, similar to Golden Bow's. (In the old days, Mace used to repackage and distribute Golden Bow's caching programs.) They all are device drivers, installed in CONFIG.SYS. Unlike Vcache, they cannot be unloaded from memory.

The three caching drivers are MCACH.SYS, MCACH-EM.SYS, and MCACH-AT.SYS. You optionally can specify the size of the cache and the drives to be cached when the driver is loaded. A command line program, CACHCTRL, can be used to monitor and tune the cache's performance after it's been loaded, as well as turn caching on or off. An interesting TEST option reports on the cache's performance, as seen in Fig. 20-4.

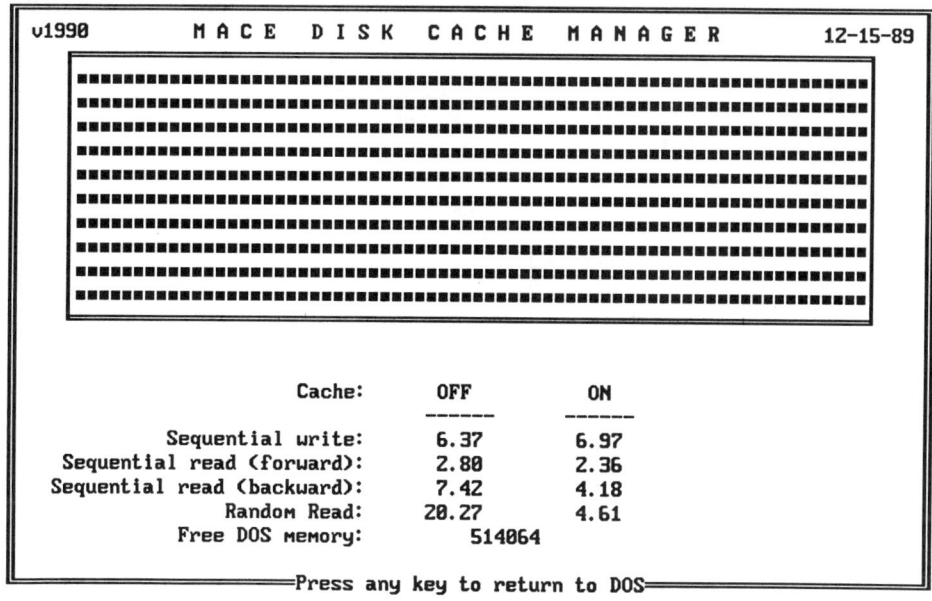

	Cache:	OFF	ON
		-------	-------
Sequential write:		6.37	6.97
Sequential read (forward):		2.80	2.36
Sequential read (backward):		7.42	4.18
Random Read:		20.27	4.61
Free DOS memory:		514064	

20-4 Mace's Cache Control program reports that all's well in disk caching land.

Summary

Although this is a hard disk book, this chapter dealt with RAM and the various ways RAM can be used to optimize hard disk performance. With DOS 5, RAM is saved rather than used. Device drivers, memory-resident programs, and even DOS itself can be removed from conventional memory, giving your applications more breathing room in that puny

640 K. Beyond that, extended and expanded memory can be put to work as a RAM drive or as a general disk speed-up tool, the cache.

The next chapter wraps up this part of the book on hard disk optimization with a look at different and unusual types of hard drives, as well as the topic of upgrading your hardware.

21

Upgrading your hardware

The final toss-in-the-towel decision and ultimate cure for a slow or low-capacity hard drive is to buy a new one. On one hand, this seems like a royal pain. Aside from the expense, you also have to back up your original hard drive, remove it, go through the rigors of installing the new drive, and then restore your files to it. On the other hand, it's an exciting and practical thing to do, not terribly expensive, and with definite benefits.

This chapter is about upgrading your hardware, plus some other options you might want to consider as hard drive replacements or add ons. The typical PC has room for two hard drives, so why not take advantage of it? Further, you can add other interesting devices to your system to increase your storage, back up data, or give you online access to megabytes of information.

Adding or replacing a hard drive

The physical job of adding or replacing a hard drive isn't that hard. Anyone can do it using a screwdriver and maybe an hour of time. Before making this or any hardware modification to your PC, I recommend you take the following steps:

Backup Making a backup is obvious if you're replacing your hard drive, but what might not be obvious is copying your backup software to a floppy diskette. Why? Because you'll need to restore from somewhere and the new drive probably won't have any RESTORE program installed. Also, if you are adding only a drive, it helps to have that backup copy just in case.

Give yourself plenty of time You should never rush through anything. PC users (and their owners) are always pressed for time. Yet, doing something quickly ensures only sloppiness. There's never time to do something right but always time to do it over.

Make sure you have a work area Most PCs are surrounded by clutter. If not, then they're not used or are used by people who haven't a clue. You'll need a big work space to do hardware upgrading.

Have a purpose You should never venture into your PC without a purpose. Sometimes the purpose is simply to familiarize yourself with a PC's guts. I've taken the lid off more than one PC while teaching classes. I also have written about it in several books, but the purpose is a guided tour—education. Your purpose here is to upgrade to a hard drive, or add a second one to your system.

Selecting a hard drive

Hard drives come in two pieces. First, there's the hard disk itself, which is basically a mechanical device—a set of platters on a spindle with a motor. Second, there's the hard disk controller, the brains of the operation.

In the traditional PC, the hard disk and controller are two required elements for a hard disk system. The controller could handle up to two drives, but both drives had to be of the same type and capacity (although not necessarily the same model number). These drives and their controllers are referred to as MFM, RLL, or ERLL system.

The MFM, RLL, and ERLL acronyms refer to the way the controller encodes data on the drive. MFM stands for Modified Frequency Modulation. It's the cheapest and most traditional type of controller. It stores the least amount of information and is a slug. RLL stands for Run Length Limited. It's a faster and denser encoding scheme, offering about a 3:2 ratio of storage space improvement over MFM drives. However, you need an RLL drive for an RLL controller. If not, the format won't hold.

The ERLL drives appeared for a time and still might be popular. ERLL stands for Extended Run Length Limited and was yet another attempt at developing a fast and high-capacity hard drive controller. However, it eventually was overshadowed by the integrated drive controllers.

All three of these controllers (MFM, RLL, and ERLL) require compatible hard drives in order to work. If the hard drive is not compatible, don't expect the format to hold. Your dealer is responsible for selling you the proper parts, so always inquire about matching drives and controllers.

Today's PCs mostly use integrated hard drives. There might be a controller card involved or some type of hard disk connection on the motherboard, but most of the smarts usually are included on the hard drive itself. The drives of this type are the IDE, Integrated Drive Electronics, drives; the ESDI, Enhanced Small Device Interface, drives; and the SCSI, scuzzy or Small Computer System Interface, drives.

If you're adding a hard disk to your system for the first time, then your choice is fairly liberal. As long as your system doesn't have a hard disk controller in it already, you can choose anything. For my personal recommendations, I have no preference. I'd like to side with SCSI, but the SCSI interfaces on a PC require extra device drivers and tend to be slow. ESDI or IDE would be a better choice in my opinion (although the IDE drives are all low-level formatted by the factory and disk utilities cannot access the drive at that level).

For brand names—I haven't a clue. It's one of the questions most often asked on my radio talk show. Some caller will rattle off a brand name and a series of numbers and letters and ask me if I trust the drive. I could tell you more about a company's stock than their disk drive serial numbers.

If you already have a hard drive and controller, you must pick up a second hard drive (or a replacement) that works with the same controller. For the earlier MFM and RLL drives, this also implied a second drive of the same capacity as the first. There were a few exceptions; however, for the most part, you could add a second 40 megabyte drive only if you already had one. For ESDI, SCSI, and IDE, the second drive can be any capacity, although you probably will vie for a larger capacity (I know I would).

One thing to scout for is a drive with the same form factor as the drive you're removing or as dictated by your PC's case. A form factor is nothing more than the physical dimensions of a drive. For example, you can't put a full height drive into a half height drive bay. You can't fit a full $5^1/4$-inch drive into a laptop's $3^1/2$-inch form factor. However, you can mount a smaller drive in a larger bay; brackets are available for doing this. So, inquire about a form factor before you buy the drive.

As for shopping hints, you can turn to your PC's manufacturer. However, for me to replace my laptop's piddly little 40 Mb drive with the 120 Mb jobbie, I'll have to pay $999. The same drive by the same company is available from a hard disk broker for $350. (I found it in a magazine ad in the back of *BYTE*.) The difference? Only $649! Because I would install the drive myself, why go with the manufacturer?

If mail order disk drives make you queasy (and it shouldn't), then you can try a local dealer. If they don't have the part, they usually can order it. You'll pay a bit more. I'd recommend having them install it as well, because they'll charge you only about $15 or so labor.

When you end up ready to install the drive yourself, make sure you order it properly configured as your first or second hard drive. There is a difference. Once that's done, you can heed the instructions offered in the next two sections. The first is for removing a drive; the second for installing. Good luck and lots of patience.

Removing a drive

Removing a drive is required under several circumstances. Primarily, if you're doing a straight-across hard disk replacement. However, if possible, I recommend adding a second drive if your system has room. If it doesn't, then what you might be removing is a floppy drive in order to replace it with a hard drive. In any case, the steps below are the same.

For this operation, you will need a screwdriver, typically a Phillips head. Make sure you've done your backup before starting. Always unplug the computer from the wall whenever you venture inside.

Remove the lid   Start the operation by powering down your computer and removing its lid. There are anywhere from two to five screws that must be removed from the back of the case, on the outside edge.

As you're facing the machine, pull the lid slowly toward you, checking under it for any snagged cables. If the lid doesn't move, check for any stray screws you might have forgotten. Make sure the key is unlocked.

Look for the drive to remove   The drive that you want to remove will be in the lower right corner as you look down on the PC from the front.

Remove the drive   There will be two mounting screws on the side of the drive. Unscrew them and slide the drive forward just a bit.

You'll need to remove three cables from a hard drive, two from a floppy drive. The controller cables will be flat ribbons connected to the drive's rump. A flat square power supply cable also should be removed.

Once the drive is free of its cables, slide it all the way forward and out of the PC. Check the drive to see if it has mounting rails on the sides. If so, remove the rails and attach them to the new hard drive. Make sure they're in the same orientation: pointy end toward the back of the drive.

The next step is to install the new drive in its place.

Installing a drive

If you're not continuing from the previous section, then refer to the start of that section for instructions on powering down your PC and removing its lid.

Inspect the new drive   If you're adding a second hard drive to your system, you'll need to make sure the jumpers on the drive are properly configured for DS1. The drive also should have a terminating resistor. If you're in doubt about this, phone up your dealer. (They should have sent you the proper drive configuration. Also, the drive might be smart enough to assume this configuration.)

If your system uses the mounting rail method of installing a drive, attach the mounting rails to the drive at this stage. One rail is screwed into either side of the drive. Make sure the pointy parts of the rails go toward the back of the PC's case.

Insert the new drive   Position the drive right side up (the drive light and vents are always on the bottom half) and slide it into the drive bay.

Attach cables   Hard drives have three cables attached. All of these cables are notched so you cannot install them backwards (if you did, it probably wouldn't damage the drive anyway; it just wouldn't work). The three cables are the power supply, the narrow 20-line data cable, and the wider 34-line control cable.

Secure the drive   With all the cables attached, slide the drive all the way into the bay. Tighten whatever additional mounting screws are required to anchor the drive.

Before testing the drive, double check all of your connections. I once thought my drive was DOA, but it turned out I'd forgotten to reconnect the data cable.

Test   Fire up your PC with the lid still off. Make sure the drive comes online. You'll see its light blink and hear the drive's chipmunks squeak away. If the light constantly flashes or your computer beeps more than once, you might have a problem.

On AT-class machines, don't be alarmed by a CMOS or Setup error. That always occurs when you add new hardware. Run your setup program and inform the computer's battery-backed up RAM about the new drive, using the drive type value supplied with the drive.

Close up   If everything proceeded as planned, power off your PC. Attach the lid, carefully gliding it on so that you don't snag any cables. Screw in the five or so mounting screws and reassemble your desk.

The job isn't really done yet. You still will need to perform further hard disk setups, as described in chapter 2. If any instructions came with the drive, follow them as well (unless they're written in Chinglish).

Removable hard disks and other interesting hardware

People who grew up as floppy drive users have an assortment of interesting questions regarding hard disks. For example, floppy-only users want to know why you can't take the disks out of a hard drive. The easily-paranoid find it hard to believe data will stick to the hard disk even when the computer is off. They want that data on a disk in their hands, not in some hermetically sealed black box at the mercy of the wicked machine.

The reasons why hard disks are rigid fixed media were discussed earlier in this book. The disk must spin at an extremely fast rate. The read/write head is only microns away from the disk surface. As an interesting aside, you might have heard the term *flying head* when referring to the read/write head of a hard disk. This is because, with the read/write head so close to the spinning disk, it creates a physical phenomenon where it actually does fly over the surface of the disk.

The same performance could be obtained from a floppy diskette if it weren't for two problems. First, the diskette would have to spin at the same speed as the hard disk, upwards of 3000 RPM, or 10 times faster than it spins in a floppy drive. At this speed, the flexible media flutters like a pinwheel. This does not make for good contact with the read/write head.

Secondly, the read/write head would need to be just as close to the surface of the disk as it would with a hard disk. It's the close distance that causes more information to be stored on a hard disk than a floppy. With the head so close and the speed of the drive so great, a head crash would be inevitable on a floppy.

Because of these two reasons, hard disks are constructed the way they are. The rigid media provides stability at high spin rates. The hermetically sealed black box provides a safe air-tight environment to prevent disk crashing.

Still, there are valid reasons for wanting a removable hard disk. Some of the oldest types of hard disks were called packs. The entire pack of disk platters was removable from the system. The packs could be removed, cleaned, taken to another site, stored away—all without damage to the media. Yet, this form of removable hard disk proved too costly for microcomputers.

The advantages of removing a hard disk are many, with security first among them. Nothing is safer than removing a hard disk from the computer and locking it up in a safe overnight. This avoids the potential problems of theft, vandalism, even fire. No password system, lock and key, or chain is as good as removing the hard disk from the computer.

Removable hard disks also are handy. Taking work home from the office or from one branch to another is as easy as slipping out the hard disk. If many users all use the same computer, each of them can have their own hard disk. They simply sit down, plug the disk into the slot, then use the computer. When they're done, they remove the hard disk media and let others use the machine.

Backups are relatively easy with removable hard disks. Because they can be treated like floppies, copying a removable hard disk is conceivably as simple as typing XCOPY C: \ *.* D: /S /E. If the backed up disk is a system disk, then you have two working copies of your hard disk. Unlike other forms of backup (floppy and tape), with a second copy of a removable hard disk, you simply slide it into the slot and you're ready to work.

Possibly the best advantage to removable hard disks is the potential limitless size of storage. Rather than buy yourself a second hard drive, you just buy a second removable disk—or a third or a fourth. Typically, the cost of the media is far less expensive than buying the entire hard disk mechanism.

Bernoulli drives

Daniel Bernoulli was an 18th century Swiss mathematician and inventor who discovered a number of interesting things, primarily dealing with the flow of fluids around certain interesting objects (and air is considered a fluid). One of his theories states that the pressure in a stream of fluid is reduced as the speed of the flow is increased. This usually is illustrated using an airplane wing; the pressures created by the airflow around the wing cause the wing to lift in the air. Because air takes longer to get around the top of the wing, the air pressure is less than it is below the wing and the wing rises.

As Bernoulli was toying around with air pressure flow over certain objects, he discovered that, if you spin a flexible disk fast enough, it will wobble like a pinwheel (not his words). He then discovered that, if you spin that same flexible disk next to a flat rigid surface, the disk stabilizes. The airflow causes the flexible disk to become as smooth as a solid disk. It's on this principle that the Bernoulli box operates.

In the early days of personal computing, the Bernoulli drive was an inexpensive alternative to a hard disk. For a comparative price, you got a faster disk drive (twice as fast as the original PC/XT's hard disk). You also got removability. You could take the media out of the drive. You also could buy a lot of media. Instead of only having a 10 Mb drive, you could have as many megabytes of storage as you had removable disks.

The Bernoulli box consists of an external or internal unit and the actual disk itself. The disk is a flexible floppy disk, contained in a hard plastic case. The disk spins next to a solid surface creating the Bernoulli effect and enabling the Bernoulli box to behave just like a hard disk.

The external Bernoulli box comes in a variety of configurations. The most important thing to look for is whether or not the disk is bootable. A bootable Bernoulli disk means it's treated just like a hard disk; you start the computer and the computer looks at the Bernoulli drive just like a hard disk. Computers with non-bootable Bernoullis are booted from a floppy disk.

Like external hard disks or tape drives, the external Bernoulli box needs to interface with the computer via an adapter card. The externals come in several sizes; one or two drives can fit into one unit. The Bernoulli box plus contains an 80 Mb hard disk plus two 20 Mb Bernoulli disks.

The internal Bernoulli drive is the same size as a half-height disk drive. It uses the SCSI interface to connect to the computer (so your computer must have an SCSI card installed). It sports a smaller removable cartridge than the external Bernoulli boxes, roughly $5^1/2$ inches square.

The cartridges for the external Bernoulli boxes are about the size of a sheet of paper, 8 × 11 inches and about $1/2$ inch thick. They contain the flexible media and the rigid surface it spins next to. The cartridge doesn't need to be hermetically sealed. Because of another interesting aspect of the Bernoulli effect, any foreign material which comes into contact with the disk does not cause a disk crash. A dust particle on the spinning disk creates a dimple. The dimple temporarily wrecks the Bernoulli effect, causing the disk to momentarily flutter. The flutter dislodges the dust and returns the disk back to normal. (It's incredible no one else ever thought of the Bernoulli box before IOMEGA—pure genius.)

The speed of the Bernoulli drives is comparable to the best of hard disks. In terms of millisecond (ms) access time, Bernoulli drives average about 35 ms; most typical hard drives are rated at 40 ms, although 18 ms is common on high-performance systems. The error rate also is impressively low when compared to traditional fixed disks.

The only drawback to the Bernoulli box is the price. Hard disk prices literally have gone through the floor in recent years. Yet, the Bernoulli box is comparatively expensive. This makes it look a little odd to purchase a Bernoulli box—even with its advantages of removable media, easy backups, and speed—when hard disks are so cheap.

The pay off comes with volume of information and security. When fixed disk sizes climb into the 100 Mb range, the prices really shoot up. For less than half the cost of a 100 Mb hard disk you could purchase a single Bernoulli box and a number of 10 Mb cartridges. Not only will you have saved some money, but you have the added bonus of security and quick backup protection, with a reliable removable disk system.

The SyQuest removable drive

Here is something you probably thought couldn't be done. The folks at SyQuest Technology have developed an actual removable hard disk drive (Fig. 21-1). It slides into a slot and is read just like any other disk, but it's more like a floppy than a hard drive.

As with all removable hard disks, the SyQuest removable drive is more expensive than static hard drives. Yet, you buy the drive once and your only additional expense is buying more disk cartridges. This is the exact technology many of the early hard disk owners wanted to see. Is it too late, however? With large, fast, and reliable hard drives and tape backup systems popular, the time for the SyQuest drive might have passed. Still, it's worth looking into, especially if the concept of a Bernoulli box doesn't meet your fancy.

You can contact SyQuest Technology at (415) 226-4000.

The hard card

A *hard card* is an interesting solution for hard disk expansion, especially for older PCs or those that don't have room to add a hard drive. Basically, the hard card is a hard disk mounted vertically on the tail of the hard disk controller card. The only true hard card is the Hardcard II put out by Plus Development. It's the offspring of the original solution to adding a hard disk to the first PC without the necessity of sacrificing one or more floppy drives.

For a while there, hard carding was a hobby by every joker who sold hard disks. They simply used flimsy mounting brackets to copy Plus' original Hardcard, sticking their

21-1 SyQuest's removable hard disk system.

bulky hard drives at the end of a wobbly controller card. For this sin, they were all severely sued by Plus Development. Presently, Plus is the only maker of such cards.

The Hardcard II is fast and light and offers high performance. It comes in many capacities, although the drive still takes up only a single expansion slot. To add a Hardcard to your system, you simply plug it in. There are no cables to mess with or power supply line to sacrifice. The rest is all software setup, which makes the Hardcard an excellent solution for hard disk users in dire need of expansion. There's more, however.

Plus has an outstanding reputation for after-sales support. They really bend over backwards to help all Hardcard owners. This policy puts them above the level of most hardware vendors in my book. (A removable drive system, the Passport, also is available.)

Plus Development
1778 McCarthy Blvd.
Milpitas, CA 95035
(408) 434-6900
(800) 624-5545

Other types of storage devices

Alternative storage devices thrive for the PC. The standard floppy and hard drive setup still is common, with a few removable drives thrown in. Yet, there's always that *what's next* coming over the horizon. What it could be is anyone's guess. Some hot contenders, available today, are listed below.

Optical disks   One rage in high-capacity storage devices is the optical disk, which uses light to store information on a reflective surface. The supposed advantage to this form of storage is that the optical disks last an eternity if properly maintained. This is opposed to magnetic storage technology, where the magnetic particles tend to reorient themselves to the earth's magnetic pole after a dozen or so years.

While optical storage might be eternal, it's slow. In addition to being expensive, reading and writing from an optical drive happens at about 80 ms. The old 20 Mb hard drives were considered slow if they accessed disk at 65 ms. Today's fast drives cruise along at 16 ms.

Even the revolutionary NeXT computer gave up the ghost with its magneto-optical storage after the first generation machine. Sure, it stored a lot of information and was relatively cheap on a per-disk basis (about $150 per disk for 300 Mb of storage). However, too many users screamed for the hard drive with floppy disk support, so the optical disk remained an interesting but impractical alternative.

WORM drives   Nothing beats telling a computer illiterate friend that you have a WORM drive with a SCSI (scuzzy) connection on your PC.

WORM actually stands for Write Once/Read Many. It's an optical drive that can be written to—but only once. Sure, you can read from the drive as many times as you like, but nothing can be erased or replaced.

The WORM drive is ideal for backup and long-term archival storage. If I had one, I'd put all my old book archives on it, as well as some computer games that take up way too much disk space. However, because you can write only once to a WORM drive (and you cannot erase), they'll never replace a hard disk system. (I'm not even going to mention how much they cost, although over $1500 is typical.)

CD-ROMs   The most popular type of optical disk is the CD-ROM. The CD means *compact disc*, which is exactly like the type of media that replaced the 33 rpm LP record. The only difference is that this CD stores computer information (and while you can play it on your music CD, it sounds like someone scratching a chalkboard with a fork). The ROM part of CD-ROM means *read-only memory*. This type of drive can be read from only. You cannot write to it or store your own data there.

CD-ROMs have grown in popularity, primarily as storage devices for volumes of information, such as medical and legal references, books in print, and graphics libraries. One computer game even comes on a CD-ROM (as opposed to 12 Mb of floppy diskettes).

There are drawbacks to CD-ROM. The first is the price. You pay a lot for a storage-only device and interface. No, you cannot use your music CD player no matter what gizmos you attach to it. The second drawback is the lack of a standard. Microsoft has worked hard to create a standard. However, what their group came up with is a non-standard that pleases everyone but doesn't solve any problems. When that issue is resolved and the price drops, having a CD-ROM on a PC will be similar to owning a printer; you wouldn't think of buying a PC without it.

Summary

The most important point of this entire chapter is that you're not limited to your current hard disk/floppy drive arrangement on your computer. Many hardware manufacturers offer interesting and productive options for hard disk storage. The really neat part about these alternative devices, as well as hard disks and floppy drives, is that you can install and upgrade your system by yourself. It's all quite painless.

This wraps up the discussion of hard disk optimization, as well as this book. Your hard disk is an interesting and highly useful tool. I hope that you've picked up several useful tricks for making your hard disk system more useful and more productive. Please take a second to leaf through some of the appendices, especially the one on the supplemental diskette.

If you wish to get in touch with me or have comments regarding this book, please feel free to write to me in care of:

TAB Books
13311 Monterey Lane
Blue Ridge Summit, PA 17294-0850

I answer all my mail, promise!

Appendix A
Summary of DOS commands

Below are listed all the major DOS commands through MS-DOS version 5.0. Each command is listed alphabetically by name. You are told whether it's internal, external, or both. Then, you are given the command's format and a brief description of how the command works and what it does. Where applicable, there are references to individual chapters in the book where the command is dealt with.

APPEND   Internal/External

APPEND *d:path*[;[*d:path*]] . . . [/X[:on | off]] [/*path*:on | /*path*:off] [/E]

The APPEND command controls a special search path used to find data files as opposed to PATH, which locates only programs. APPEND works a lot like PATH.

ASSIGN   External

ASSIGN [*d:* = *d:*]

ASSIGN is used to reassign a drive letter to a certain drive. For example, ASSIGN A: = B: redirects all attempts to access drive A, sending them off to drive B. It's like pretending one drive works like another. By using ASSIGN alone on the command line, all drive assignments will be reset to normal.

ATTRIB   External

ATTRIB [±R][±A][±S][±H] *pathname* [/S]

The ATTRIB command changes attributes of a file or group of files. It can be used to protect files from accidental modification or deletion or, in conjunction with BACKUP or XCOPY, to specifically target certain files. See chapter 18.

BACKUP   External

BACKUP *filename* d:
[/S][/M][/A][/D:*date*][/T:*time*][/F:*size*][L:*filename*]

The BACKUP command is used to archive files, typically from a hard disk onto floppies for safe keeping. This command is covered in detail in chapter 16.

377

BREAK   Internal

BREAK [ON | OFF]

The BREAK command is used to turn monitoring of the Ctrl−Break keystroke on or off, as specified by ON or OFF following BREAK on the command line. When used alone, BREAK displays the status of the Ctrl−C and Ctrl−Break monitoring.

CHCP   Internal

CHCP [nnn]

The CHCP command changes the current code page, which determines formats for the date and time, as well as currency symbol. When specified, the number nnn activates a new code page. CHCP used by itself displays the current code page.

CHDIR/CD   Internal

CHDIR [d:][path]

The CHDIR command, also abbreviated CD, is used to specify a new subdirectory in which to work. When used by itself, CHDIR simply displays the name of the current sub-directory. CHDIR is covered in detail in chapter 5.

CHKDSK   External

CHKDSK [filename] [/F][/V]

The CHKDSK program is used to display statistical information about a disk and memory, as well as examine files on the disk for noncontiguous blocks and bad files. CHKDSK is covered in detail in chapter 4 and also is mentioned in chapter 19.

CLS   Internal

CLS

The CLS command clears the screen. The command is introduced in chapter 4.

COMMAND   External

[path] [device] [/E:nnnn] [/P] [/C command] [/msg]

COMMAND is COMMAND.COM, DOS's command processor. It can be run more than once to invoke a new copy of the command shell. This is primarily done with older versions of DOS to call batch files. See chapter 7.

COMP   External

COMP file1 file2 [/D][/A][/L][/N = num][/C]

The COMP command is used to compare two files. Any differences in the files are noted and displayed on the screen.

COPY   Internal

COPY *source* [*destination*] [/A | /B][/V]

COPY is used to copy from one device to another, usually copying one file or a group of files (specified by wildcards) from one disk drive or subdirectory to another. COPY is covered in detail in chapter 4.

CTTY   Internal

CTTY *device*

The CTTY command is used to specify another device as the console. For example, CTTY AUX causes the AUX device, the serial port, to be used as the console, both keyboard and screen.

DATE   Internal

DATE [*mm-dd-yy*]

The DATE command is used to enter a new date for DOS. DOS uses that date to time-stamp all files created or updated. If the current date isn't specified after the DATE command, DOS will prompt you for it. See chapters 4 and 14.

DEBUG   External

DEBUG [*filename*]

DEBUG is used to examine memory, change memory, load sectors or files from disk, and optionally edit them and write them back to disk. Debug also can be used to trace through a program as it's executed.

DEL/ERASE   Internal

DEL *filename* [/P]

The DEL command is used to delete files from disk. The ERASE command does the same thing. See chapter 4.

DIR   Internal

DIR [*pathname*] [/P][/W][/A:*attrib*][/O:*sort*][/S][/B][/1]

DIR, the most commonly used DOS command, displays a list of files in the current directory. See chapter 3.

DISKCOMP   External

DISKCOMP [*d:*] [*d:*] [/1][/8]

The DISKCOMP command compares two diskettes for any differences. It is similar to the way COMP works to compare files.

DISKCOPY   External

DISKCOPY [*d:*] [*d:*]

DISKCOPY is used to copy, or make an exact duplicate of, a floppy diskette. Two floppy drives can be specified for the DISKCOPY, but both disks must be of the same type and size.

DOSKEY   External

DOSKEY [*/reinstall*] [*/bufsize = size*] [*/insert | /overstrike*]
DOSKEY [*/history*] [*/macros*]
DOSKEY [*macroname = [text]*]

DOSKEY is a memory-resident keyboard enhancement, history, and macro command.

DOSSHELL   External

DOSSHELL [*/T[:resolution[n]]*] [*/B*]

DOSSHELL runs the DOS Shell program. See chapter 13.

EDIT   External

EDIT [*filename*]

EDIT activates the DOS Editor. See chapter 6.

EXIT   Internal

EXIT

The EXIT command is used to leave a command shell (invoked by COMMAND.COM). It also will return to certain software applications that shell to DOS.

FASTOPEN   External

FASTOPEN *d:*[*= nnn*] . . . [*/X*]

The FASTOPEN command is used to speed access to commonly used files. FASTOPEN keeps track of recently opened files and their locations. Any additional access to those files will be quicker. I don't recommend using this program at all; instead run SMARTDrive, as covered in chapter 20.

FC   External

FC [*/A*][*/C*][*/L*][*/LBn*][*/N*][*/T*][*/W*][*/nnnn*] [*file1*] *file2*

FC is used to compare files on a more technical basis than the simple COMP program.

FDISK   External

FDISK

The FDISK command is used to initialize and partition a hard drive for use with DOS. FDISK is the step done after a low-level format and before the DOS format. After using FDISK, the computer is reset. See chapter 2.

FIND   External

FIND [/V][/C][/N][/I] "string" filename . . .

FIND is a filter used to search through text files for specific strings of text. See chapters 3 and 16.

FORMAT   External

FORMAT d:[/S][/V:"label"][/B][/F:size][/Q][/U]
[/N:xx][/T:xx][/1][/4][/8]

The FORMAT command is used to initialize disks, preparing them for use with DOS. Formatting disks is discussed in chapters 1 and 2; a table of formatting commands appears in chapter 15.

GRAFTABL   External

GRAFTABL [437 | 850 | 852 | 860 | 863 | 865] [/status]

The GRAFTABL command is used to load a graphics character set into memory, dependent on a specific country code specified after the GRAFTABL command.

GRAPHICS   External

GRAPHICS [type] [filename] [/R][/B][/LCD] [/printbox:[std | lcd]]

The GRAPHICS command sets your computer to display graphics on a specific type of monitor or sets your printer type to work with the IBM graphic character set.

HELP   External

HELP [command]

The HELP command displays helpful information about all DOS commands or a specific command. Help is available for each command individually, using the /? switch.

JOIN   External

JOIN [d:] [/D] [d: \ path]

The JOIN command is used to assign a subdirectory name to a disk drive, making DOS think that drive really is a subdirectory. JOIN by itself lists all drives assigned in such a manner. The /D switch is used to disable the JOINed drives.

KEYB   External

KEYB [xx],[yyy] [*filename*] [/E][/ID:*nnn*]

KEYB is used to load a keyboard driver for another country or language into memory. By using KEYB, you can access special characters used in foreign languages.

LABEL   External

LABEL [*d:*][*label*]

The LABEL command allows you to set, change, or examine a disk's volume label. See chapter 2.

LOADHIGH/LH   Internal

LOADHIGH *program*

The LOADHIGH, or LH, command is used to load a memory-resident program into an upper memory block. See chapter 20.

MEM   External

MEM [/P | /PROGRAM] [/D | /DEBUG] [/C | /CLASSIFY]

The MEM command is to your computer's memory as CHKDSK is to disk. MEM displays a list of items in your system's memory, their location and size, and what they are. See chapter 20.

MIRROR   External

MIRROR /*partn*
MIRROR /U
MIRROR *drive*: . . . [/1] [/T*drive*[– files]] . . .

The MIRROR program provides a safety net for your hard drives and the data on them. It also can aid the UNDELETE and UNFORMAT commands in file and disk recover. See chapter 15.

MKDIR/MD   Internal

MKDIR *pathname*

The MKDIR command, also abbreviated MD, is used to create a new subdirectory on disk. MKDIR is covered in detail in chapter 5.

MODE   External

MODE [. . .*various*. . .]

The MODE command has seven separate uses, most of which are associated with the mode of operation of certain devices in the computer: the display, keyboard, printer, and communications port.

MORE External

> command ¦ MORE
> MORE < textfile

MORE is a filter used to page the output of files, pausing after each screen of text to display the message —more— and wait for a keystroke. See chapter 3.

NLSFUNC External

> NLSFUNC [filename]

The NLSFUNC command is used in conjunction with CHCP to supply code page information. The filename specified is the COUNTRY.SYS file that comes with DOS.

PATH Internal

> PATH [;] [d:path][;d:path]...

The PATH command is used to specify a series of subdirectories DOS will look through for programs. The PATH command is covered in detail in chapter 9.

PRINT External

> PRINT [/D:x][/B:x][/U:x][/M:x][/S:x][Q:x][/C][/T][/P] [filespec]

The PRINT command activates DOS's printing queue, which is like a print spooler but only for text files specified by the PRINT command. In my opinion, this command is poor and you shouldn't use it.

PROMPT Internal

> PROMPT [prompt text]

The PROMPT command changes DOS's system prompt. You can include the date, time, path, directory, or any of a number of text characters in your system prompt, all via the PROMPT command. PROMPT is fleshed out in chapter 9, but also check chapter 12.

QBASIC External

> QBASIC [program[.BAS]] [/RUN]

QBASIC runs the QuickBASIC interpreter included with DOS. See chapter 18.

RECOVER External

> RECOVER filename

RECOVER is used to rescue files, as best DOS can, from damaged diskettes. The files recovered must be renamed and typed at the DOS prompt to determine their former contents. In my opinion, you should never use this command. Not ever.

RENAME/REN   Internal

RENAME [*path*]*orgname newname*

The RENAME command, which can be abbreviated to REN, is used to change the name of a file on disk. RENAME is covered in detail in chapter 4.

REPLACE   External

REPLACE *source destination* [/A][/P][/R][/S][/W]

REPLACE is used to locate files on one disk and replace them with similarly named files on another disk. REPLACE seeks out the older files and replaces them, saving you time when updating software and DOS.

RESTORE   External

RESTORE *d: filename* [/P][/M][/S][/N][/D][/B:][/A:][/E:][/L:]

The RESTORE command is used to restore files from a backup diskette back to the original. It is the complement of the BACKUP command and is covered in detail in chapter 16.

RMDIR/RD   Internal

RMDIR [*d:*][*path*]

The RMDIR command, also abbreviated RD, removes a subdirectory from disk. The subdirectory must be empty before it can be removed. RMDIR is covered in detail in chapter 5.

SET   Internal

SET [*name*[= *parameter*]]

The SET command is used to place a variable and its associated string into DOS's environment. When used by itself, SET displays the current contents of the environment. SET is covered in chapter 9.

SETVER   External

SETVER [*program n.nn*] [/DELETE] [/QUIET]

SETVER is used to display the DOS 5 version table and, additionally, to add or remove a program from it. This keeps older stubborn programs running even if they don't recognize DOS 5.

SHARE   External

SHARE [/F:*space*] [/L:*locks*]

SHARE is a command used in file sharing, primarily to secure access to one file by more than one program or individual. This command is not needed under DOS 5 unless one of your applications specifically requests it.

SORT External

SORT [/R][/ + n] < textfile
command ¦ SORT [/R][/ + n]

SORT is a filter used to order the lines in a text file alphabetically or reverse alphabetically. SORTing also might be done on a specific column of text using the / + n switch. See chapter 3.

SUBST External

SUBST [d:] [/D] [d: \ path]

The SUBST command is used to assign a drive letter to a subdirectory. This makes DOS treat the subdirectory just as if it were its own independent disk drive. (SUBST is kind of the opposite of the JOIN command.) SUBST by itself lists all subdirectories assigned as disk drives. The /D switch disables the substituted drives.

SYS External

SYS d:

The SYS command is used to transfer the system (the basic DOS files) to another disk, typically a freshly formatted disk or one with enough space for the system files. SYS is covered in chapter 2.

TIME Internal

TIME [hh:mm[:ss[.xx]]]

The TIME command is used to enter a new time for DOS. DOS uses that time to time-stamp all files created or updated. If the time isn't specified after the TIME command, DOS will prompt you for it. See chapters 4 and 14.

TREE External

TREE [pathname] [/A][/F]

TREE is a command used to display the tree structure of a disk drive, optionally listing any files found in any subdirectories (with the /F option). See chapter 5.

TYPE Internal

TYPE filename

The TYPE command lists the contents of a file on the screen. It normally is used for viewing text files, although any file can be typed (non-text files just don't look pretty, that's all). See chapter 4.

UNDELETE External

UNDELETE [*filename*] [*/list* | /ALL] [/dos | /dt]

The UNDELETE command is used to recover a file deleted by the DEL or ERASE commands. When used with the MIRROR command's deletion tracking feature, files can be recovered quite readily. See chapter 15.

UNFORMAT External

UNFORMAT *drive* [/J] [/U][/L][/TEST][/P]
UNFORMAT */partn* [/L]

The UNFORMAT command is used to recover a freshly formatted floppy diskette or hard drive. Recovery is almost guaranteed if the MIRROR command was used on the drive. See chapter 15.

VER Internal

VER

The VER command displays the current version of DOS.

VERIFY Internal

VERIFY [ON | OFF]

The VERIFY command is used to turn automatic verification of disk writes on or off. Used by itself, VERIFY displays the current verify status.

VOL Internal

VOL [*d:*]

VOL displays the volume label for the current disk or a disk drive specified.

XCOPY External

XCOPY *source* [*destination*] [/A | /M] [/D:*date*] [/E][/P][/S][/V][/W]

XCOPY is a super-COPY program, but it basically works by quickly copying files by putting them all in memory rather than copying one at a time (as COPY does). XCOPY also contains a number of switches, which makes it far more versatile than the vanilla COPY command. XCOPY is covered in chapter 5.

Appendix B
Summary of EDLIN commands

EDLIN is DOS's text editor. You would have thought DOS 5's Editor would have killed it off. However, EDLIN still is with us.

EDLIN is clunky, inconvenient, and awkward to use. Its only saving grace is that it's free with DOS and that all versions of DOS have it. This makes EDLIN a common base for all DOS users. However, because I dislike EDLIN, it's been banished to this appendix. (All my publishers tell me that no one ever reads appendixes. Write to them and tell them why you're here.)

EDLIN is a line editor, working on text one line at a time. It can edit or create only text, or ASCII, files.

You must always start EDLIN with the name of a file to edit. If the file exists, it's loaded. If the file doesn't exist, EDLIN creates it. EDLIN also makes automatic backup files (*.BAK) if the file loaded is modified and saved to disk.

Once you're in EDLIN, you'll see EDLIN's drastic prompt: the asterisk. There you can issue one of EDLIN's commands, which all are conveniently listed in this appendix. Keep this in your head: you must tell EDLIN which line you want to edit or where you want to insert text. The asterisk is a prompt; it doesn't mean you're editing text.

To leave EDLIN and return to DOS, the E command is used. That command saves the file you're working on to disk, backing up the original with a BAK extension. If you use the Q command instead, all edits will be forgotten and the file will remain the same on disk (and no BAK file will be created).

The following sections list EDLIN's commands. Good luck.

Insert line

I   Inserts a new line at the current line. When creating a new file, I inserts line 1.

nI   Inserts a new line number *n*.

.I   Inserts a new line at the current line.

#I   Inserts a new line at the bottom of the file.

+nI   Inserts a new line *n* lines down from the current line number.

−nI   Inserts a new line *n* lines up from the current line number.

List

L   Lists the 11 lines before the current line, the current line, and 11 lines after the current line.

xL   Lists 23 lines starting with line x.

,yL   Lists the 11 lines before line y, line y, and the 11 lines after line y.

x,yL   Lists the lines from x through y.

P   Page or print from the current line down 23 lines.

,yP   Print from the current line through line y.

x,yP   Print from line x through line y.

Delete

D   Deletes the current line.

xD   Deletes line x.

x,yD   Deletes lines x through y.

,yD   Deletes all lines from the current line through line y.

x,.D   Deletes all lines from x through the current line.

Copy

x,y,zC   Copies the block of lines from x through y and places them at line number z.

x,x,zC   Copies the single line x to line number z.

Move

x,y,zM   Moves the block of lines from x through y and places them at line number z.

x,x,zM   Moves line x to line number z.

Search and Replace

S string   Searches for the characters in string.

x,ySstring   Searches for the characters in string between lines x and y.

x,y?Sstring   Searches for the characters in string between lines x and y and stops and asks OK? for each occurrence. Pressing Y continues the search, N cancels.

Rstr1^Zstr2   Replaces all occurrences of str1 with str2. ^Z is Ctrl−Z.

x,yRstr1^Zstr2   Replaces all occurrences of str1 with str2 in the range of lines from x through y.

x,y?Rstr1^Zstr2   Replaces all occurrences of str1 with str2 in the range of lines from x through y. When str1 is found, replace stops and asks OK? Pressing Y replaces, pressing N cancels.

Edit

    n Selects line *n* for editing.

    −*n* Selects line *n* lines up for editing.

    +*n* Selects line *n* lines down for editing.

    • Selects current line for editing.

Disk

    *n*A Appends lines from the disk file into memory. (This command works only if the file being edited is too big to fit into memory.)

    *n*T Transfers text to disk starting with line *n*. If *n* is omitted, the current line is used.

    *n*W Writes a specific number of lines to disk. (Used only for files too large to fit into memory at once.)

End

    E Ends edit, saves file, and renames the original file to *.BAK.

    Q Cancels edit, without saving changes

Appendix C
Extended ASCII chart

ASCII (pronounced *ASK-ee*) is an acronym for the American Standard Code for Information Interchange. The ASCII codes from 0 through 127 are assigned to letters, numbers, special characters, and other symbols. ASCII codes 128 through 255 vary from computer to computer. On IBM PCs and compatibles, these characters are referred to as the *Extended ASCII set*. The actual characters displayed on the screen are in the chart at the end of this appendix.

Code/Char		Code/Char		Code/Char		Code/Char	
0	^@	24	^X	48	0	72	H
1	^A	25	^Y	49	1	73	I
2	^B	26	^Z	50	2	74	J
3	^C	27	^[	51	3	75	K
4	^D	28	^\	52	4	76	L
5	^E	29	^]	53	5	77	M
6	^F	30	^^	54	6	78	N
7	^G	31	^_	55	7	79	O
8	^H	32	*blank*	56	8	80	P
9	^I	33	!	57	9	81	Q
10	^J	34	"	58	:	82	R
11	^K	35	#	59	;	83	S
12	^L	36	$	60	<	84	T
13	^M	37	%	61	=	85	U
14	^N	38	&	62	>	86	V
15	^O	39	'	63	?	87	W
16	^P	40	(	64	@	88	X
17	^Q	41	)	65	A	89	Y
18	^R	42	*	66	B	90	Z
19	^S	43	+	67	C	91	[
20	^T	44	,	68	D	92	\
21	^U	45	–	69	E	93	]
22	^V	46	.	70	F	94	^
23	^W	47	/	71	G	95	_

Code	Char	Code	Char	Code	Char	Code	Char
96	'	104	h	112	p	120	x
97	a	105	i	113	q	121	y
98	b	106	j	114	r	122	z
99	c	107	k	115	s	123	{
100	d	108	l	116	t	124	|
101	e	109	m	117	u	125	}
102	f	110	n	118	v	126	~
103	g	111	o	119	w	127	⌂

The following table contains the complete set of Extended ASCII characters and their respective ASCII code values.

Code/Char		Code/Char		Code/Char		Code/Char	
128	Ç	160	á	192	└	224	α
129	ü	161	í	193	┴	225	β
130	é	162	ó	194	┬	226	Γ
131	â	163	ú	195	├	227	π
132	ä	164	ñ	196	─	228	Σ
133	à	165	Ñ	197	┼	229	σ
134	å	166	ª	198	╞	230	µ
135	ç	167	º	199	╟	231	τ
136	ê	168	¿	200	╚	232	Φ
137	ë	169	⌐	201	╔	233	Θ
138	è	170	¬	202	╩	234	Ω
139	ï	171	½	203	╦	235	δ
140	î	172	¼	204	╠	236	∞
141	ì	173	¡	205	═	237	φ
142	Ä	174	«	206	╬	238	ε
143	Å	175	»	207	╧	239	∩
144	É	176		208	╨	240	≡
145	æ	177	▒	209	╤	241	±
146	Æ	178	▓	210	╥	242	≥
147	ô	179	│	211	╙	243	≤
148	ö	180	┤	212	╘	244	⌠
149	ò	181	╡	213	╒	245	⌡
150	û	182	╢	214	╓	246	÷
151	ù	183	╖	215	╫	247	≈
152	ÿ	184	╕	216	╪	248	°
153	Ö	185	╣	217	┘	249	•
154	Ü	186	║	218	┌	250	·
155	¢	187	╗	219	█	251	√
156	£	188	╝	220	▄	252	η
157	¥	189	╜	221	▌	253	²
158	₧	190	╛	222	▐	254	■
159	ƒ	191	┐	223	▀	255	blank

─────────Appendix D─────────
ANSI.SYS commands

In the following text, the italic *n* represents an integer ASCII value. For example, if you want *n* to represent the value 42, replace it with the ASCII characters 42 not the byte value 42. If more than one replaceable integer value appears in a command string, they are numbered n1, n2, and so on. The ← represents the escape character, ASCII 27 (1B hexadecimal, or ^[).

Locate cursor

←[n1;n2H

n1 is a row number; *n2* is a column number. After the previous command, the cursor will be positioned at row *n1* and column *n2*. If both parameters are omitted, as in ←[;H, the cursor is sent to position 1,1—the upper left corner of the screen.

Position cursor

←[n1;n2f

operates the same as the previous command, although it's not as common and is rarely used.

Move cursor up

←[nA

moves the cursor up *n* number of rows. If *n* is omitted, the cursor moves up one row. If the cursor is at the top row, this command is ignored.

Move cursor down

←[nB

moves the cursor down *n* number of lines. If *n* is omitted, the cursor moves down one row. If the cursor is at the bottom row, this command is ignored.

Move cursor right

←[nC

moves the cursor right *n* number of columns. If *n* is omitted, the cursor moves right one column. If the cursor is at the far right column, this command is ignored.

Move cursor left

←[nD

moves the cursor left *n* number of columns. If *n* is omitted, the cursor moves left one column. If the cursor is at the far left column, this command is ignored.

Save cursor position

←[s

The current cursor position is saved. To restore it, use the following command.

Restore cursor position

←[u

restores the cursor to its position as saved by the ←[S command sequence.

Erase display

←[2J

This sequence clears the screen and puts the cursor into the upper left corner.

Erase line

←[K

The line the cursor is on will be erased from the cursor's position to the end of the line.

Set graphics rendition

←[nm

n takes on a number of values, each changing the foreground and background color attributes of the screen:

    0   Normal text
    1   High-intensity
    2   Low-intensity
    4   Underline on (monochrome displays only)
    5   Blinking on
    7   Inverse video on
    8   Invisible text
    30 Black foreground

31 Red foreground
32 Green foreground
33 Yellow foreground
34 Blue foreground
35 Magenta foreground
36 Cyan foreground
37 White foreground
40 Black background
41 Red background
42 Green background
43 Yellow background
44 Blue background
45 Magenta background
46 Cyan background
47 White background

For example, ←[34m turns on a blue foreground color.

Two or more of the attributes can be selected at once using the following format:

←[n1;n2;. . .nnm

Different color attributes can be specified by separating each of them with a semicolon. The final attribute is followed by the lowercase m. For example:

←[37;44m

This command sets white characters on a blue background.

Set/reset mode

←[=nh

The mode in this case is the screen mode, the resolution of characters or graphics pixels. *n* carries 7 values, from 0 through 6:

0 Monochrome text, 40 × 25
1 Color text, 40 × 25
2 Monochrome text, 80 × 25
3 Color text, 80 × 25
4 Medium-resolution graphics (four color), 320 × 200
5 Same as 4, but with color burst disabled
6 High-resolution graphics (two color), 640 × 200
14 Color graphics, 640 × 200
15 Monochrome graphics, 640 × 350
16 Color graphics, 640 × 350
17 Color graphics, 640 × 480
18 Color graphics, 640 × 480
19 Color graphics, 320 × 200

These commands are useful when creating special large character screens (for example, for children or the handicapped who have trouble reading the regular display).

Character wrap on

←[=7h

Part of ANSI's VT100 legacy is the ability to wrap characters on the screen. That is, if a character is displayed in column 80 (the far right hand column), the next character will be displayed on the next row in the first column. This feature is called *character wrap.*

If character wrap is disabled, then all characters displayed after the 80th character on a line and before a carriage return character will be displayed in column 80.

Character wrap on is the default of the ANSI.SYS driver.

Character wrap off

←[=7l

This command disables character wrap. Note that the final character in the command string is a lowercase *L*, not a one.

Keyboard key reassignment

←[n1;n2p

n1 is the ASCII code for a key to redefine. *n2* is the ASCII code that will be produced when *n1* is pressed. For example:

←[71,84p

assigns capital *G* (ASCII 71) as capital *T* (ASCII 84). Whenever a capital *G* key is typed, DOS will display a *T.* To reassign the lowercase characters, use the following:

←[103;116p

Keyboard string reassignment

←[0;n;"string"p

n is an extended keyboard code. *string* is a string of characters that will be produced every time the specified key is pressed. For example:

←[0;113;"DIR"p

assigns the string DIR to the key combination Alt−F10. To add a carriage return after the DIR command, use:

←[0;113;"DIR";13p

(See chapter 12 for a complete example of keyboard reassignment.)

Note that you can only un-assign the keys by rebooting your computer or by running an un-assign program. Also, note that, because most applications do not use DOS routines to read the keyboard, these reassignments probably will not take effect in any of your programs.

Appendix E
About the companion diskette

A diskette is offered in conjunction with this book. On that diskette, you'll find all the batch file programs, plus a few special utilities, as mentioned in this book. This appendix will describe the companion diskette and how you can install it and its programs onto your hard drive.

None of the files on the disk are shareware. Buying this book means you've paid for whatever is on the diskette. Because I've written all of the programs, this is no problem with me. However, please do not include any of these programs on any other shareware diskette, nor should you upload them to any online system, distribute them at a user group meeting, or give them away. Thanks.

Companion diskette structure

The companion diskette contains 12 directories:

BATUTIL	CHAP14
CHAP08	CHAP17
CHAP09	CHAP18
CHAP10	CHAP19
CHAP11	MENU
CHAP12	UTIL

All directories starting with CHAP contain files mentioned in those chapters. The three additional directories contain files according to certain categories: MENU contains the Menu Maker programs, as discussed in chapter 14; BATUTIL contains various batch file utilities that might come in handy; and UTIL contains general hard disk utilities and programs.

Files on the disk

Every file on the disk, except for the batch files and other programs described in this book, has an accompanying DOC file. That's a text file that describes how the program works and all about its features. Type the DOC file to the display with the following:

```
TYPE filename.DOC | MORE
```

The VIEW command has an interesting look on files. To see what it can do, move to the MENU directory and type the following:

```
VIEW VIEWME
```

Installing on your hard drive

If you have a hard disk shell or file tool, such as PC Shell or XTree, then you can pick and choose which files to install and use on your system. You don't have to copy everything. However, useful batch files could be copied to your BATCH directory, utilities to your UTIL directory, and the Menu Maker programs would like their own MENU subdirectory. I only can make suggestions here; you should find a solution that works best with your own personal hard disk organization.

The original book's diskette

Previous versions of this book came with a different diskette. That diskette was offered through the PC-SIG library. If you'd like to order that diskette (it still is a good deal), dial up PC-SIG at (800) 245-6717 or (800) 222-2996 in California and ask for diskette #786.

_____Appendix F_____
Country and code page information

Table F-1 contains codes used by CONFIG.SYS's COUNTRY configuration command, as well as the KEYB command.

Table F-1   Country codes, keyboard codes, and accepted code page values.

Country/ language	Country code	Keyb code	Code pages
Australia	—	us	437,850
Belgium	032	be	437,850
Brazil	055	—	850,437
Canadian-French	002	cf	863,850
Czechoslovakia	042	cz	850,852
Czech.-Slovak	042	sl	850,852
Denmark	045	dk	865,850
English (Int'l)	061	—	437,850
Finland	385	su	437,850
France	033	fr	437,850
Germany	049	gr	437,850
Hungary	036	hu	852,850
Italy	039	it	437,850
Latin America	003	la	437,850
Netherlands	031	nl	437,850
Norway	047	no	865,850
Poland	048	pl	852,850
Portugal	351	po	860,850
Spain	034	sp	437,850
Sweden	046	sv	437,850
Swiss-French	041	sf	437,850
Swiss-German	041	sg	437,850
United Kingdom	044	uk	437,850
United States	001	us	437,850
Yugoslavia	038	yu	852,850

Table F-2 contains code page descriptions. The code pages listed are used with the COUNTRY configuration command, as well as the CHCP, GRAFTABL, and MODE DOS commands, plus the DISPLAY.SYS and PRINTER.SYS device drivers.

Table F-2   Code page descriptions.

Code page	Value
Canadian-French	863
Multilingual	850
Nordic	865
Portuguese	850
United States	437
Slavic	852

Hardware keyboard configurations used with the KEYB command are shown in Table F-3.

Table F-3   KEYB command hardware arrangement codes.

Country/ Language	Codes
France	120,189
Italy	141,142
United Kingdom	166,168

Code page information (CPI) files used with various commands are listed in Table F-4.

Table F-4   Code page information files for various IBM equipment.

4201.CPI	IBM Proprinter, Proprinter XL
4208.CPI	IBM Proprinter X24 & XL24
5202.CPI	IBM Quietwriter III
EGA.CPI	EGA display
LCD.CPI	The IBM PC Convertible laptop display

Index

backup procedures (*cont.*)

PC Tools CP Backup, 286-287

reasons to back-up, 271-272

RESTORE, 279-284, 285

RESTORE, date and time switches, 282

RESTORE, directories and sub-directories, 281

RESTORE, full hard drive restoration, 279-280

RESTORE, individual file restoration, 280

RESTORE, notes on use, 282-283

RESTORE, switches, options, 281

streaming tape backup systems, 288-289

tape backup systems, 288-291

virus protection, 296

work-area backups, 277

bad sectors, 45

bases, number systems, 4

batch files, 131-141, 161-187

= = testing, 170

application-program loading batch files, 133-134

backup-batch file, SHUTDOWN-.BAT, 283-284

chaining, 162, 171-172

conditional branching, IF, 167-168

conditional loops, 164, 166-167

conditional statements, 162

creation, COPY CON, 132-133

directory for batch files, 133

encryption, CRYPT.BAS, 323-324

environmental variables, 154-155

equality conditional test, 168-169

ERRORLEVEL testing, 166-167, 170

EXIST conditional testing, 168

FOR loops, 164-165

GOTO command, 163-165

infinite loops, 162

labels, 163

looping, 162-167

menu system using batch files, 181-182

messages, 135

NOT conditional testing, 170

operation of batch files, 132

programming techniques, 161-171

remarks, REM, 114, 123

replaceable parameters, 139-140

sequential execution, 161

show execution on screen, ECHO commands, 135-137

subroutines, 162

subroutines, CALL command, 172

suppress screen display, @ prefix, 137-138

suspend execution, PAUSE , 138-139

syntax errors, 169-170

termination, 134-135

time-logging program, 242-243

Bernoulli disks, 13, 372-373

Bernoulli, Daniel, 372

BIN branch organization, 87-89

binary numbers, 4, 6-7

BIOS, 111-112

bits, bytes, 4-5

block-text operations, Editor, EDIT, 104-107

boot record, 21

boot-disk creation, 30-33, 295

boot-up process, 111-113

BOOTLOCK, 305-307

borders for menus, ASCII codes, 190-193

branching, conditional, IF, 167-168

BREAK, 116, 378

BUFFERS, 114, 117

C

caching, disk caching, 363-365

CALL, 172

categorical organization, 86-87

CD-ROM, 375

Certus virus protection, 299-304

chaining, 162, 171-172

CHCP, 378

CHDIR or CD, 83-84, 378

child directories, 83

CHKDSK, 68-71, 337-338, 378

clock setting, AUTOEXEC.BAT, 156

CLS, 65, 378

clusters, 44

code pages

change current code page, CHCP, 378

country codes, keyboard codes, code page values, 399-400

foreign language use, COUNTRY, 117-118

show information about code pages, NLSFUNC, 383

color selection

ANSI.SYS commands, 200-201

DOS Shell, 212

Menu Maker menu generator, 239-240

COM devices, 59

command format, 57

command interpreter, selection, SHELL, 114, 123-124

command processors, COMMAND, COMMAND.COM, 55-56, 378

command summary, 55-75, 377-386

COMMAND, COMMAND.COM, 55-56, 112, 123-124, 378

virus protection, 297

Commander, Norton shell, 251-252

communications ports, 59-60

COMP, 378

companion diskette, xiii, 397-398

directories on the disk, 397

files on the disk, 397-398

installation, 398

obtaining copies of diskette, 398

Compress by PC Tools, 336, 342-343

compressing files, 336

COMSPEC, 152

CON devices, 59

conditional branching, IF, 167-168

conditional execution, 162, 164, 166-167

= = testing, 170

branching, IF, 167-168

equality conditional test, 168-169

EXIST conditional testing, 168

NOT conditional testing, 170

conditional loops, ERRORLEVEL testing, 166-167, 170

CONFIG.SYS, 111-129

80286 CONFIG.SYS example, 126-127

80386 CONFIG.SYS example, 127-128

8088/8086 CONFIG.SYS example, 125-126

AUTOEXEC.BAT, 112

BIOS and ROM, 111-112

boot-up process, 111-113

command interpreter selection, SHELL, 114, 123-124

command summary, 115

COMMAND.COM, 112

copy, create backup, COPY, 129

creating and updating CONFIG.SYS, 125-129

device driver, load to extended memory, DEVICEHIGH, 119-120, 357, 358

device driver, load to memory, DEVICE, 114, 118-119

drive designations, highest letter allowable, LASTDRIVE, 122-123

editing CONFIG.SYS, 115

experimenting with new configurations, 128-129

external-drive configurations, DRIVPARM, 121

file control blocks, FCBS, 121

files, maximum number open, FILES, 114, 121

foreign language use, COUNTRY, 117-118

form factors, 121

load DOS to high memory area (HMA), DOS command, 114, 120-121

memory buffer settings, BUFFERS, 114, 117

memory stack configuration,

Hard Disk Management with DOS 5
3rd ed.
Dan Gookin

The enclosed disk contains the programs used in *Hard Disk Management with DOS 5—3rd ed.* (Windcrest Book 4072), ©1992 by Dan Gookin. These programs are the same as the programs shown and discussed in this book. You can run these programs to follow along with the instruction in the book.

These programs can be run under DOS version 5.0 on an IBM or compatible computer. The files are contained in the following subdirectories:

BATUTIL	CHAP11	CHAP18
CHAP08	CHAP12	CHAP19
CHAP09	CHAP14	MENU
CHAP10	CHAP17	UTIL